# FOXE'S BOOK OF MARTYRS

## SELECT

T0115586

JOHN FOXE (1516/17–8 ...
During his youth, England ...
cerning the advent of new I ...
thorized effort to produce a translation of the New Testament, and
Henry VIII's endeavour to divorce Catherine of Aragon. Foxe began
his studies at the University of Oxford c.1534, close to the time
when England broke from the Church of Rome and Henry VIII
united church and state. Having become a Protestant, Foxe resigned
his fellowship at Magdalen College and then began a career as a
publicist during the reign of Edward VI. At the same time, Foxe
entered into service to the Duchess of Richmond as tutor to the
orphans of her brother, the recently executed Henry Howard, Earl
of Surrey, who had joined his father, the 3rd Duke of Norfolk, as a
leader of the Roman Catholic faction. When Edward's Roman
Catholic half-sister, Mary I, acceded to the throne she instituted a
reign of terror during which hundreds of Protestants were burnt
alive as heretics. From exile in Europe, Foxe began to publish martyrological histories in Latin. When he returned to England following the cessation of persecution of Protestants, he entered into
collaboration with the London printer, John Day, who published a
sequence of four vernacular editions of the *Book of Martyrs* (1563,
1570, 1576, and 1583). At about four times the length of the Bible, the
fourth edition is the most physically imposing, complicated, technically demanding, and best illustrated book of the Shakespearean age.
Although it contains an impressive array of genres, it is best remembered for its many moving accounts of the apprehension, imprisonment, interrogation, and execution of Protestants who had been
condemned as heretics.

JOHN N. KING is Distinguished University Professor and Hu-
manities Distinguished Professor of English and of Religious
Studies at The Ohio State University. His publications include
*English Reformation Literature: The Tudor Origins of the Protestant
Tradition* (1982); *Tudor Royal Iconography: Literature and Art in an
Age of Religious Crisis* (1989); *Spenser's Poetry and the Reformation
Tradition* (1990); *Milton and Religious Controversy: Satire and Polemic
in* Paradise Lost (2000); *Voices of the English Reformation: A
Sourcebook* (2004); and *Foxe's* Book of Martyrs *and Early Modern
Print Culture* (2006). He serves as Editor of *Reformation* and Co-
editor of *Literature and History*.

# OXFORD WORLD'S CLASSICS

*For over 100 years Oxford World's Classics have brought
readers closer to the world's great literature. Now with over 700
titles—from the 4,000-year-old myths of Mesopotamia to the
twentieth century's greatest novels—the series makes available
lesser-known as well as celebrated writing.*

*The pocket-sized hardbacks of the early years contained
introductions by Virginia Woolf, T. S. Eliot, Graham Greene,
and other literary figures which enriched the experience of reading.
Today the series is recognized for its fine scholarship and
reliability in texts that span world literature, drama and poetry,
religion, philosophy, and politics. Each edition includes perceptive
commentary and essential background information to meet the
changing needs of readers.*

OXFORD WORLD'S CLASSICS

# Foxe's Book of Martyrs
## Select Narratives

*Edited with an Introduction and Notes by*
JOHN N. KING

OXFORD
UNIVERSITY PRESS

# OXFORD

UNIVERSITY PRESS

Great Clarendon Street, Oxford OX2 6DP

Oxford University Press is a department of the University of Oxford.
It furthers the University's objective of excellence in research, scholarship,
and education by publishing worldwide in

Oxford  New York

Auckland  Cape Town  Dar es Salaam  Hong Kong  Karachi
Kuala Lumpur  Madrid  Melbourne  Mexico City  Nairobi
New Delhi  Shanghai  Taipei  Toronto

With offices in

Argentina  Austria  Brazil  Chile  Czech Republic  France  Greece
Guatemala  Hungary  Italy  Japan  Poland  Portugal  Singapore
South Korea  Switzerland  Thailand  Turkey  Ukraine  Vietnam

Oxford is a registered trade mark of Oxford University Press
in the UK and in certain other countries

Published in the United States
by Oxford University Press Inc., New York

British Library Cataloguing in Publication Data

Data available

Library of Congress Cataloging-in-Publication Data

Data available

Typeset by Cepha Imaging Private Ltd., Bangalore, India
Printed in Great Britain
on acid-free paper by
Clays Ltd., Elcograf S.p.A.

ISBN 978–0–19–923684–8

12

In memory of my parents
Revd Dr Luther Waddington and Alba Iregui King
and my grandparents
Revd William Luther and Mary Ann Waddington King
and
Salvador Enrique and Maria Luisa Burgos Iregui

# ACKNOWLEDGEMENTS

I owe a debt of gratitude to Mark Greengrass and David M. Loades, who serve respectively as Project Director and Editorial Director of *Foxe's* Book of Martyrs *Online*, a new digital edition published by the Humanities Research Institute at the University of Sheffield under sponsorship from the British Academy and Humanities Research Institute. I have incurred debts to others who have been associated with this massive scholarly endeavour. They include Patrick Collinson and the late J. B. Trapp. Editors at Oxford University Press—Judith Luna, Andrew McNeillie, and Rowena Anketell—have contributed greatly to advancing this edition towards publication. I am further indebted to other individuals on both sides of the Atlantic Ocean, who include Steven Galbraith, the late Ruth Samson Luborsky, and Alexandra Walsham. At my home institution, I am indebted to James Bracken, with whom I have collaborated on projects related to John Foxe, early modern printing, and the history of the book for many years. For good conversation, wise counsel, and unfailing support, I am grateful to Joseph Branin, Richard Dutton, Christopher Highley, Valerie Lee, James Phelan, John Roberts, Geoffrey Smith, and Luke Wilson. In particular, I am grateful to Mark Rankin for wise counsel and assistance in transcribing the textual contents of this edition and to Erin Kelly, Erin McCarthy, Aaron Pratt, and Seth Reno for their gracious support in preparing this edition. Of course, I remain responsible for all errors in this edition.

By permission of John N. King, illustrations are reproduced from his privately owned copy of the 1583 edition of *Book of Martyrs*.

Above all, I am grateful for the support of my wife, Pauline, and son, Jonathan Paul.

JOHN N. KING

*The Ohio State University*

# CONTENTS

# LIST OF ILLUSTRATIONS

# INTRODUCTION

John Foxe's *Acts and Monuments* is a vast collection of unforgettable accounts of religious persecution. Best remembered by the popular title of the *Book of Martyrs*, this sensational book serves as a window into early modern English cultural history. This compilation came to exert a greater influence upon the consciousness of early modern England and New England than any other book aside from the English Bible and Book of Common Prayer. It is recognized to have been one of the most influential texts in the formation of English national consciousness between 1560 and 1700. As such, it influenced writers as various as Raphael Holinshed, William Shakespeare, Ben Jonson, Thomas Heywood, John Selden, William Prynne, John Bunyan, John Milton, Andrew Marvell, Cotton Mather, and many others. Not only did it encourage the development in England of a sharply defined Protestant identity, it strongly influenced the nationalistic association between Roman Catholicism and foreign political domination. At the level of popular culture, it generated centuries of emotional anti-Catholicism that was especially strong during the time of the Gunpowder Plot, Civil Wars, and Popish Plot. Its impact upon worldwide anglophone culture endures in scores of poorly edited and inaccurate abridgements and websites. Woodcuts that it contains are among the most famous and often reproduced early modern English pictures.

A graduate of Brasenose College and onetime fellow of Magdalen College, Foxe designed the *Book of Martyrs* to supplant late medieval legends of saints, which celebrated their subjects' alleged ability to work miracles, cures, and supernatural feats. He believed that his martyrologies differ from old-fashioned saints' lives because they are not filled with fabulous elements. Although the *Book of Martyrs* contains a myriad of documents in an extraordinary array of genres (e.g., poems, speeches, tracts, biographies, spiritual memoirs, letters, historical documents, state papers, genealogies, papal bulls, and more), its main appeal for the modern reader lies in scores of highly affective narratives concerning the experience of hundreds of people who were burnt alive for their religious beliefs during the reign of Mary I, who is still best known by the sobriquet of 'Bloody Mary'.

These rousing stories incorporate unforgettable accounts of heresy hunts, apprehensions, interrogations, condemnations, imprisonments, and dying speeches.

Foxean martyrologies include stirring tales about the pacifistic response of low-born women, children, and men who died because they insisted on reading the vernacular Bible; an infant who was thrown into the fire that consumed its mother; a preacher who cut short a letter of pastoral instruction by noting that officials had arrived to lead him to the site where he would be burnt alive; and many more. At times prisoners attested to their confidence in salvation by playing chess or consuming cakes and ale as they awaited execution. Some martyrologies incorporate letters that individuals condemned for heresy composed, despite surveillance, in order to offer consolation to fellow prisoners and to extend advice on how to resist inquisition. The *Book of Martyrs* is famous for recounting the last words of victims who were about to perish in fire such as Thomas Cranmer, former Archbishop of Canterbury. After undergoing interrogation for heresy at the church of St Mary the Virgin at the University of Oxford, he was escorted hastily to the pyre in Broad Street, where he thrust his right hand into the flame to atone for having recanted his religious beliefs. At this time, he uttered the prayer of St Stephen, the protomartyr who led the way for ensuing Christian martyrs when a mob in Jerusalem stoned him to death (Acts 7: 59; see p.196).

Numerous well-crafted woodcuts made this collection the best-illustrated English book of its age. In the popular imagination, the *Book of Martyrs* is renowned for its spectacular portrayals of the 'roasting' of Sir John Oldcastle, hangings of Lollards, and the burnings of Protestant martyrs. Like the text that they illustrate, these pictures appealed to a broad popular audience. Indeed, they functioned as visual arguments that even the illiterate could understand. Functioning as illustrations for specific martyrologies, realistic narrative woodcuts incorporate details mentioned in the text. Word balloons frequently contain dying speeches attributed to martyrs.

The present Oxford World's Classics edition contains twenty-nine selections, accompanied by a selection of some of the original woodcuts, which concentrate on presenting only a tiny proportion of narrative component of this book. Foxe oversaw expansion of the text from about 1,900,000 to 3,800,000 words in four English-language editions published in 1563, 1570, 1576, and 1583.[1] (Five more unabridged editions and dozens of abridgements were published across the seventeenth and eighteenth centuries.) The fourth edition was the most physically imposing and complex English book of its era. Ordinary people read chained copies of the Bible and the *Book of Martyrs* side by side in many parish churches. Copies also found places in schools, guildhalls, cathedrals, royal palaces, and private libraries. Each edition reflects its historical moment both as an ideological construction and as an artifact of the hand-operated press.

## Foxe's Life and Times

John Foxe lived from 1516/17 until 1587, during a time of momentous change in English religion and government.[2] Shortly before his birth, an obscure Augustinian monk named Martin Luther ignited controversy over the relative merit of justification by faith versus justification by good works when he tacked his Ninety-Five Theses on the door of Castle Church at Wittenberg, an event that is conventionally viewed as the starting point of the Protestant Reformation. Based upon his understanding of St Paul's Letter to the Romans, this German theologian argued that Christian believers are wholly reliant on religious faith that comes not from within, but as a divine gift. He took particular exception to the theological principle that good works such as the purchase indulgences (i.e., remissions of temporal punishment for sin), giving of alms, or veneration of saints played any role in justifying souls for salvation. Luther's challenge met with staunch resistance from adherents of the Church of Rome, and the repercussions of this controversy reverberated throughout Western Europe. By contrast, 1516 seems remarkably tranquil. It witnessed the birth of Princess Mary by Catherine of Aragon and publication of Desiderius Erasmus' Latin–Greek New Testament and Sir Thomas

---

[1] I am indebted to Mark Greengrass for this information.

[2] For helpful overviews of historical events, see David M. Loades, *The Reign of Mary Tudor* (London, 1991); and Alan G. R. Smith, *The Emergence of a Nation State: The Commonwealth of England, 1529–1660*, 2nd edn. (London, 1997), pts. 1–2. Basic sources concerning Foxe's life and times include John N. King, 'John Foxe', in David A. Richardson (ed.), *Sixteenth-Century British Nondramatic Writers: First Series* (Detroit, 1993), 131–40; Thomas S. Freeman, 'John Foxe: A Biography', in *Foxe's Book of Martyrs Online (FBMO)*; and the *Oxford Dictionary of National Biography*.

More's *Utopia*, which contain no foretaste of Luther's challenge to the Church of Rome.

We know little about Foxe's family background or how he spent his boyhood in the town of Boston in Lincolnshire. He was quite young when church authorities burnt Lutheran books and Henry VIII published his defence of the traditional system of seven sacraments, *Assertio septem sacramentorum* (1521), in opposition to the attack mounted in Luther's *Babylonian Captivity of the Church* (1520). These sacraments consisted of the Eucharist, baptism, confirmation, penance, marriage, ordination, and extreme unction. By the time that Foxe was 10 years of age, William Tyndale had succeeded at overcoming many obstacles to the publication of his English translation of the New Testament. The disapproval of ecclesiastical and secular authorities, who believed that ordinary people ought not read and interpret the Bible for themselves, forced this translator to go into exile in order to accomplish his life's work. Although his New Testament was publicly burned, smuggled copies poured into England. Furthermore, illicit copies of Tyndale's scriptural commentaries and polemical tracts exerted a powerful influence on the domestication of Lutheran ideas.

Foxe began his studies at the University of Oxford by about 1534. During this momentous year, the Acts of Succession and Supremacy settled inheritance of the throne on the offspring of Henry VIII and Anne Boleyn, and pronounced the king Supreme Head on Earth of the Church of England. In taking control of the ecclesiastical establishment as a kind of 'English pope', the king united church and state after centuries of dispute concerning whether papal authority is superior to royal power. These events capped years of turbulence dominated by Henry VIII's petition for a divorce from Catherine of Aragon, who had failed to deliver his long-sought-for male heir. Sitting from 1529 until 1536, the Reformation Parliament promulgated a stream of statutes that brought the ecclesiastical hierarchy under royal control. When Cardinal Thomas Wolsey fell from favour over his failure to secure papal approval for a royal divorce, Sir Thomas More succeeded him as Lord Chancellor only to resign soon afterwards. Having risen in favour due to his support of the royal divorce, Thomas Cranmer became Archbishop of Canterbury in 1533, a year that also witnessed Henry VIII's marriage to Anne Boleyn while she was pregnant with Princess Elizabeth. During the mid-1530s

Henry VIII appointed Protestants such as Hugh Latimer to serve as bishops.

Foxe completed his undergraduate studies against the backdrop of continuing turbulence. Having become a Protestant while at Oxford, he moved within a circle of reformists who included Alexander Nowell and Robert Crowley. Sharing evangelical sympathies in common with Cranmer, Thomas Cromwell was the chief agent in promoting ecclesiastical reform as the king's chief minister and vicegerent for religious affairs. Not only did he initiate the Dissolution of the Abbeys, but he also patronized evangelical reformers who included John Bale, a former friar who composed militantly propagandistic plays, and Miles Coverdale, who compiled the first printed translation of the English Bible. Published in Antwerp in 1535, the Coverdale Bible completed the translation of the Bible that Tyndale had undertaken. He was executed near Antwerp soon afterwards. Having lost favour due to her failure to deliver a male heir, Anne Boleyn was beheaded on the grounds that she had committed adultery and incest. Henry VIII then married Jane Seymour, who died soon after she delivered the heir apparent, Prince Edward, on 12 October 1537.

Foxe received his Bachelor of Arts degree during the same year. A year later he became probationary fellow at Magdalen College. These events took place against the backdrop of the production of an unauthorized Bible translation by John Rogers, who employed the pseudonym of Thomas Matthews. It incorporated work by Tyndale. Building upon prior translations, the Great Bible (1539) was then printed under the patronage of Thomas Cromwell. Specifically ordering its use, the Royal Injunctions of 1538 ordered the acquisition of 'one book of the whole Bible of the largest volume, in English' by every parish church, where chained copies were to be freely accessible for the 'reading or hearing' of parishioners.[3] Combination of Tyndale's suspect work and that by Coverdale in this officially authorized version attests to how far Cromwell and Cranmer had led England in the direction of religious reform.

In 1539, Foxe became a full fellow of Magdalen College. During the same year, a conservative reaction favoured by the members of the Catholic faction led by Thomas Howard, 3rd Duke of Norfolk, and Stephen Gardiner, Bishop of Winchester, resulted in parliamentary

[3] A. G. Dickens and Dorothy Carr (eds.), *The Reformation in England to the Accession of Elizabeth I*, Documents of Modern History (London, 1967), 82.

passage of the Act of Six Articles. Even though Henry VIII countenanced administrative reforms introduced by Cranmer and Cromwell, his theological views were conservative, and he favoured retention of the Roman-rite Mass. Because of the stringent penalties that this legislation imposed, the *Book of Martyrs* terms it the 'whip with six strings'.[4] The statute reaffirmed Catholic orthodoxy concerning transubstantiation, celebration of the Mass in one kind (i.e., with reservation of the wine solely for the priest), clerical marriage, and other doctrines. Protestants such as Foxe were united in opposition to a reactionary swerve that foreshadowed the fall and execution of Cromwell. Cranmer retained favour despite conservative attack, but Hugh Latimer resigned as Bishop of Worcester and figures such as Miles Coverdale and John Bale went into exile. In 1543, the year during which Foxe received the degree of Master of Arts, Parliament went on to withdraw permission for commoners to read and interpret the Bible, even though individuals with evangelical sympathies had come into ascendancy at court, most notably Edward Seymour and Henry VIII's sixth wife, Catherine Parr. The conservative faction attempted to counter their influence by lodging heresy charges against Anne Askew, a dissident Protestant who engaged in open disputation concerning biblical interpretation. She was apparently associated with Hugh Latimer and noblewomen in the circle of Catherine Parr.

Foxe resigned his fellowship at Magdalen College in 1545, the year during which Askew underwent her first heresy examination (i.e., formal inquiry to determine whether an individual is guilty of heresy under ecclesiastical and/or civil law). He left Oxford because of his refusal to comply with the college requirement that he take a vow of celibacy and become a priest. His associate, Robert Crowley, had already resigned his fellowship. From a safe haven in the Rhineland, John Bale fuelled Protestant antipathy by publishing detailed accounts of the interrogation, condemnation, and execution of Askew on 16 July 1546. Late in this year Edward Seymour thwarted the conservatives, with the result that the Duke of Norfolk and his son, Henry Howard, Earl of Surrey, were condemned to death. The younger Howard was decapitated little more than one week before Henry VIII died on 28 January 1547. His father survived

---

[4] Foxe's *Book of Martyrs* (1583), 1136.

the late king, but he was imprisoned in the Tower of London throughout the reign of Edward VI.

During the same year, Foxe married Agnes Randall, with whom he had six children. He was employed at this time as tutor to the children of William Lucy, who resided at Charlecote in Warwickshire. Foxe moved on to London early during the minority of Edward VI, at a time when Protestant lords who controlled the king and his government were advancing a thoroughgoing programme of ecclesiastical reform. Edward Seymour, who became Protector of the Realm and Duke of Somerset, led the way, only to be deposed in 1549 by John Dudley, Earl of Warwick and later Duke of Northumberland. The Privy Council and Parliament reversed the policy of religious reaction that marked the last years of Henry VIII. Among other measures, Parliament abrogated legislation including the notorious *De haeretico comburendo* ('Concerning the burning of heretics'), which dated back to 1401. It imposed the death penalty on those who translated or owned translations of the Bible.

The heady years of the reign of Edward VI, during which Protestants enjoyed unprecedented freedom of expression, were conducive to Foxe's undertaking of historical research that would become his life's work. He attracted the attention of the Duchess of Richmond, the widow of Henry Fitzroy, Henry VIII's natural son. A notable patroness of Protestant reformers, this peeress lodged Foxe at Mountjoy House, her household in London, where he forged a long-standing acquaintance with John Bale, a fellow guest who had by now returned from exile. The duchess further arranged for Foxe to tutor the newly orphaned offspring of her brother, Henry Howard, at Reigate Castle. During these years Foxe completed *De non plectendis morte adulteri consultatio* (1548), a treatise opposed to the execution of adulterers. This work attests to his long-standing opposition to capital punishment. *De censura sive excommunicatione ecclesiastica* (1551) then called for the use of excommunication in order to punish religious and social infractions. His dedication of this learned appeal to Cranmer suggests that Foxe had gained entrée to high-ranking circles due to the patronage of the Duchess of Richmond. He was associated with William Cecil, the Principal Secretary to Edward VI, and ordained a deacon by Nicholas Ridley, Bishop of London. Foxe also made the acquaintance of the future martyrs John Hooper and John Rogers. Foxe's evangelical convictions are further apparent in his translations of tracts by Martin Luther, Johannes Oecolampadius, and Urbanus Rhegius.

Everything changed with the death of Edward VI on 6 July 1553. After the failure of the Duke of Northumberland's effort to engineer the succession to the throne of his daughter-in-law, Lady Jane Grey (the 'nine-day queen'), Mary I was acclaimed Queen of England. Her profound Roman Catholic convictions and the likelihood of her marrying her cousin, Philip of Spain, triggered the rebellion led by Sir Thomas Wyatt the Younger (January–February 1554). As the apparent beneficiary of this plot, Princess Elizabeth was imprisoned in the Tower of London and then placed under house arrest at Woodstock.

Foxe joined Bale, Crowley, and like-minded Protestants in fleeing to the Continent with his wife and family. He gravitated to Strasbourg, where Wendelin Rihel printed the first Latin instalment of his martyrological history of the martyrs, *Commentarii rerum in ecclesia gestarum* (1554). Dealing with events that took place before 1500, this work focuses on those whom Foxe regards as forerunners of the Reformation. They included John Wyclif, the Lollards, and Jan Hus. Foxe soon moved on to Frankfurt, where he sided with John Knox's effort to extend liturgical reform beyond the second Edwardian Book of Common Prayer (1552). Foxe then departed for Basle, where he spent the remainder of his exile in the company of Lawrence Humphrey and his friend John Bale. They earned a living by working as learned correctors for printers in Basle, notably Johannes Oporinus. At this time, Foxe and Bale continued to labour on their own historical and theological projects.

Revalidation of heresy legislation including the *De haeretico comburendo* ('Concerning the burning of heretics') led the way to prosecution of Protestants, about three hundred of whom were burnt at the stake from February 1555 onward. These executions left an indelible imprint upon Foxe, who joined other Protestants in vilifying Stephen Gardiner and Edmund Bonner, Bishop of London, for promoting persecution. Foxe was the recipient of manuscript transcriptions of interrogations and dying testimonials of the martyrs, many of which were passed on to him by his fellow exile, Edmund Grindal, later Archbishop of Canterbury under Elizabeth I. As Foxe collected these materials with the intention of incorporating them into his forthcoming martyrological history, he published *Christus triumphans* (1556), a Latin closet drama (i.e., a play designed to be read rather than performed) in five acts. This 'apocalyptic comedy' enfolds the 'tragic' sufferings of 'true' Christians within the over-arching trajectory of providential history as it is prefigured in the Book of Revelation. The fifth act alludes to the double execution of Hugh Latimer and Nicholas Ridley, who were burnt alive at Oxford on 16 October 1555. This dramatization of the persecution of 'true' believers by the Church of Rome is aligned with John Bale's influen-tial commentary upon Revelation, *The Image of Both Churches* (1545?), whose vision of enduring conflict between 'true' and 'false' churches would permeate the *Book of Martyrs*.

When Queen Mary died in 1558, the accession of Elizabeth I allowed for the homecoming of the Protestant exiles and the renewal of expectations for the reform of the English church. Shortly before Foxe returned to England, Oporinus and Nicolaus Brylinger pub-lished *Rerum in ecclesia gestarum . . . commentarii* (1559), an expansion of Foxe's *Commentarii*. Focusing on the persecution of 'true' believ-ers from the time of the Lollards to the early years of the Marian persecutions, *Rerum* is heavily indebted to manuscripts gathered by Grindal; John Bale's biographical bibliography of British authors, *Scriptorum illustrium maioris Brytanniae . . . catalogus* (1557–9); and related materials. Upon his return to London, Foxe lodged at the home of Thomas Howard, 4th Duke of Norfolk, whom he had tutored during the reign of Edward VI. In 1560 Grindal, who had received appointment as Bishop of London, ordained Foxe as a priest. He later received a prebend (i.e., revenue granted to canon or mem-ber of a chapter house at a collegiate church or cathedral) at Salisbury Cathedral in addition to patronage from John Parkhurst, who served as Bishop of Norwich. Nevertheless, Foxe's opposition to the wear-ing of ecclesiastical vestments during the first outbreak of Puritan controversy in the 1560s appears to have blocked him from further advancement in the ecclesiastical hierarchy.

From the time of his return to England in late 1559 until close to the end of his life, Foxe worked closely with John Day, who was a committed publisher of Protestant books. On 20 March 1563, Day published the first edition of *Book of Martyrs* at his Aldersgate print-ing establishment.[5] It is now clear that Foxe did not work alone, but

---

[5] On the publication history of editions of the *Book of Martyrs* published during the lifetime of Foxe and Day, see John N. King, *Foxe's* Book of Martyrs *and Early Modern Print Culture* (Cambridge, 2006), 92–135.

engaged in a collaborative enterprise in constructing this martyro-logical history.[6] This initial publication reflects the optimistic mood of the opening years of the reign of Elizabeth I, when nationalistic Protestants welcomed the cessation of religious persecution and expectations were high for completion of the programme of ecclesiastical reform embarked upon during the reign of Edward VI. Drawing heavily upon *Rerum . . . commentarii*, this edition emphasizes ecclesiastical history from roughly 1000 CE, with particular emphasis on the period since the time of John Wyclif. By positioning his account of the imprisonment of Elizabeth when she was a princess close to the conclusion of this book, Foxe reinforces his claim that she miraculously survived to succeed her half-sister due to the intervention of divine providence.

In 1570 John Day published the second edition of the *Book of Martyrs*. During the preceding seven years, this compilation almost doubled in size to about 3,500,000 words. It established an enduring model for succeeding editions overseen by Foxe and Day in addition to five more unabridged editions published up to 1684. Not only did Foxe engage in substantial revision of the original text and deletion of previously published material, he expanded the collection in response to stinging assault by Roman Catholic critics, most notably Nicholas Harpsfield, whose *Dialogi sex* (Antwerp, 1566) attacked Protestant historians including Foxe under the pseudonym of Alan Cope. Foxe broadened the scope of his inquiry by going back to the early days of the Christian church in order to place the martyrdoms of Christian believers from the Roman persecutions onwards within the context of the evolving relationship between ecclesiastical and secular authority. Like Bale, Foxe was convinced that the Church of Rome had diverged from the 'true' church from the late Middle Ages onwards. In collaboration with associates such as Henry Bull, he expanded this heterogeneous collection through the addition of a multitude of letters written by the martyrs, manuscript accounts, and oral testimony.

High-ranking officials encouraged the acquisition of copies of the 1570 version for reading in public places. Chained copies were

---

[6] Patrick Collinson, 'John Foxe and National Consciousness', in Christopher Highley and John N. King (eds.), *John Foxe and His World* (Aldershot, 2002), 14; King, *Foxe's Book of Martyrs and Early Modern Print Culture*, 25–37; and Editorial Commentary in *FBMO*.

placed in English cathedrals under order from the Convocation, and the Privy Council called for its acquisition by parish churches. Foxe's intensification of anti-papal animus as the second edition was in press was in keeping with the nationalistic reaction against the recent Roman Catholic challenge to the Elizabethan religious settlement. As Foxe and Day laboured on this edition, a number of northern earls rose in rebellion during October 1569. Plotting to promote a Roman Catholic succession, they aimed to secure the freedom of Mary, Queen of Scots, and to marry her to the 4th Duke of Norfolk. A decade of relative toleration of English Catholics came to a close in February 1570, when Pope Pius V promulgated *Regnans in Excelsis*, a bull in which he excommunicated Queen Elizabeth and urged her subjects to overthrow her. At a time when English Catholics fell under suspicion of complicity with the intrigues of foreign Catholic powers, Foxe enhanced the anti-papal content of the *Book of Martyrs*.

Foxe immersed himself in a variety of projects following publication of the second edition of the *Book of Martyrs*. Among other endeavours, he edited *The Whole Works of William Tyndale, John Frith, and Doctor [Robert] Barnes* (1573) in collaboration with John Day. This edition accords with Foxe's high praise of Tyndale in the laudatory account of his life and death that he incorporated into the *Book of Martyrs*. Published on 27 June 1576, the third edition of the *Book of Martyrs* followed along lines similar to those of the previous version even though it is somewhat shorter and contains revisions. The major change involved John Day's decision to place its production under the supervision of his son, Richard. The employment of cheaper paper and smaller type sizes appears to be the product of a concerted effort to produce a more affordable book. A homily by Foxe and an attack on the papacy were published under the titles of *A Sermon Preached at the Christening of a Certain Jew* (1578) and *The Pope Confuted* (1580). Having published the fourth edition of the *Book of Martyrs* in October 1583, John Day died during July of the following year. At a length of about 3,800,000 words, it is the longest and most complete version of this collection. This collection follows along the lines of the 1570 version, but Foxe continued to add new material and restore some of the material excised from previous editions. At the time of Foxe's death on 18 April 1587, his son, Samuel, and Abraham Fleming were assisting the martyrologist in preparing *Eicasmi seu meditationes, in sacram Apocalypsin*

(1587) for publication. It contains an extended commentary on Revelation 1–17.

## Theology and Religion

Foxe and like-minded Protestants regarded the reign of Edward VI as the high water mark of religious reformation. It represented a radical departure from ecclesiastical reform under Henry VIII, when theology and ritual underwent little change. Earlier changes were largely administrative, because they involved schism from the Church of Rome, submission of the clerical hierarchy to royal authority, the Dissolution of the Monasteries, and so forth. The Roman-rite Mass, wearing of clerical vestments, and religious ceremonies and ritual remained essentially unchanged. The Act of Six Articles upheld traditional doctrinal belief in clerical celibacy; auricular confession (i.e., one heard by a priest); and transubstantiation, whereby the *substance* (i.e., essential nature) of the elements of bread and wine undergo transformation into the body and blood of Christ even though the *accidents* (i.e., material attributes) remain the same.

Everything changed under Edward VI, when Archbishop Cranmer presided over sweeping change of English worship. According to the *Book of Martyrs*, this time represents the benchmark for evaluating the state of 'true' religion. This is the case, for example, in the account of John Rogers, who remained abroad 'until such time as it pleased God, by the faithful travail of his chosen and dear servant King Edward the sixth, utterly to banish all popery forth of England, and to receive in true religion, setting God's gospel at liberty' (p. 35). Not only did exiled preachers return home, but England also became a haven for foreign reformers including Martin Bucer and Pietro Martire Vermigli. Having resumed his preaching career, Hugh Latimer joined John Hooper and others in preaching on behalf of ecclesiastical reform at Paul's Cross and other pulpits. In addition to sanctioning unrestricted public access to the vernacular Bible, the Royal Injunctions of 1547 ordered all clergy except those licensed to write their own sermons to preach out of the Book of Homilies, a set of government-authorized sermons, and to study Erasmus' *Paraphrases of the New Testament*. The same orders endorsed widespread iconoclastic attack on relics, religious images, and shrines. Standing almost alone in opposition to the imposition of changes in religion during a royal minority, Stephen Gardiner was imprisoned in the Tower of London.

Within a year of the accession of Edward VI, Parliament had swept away the chantries, the Act of Six Articles, and prior heresy legislation. Doctrines concerning purgatory and clerical celibacy were abandoned. During 1548, the government abolished many religious ceremonies. In a radical departure from the traditional Latin rite, Cranmer oversaw the gradual introduction of an English church service. Parliament authorized the first Book of Common Prayer, which came into use throughout England on 9 June 1549 (Whitsunday). Although it rejected transubstantiation, this document retained a vernacular version of the Mass, clerical vestments, and other elements of traditional ritual. Following the fall of Protector Somerset, John Hooper used his enhanced prominence at the royal court to advance Zwinglian ideas concerning the commemorative nature of Holy Communion. Conservative bishops, notably Bonner and Gardiner, were deprived of their sees and replaced with evangelical successors such as Hooper and Ridley. They led the way in ordering the removal of rood screens and replacing altars with communion tables placed in chancels of churches. Hooper opposed the wearing of clerical vestments and was a leader of opposition to the first prayer book that resulted in a revised second edition of the Book of Common Prayer. Introduced in 1552, the new church service did away with the Mass, elevation of the host, altars, and chasubles. Revision of the canon of the Mass made it clear that the sacrament was not an object of veneration. The Privy Council overruled Cranmer when it inserted the 'Black Rubric', which denied that kneeling at communion implied adoration, transubstantiation, or the Real Presence of Christ. Not long before the death of the boy king, the government issued the Forty-Two Articles, which imposed an essentially Protestant settlement of religion.[7]

The reign of Mary I represented a catastrophe for Protestant reformers. Two Acts of Repeal undid first the Edwardian and then the Henrician Reformation. Clerics such as John Rogers and Rowland Taylor ran afoul the authorities for preaching in favour of the religious settlement under Edward VI in violation of this legislation and the Marian proclamation against unlicensed preaching. The *Book of*

---

[7] See Smith, *Emergence of a Nation State*, 64–76.

*Martyrs* praises the latter preacher, for example, because he opposed reinstatement of the Roman-rite Mass: 'For as yet Doctor Taylor, as a good shepherd, had retained and kept in his church, the godly church service and reformation made by King Edward, and most faithfully and earnestly preached against the popish corruptions, which had infected the whole country round about' (p. 74).

The revival of legislation against heresy resulted in the deaths of hundreds of Protestants who remained resolute in their denial of transubstantiation and insistence that Holy Communion represents a commemorative service rather than a repeated sacrifice effected through the officiation of unmarried priests. Attack on celibacy represents a minor concern, but an important one, in these narratives. Ministers such as Rowland Taylor, John Hooper, and John Rogers receive praise for maintaining 'godly' households in adherence to the Protestant position that celibacy is not mandatory and that it is advisable for clerics to marry.

The doctrinal issue over which scores of alleged heretics were willing to die was their denial that the elements of bread and wine undergo transubstantiation into the body and blood of Christ during the Mass. It should come as no surprise to note that underlying this dispute is a controversy over biblical interpretation, namely the correct meaning of Jesus' words at the time of the Last Supper: 'During supper he took bread, and having said the blessing he broke it and gave it to them, with the words "Take this; this is my body". Then he took a cup, and having offered thanks to God he gave it to them; and they all drank from it. And he said to them, "This is my blood, the blood of the covenant, shed for many"' (Mark 14: 22–4). Zwingli's understanding of these words wholly in a figurative sense underlies his view that Holy Communion represents a commemorative rite. This interpretation represented a major crux of this controversy.

During heresy examinations, Roman Catholic interrogators attempt over and over again to persuade alleged heretics to recant the Zwinglian position. The martyrs are equally vehement, however, in the manner of William Hunter, who responds to his interrogator that the scriptural text categorically states that '"Christ took bread but not that he changed it, into another substance, but gave that which he took, and brake that which he gave, which was bread, as is evident by the text. For else he should have had two bodies, which to affirm I see no reason"' (p. 107). In the manner of other martyrs, Hunter elaborates his position thus: 'And also though Christ call the bread his body, as he doeth also say, that he is a vine, a door, et cetera. Yet is not his body turned into bread, nor more than he is turned into a door, or vine. Wherefore Christ called the bread his body by a figure' (p. 107). It should come as no surprise to note that William Tyndale articulates the hermeneutical basis for this controversy in his *Obedience of a Christian Man*, which rejects the fourfold mode of Scholastic interpretation on the ground that the meaning of the Bible is wholly literal, even though its language is filled with metaphorical usages: 'So in like manner the scripture borroweth words and sentences of all manner things, and maketh proverbs and similitudes or allegories. . . . So when I say, "Christ is a lamb", I mean not a lamb that beareth wool, but a meek and patient lamb which is beaten for other men's faults. Christ is a vine, not that beareth grapes, but out of whose root the branches that believe, suck the spirit of life, and mercy, and grace, and power to be the sons of God and do his will. The similitudes of the gospel are allegories borrowed of worldly matters to express spiritual things."'[8]

## Martyrological Narratives

Although the *Book of Martyrs* is filled with many kinds of documents, its best-remembered parts consist of detailed narratives concerning the lives of 'true' Christian believers who were condemned to death because of their religious convictions. These martyrologies include moving accounts of William Tyndale's career from his university days until his execution in the Low Countries; Anne Askew's refusal to remain silent concerning biblical interpretation; the death of John Rogers, the proto-martyr who stands at the head of the list of victims of Marian heresy inquisitions; the career of Thomas Cranmer, the all-too-human prelate who wavered in his beliefs only to reaffirm his faith, as he was consumed with flames, by first burning the hand that signed his recantation; the poignant account of the execution of the Protestant heroes Nicholas Ridley and aged Hugh Latimer, who were burnt alive in the same pyre in Broad Street at the University of Oxford; and many more.

[8] John N. King (ed.), *Voices of the English Reformation: A Sourcebook* (Philadelphia, 2004), 41. See John 1: 29, 36; and 15: 1.

These accounts are disturbing even to readers who are not squeamish, but they provide opportunities for enjoying good, indeed often exciting, stories involving black-and-white confrontations between 'heroes' and 'villains'. We see this, for example, when Anne Askew talks back to interrogators including Bishop Bonner, all of whom are male. When he questions her concerning Mass bread— '"What if the scripture do say that it is the body of Christ?"'—she comes back with a quibbling retort that appears to pay lip service to the patriarchal expectation that women should remain chaste, silent, and obedient: '"I believe," said I, "as the scripture doth teach me"' (p. 27). Foxe or informants whose narratives he collects employ all of the devices of good storytelling to enthrall the audience, gruesome detail being one of them. This is the case, for instance, in the description of the prolonged suffering of John Hooper, when he is burnt on a pyre of green wood that requires rekindling three times:

But when he was black in the mouth, and his tongue swollen, that he could not speak, yet his lips went till they were shrunk to the gums: and he knocked his breast with his hands, until one of his arms fell off, and then knocked still with the other, what time the fat, water, and blood dropped out at his fingers' ends, until by renewing of the fire, his strength was gone, and his hand did cleave fast in knocking to the iron upon his breast. So immediately bowing forwards, he yielded up his spirit. (p. 70)

These stories are disturbing partly because their unflinching descriptions are so fascinating.

Because of Foxe's unsubtle propagandizing and vilification of Roman Catholics as superstitious persecutors, his history immediately came under attack from hostile critics for being a thin tissue of fictions and lies. Although questioning of the truthfulness of the *Book of Martyrs* lasted well into the nineteenth century, this kind of inquiry has lost favour with late twentieth- and twenty-first-century historiographers. It seems reasonable to claim, then, that Foxe was notable not so much for his truthfulness, but for his masterly ability to construct powerful myths.[9] His imaginative embellishments were of less concern at a time when the line between 'history' and 'story'

[9] Patrick Collinson, 'Truth and Legend: The Veracity of John Foxe's *Book of Martyrs*', in A. C. Duke and C. A. Tamse (eds.), *Clio's Mirror: Historiography in Britain and the Netherlands* (Zutphen, 1985), 151–2.

was less clearly demarcated than it became in later centuries.[10] What mattered was Foxe's effectiveness as a popularizer and skill in lodging highly polemical arguments in a compelling fashion.

Like his Roman Catholic opponents, Foxe subscribes to the Augustinian dictum that 'It is the cause, not the suffering, which makes a martyr'. In line with this sentiment, he excludes those who profess religious beliefs alien to his own. As such, he designs 'true' martyrologies in order to supplant medieval legends of saints, which celebrated their subjects' alleged ability to work miracles, cures, and magical feats. Denying that the *Book of Martyrs* contains 'anything fabulous', the martyrologist declares that he tells the truth because he has drawn his documents 'from the archives and registers of bishops and from the letters of the martyrs themselves, drawn together to be seen side by side'.[11] The suffering experience of saints is a common element in Protestant and Catholic martyrologies, but Foxe and his co-religionists insist that sainthood means risking even life itself to testify on behalf of Christ, rather than in the marvellous elements emphasized in late medieval saints' legends. Instead of the older belief that saints are exceptional individuals who possess miraculous power to intercede on behalf of sinners (e.g., Saints Barbara and Catherine of Alexandra), Protestants believed that sainthood is accessible to any 'true' believer, including Lollard dissidents of the late Middle Ages and lowly peasants and artisans, many of whom died for their faith under Mary I.[12]

Stories about the martyrs constitute the fundamental narrative units of the *Book of Martyrs*. Even though Foxe relies on first-person narratives, manuscripts written by eyewitnesses, and oral testimony, he or his sources attempt to impose an orderly shape on disparate materials. Typical of the martyrologist's active role in the framing of narrative is 'A notable history of William Hunter, a young man of nineteen years'. The brief account in early versions of the *Book of Martyrs* underwent considerable expansion in the second edition due to the addition of a highly circumstantial eyewitness report written

---

[10] See William Nelson, *Fact or Fiction: The Dilemma of the Renaissance Storyteller* (Cambridge, Mass. 1973).

[11] Foxe's *Book of Martyrs* (1583), *1ᵛ–2ᵛ; trans. supplied.

[12] See Helen C. White, *Tudor Books of Saints and Martyrs* (Madison, 1963), ch. 1. For a helpful approach to the construction of narrative in Foxe's *Book of Martyrs*, see John R. Knott, *Discourses of Martyrdom in English Literature, 1563–1694* (Cambridge, 1993), chs. 1–2.

by the victim's own brother, Robert, 'who being present with his brother William, and never left him till his death'. Making no claim to original authorship, Foxe indicates that he 'with like faithfulness placed and recorded the same' within his martyrological history (p. 102). In the instance of Rawlins White, a Cardiff fisherman, Foxe initially included a simple notice concerning the death of this martyr. In the 1570 version, however, he adds a moving eyewitness account supplied by John Dane, whose mother aided the prisoner by providing him with 'money and other relief' (p. 117). In the 1576 and 1583 editions, these narratives remained wholly or almost wholly the same.[13]

Foxe emphasizes the importance of organizing narratives in a clear and compelling manner. This is the case in one of the most interesting stories in the *Book of Martyrs*, for example, that of Richard Woodman. By drawing on the martyr's own accounts of his experience and transcriptions of his heresy examinations, Foxe enables Woodman to address the reader directly in a very appealing and convincing voice. The martyrologist indicates that it is inclusion of Woodman's own words that gives weight to a narrative that might otherwise seem unbelievable: 'Touching the whole discourse whereof, for so much as the matter is something strange, and will peradventure scarce find credit upon my narration, with them which deny all things, that like them not to believe, ye shall hear himself speak, and testify both of the manner of his troubles, and also his own examinations by himself recorded, in order as followeth' (p. 213). This narrative contains many colourful details about Woodman's concealing of himself from heretic hunters by hiding in a concealed chamber within his home and in nearby woods. Foxe notes, furthermore, that it is important to follow chronological order, as in the story about Thomas Haukes, a courtier whose patron turned him in to authorities for religious heterodoxy: 'first, beginning briefly with his godly conversation and institution of life, then showing of his troubles, also of his examinations and conflicts with the bishop and other adversaries according as the order of his story doth require' (p. 133).

Formulaic elements in martyrological narratives include the apprehension of alleged heretics, imprisonment, heresy examination (sometimes in the presence of torture), clerical appeal for recantation,

---

[13] For detailed accounts of the sources for individual narratives, see the Editorial Commentary in *FBMO*.

refusal to recant (sometimes after an initial recantation), conviction, chaining to the stake, recitation of Psalm 51 (a confession of sin and penitential lamentation), and final prayerful utterances. Either through negligence or a desire to save money, executioners sometimes failed to provide an adequate supply of wood or used unseasoned green wood. Martyrs such as Lawrence Saunders accordingly suffered agonizingly drawn-out death over slowly smouldering flames.

Notes that fill the margins of early editions of the *Book of Martyrs* function not only as place indicators, but also as markers that outline progressive stages in narratives. Foxe also editorializes by introducing evaluative comments within marginal glosses. In the account of the imprisonment and release of Princess Elizabeth, for example, these notes enforce Foxe's thesis that she was the recipient of the 'blessed protection of almighty God . . . in her manifold dangers and troubles' and that she was 'preserved by the Lord's providence from execution in the Tower'. An added comment asserts that divine intervention shielded her from Stephen Gardiner: 'Winchester's platform overthrown' (pp. 265, 272).

The account of Rowland Taylor constitutes an exemplary martyrology that contains familiar components that we witness in many other narratives. Building upon a set of documents contained in *Rerum . . . commentarii*, Foxe relied on oral testimonials in expanding his story in the 1563 *Book of Martyrs*. After the addition of further material in 1570, this account remains largely the same in later editions. Opening with an idealized account of Taylor's pastoral career at Hadleigh, Foxe draws on a variety of local witnesses in portraying this minister as a clerical paragon who was 'void of all pride, humble, and meek as any child' in the course of instructing his parishioners in knowledge of the Bible and 'true' religion. Nevertheless, 'he would be stout in rebuking the sinful and evil doers . . . with such earnest and grave rebukes as became a good curate and pastor' (p. 73). After his highly dramatic resistance to the reinstatement of the Mass following the accession of Mary I, his Roman Catholic opponents report him to clerical authorities. Instead of fleeing, he resolutely submits to interrogation by Stephen Gardiner and other bishops concerning his views on the sacrament. After being remanded to prison, he remains true to his clerical vocation by preaching, praying, and engaging in biblical interpretation with fellow prisoners. Following repeated examinations by bishops and condemnation for heresy, he receives a visit from Bishop Bonner. In order to deprive him of office, the bishop requires him to don episcopal vestments prior to their symbolic removal. Bonner backs down from a threat to strike the prisoner with his episcopal crook when his chaplain restrains him on the ground that Taylor, a heavily built man, would assault him. Indeed, the prisoner indicates that he would emulate St Peter in fighting on behalf of Christ as his master.

After spending a night at an inn outside London Wall, Taylor and his guards set out for Hadleigh on horseback. Constituting an important formulaic element in martyrological narratives, his cheerful readiness to die functions as a mark of martyrological sanctity. En route to Hadleigh, he was accordingly 'joyful and merry, as one that accounted himself going to a most pleasant banquet or bridal' (p. 87).[14] A marginal note calls attention to his jesting anticipation of his consumption by fire:

I am as you see, a man that hath a great carcass, which I thought should have been buried in Hadleigh churchyard if I had died in my bed, as I well hoped I should have done: but herein I see I was deceived: and there are a great number of worms in Hadleigh churchyard, which should have had jolly feeding on this carrion, which they have looked for many a day. But now I know we be deceived, both I and they: for this carcass must be burnt to ashes and so shall they lose their bait and feeding, that they looked to have had of it. (p. 88)

Taylor quibbles on the deceitfulness of death in denying scavengers an opportunity to feast upon his not inconsiderable flesh. Another marginal stresses the condemned man's embrace of death as a heavenly homecoming: 'now I know I am almost at home. I lack not past two stiles to go over, and I am even at my father's house' (p. 89). In styling his forthcoming suffering as an imitation of Christ, these words constitute a witty variation of Jesus' final discourse with the

[14] Among other instances of composure in the face of death, we may take note of Thomas Bilney's enjoyment of 'an ale brew with . . . a cheerful heart and quiet mind' on the day before his execution (p. 9); John Rogers's composure during imprisonment, when he was 'merry and earnest in all he went about' (p. 37); John Bradford's consoling words—'"Be of good comfort, brother; for we shall have a merry supper with the Lord this night"'—to the young man with whom he was burnt alive (p. 149); John Hooper's decision '"to tarry and to live and die with my sheep"' rather than flee from his episcopal see (p. 59); and Thomas Haukes's agreement with his friends that he would provide a sign within the flames 'if the rage of the pain were tolerable and might be suffered' (p. 136).

disciples: 'There are many dwelling-places in my Father's house; if it were not so I should have told you: for I am going to prepare a place for you' (John 14: 2).

The tight management of the execution site is typical. Guards in attendance deny this gifted preacher an opportunity to exhort bystanders when they force a pointed weapon into his mouth. He has an added incentive to acquiesce if rumour is correct that the Privy Council has threatened to have martyrs' tongues cut out unless 'they would promise, that at their deaths they would keep silence, and not speak to the people' (p. 91). After all, he wishes to retain the power of speech in the hope that he may deliver a final prayerful testimonial to his religious faith from within the flames. In the manner of other martyrs, he doffs his attire until no more than his 'shirt' (an under-garment) remains. He gives away his clothing and books as a form of alms. As an act of mercy, one bystander provides Taylor with a bag of gunpowder in order to enable him to die swiftly when the fire causes it to explode. The cruelty of the executioners, one of whom draws blood by striking him on the head with a faggot, is not un-usual. Another one strikes the doomed man on the lips when he recites Psalm 51 in English, rather than the authorized Latin Vulgate version. At the climactic moment, as the flames rise upwards, Taylor delivers his last words: '"Merciful father of heaven, for Jesus Christ my Saviour's sake, receive my soul into thy hands"' (p. 93). In a final act of cruelty, the recipient of the gift of Taylor's boots dashes out his brains with a halberd.

The *Book of Martyrs* is renowned for recording last words of the kind that Rowland Taylor spoke. Their conventional character is apparent in the recurrence of formulaic utterances. For example, the reader encounters variations of his final prayer in accounts of the burnings of John Hooper, Thomas Haukes, Thomas Cranmer, and others (see pp. 70, 138, 196). These words are appropriate because they are modelled on a prayer uttered by St Stephen. In rehearsing their final performance only moments before they were burnt alive, martyrs behaved in accordance with the *ars moriendi* ('art of dying'), which presumed that a 'good death' functioned as a testimonial to dying in a state of grace.[15] In attempting to silence martyrs, bailiffs acknowledged the power of final words. The sententiousness of dying

---

[15] Mary Hampson Patterson, *Domesticating the Reformation: Protestant Best Sellers, Private Devotion, and the Revolution of English Piety* (Teaneck, NJ, 2007), 101–54, *passim*.

speeches accords with the widespread belief that last words should command attention because individuals on the verge of death lack any incentive to lie. A preface added to the seventh edition of the *Book of Martyrs* acknowledges the rhetorical impact of last words in declaring 'the most pathetical speeches of dying saints' afford a good means 'to win the affections' of readers or hearers of its stories'.[16] On reading these affective declarations, many early readers must have experienced a frisson that combined religious instruction with entertainment.

Aphorisms, maxims, and other witty sayings abound in words uttered by martyrs before being burnt alive. For example, all but the first edition of the *Book of Martyrs* ascribes to Hugh Latimer what may be the best-remembered speech in the entire collection. Of the immolation that he was about to share with Nicholas Ridley, the aged cleric is said to have made this epitaphic utterance: 'Be of good comfort Master Ridley, and play the man: we shall this day light such a candle by God's grace in England, as (I trust) shall never be put out' (p. 154). These words are famous as a rallying cry of the English Reformation. Latimer's punning allusion to wording in the Sermon on the Mount (Matthew 5: 14–15) declares that their martyrdom will contribute paradoxically to the endurance of 'true' faith.

In the manner of Hugh Latimer, many martyrs articulated spiritual testaments at the point of death. When Lawrence Saunders arrived at the stake to which he was about to be chained, for example, he embraced and kissed it with the exclamation that styles his death as an imitation of Christ: 'Welcome the cross of Christ; welcome everlasting life'. John Bradford bade farewell to the companion with whom he shared a pyre by paraphrasing an eschatological warning from the Sermon on the Mount: 'Strait is the way, and narrow is the gate that leadeth unto life eternal, and few there be that find it' (Matthew 7: 13–14). Other remarks that gained considerable fame include John Philpot's apostrophe to the site of his burning north-west of London Wall: 'I will pay my vows in thee O Smithfield' (pp. 51, 149, 167).

## The Bible

The Bible is the most important influence on narratives in the *Book of Martyrs*. Not only do scriptural quotations and allusions fill stories

---

[16] *Book of Martyrs* (1631), vol. 1, sig. ()6$^{r-v}$.

about the martyrs, but they often receive explicit citations within the text or among the marginal glosses. Even more, Foxe and the informants on whom he draws have absorbed biblical phraseology into their own prose in a manner that often goes without acknowledgement.[17] This habit of mind reflects the mentality of an era during which individuals engaged in methodical reading of the Bible and often knew large sections or even the whole of the Bible by heart.

One of the major themes of the *Book of Martyrs* concerns how laypersons ignorant of learned languages became empowered to read and interpret the Bible in the vernacular without the intercession of clerics. This development originates in the humanistic insistence upon returning to original sources in an effort to recover the original state of biblical texts in Hebrew, Greek, and Aramaic. It accords, furthermore, with Erasmus' influential appeal in *Paraclesis* ('Exhortation'), one of the prefaces to his Latin–Greek edition of the New Testament, for translation of the Bible so that 'even the lowliest women' could study the scriptures for themselves.[18]

In constructing the first biography of William Tyndale for inclusion in the *Book of Martyrs*, Foxe praises this humanistic scholar as a Reformation hero for undertaking translation of the New Testament into the English language. Building upon a lost manuscript account presumably written by Richard Webb[19] and autobiographical comments in Tyndale's own non-translation prose, the martyrologist narrates a colourful story about how Tyndale exposed the ignorance of unlearned clerics when he served as a tutor to the children of Sir John Walsh of Little Sodbury, Gloucestershire. The central incident demonstrates the translator's adherence to the Lutheran doctrine of *sola scriptura* ('by scripture alone') when he countered the words of one who subordinated the authority of the Bible to that of the pope with the zealous rejoinder that 'ere many years he would cause a boy that driveth the plough to know more of the scripture, than he did' (p. 15). It seems certain that this speech recalls the following appeal for translation of scriptural texts in Erasmus' *Paraclesis*: 'Would that, as a result, the farmer sing some portion of them at the plow'.[20]

[17] The Explanatory Notes below identify many quotations and allusions that receive no explicit acknowledgement within narratives in this text.

[18] Desiderius Erasmus, *Christian Humanism and the Reformation: Selected Writings*, ed. John C. Olin (New York, 1965), 97.

[19] David Daniell, *William Tyndale: A Biography* (New Haven and London, 1994), 61.

[20] Erasmus, *Christian Humanism*, 97.

Of course, a gulf yawns between Erasmus' use of 'Would that' as opposed to Tyndale's 'I will cause'. Tyndale sets out to accomplish what Erasmus expresses only in the form of a wish.[21] The remainder of the Tyndale martyrology incorporates other materials including an account of his residence in Antwerp that appears to have been written by Thomas Poyntz, a kinsman of Lady Anne Walsh, with whom Tyndale lodged at Antwerp prior to his apprehension and execution.

The *Book of Martyrs* contains many stories about martyrs of lowly status who learn to understand the vernacular Bible in fulfilment of Erasmus's appeal and Tyndale's prophecy. This ideal informs Rowland Taylor's ministry at Hadleigh, where many parishioners 'became exceeding well learned in the holy scriptures, as well women as men. . . . Their children and servants were also brought up and trained so diligently in the right knowledge of God's word, that the whole town seemed rather an university of the learned, than a town of cloth-making or labouring people' (p. 72). In the account of William Hunter, one reads about an apprentice weaver who debates scriptural interpretation with a cleric.[22] Illiterate martyrs who absorb the Bible through hearing it read aloud by others include Joan Waste, a blind weaver and rope maker, and Rowland White, a Welsh fisherman. Lowly women other than Waste include a spinner who is remembered only as the wife of a man whose surname is Prest. According to the transcription of her examination for heresy, she is able to employ language laced with Bible quotations and allusions in debating with the Bishop of Exeter concerning the Eucharist (p. 206). Her abandonment of her husband and children recalls the behaviour of Anne Askew, a gentlewoman who recounts how she flouted patriarchal authority by going to Lincoln Minster to engage in public reading of the Bible: '"I remained there nine days to see what would be said unto me"' (p. 28). Not only does Rowland White hear readings from the Bible, but he learns it by heart and becomes an

---

[21] Stephen Greenblatt, *Renaissance Self-Fashioning: From More to Shakespeare* (Chicago, 1980), 106. On Foxe's engagement with Tyndale, see John N. King, '"The Light of Printing": William Tyndale, John Foxe, John Day, and Early Modern Print Culture', *Renaissance Quarterly* 54 (2001), 52–85.

[22] Dialogues between learned lay people and ignorant clerics are a familiar component of Protestant propaganda in Germany and England. See John N. King, *English Reformation Literature: The Tudor Origins of the Protestant Tradition* (Princeton, 1982), 258–62, 286–7.

itinerant preacher in the hills of Wales. In yet another variation of Tyndale's plowboy, George Eagles is an unlearned tailor who is also known by the name of Trudgeover because of his habit of wandering as an itinerant preacher. As he is dragged on a sledge to the site of his execution, he reads from the Book of Psalms 'all the way with a loud voice till he came there' (p. 234). Bible reading played a transformative role in the life of a dissident ironmaker, Richard Woodman, whose speech is laced with scriptural quotations and allusions. When authorities force him to go into hiding in a forest, he considers it essential to bring with him 'even under a tree . . . my Bible, my pen and mine ink, and other necessaries' (p. 217).

Underlying many of the Bible quotations and allusions in the *Book of Martyrs* is the typological application of scriptural texts to ecclesiastical history and the experiences of individual believers. Foxe, his informants, and many of the martyrs believed that later events are prefigured by and patterned upon happenings recorded in the Old and New Testaments. These correspondences contribute to a prevailing manner in which martyrs such as Anne Askew, Rowland Taylor, and Richard Woodman speak in parables and employ language infused with scriptural imagery and symbolism. In the *Obedience of a Christian Man*, Tyndale describes typological application in terms of the borrowing of 'likenesses or allegories of the scripture, as of Pharaoh and Herod and of the scribes and Pharisees, to express our miserable captivity and persecution under Antichrist the Pope'.[23]

The reader encounters repeated examples of the most pervasive typological application, imitation of Christ. For example, Thomas Bilney intimates to his friends that 'he would go to Jerusalem, alluding belike to the words and examples of Christ in the Gospel going up to Jerusalem, what time he was appointed to suffer his passion' (p. 6). According to the narrator of the story of Rowland Taylor, this martyr discharged his ministry on the model of Jesus Christ as the Good Shepherd: 'Where he as a good shepherd, abiding and dwelling among his sheep, gave himself wholly to the study of holy scriptures most faithful endeavouring himself to fulfil that charge, which the Lord gave unto Peter, saying, "Peter, lovest thou me? Feed my lambs, feed my sheep, feed my sheep"' (p. 72). In refusing to save his life by taking flight, furthermore, Taylor himself declares

---

[23] King (ed.), *Voices*, 43.

to his servant: '"Remember the good shepherd Christ, which not only fed his flock, but also died for his flock".'[24]

A related cluster of pastoral metaphors is grounded upon the messianic prophecy concerning the suffering servant who is 'like a sheep led to the slaughter' (Isaiah 53: 7). Christians interpret this text as a prefiguration of the crucifixion of Jesus as the 'Lamb of God' (John 1: 29, Acts 8: 26–39). Lamenting the imprisonment of Protestant ministers 'as lambs waiting when the butchers would call them to the slaughter', for example, the narrator of Taylor's story indicates that the consciences of persecutors 'told them, that they led innocent lambs to the slaughter' (p. 86). As members of Christ's 'flock', Christian believers also undergo comparison to lambs or sheep. John Hooper accordingly affirms that he will not flee, but instead '"tarry and to live and die with my sheep"'. The narrator notes that he proceeds to the site of his execution 'as it were [as] a lamb to the place of slaughter' (p. 67). Beleaguered Protestants likened inquisitors and executioners, furthermore, to butchers of innocent lambs. Chief among them is the Bishop of London whom Protestants vilified as 'Butcher Bonner'. A related concern elaborates upon an admonition from the Sermon on the Mount: '"Beware of false prophets, who come to you dressed up as sheep while underneath they are savage wolves"' (Matthew 7: 15). When friends would come to visit Rowland White during his imprisonment at Cardiff Castle, for example, this fisherman-preacher 'would pass away the time in prayer and exhortations, admonishing them always to beware of false prophets which come in sheep's clothing'. Jesus' warning against dissimulators within the church stuck like pitch to Stephen Gardiner, the cunning Bishop of Winchester whom Protestants maligned with the unforgettable alliterative epithet: 'Winchester Wolf'.[25]

Christological overtones come into play in other forms. For example, a marginal gloss likens the manner in which Edmund Bonner sends Lawrence Saunders to Stephen Gardiner to the action of Annas in sending Jesus for interrogation by Caiaphas, the high priest, prior to the crucifixion (p. 47; see John 18: 19, 24). When Woodman speaks of his ability to elude his pursuers—'And yet all mine enemies could lay no hands on me till the hour was full come'—he alludes to Jesus' declaration to the disciples, prior to the crucifixion, that

[24] See John 10: 1–18.
[25] See King (ed.), *Voices*, 293.

'"The hour has come for the Son of Man to be glorified"' (John 12: 23). Continuing in a similar vein when he is apprehended, Woodman applies another declaration of Jesus concerning the crucifixion—'"The Son of Man is going the way appointed for him in the scriptures; but alas for that man by whom the Son of Man is betrayed! It would be better for that man if he had never been born"' (Matthew 26: 24)—to his own condition: 'This way was appointed of God for me to be delivered into the hands of mine enemies, but woe unto him by whom I am betrayed. It had been good for that man, that he had never been born' (p. 220).

In other cases, martyrs envision their suffering not in terms of imitation of Christ, but as a means of attaining union with Christ after death. This is the case when Rawlins White requested that his sorrowful wife 'send unto him his wedding garment, meaning a shirt, which afterward he was burned in' (p. 120). In a similar vein, John Bradford uttered a 'prayer of the wedding garment' when he 'shifted himself with a clean shirt that was made for his burning (by one Master Walter Marlar's wife, who was a good nurse unto him, and his very good friend)' (p. 145–6). The apocalyptic expectations associated with Christ as the Bridegroom and the Spouse as a figure for the faithful Christian (Revelation 19: 7–8) become explicit when the narrator praises the 'cheerful countenance' of Prest's wife 'as though she had been prepared for that day of her marriage to meet the Lamb' (p. 253).

Moreover, a variety of biblical texts offer prefigurations for the experience of a variety of believers. Not only does Princess Elizabeth take solace in reading her Bible upon her entry into the Tower of London, she models her demeanour on the Parable of the Two Houses (Matthew 7: 24–7) when she desires that 'God not to suffer her to build her foundation upon the sands but upon the rock' (p. 271). The narrator furthermore likens Stephen Gardiner to Ahithophel, a counsellor who betrayed King David, when he blames the Bishop of Winchester for seeking Elizabeth's execution (p. 272).[26] Marginal glosses liken both Lawrence Saunders and Rowland Taylor to the prophet, Elijah, at the time of his confrontation with the priests of Baal during the reign of King Ahab, who functions as a type for Mary I (pp. 51, 75); see 1 Kings 18). When Foxe praises Hooper

---

[26] See 2 Samuel 15–17.

as an ideal bishop, he assigns to him 'virtues and qualities required of Saint Paul in a good bishop in his epistle to Timothy' (p. 55).[27] In praising the power of Tyndale's religious faith, Foxe transmits hearsay that 'he converted his keeper, his daughter, and other of his household' during imprisonment that preceded his execution (p. 20). In so doing, he likens the Bible translator to St Paul, who joined Silas in converting their jailer during imprisonment at Phillippi (Acts 16: 25–34). In a similar vein, Pauline associations may underpin the conversion of John Bowler, 'a very perverse papist' who served as a keeper at the Tower of London, to whom Edwin Sandys and John Bradford ministered during their imprisonment (p. 258). In a sermon that he had preached after the death of Edward VI, Sandys himself had applied the Israelites' declaration of allegiance to Joshua after the death of Moses (Joshua 1: 16–18) as a precedent for the legality of the succession of Lady Jane Grey as the late king's heir (p. 254).

## *Woodcut Illustrations*

Any overview of the *Book of Martyrs* would be incomplete if it failed to mention its woodcut illustrations. John Day illustrated the 1583 version with more than 100 woodcuts, many of which occurred more than once, adding up to a total of more than 150 illustrations.[28] Representing one of the best-remembered features of Foxe's martyrological history, they attracted a lot of attention from readers, who often wrote inscriptions or marked them in other ways. In addition to the imposing title-page border (Illustration. 1) and printer's device (Illustration 2), which portrays the publisher, many of these pictures are large illustrations that illustrate specific narratives. These woodcuts characteristically illustrate executions that constitute the climactic moment in martyrologies. The woodcut illustrating the execution of Hugh Latimer and Ridley, for example, portrays the martyrs secured to the stake as attendants pile up faggots only moments before the ignition of fire (Illustration 14). In other cases,

---

[27] See 1 Timothy 3: 1–7.
[28] Ruth Samson Luborsky and Elizabeth Ingram, *A Guide to English Illustrated Books, 1536–1603*, 2 vols. (Tempe, Ariz., 1998), 382. Luborsky's total of 'one hundred woodcuts in 153 occurrences' underestimates the actual numbers according to Mark Rankin.

martyrs are portrayed within flames. Within this woodcut, the portable pulpit from which Dr Richard Smith delivers a sermon, the cityscape in the background, and the open oval space with a crowd of spectators at its edge constitute distinctive motifs in Day's martyrological woodcuts. This naturalistic scene incorporates horses, which often function as symbols for injustice on the part of officials borne on these steeds. Banderoles (i.e., sinuous word streamers) contain typesettings for the martyrs' last words. Alluding to the dying words of St Stephen and Jesus Christ, Latimer and Ridley respectively pray 'Father of heaven receive my soul' and a Latin version of Jesus' last words on the Cross: 'Father, into thy hands I commit my spirit' (Luke 23: 46). Other banderoles contain the biblical text for Smith's sermon and a remark made by an observer. In a fanciful detail, Thomas Cranmer prays atop Bocardo Prison: 'O Lord strengthen them'.

Other woodcuts portray unforgettable moments such as the moment when Thomas Bilney tested his resolve to suffer being burnt alive by burning his finger in his prison cell. The radiance of the candle flame and the Bible open before him symbolize his adherence to scriptural 'truth'. Other hand-burning scenes feature in woodcuts illustrating the torture of Thomas Tompkins and Rose Allin, in addition to Thomas Cranmer's thrusting into the flames of the hand that signed his recantation. Bishop Bonner's predilection for brutality is notable in the portrayal of his cruelty to Tompkins and scourging of Thomas Hinshaw. In portraying the constancy of martyrs *in extremis*, other woodcuts provide a visual complement to memorable narratives concerning William Tyndale, Anne Askew, John Rogers, Lawrence Saunders, John Hooper, Rowland Taylor, and other victims.

Foxe's *Book of Martyrs* has attracted the attention of readers, influenced politicians and writers, and aroused controversy ever since its initial publication during the aftermath of the reign of terror experienced by Protestants who suffered under Mary I. Surviving copies that contain bits of candle wax, nutshells, and scribbled responses from outraged readers suggest that many of them nibbled food as they stayed up late at night in order to read about the religious constancy of martyrs, their witty mockery of executioners, and gruesome accounts of their last moments of life. From the beginning, the *Book of Martyrs* influenced low-born individuals such as Sir Francis Drake, who read from it as he circumnavigated the globe on the

*Golden Hind.* At the other end of the social scale, aristocrats such as Sir John Harington, the godson of Queen Elizabeth who earned a well-deserved reputation as a court wit, read from it. He recounts how he translated the story about her imprisonment and threatened execution into Latin when he was a schoolboy at Eton College.[29] Elizabethan and Jacobean dramatists alluded to it, as is the case in Christopher Marlowe's *Tamburlaine the Great* and plays by lesser-known playwrights. In *Henry VIII*, William Shakespeare and John Fletcher model their dramatization of courtly plotting against Thomas Cranmer on the *Book of Martyrs*. Even though we have had to wait until the twenty-first century for the completion of a definitive modern edition of this extraordinary book, readers over the centuries have been lured to corrupt and sometime bowdlerized versions of this book in a host of unabridged editions, abridgements, or transmogrifications that include one that expands and 'updates' Foxe's collection by interpolating accounts of the suffering of Quakers in colonial New England, a sketch of the French Revolution, persecution of Protestant missionaries in nineteenth-century India and the West Indies, and other lurid events.[30] The *Book of Martyrs* remains to the present day a propagandistic book of considerable historical, literary, and cultural importance.

---

[29] King, *Foxe's* Book of Martyrs *and Early Modern Print Culture*, 285, 297–303.

[30] *Fox's Book of Martyrs, Or A History of the Lives, Sufferings, and Triumphant Deaths of the Primitive Protestant Missionaries* (Philadelphia: Porter and Coates, n.d.).

# NOTE ON THE TEXT

John Foxe's *Book of Martyrs* is the popular title of a famous martyrological history that the London printer, John Day, initially published
under the title of *Acts and Monuments of These Latter and Perilous
Days, touching matters of the Church*. Foxe oversaw expansion of his
martyrological history from about 55,000 words in the first of two
Latin precursors to a text that ballooned from about 1,880,000 words
to 3,775,000 words in four vernacular editions.[1] Published in 1563,
the first edition is a large folio volume that contains nearly 1,800
pages. It underwent major revision and expansion in 1570, minor
revision in 1576, and further expansion in 1583. Foxe deleted and
added material in each of these editions. In some cases, he restored
previously deleted material. The 1583 version is made up of two volumes of about two thousand folio pages in double columns. At nearly
four times the length of the Bible,[2] the monumental fourth edition is
the most physically imposing, complicated, and technically demanding English book of its era. It seems safe to say that it is the largest
and most complicated book to appear during the first two or three
centuries of English printing history. The sheer size of the work
staggers the imagination. Taking on a life of its own after the death
of Foxe and Day, this collection appeared in five more unabridged
editions by 1684. Published in 1631–2, the seventh edition underwent reconfiguration due to further subdivision into three volumes
and the addition of a 108-page-long 'Continuation of the Histories of
Foreign Martyrs' that updates Foxean history by accounting for
events up to the 1620s. In addition to these nine unabridged editions,
numerous abridgements and selections were published.

Even though investigations of the *Book of Martyrs* often cease in
1684, the manufacture of folio editions continued unabated after the
Company of Stationers published the ninth edition in that year. It
was the final unabridged version that reflected the original design of
Foxe and Day. When the Licensing Act lapsed in 1695, the Company

---

[1] Word estimates for the English editions are based on personal communication from
Professor Mark Greengrass. They exclude headlines and marginal notes.

[2] The length of the Authorized Version of 1611 (the 'King James' Version'), including the Apocrypha, approximates 900,000 words.

lost its monopoly on publication of this book. Passage of the
Copyright Act of 1710 then deprived the Company of its copyright.
These changes enabled booksellers to print competing versions of
this book in forms that underwent a variety of fundamental transform-
ations in dozens of revisions, abridgements, and selections. Publishers
continued to produce folio editions, despite the general shift to
quarto format for serious literature during the eighteenth century. In
1732, John Hart and John Lewis printed a folio that truncates the
*Book of Martyrs* into a 900,000-word-long chronicle concerned almost
wholly with the persecution of Marian martyrs. When eighteenth-
century readers encountered the *Book of Martyrs*, they typically read
a version that omitted Foxe's extended history of the Christian
Church that preceded the reign of Mary I.[3]

During the nineteenth century, five unabridged editions were
based upon the edition produced in eight volumes by Stephen R.
Cattley (London, 1837–41), with a preliminary dissertation by George
Townsend. The 1965 facsimile reprint of Cattley's second edition
(London, 1843–9), long out of print, is the version of the work that
is most readily accessible in academic libraries, but it is relatively
inaccessible. This edition provides a faulty basis for scholarship because
the text that it contains is inaccurate. Claiming to base his moderniza-
tion on the 1583 edition, Cattley incorporates some but not all of the
material in the 1563 version that Foxe revised or eliminated in later
editions. He disrupts the compiler's organization by rearranging
material found in the original texts; haphazardly moves material to
different places within the work, or to appendices, or to footnotes; and
edits, condenses, and amends marginal glosses with extreme freedom, and often moves them into footnotes or into the text as sub-
titles. Latin extracts find their way into footnotes. Cattley therefore
produces a composite text that bears a highly imperfect relationship
to Foxe's configuration of his work. The nineteenth-century editions
are an unreliable guide to investigation of the substantial differences
among the four editions overseen by Foxe because they fail to indicate the edition in which a particular document originated, whether
it underwent revision, or whether it was ever eliminated from or
restored to particular editions.

---

[3] See John N. King, 'Eighteenth-Century Folio Publication of Foxe's *Book of
Martyrs*', *Reformation*, 10 (2005), 99–105.

At the present moment, a new digital edition of the *Book of Martyrs* is in progress: *Foxe's Book of Martyrs Variorum Edition Online* (hereafter cited as *FBMO*). This edition is published by the Humanities Research Institute Online, University of Sheffield, under sponsorship from the British Academy and the Arts and Humanities Research Board. Professors Mark Greengrass and David Loades serve respectively as the Project Director and Editorial Director. *FBMO* represents a great boon to scholarship, because it provides reliable, searchable transcriptions of the first four editions. They permit scholars to engage in detailed comparison of the four different versions produced by Foxe and Day. For material concerning the reign of Mary I, the apparatus consisting of general introductions; commentaries that identify sources, persons mentioned, and textual variations in the first four editions; and other materials is now complete. The commentary dealing with material before the reign of Queen Mary approaches completion. The online edition incorporates facsimiles of the woodcut illustrations and initial capital letters on the relevant pages of each edition.

The present Oxford World's Classics edition aims to present a much-abridged version of the *Book of Martyrs* that is designed to address the needs of modern readers. Selections consist of highly readable and moving stories drawn from the narrative component of accounts of three individuals who were executed during the reign of Henry VIII, in addition to accounts of the prosecution and death of many Marian martyrs. Other selections concern Princess Elizabeth and Edwin Sandys, who escaped execution; Stephen Gardiner, who died of natural causes; and tales about 'providential' judgement upon persecutors. Ellipses indicate the omission of material that includes wording in Latin, letters, and other non-narrative documentation. On occasion, brief summaries within square brackets bridge over eliminated material. On a selective basis, woodcuts are located at appropriate places in narratives. Marginal glosses are included in the margins.

The text retains archaic and obsolete vocabulary. Spelling of words, places, and names is modernized. Contractions and abbreviations are silently expanded. Words appearing in square brackets represent editorial insertions not in Foxe's text and are designed as aids to comprehension. Roman and Arabic numerals are written out. Punctuation is left intact, except in rare instances where it is misleading.

Colons remain in their original locations in order to preserve subtleties of meaning that vanish when replaced by either a comma, full stop, or semicolon. Some substitutions are made for printers' symbols that are no longer in use. Upper case and lower case are employed in accordance with modern usage. Quotation marks are inserted to separate direct discourse from narration. Indirect discourse is not enclosed within quotation marks. Roman type is employed for text that may appear in black letter, italic, or roman type in the original text. When shifts in typeface in the version designate material quoted from sources, inverted commas are employed as quotation marks in the OWC edition. Running titles are not transcribed, and paragraph placement from the original text is maintained. Dates are in new style.

This edition is based on the fourth edition of the *Book of Martyrs* because it represents the most complete and final edition overseen by Foxe and Day. By courtesy of the Rare Books and Manuscripts Library at The Ohio State University, this edition contains fresh transcriptions from a copy in its collection (BR1600.F6 1583, copy 1). In a few cases where printing is unclear, wording is supplied from the editor's personal copy of this edition. Readers who wish to supplement these readings by reference to the unabridged text are advised to consult *FBMO*.

The Introduction, Explanatory Notes, and Glossaries of Persons and Places rely silently on the following resources: *New Encyclopaedia Britannica*, 15th edn., 32 vols. (Chicago, 1986); *Oxford Dictionary of National Biography (Online)* (Oxford and New York, 2004); Paul J. Achtemeier, et al. (eds.), *Harper's Bible Dictionary* (San Francisco, 1985); Alan G. R. Smith, *The Emergence of a Nation State: The Commonwealth of England, 1529–1660*, 2nd edn. (London and New York, 1997); and Ben Weinreb and Christopher Hibbert (eds.), *London Encyclopaedia* (London, 1983). Scriptural references are to *Oxford Study Bible: Revised English Bible with the Apocrypha*, ed. M. Jack Suggs, Katharine Doob Sakenfeld, and James R. Mueller (New York, 1992). The Glossary of Words and Terms is based on *The Oxford English Dictionary*, 2nd edn. (Oxford, 1989).

# SELECT BIBLIOGRAPHY

## Editions

Foxe, John, *Book of Martyrs* (London, 1563). This is the popular title of a book originally entitled *Acts and Monuments of These Latter and Perilous Days, touching matters of the Church.*
—— 2nd edn., rev. (London, 1570).
—— 3rd edn., rev. (London, 1576).
—— 4th edn., rev. (London, 1583).
—— ed. Stephen R. Cattley, with an introduction by George Townsend, 2nd edn., 8 vols. (London, 1843–9), facsimile reprint (New York, 1965).
Foxe, John, *Acts and Monuments . . . The Variorum Edition [online]* (hriOnline, Sheffield, 2004). Available from http://www.hrionline. shef.ac.uk/foxe/ [Accessed 12.06.2008]. Hereafter cited as *FBMO*.

## Reference Works

Achtemeier, Paul J., et al. (eds.), *Harper's Bible Dictionary* (San Francisco, 1985).
Bettenson, Henry, ed., *Documents of the Christian Church*, 2nd edn. (London, 1963).
Dickens, A. G., and Carr, Dorothy (eds.), *The Reformation in England to the Accession of Elizabeth I* (London, 1967).
Luborsky, Ruth Samson, and Ingram, Elizabeth, *A Guide to English Illustrated Books, 1536–1603*, 2 vols. (Tempe, Ariz., 1998). This book contains a census of the woodcuts in the first five editions of the *Book of Martyrs* (1563–96), 365–82.
*The New Encyclopaedia Britannica*, 15th edn., 32 vols. (Chicago, 1998).
*The Oxford Dictionary of National Biography* (Oxford and New York, 2004).
*The Oxford Study Bible: Revised English Bible with the Apocrypha*, ed. M. Jack Suggs, Katharine Doob Sakenfeld, and James R. Mueller (New York, 1992).
Pollard, A. W., Redgrave, G. R., Jackson, W. A., Ferguson, F. S., and Pantzer, Katharine F., compilers, *A Short-Title Catalogue of Books Printed in England, Scotland, and Ireland, and of English Books Printed Abroad, 1475–1640*, 2nd edn., rev. and enlarged, 3 vols. (London, 1976–91).
Weinreb, Ben, and Hibbert, Christopher (eds.), *The London Encyclopaedia* (London, 1983).

*Biographical Studies*

Daniell, David, *William Tyndale: A Biography* (New Haven and London, 1994).

Freeman, Thomas S., 'Life of John Foxe', in *FBMO*.

King, John N., 'John Foxe', in David A. Richardson (ed.), *Sixteenth-Century British Nondramatic Writers: First Series* (Detroit, 1993), 131–40.

Mozley, J. F., *John Foxe and His Book* (London, 1940).

*Critical and Historical Studies: Books and Collections of Essays*

Bauckham, Richard, *Tudor Apocalypse* (Oxford, 1978).

Betteridge, Thomas, *Tudor Histories of the English Reformations, 1530–1583* (Aldershot, 1999).

Christianson, Paul, *Reformers and Babylon: English Apocalyptic Visions from the Reformation to the Eve of the Civil War* (Toronto, 1978).

Collinson, Patrick, *The Reformation* (London and New York, 2003).

Covington, Sarah, *The Trail of Martyrdom: Persecution and Resistance in Sixteenth-Century England* (Notre Dame, 2003).

Dickens, A. G., *The English Reformation* (London, 1964).

Firth, Katharine R., *The Apocalyptic Tradition in Reformation Britain, 1530–1645* (Oxford, 1979).

Greenblatt, Stephen, *Renaissance Self-Fashioning: From More to Shakespeare* (Chicago, 1980).

Gregory, Brad S., *Salvation at Stake: Christian Martyrdom in Early Modern Europe* (Cambridge, Mass., 1999).

Haigh, Christopher, *The English Reformations: Religion, Politics, and Society under the Tudors* (Oxford, 1993).

Haller, William, *The Elect Nation: The Meaning and Relevance of Foxe's Book of Martyrs* (New York, 1963).

Helgerson, Richard, *Forms of Nationhood: The Elizabethan Writing of England* (Chicago, 1992).

Highley, Christopher, and King, John N. (eds.), *John Foxe and His World* (Aldershot, Hants., 2002).

King, John N., *English Reformation Literature: The Tudor Origins of the Protestant Tradition* (Princeton, 1982).

—— *Foxe's* Book of Martyrs *and Early Modern Print Culture* (Cambridge, 2006).

—— (ed.), *Voices of the English Reformation: A Sourcebook* (Philadelphia, 2004).

Knott, John R., *Discourses of Martyrdom in English Literature, 1563–1694* (Cambridge, 1993).

Lander, Jesse M., *Inventing Polemic: Religion, Print, and Literary Culture in Early Modern England* (Cambridge, 2006).

Lewis, C. S., *English Literature in the Sixteenth Century Excluding Drama* (Oxford, 1954).

Loades, David M., *Mary Tudor: A Life* (Oxford, 1989).

—— *The Oxford Martyrs* (New York, 1970).

—— *The Reign of Mary Tudor* (London, 1979).

—— (ed.), *John Foxe and the English Reformation* (Aldershot, Hants., 1997).

—— (ed.), *John Foxe at Home and Abroad* (Aldershot, Hants., 2004).

—— (ed.), *John Foxe: An Historical Perspective* (Aldershot, Hants., 1999).

Marshall, Cynthia, *The Shattering of the Self: Violence, Subjectivity, and Early Modern Texts* (Baltimore, 2002).

Oastler, C. L., *John Day, the Elizabethan Printer*, Occasional Publications of the Oxford Bibliographical Society, No. 10 (Oxford, 1975).

Olsen, V. Norskov, *John Foxe and the Elizabethan Church* (Berkeley and Los Angeles, 1973).

Patterson, Mary Hampson, *Domesticating the Reformation: Protestant Best Sellers, Private Devotion, and the Revolution of English Piety* (Teaneck, NJ, 2007).

Smith, Alan G. R., *The Emergence of a Nation State: The Commonwealth of England, 1529–1660*, 2nd edn. (London and New York, 1997).

White, Helen C., *Tudor Books of Saints and Martyrs* (Madison, 1963).

Wooden, Warren W., *John Foxe* (Boston, 1983).

Yates, Frances A., *Astraea: The Imperial Theme in the Sixteenth Century* (London, 1975).

### Critical and Historical Studies: Articles and Chapters in Books

Betteridge, Thomas, 'Truth and History in Foxe's *Acts and Monuments*', in Highley and King (eds.), *John Foxe and His World*, 145–59.

Burks, Deborah, 'Polemical Potency: The Witness of Word and Woodcut', in Highley and King (eds.), *John Foxe and His World*, 263–76.

Collinson, Patrick, 'John Foxe and National Consciousness', in Highley and King (eds.), *John Foxe and His World* (Aldershot, Hants, 2002), 10–36.

—— 'Truth and Legend: The Veracity of John Foxe's *Book of Martyrs*', in A. C. Duke and C. A. Tamse (eds.), *Clio's Mirror: Historiography in Britain and the Netherlands* (Zutphen, 1985), 31–54.

—— 'Truth, Lies, and Fiction in Sixteenth-Century Protestant Historiography', in Donald R. Kelley and David Harris Sacks (eds.), *The Historical Imagination in Early Modern Britain: History, Rhetoric, and Fiction 1500–1800* (Washington, DC, 1997), 37–68.

Covington, Sarah, 'The Heresy Examinations of John Philpot: Defiance, Bold Speaking, and the Making of a Martyr', *Reformation* 7 (2002), 79–133.

Evenden, Elizabeth, and Freeman, Thomas S., 'John Foxe, John Day and the Printing of the "Book of Martyrs"', in Robin Myers, Michael Harris, and Giles Mandelbrote (eds.), *Lives in Print: Biography and the Book Trade from the Middle Ages to the 21st Century* (London, 2002), 23–54.

Fox, Alistair, 'John Foxe's *Acts and Monuments* as Polemical History', *Parergon* 14 (1976), 43–51.

Freeman, Thomas S., 'Fate, Faction, and Fiction in Foxe's *Book of Martyrs*', *Historical Journal*, 43 (2000), 601–23.

—— 'Providence and Prescription: The Account of Elizabeth in Foxe's "Book of Martyrs"', in Susan Doran and Thomas S. Freeman (eds.), *The Myth of Elizabeth* (London, 2003), 27–55.

—— 'Publish and Perish: The Scribal Culture of the Marian Martyrs', in Julia Crick and Alexandra Walsham (eds.), *The Uses of Script and Print, 1300–1700* (Cambridge, 2004), 235–54.

—— 'Texts, Lies and Microfilm: Reading and Misreading Foxe's "Book of Martyrs"', *Sixteenth Century Journal: Journal of Early Modern Studies*, 30 (1999), 23–46.

Hickerson, Megan, 'Negotiating Heresy in Tudor England: Anne Askew and the Bishop of London', *Journal of British Studies*, 46 (2007), 774–95.

King, John N., 'Fiction and Fact in Foxe's *Book of Martyrs*', in Loades (ed.), *John Foxe and the English Reformation*, 12–35.

—— 'John Day: Master Printer of the English Reformation', in Peter Marshall and Alec Ryrie (eds.), *The Beginnings of English Protestantism* (Cambridge, 2002), 180–208.

—— 'John Foxe and Tudor Humanism', in Jonathan Woolfson (ed.), *Reassessing Tudor Humanism* (Houndmills, 2002), 174–85.

—— '"The Light of Printing": William Tyndale, John Foxe, John Day, and Early Modern Print Culture', *Renaissance Quarterly*, 54 (2001), 52–85.

Knott, John R., 'John Foxe and the Joy of Suffering', *Sixteenth Century Journal*, 27 (1996), 721–34.

Luborsky, Ruth, 'The Illustrations: Their Pattern and Plan', in Loades (ed.), *John Foxe: An Historical Perspective*, 67–84.

Robinson, Marsha S., 'Doctors, Silly Poor Women, and Rebel Whores: The Gendering of Conscience in Foxe's *Acts and Monuments*', in Highley and King (eds.), *John Foxe and His World*, 235–48.

Wooden, Warren, 'Recent Studies in Foxe', *English Literary Renaissance*, 11 (1981), 224–32.

# A CHRONOLOGY OF FOXE'S LIFE AND TIMES

Events in Foxe's life are printed in **bold** type.

**1516/17 Foxe born at Boston in Lincolnshire.**

1517 Martin Luther's *Ninety-Five Theses* initiate the Protestant Reformation.

1520 Luther's *Babylonian Captivity of the Church*. Publication of the Complutensian Polyglot Bible (completed in 1522).

1521 Lutheran books burnt in London. Henry VIII's *Assertio septem sacramentorum*. Diet of Worms. Birth of John Day in this year or 1522.

1522 Luther's German New Testament.

1525 Printing of William Tyndale's English New Testament thwarted in Cologne.

1526 After publication of Tyndale's New Testament in Worms, smuggled copies are prohibited and burnt in England. Persecution of English Protestants (1526–7).

1527 Henry VIII pursues divorce from Catherine of Aragon. Emperor Charles V sacks Rome and curtails authority of Pope Clement VII. Thomas Cranmer enters royal service.

1528 Tyndale's *Parable of the Wicked Mammon* and *Obedience of a Christian Man*. More's *Dialogue Against Heresy*.

1529 Cardinal Thomas Wolsey fails to resolve the divorce question and resigns as Lord Chancellor. Sir Thomas More appointed Lord Chancellor. Opening session of Reformation Parliament pursues ecclesiastical reform. Simon Fish's *Supplication for Beggars*.

1531 The House of Commons acknowledges Henry VIII as the Supreme Head of the Church 'as far as the law of Christ allows'. Thomas Bilney burnt alive at Norwich (19 August).

1532 Submission of the Clergy acknowledges that Henry VIII's authority exceeds that of the pope. More resigns Lord Chancellorship. Thomas Cromwell serves as Chief Minister. William Thynne's edition of collected works of Chaucer.

1533 Thomas Cranmer becomes Archbishop of Canterbury. Henry VIII divorces Catherine of Aragon. Clement VII excommunicates Henry VIII, who marries Anne Boleyn. Act in Restraint of Appeals nullifies authority of the Church of Rome. Anne Boleyn gives birth to Princess Elizabeth.

1534 **Foxe matriculates at Brasenose College, Oxford** (c.1534). Act for the Submission of the Clergy. Act of Succession mandates inheritance of the Crown by offspring of Henry VIII and Anne Boleyn. Act of Supremacy declares Henry VIII Supreme Head on Earth of the Church of England.

1535 Henry VIII appoints Cromwell vicegerent for religious affairs. Cromwell extends patronage to evangelical propagandists and initiates the Dissolution of the Monasteries. Beheadings of More and Bishop John Fisher. Publication of Coverdale Bible in Antwerp, the first complete version printed in English.

1536 Beheading of Anne Boleyn. Henry VIII marries Jane Seymour. Act for the Dissolution of the Lesser Monasteries. Pilgrimage of Grace begins. Ten Articles approves compromise with Lutheran theology, notably the reduction of the seven sacraments to the three sacraments of the Eucharist, baptism, and auricular confession. The Royal Injunctions discourage devotion to saints' images and shrines. Tyndale executed in Brabant (presumably on 6 October). Calvin's *Institution of Christian Religion*.

1537 **Foxe receives Bachelor of Arts degree**. Birth of Prince Edward and death of Jane Seymour. Birth of Lady Jane Grey. Publication of an English translation of the Bible under the pseudonym of Thomas Matthew. John Bale arrested for heresy and released through intervention of Cromwell.

1538 **Foxe becomes probationer fellow at Magdalen College.** Royal Injunctions order the acquisition of the English Bible by parish churches and prohibit pilgrimages and other ritual practices. Destruction of the shrine of St Thomas Becket at Canterbury. Bale writes and acts in propagandistic plays performed by a troupe that he led under patronage from Cromwell. John Lambert burnt alive for heresy (22 November).

1539 **Foxe becomes fellow of Magdalen College**. Greater abbeys dissolved. Act of Six Articles restores orthodox Catholic doctrine concerning transubstantiation, communion in one kind for the laity, clerical celibacy, inability to marry by those who have left religious orders, private Masses, and auricular confession. This legislation imposed stringent penalties for violation of its provisions. Hugh Latimer resigns appointment as Bishop of Worcester. Publication of the Great Bible. Robert Crowley admitted as a scholarship student at Magdalen College, where he associates with Foxe.

1540 Annulment of Henry VIII's marriage to Anne of Cleves. Fall and execution of Cromwell. John Bale, Miles Coverdale, and others exile themselves to the Continent. Following his criticism of Bishop Stephen Gardiner, Robert Barnes is burnt alive for heresy. Henry VIII marries Catherine Howard, niece of Thomas Howard, 3rd Duke of Norfolk.

1541 Order for destruction of religious shrines.

1542 Beheading of Catherine Howard (13 February). Birth of Mary, Queen of Scots. Crowley resigns fellowship at Magdalen College, in apparent protest against religious conservatism.

1543 **Foxe receives degree of Master of Arts.** Henry VIII weds Catherine Parr (12 July) and protects Cranmer against accusations of heresy. Act for the Advancement of True Religion denies commoners access to English Bible.

1544 Sympathizers with evangelical reform threaten Gardiner on the Privy Council. Sir John Cheke, a Protestant humanist, appointed tutor to Prince Edward. Led by Edward Seymour, Earl of Hertford, the English army invades the Scottish lowland.

1545 **Foxe resigns fellowship in response to the requirement that he take a vow of clerical celibacy.** First heresy examination of Anne Askew. Council of Trent begins. Likely date of publication of John Bale's *Image of Both Churches* in Antwerp.

1546 Henry VIII in declining health. Thomas Howard, 3rd Duke of Norfolk, and son, Henry Howard, Earl of Surrey, imprisoned in Tower of London. Second examination of Anne Askew, who is burnt at Smithfield along with three others condemned for heresy (16 July). In anticipation of death, Henry VIII appoints a Council of Regency to govern during the minority of his son, Edward. John Day begins career as London printer-publisher. Bale's edition of *First Examination of Anne Askew* published abroad (November).

1547 **Foxe employed as tutor by Sir William Lucy at Charlecote, Warwickshire. Marriage to Agnes Randall. The Duchess of Richmond appoints Foxe to serve as tutor to Thomas Howard, later 4th Duke of Norfolk, and the other orphans of Henry Howard, her late brother.** Bale's edition of *Latter Examination of Anne Askew* published abroad (16 January). Beheading of Henry Howard (19 January). Death of Henry VIII and accession of Edward VI (28 January). Edward Seymour appointed Lord Protector of the Realm (1 February) and then Duke of Somerset (17 February), with authority to act on the king's behalf from 12 March. Edward VI, Seymour, and Cranmer extend patronage to Protestant propagandists and booksellers. Royal Injunctions begin to introduce Protestant reforms (31 July). Publication of the Book of Homilies for use by unlicensed preachers. Gardiner imprisoned because of his opposition to these events. Parliament sits in November and December and abrogates of the Act of Six Articles, *de haeretico combu-rendo* (promulgated in 1401), and other heresy legislation. Suspension of prior censorship and extension to Protestants of relative freedom of publication and reading. Widespread publication of Protestant propaganda. Initial steps toward a Protestant settlement of religion. Publication of plays by John Bale at about this year or 1548.

1548  Foxe encounters John Bale as guest at the London house of the Duchess of Richmond. Hugh Singleton publishes Foxe's appeal against the imposition of capital punishment for adultery, *De non plectendis morte adulteris consultatio*. At about this year Singleton also publishes Foxe's translations of Martin Luther's *Sermon of the Angels*, Johannes Oecolampadius' *Sermon to Young Men and Maidens*, and Urbanus Rhegius' *An Instruction of Christian Faith*. Latimer's 'Sermon on the Plowers' (18 January). Gardiner released from prison and imprisoned once again for preaching against religious reform. Royal proclamations order elimination of many religious ceremonies and iconoclastic destruction of religious images and altars. Explosion in publication of Protestant propaganda, including a spate of anti-Mass tracts. Compilation of an English church service despite resistance by bishops who included Edmund Bonner and Cuthbert Tunstall. Chained copies of Erasmus' *Paraphrases of the New Testament*, volume 1 (31 January), ed. Nicholas Udall, were placed in churches. From this year until 1551, Robert Crowley is active as bookseller, editor, and writer of satires and tracts favourable to religio-social reform. Bale's *Illustrium maioris Britanniae scriptorum summarium*. Pietro Martire Vermigli appointed Regius Professor of Divinity at Oxford. The Act of Uniformity mandates the use of the forthcoming Book of Common Prayer.

1549  The Book of Common Prayer replaces the old Latin rite with an English church service on 9 June. Western Rebellion (June). Kett's Rebellion (12 July to 27 August). Volume 2 of Erasmus' *Paraphrases*, ed. Miles Coverdale (16 August). Edmund Bonner imprisoned and deprived of office as Bishop of London. Protector Somerset deposed (11 October) and imprisoned in Tower of London. John Dudley, Earl of Warwick, supplants him as leading peer in England. Appointment of Martin Bucer as Regius Professor of Divinity and Paulus Fagius as Reader in Hebrew at Cambridge.

1550 **Foxe ordained as deacon.** Seymour released from imprisonment (6 February). John Hooper appointed Bishop of Gloucester, but his consecration is delayed until 1551 because of his opposition to episcopal vestments. Parliamentary legislation mandates destruction of religious images and Roman-rite service books. Gardiner placed on trial (15 December). Burning of Catholic books at Oxford. Robert Crowley's editions of *Piers Plowman*. Joan Bocher, who was also known as Joan Knell and Joan of Kent, was burnt alive because of her Anabaptist convictions (2 May).

1551 **Foxe publishes *De censura sive excommunicatione ecclesiastica*, an argument in favour of the propriety of imposing excommunication on adulterers.** John Dudley becomes Duke of Northumberland. John Ponet becomes Bishop of Winchester in succession to Stephen Gardiner (8 March). George van Paris, a Flemish dissident, burnt alive for heresy (24 April). John Hooper appointed bishop of the united diocese of Worcester and Gloucester. Second arrest of Edward Seymour (16 October) and trial for treason (December). Thomas More's *Utopia* published in English translation.

1552 Edward Seymour beheaded at Tower (22 January). Revised under the influence of Hooper and other radicals, the Second Book of Common Prayer abolishes the Mass, wearing of surplices, and many ceremonies retained in the first prayer book. The 'Black Rubric' declares that kneeling during the communion service does not signify the Real Presence of Christ. Altars are dismantled and replaced by communion tables set up in the naves of churches Edmund Spenser born (?).

1553 William Baldwin composes a religious satire entitled *Beware the Cat*, but it remains in manuscript presumably because of the change in religious policy that followed the death of King Edward. Lady Jane Grey weds Lord Guildford Dudley (21 May). The Forty-Two Articles define a Protestant settlement of religion that includes the doctrine of justification by faith alone and a Zwinglian formulation of the Eucharist as a memorial celebration (19 June). Death of Edward VI (6 July). John Dudley, Duke of Northumberland, attempts to alter the succession in favour of Lady Jane Grey, who is acclaimed Queen of England (10 July). Lady Jane Grey deposed and imprisoned in the Tower of London; accession of Mary I (19 July). Thomas Howard, 3rd Duke of Norfolk, released from prison. For support of Lady Jane Grey, Edwin Sandys is imprisoned in the Tower (25 July). Many prominent English Protestants join foreign reformers in fleeing England. Gardiner and Bonner released from prison. Deprivation from office and imprisonment of Protestant bishops including Cranmer,

Latimer, Ridley, Hooper. First Act of Repeal abrogates legislation that implemented the Edwardian settlement of religion. Surreptitious publication of anti-Marian propaganda under the false imprint of Michael Wood of Rouen (possibly John Day) (October 1553–May 1554). Performance of Udall's masque, *Respublica*, during Christmas revels at the royal court.

1554 **Foxe in exile on the Continent. Wendelin Rihel publishes Latin precursor of the *Book of Martyrs* in Strasbourg, under the title of *Commentarii rerum in ecclesia gestarum*.** Continued flight of English Protestants. In opposition to the announced marriage of Mary I and Philip of Spain, Sir Thomas Wyatt the Younger leads rebels from Kent to London (January). He surrenders after getting as far as Ludgate (7 February). Lady Jane Grey and Guildford Dudley are beheaded as traitors (12 February). Royal Injunctions order bishops to suppress heresy and restore saints' days, religious ceremonies, and processions (March). Princess Elizabeth imprisoned in the Tower of London on suspicion of complicity in Wyatt's Rebellion (18 March). Wyatt executed (11 April). Edwin Sandys escapes to the Continent. Elizabeth sent from Tower to house arrest at Woodstock (19 May). Parliament revalidates heresy legislation, but disallows restoration of monastic land. Marriage of Mary I and Philip of Spain (25 July). Cardinal Reginald Pole returns from Rome as papal legate (November). Second Act of Repeal abrogates Act of Supremacy, Act of Succession, and all other Henrician legislation related to the schism from Rome. John Day imprisoned at Tower (16 October). Republication of Stephen Hawes's *The Pastime of Pleasure*. Sir Philip Sidney born.

1555 **Foxe resident at Basle, where he lives in the same community as John Bale, with whom he works as a corrector at the printing house of Johannes Oporinus.** John Day encounters John Rogers at Newgate Prison. Burning of martyrs including John Rogers (4 February), Lawrence Saunders (8 February), John Hooper and Rowland Taylor (9 February), Rawlins White (March), Thomas Tomkins (16 March), William Hunter (26 March), George Marsh (24 April), Thomas Haukes (10 June), John Bradford and John Leaf (1 July), Hugh Latimer and Nicholas Ridley (16 October), and John Philpot (18 December). Elizabeth released from Woodstock and then received by Mary I at Hampton Court (21 May). Gardiner suppresses *The Mirror for Magistrates*. Death of Gardiner (12–13 November). Cranmer formally deprived of archiepiscopal office (13 November). Cardinal Pole appointed Archbishop of Canterbury (December).

1556 **Oporinus publishes Foxe's apocalyptic comedy, *Christus triumphans*.** Accession of Philip II as King of Spain (January).

Burning of martyrs including Bartlett Green (27 January), Thomas Cranmer (21 March), Guernsey Martyrs (18 July), and Joan Waste (1 August). John Day again involved in London book trade. John Heywood's *The Spider and the Fly*. John Ponet's *Short Treatise of Politic Power*.

1557 Oporinus publishes Foxe's *Ad inclytos ac praepotentes Angliae*, which appeals to the British nobility for cessation of persecution, and *Locorum communium*, which concerns the art of memory. Burning of martyrs including Richard Woodman and nine companions (22 June), Rose Allin (2 August), and George Eagles. Incorporation of the Stationers' Company. Richard Tottel's *Songs and Sonnets* ('Tottell's Miscellany') incorporates poems by Thomas Wyatt the Elder; Henry Howard, Earl of Surrey; and others. *Works of Sir Thomas More Knight*, ed. William Rastell. Volume 1 of Bale's *Scriptorum illustrium maioris Brytanniae . . . catalogus*.

1558 Burning of martyrs including the wife of a man whose surname was Prest (November). Death of Mary I, accession of Elizabeth I, and death of Cardinal Pole (17 November). John Knox's *First Blast of the Trumpet Against the Monstrous Regiment of Women*.

1559 Foxe contributes to *Germaniae ad Angliam*, a celebration of the restoration of 'true' religion in England. Oporinus and Nicolaus Brylinger publish an expanded Latin precursor of the *Book of Martyrs* under the title of *Rerum in ecclesia gestarum . . . commentarii*. Foxe returns to England (October) and resides with his former pupil, the 4th Duke of Norfolk. John Day publishes Foxe's edition of Nicholas Ridley's *A Friendly Farewell*. Coronation of Elizabeth I (15 January). Acts of Supremacy and Uniformity. Elizabeth ordained 'Supreme Governor' of the Church of England. Third Book of Common Prayer imposes English church service based largely on the 1552 version. Opposition to the wearing of clerical vestments revives. Catholic bishops deprived of office. Matthew Parker becomes Archbishop of Canterbury (July). Public reading of English Bible permitted. Iconoclasts destroy religious images. Volume 2 of Bale's *Catalogus*. First complete edition of *The Mirror for Magistrates* published without hindrance.

1560 Foxe ordained a priest. Geneva Bible.

1561 Lady Catherine Grey, sister of Lady Jane Grey, imprisoned in Tower of London for marrying Edward Seymour, Earl of Hertford, without royal consent. Castiglione's *Book of the Courtier*, translated by Sir Thomas Hoby. Calvin's *Institution of Christian Religion*, translated by Thomas Norton.

1562 John Jewel's *Apology of the Church of England*. John Day publishes Latimer's collected sermons, ed. Augustine Bernher.

1563 John Day publishes the first edition of Foxe's *Book of Martyrs* (20 March) and an exposition of the Eucharist, *Syllogisticon* (1563?). Foxe receives prebendary at Salisbury Cathedral. Thirty-Nine Articles of Religion (a revision of the Edwardian Forty-Two Articles) reimpose Protestant settlement of religion. First edition of More's collected Latin writings published at Basle. Death of John Bale. William Shakespeare and Christopher Marlowe born.

1565 Foxe opposes the wearing of clerical vestments. Foxe's friend, Robert Crowley, active in vestiarian controversy.

1566 Nicholas Harpsfield questions veracity of the *Book of Martyrs* in *Dialogi sex*.

1567 Abdication of Mary, Queen of Scots and accession of James VI of Scotland (July). Revolt of the Netherlands.

1568 William Allen founds seminary for training of English missionary priests at Douai. Mary, Queen of Scots flees to England. Death of Miles Coverdale. Bishops' Bible. John Skelton, *Pithy Works of*, ed. John Stow.

1569 Plot to marry Mary, Queen of Scots to Thomas Howard, 4th Duke of Norfolk (spring). Howard imprisoned in Tower of London (October). Rebellion of the Northern Earls (October).

1570 John Day publishes the 2nd edition of the *Book of Martyrs*. Foxe preaches a Good Friday homily, which Day publishes as *A Sermon of Christ Crucified*. In this address, the martyrologist defends Elizabeth I during the aftermath of her excommunication by Pope Pius V, whose bull *Regnans in Excelsis* orders her subjects to depose her. Thomas Cartwright advocates Presbyterianism. Roger Ascham's *The Schoolmaster*. Publication of William Baldwin's *Beware the Cat*.

1571 Day publishes *De Christo crucifixo concio*, a translation of Foxe's Good Friday sermon. He edits the *Gospels of the Four Evangelists*, with parallel texts in Anglo-Saxon and the translation from Bishops' Bible. Convocation calls for placement of *Book of Martyrs* in cathedral churches and the homes of prelates. Parliament declares it a treasonous offence to deny the Royal Supremacy or to accuse Elizabeth I of heresy.

1572 Foxe's *Pandectae locorum communium*, a blank commonplace book, published by Day. Foxe in attendance at the execution of his former pupil, the 4th Duke of Norfolk, for complicity in the Ridolfi Plot. Massacre of Huguenots on St Bartholomew's

Day (24 August). John Field and Thomas Wilcox, *Admonition to Parliament*. John Whitgift's *Answer to a Libel Entitled an Admonition*.

1573 Foxe edits *The Whole Works of Tyndale, Frith, and Barnes*, collected and published by Day.

1574 Persecution of English Catholics begins.

1575 Foxe intercedes on behalf of Anabaptists, who were condemned to death. Death of Matthew Parker (May). Edmund Grindal becomes Archbishop of Canterbury (December). Anabaptists burnt in England.

1576 John Day publishes the *3rd* edition of Foxe's *Book of Martyrs* (27 June). Opening of the Theatre establishes England's first public playhouse. Grindal declines to execute royal order to suppress Puritan prophesyings (i.e. gatherings of clergy to study and expound the Bible).

1577 Foxe preaches at baptism of a converted Jew. Grindal suspended from executing his archiepiscopal duties. Raphael Holinshed's *Chronicles*.

1578 Publication of Foxe's sermon on the baptism of a Jew under the title of *De oliva evangelica*. Bishop James Bell translates it as *A Sermon Preached at the Christening of a Certain Jew*. Foxe contributes a prayer concerning the beleaguered state of the Church Militant to *A Book of Christian Prayers*, published by John Day and compiled by his son, Richard.

1579 Jesuits found English College at Rome. Hugh Singleton publishes Edmund Spenser's *The Shepherds' Calendar*.

1580 Foxe publishes an attack on the papacy entitled *Papa Confutatus*. Bishop Bell then translates it as *The Pope Confuted*. The Jesuit Mission to England begins with the arrival of Edmund Campion and Robert Parsons.

1581 Execution of Edmund Campion for treason.

1582 William Allen, *Brief History of the Martyrdom of Twelve Priests*. Richard Hakluyt's *Diverse Voyages*.

1583 John Day publishes the 4th edition of Foxe's *Book of Martyrs* (October). Sir William Cecil's *Execution of Justice in England* defends the imposition of capital punishment of Catholic priests as traitors.

1584 William Allen's *True, Sincere and Modest Defence of English Catholics*. Death of John Day (23 July).

1586 Trial of Mary, Queen of Scots. Approximate date of performance of Thomas Kyd's *Spanish Tragedy*.

1587 **Foxe dies on 18 April. Buried at St Giles Cripplegate.**
     **Publication of his extended commentary on Revelation 1–17,**
     *Eicasmi, seu meditationes, in sacram Apocalypsin.* **Beheading of**
     **Mary, Queen of Scots. Performance of Christopher Marlowe's**
     *Tamburlaine the Great.*

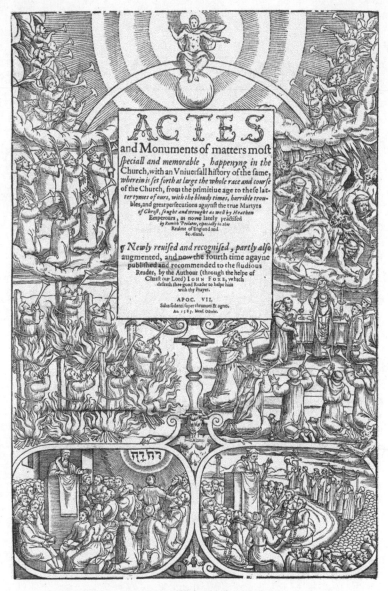

# ACTES

and Monuments of matters moſt
ſpeciall and memorable, happenyng in the
Church, with an Vniuerſall hiſtory of the ſame,
wherein is ſet forth at large the whole race and courſe
of the Church, from the primitiue age to theſe latter tymes of ours, with the bloudy times, horrible troubles, and great perſecutions agaynſt the true Martyrs
of Chriſt, ſought and wrought as well by Heathen
Emperours, as nowe lately practiſed
by Romiſh Prelates, eſpecially in this
Realme of England and
Scotland.

¶ Newly reuiſed and recogniſed, partly alſo
augmented, and now the fourth time agayne
publiſhed and recommended to the ſtudious
Reader, by the Authour (through the helpe of
Chriſt our Lord) IOHN FOXE, which
deſireth thee good Reader to helpe him
with thy Prayer.

APOC. VII.
Salus ſedenti ſuper thronum & agno.
An. 1583. Menſ. Octobr.

1. Title page

LIEFE IS DEATHE AND DEATH IS LIEFE ÆTATIS SVÆ XXXX

1562

I D

2. John Day

# 1. THOMAS BILNEY

This Thomas Bilney was brought up in the University of Cambridge, even from a child,* profiting in all kind of liberal science, even unto the profession of both laws.* But at the last, having got a better schoolmaster, even the holy spirit of Christ, who enduing his heart by privy inspiration with the knowledge of better and more wholesome things, he came at the last unto this point, that forsaking the knowledge of man's laws, he converted his study to those things which tended more unto godliness than gainfulness.

Finally, as he himself was greatly inflamed with the love of true religion and godliness, even so again was in his heart an incredible desire to allure many unto the same, desiring nothing more, than that he might stir up and encourage any to the love of Christ, and sincere religion. Neither was [sic] his labours [in] vain, for he converted many of his fellows unto the knowledge of the Gospel, amongst which number was Thomas Arthur, and Master Hugh Latimer, which Latimer at that time was cross-keeper* at Cambridge, bringing it forth upon procession days. At the last, Bilney forsaking the University, went into many places, teaching and preaching, being associate with Arthur, which accompanied him from the University. The authority of Thomas Wolsey, Cardinal of York, of whom ye heard before, at that time was great in England, but his pomp and pride much greater, which did evidently declare unto all wise men, the manifest vanity not only of his life, but also of all the bishops and clergy. Whereupon Bilney, with other good men marvelling at the incredible insolency of the clergy, which they could now no longer suffer or abide, began to shake and reprove this excessive pomp of the clergy, and also to pluck at the authority of the Bishop of Rome.

Then it was time for the Cardinal to awake, and speedily to look about his business. Neither lacked he in this point any craft or subtlety of a serpent, for he understood well enough upon how slender a foundation their ambitious dignity was grounded, neither was he ignorant that their Luciferous* and

*Master Latimer Crosskeeper in the University of Cambridge.*

*Bilney against the pride of the pope and of his cardinals.*

proud kingdom could not long continue against the manifest word of God, especially if the light of the Gospel should once open the eyes of men. For otherwise he did not greatly fear the power and displeasure of kings and princes. Only this he feared, the voice of Christ in his Gospel, lest it should disclose and detect their hypocrisy and deceits, and force them to come into an order of godly discipline: wherefore he thought good, speedily in time to withstand these beginnings. Whereupon he caused the said Bilney and Arthur to be apprehended and cast in prison . . .

After this, [on] the twenty-seventh day of November, in the year of our Lord 1527, the said Cardinal, accompanied with a *Cardinal* great number of bishops, . . . with many other both divines and *Wolsey with* lawyers, came into the Chapterhouse of Westminster, where *his* the said Master Thomas Bilney, and Thomas Arthur were *[ac]complices,* brought before them, and the said Cardinal there enquired of *against Bilney* *and Arthur.* Master Bilney, whether he had privately or publicly preached or taught to the people, the opinions of Luther or any other condemned by the Church, contrary to the determination of the Church. Whereunto Bilney answered, that wittingly he had not preached or taught any of Luther's opinions, or any other contrary to the Catholic Church. Then the Cardinal asked him, whether he had not once made an oath before, that he should not preach, rehearse, or defend any of Luther's opinions, but should impugn the same everywhere? He answered, that he had made such an oath, but not lawfully, which interrogatories so ministered, and answers made, the Cardinal caused him to swear, to answer plainly to the articles and errors preached and set forth by him, as well in the city and diocese of London, as in the diocese of Norwich and other places, and that he should do it without any craft, qualifying or leaving out any part of the truth. . . .

Thus have you the letters, the abjuration and articles of *Bilney cast* Thomas Bilney. After which abjuration made about the year *down with* of our Lord 1529, the said Bilney took such repentance and *repentance.* sorrow, that he was near the point of utter despair: as by the words of Master Latimer, is credibly testified, whose words for my better discharge, I thought here to annex, written in his seventh sermon preached before King Edward, which be these: 'I knew a man myself, Bilney, little Bilney, that blessed martyr of God, who what time he had borne his faggot, and was come again to Cambridge, had such conflicts within himself (beholding this image of death) that his friends were afraid to let him be alone. They were fain to be with him day and night, and comfort him as they could, but no comforts would serve. And as for the comfortable places of scripture, to bring them unto him, it was as though a man should run him through the heart with a sword. Yet for all this, he was revived and took his death patiently, and died well against the tyrannical see of Rome.'

*Ex. Latimer Sermon 7.*

. . . Again, the said Master Latimer speaking of Bilney in another of his sermons preached in Lincolnshire, hath these words following: 'That same Master Bilney, which was burnt here in England for God's word's sake, was induced and persuaded by his friends to bear a faggot at the time when the Cardinal was aloft, and bore the swing.* Now, when the same Bilney came to Cambridge again, a whole year after, he was in such an anguish and agony, that nothing did him good, neither eating nor drinking, nor any other communication of God's word: for he thought that all the whole scriptures were against him, and sounded to his condemnation. So that I many a time commoned with him (or I was familiarly acquainted with him) but all things whatsoever any man could allege to his comfort seemed unto him to make against him. Yet for all that, afterward he came again: God endued him with such strength and perfectness of faith: that he not only confessed his faith in the Gospel of our Saviour Jesu Christ, but also suffered his body to be burned for that same Gospel's sake, which we now preach in England'. Et cetera. . . .

Furthermore, in the first sermon of the said Master Latimer before the Duchess of Suffolk . . . he yet speaking more of Bilney, inferreth as followeth: Here I have (saith he) occasion to tell you a story which happened at Cambridge. Master Bilney, or rather Saint Bilney, that suffered death for God's word's sake, the same Bilney was the instrument whereby God called me to knowledge.* For I may thank him next to God, for that knowledge that I have in the word of God. For I was an obstinate papist as any was in England: insomuch that when I should be

*Latimer called, and converted by Bilney.*

made bachelor of Divinity, my whole oration went against Philip Melanchthon and against his opinions. Bilney heard me at that time, and perceived that I was zealous without knowledge, and came to me afterward in my study, and desired me for God's sake to hear his confession. I did so: and (to say the truth) by his confession I learned more than afore in many years. So from that time forward I began to smell the word of God, and forsake the school* doctors and such fooleries,* et cetera. . . .

By this it appeareth how vehemently this good man was pierced with sorrow and remorse for his abjuration, that space almost of two years, that is, from the year 1529 to the year 1531. It followed then that he by God's grace and good counsel, came at length to some quiet of conscience, being fully resolved to give over his life for the confession of that truth, which before he had renounced. And thus, being fully determined in his mind, and setting his time he took his leave in Trinity Hall at ten of the clock at night, of certain of his friends, and said that he would go to Jerusalem, alluding belike to the words and examples of Christ in the Gospel going up to Jerusalem, what time he was appointed to suffer his passion.* And so Bilney meaning to give over his life for the testimony of Christ's Gospel told his friends that he would go up to Jerusalem, and so would see them no more, and immediately departed to Norfolk, and there preached first privily in households to confirm the brethren and sistern, and also to confirm the anchoress whom he had converted to Christ. Then preached he openly in the fields, confessing his fact and preaching publicly that doctrine, which he before had abjured, to be the very truth, and willed all men to beware by him, and never to trust to their fleshly friends in causes of religion. And so setting forward in his journey toward the celestial Jerusalem, he departed from thence to the anchoress in Norwich, and there gave her a New Testament of Tyndale's translation, and the *Obedience of a Christian Man*,* whereupon he was apprehended and carried to prison there to remain, till the blind bishop Nix sent up for a writ to burn him.

In the mean season, the friars and religious men, with the residue of their doctors, civil and canon* resorted to him, busily labouring to persuade him not to die in those opinions,

*Marginal notes:*

*Bilney returneth again from his abjuration.*

*Nam facies eius erat euntis Hierosolyman. Bilney goeth up to Jerusalem.*

*Four orders of friars against Bilney.*

saying he should be damned body and soul, if he so continued. Among whom, first were sent to him of* the bishop Doctor Call minister: (as they call him) or provincial of the grey friars: and Doctor Stokes an Augustine friar, who lay with him in prison in disputation, till the writ came that he should be burned. Doctor Call by the word of God, through the means of Bilney's doctrine, and good life, whereof he had good experience, was somewhat reclaimed to the Gospel's side. Doctor Stokes remained obdurate, and doth yet to this day, whose heart also the Lord, if it be his will, reform and open the eyes of his old age, that he may forsake the former blindness of his youth. Another great doer against him, was one friar Byrd, with one eye, Provincial of the white friars. This Byrd was a Suffragan in Coventry, and after, Bishop of Chester, and was he that brought, apples to Bonner, mentioned in the story of Haukes.* Another was a black friar, called Hodgkins, who, after, being under the Archbishop of Canterbury, married, and afterward in Queen Mary's time, put away his wife.* These four orders of friars* were sent (as is said) to bait Bilney: who notwithstanding, as he had planted himself upon the firm rock of God's word, was at a point,* and so continued unto the end. . . .

*Doctor Call, and Doctor Stokes, sent to dispute with Bilney. Doctor Call, called by Bilney.*

*Friar Byrd busy about Bilney.*

*Friar Hodgkins a black friar, against Bilney.*

Thomas Bilney, after his examination and condemnation before Doctor Pelles, doctor of Law and Chancellor,* first was degraded by Suffragan Underwood according to the custom of their popish manner, by the assistance of all the friars and doctors of the same suit. Which done, he was immediately committed to the lay power and to the two sheriffs of the city, of whom Thomas Necton was one. This Thomas Necton was Bilney's special good friend, and sorry to accept him to such execution as followed. But such was the tyranny of that time and dread of the Chancellor and friars, that he could no otherwise do, but needs must receive him. Who notwithstanding, as he could not bear in his conscience himself to be present at his death: so, for the time that he was in his custody, he caused him to be more friendly looked unto, and more wholesomely kept concerning his diet than he was before.

*Thomas Necton Sheriff of Norwich.*

After this, the Friday following at night, which was before the day of his execution, being Saint Magnus day and Saturday [1531], the said Bilney had diverse of his friends resorting unto

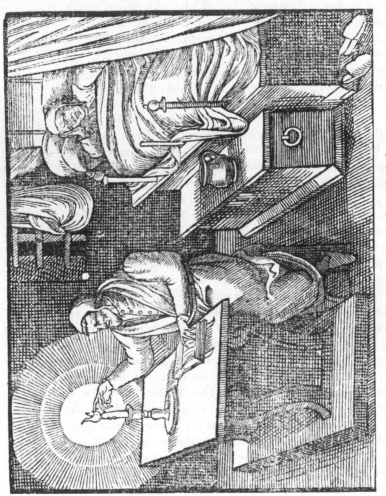

3. Thomas Bilney, proving the fire with his finger

him in the guildhall,\* where he was kept. Amongst whom one of the said friends finding him eating of an ale brew with such a cheerful heart and quiet mind as he did, said that he was glad to see him at that time, so shortly before his heavy and painful departure, so heartily to refresh himself. Whereunto he answered: 'Oh,' said he, 'I follow the example of the husbandmen of the country who having a ruinous house to dwell in, yet bestow cost as long as they may, to hold it up, and so do I now with this ruinous house of my body, and with God's creatures in thanks to him, refresh the same as ye see'. Then sitting with his said friends in godly talk, to their edification some put him in mind that though the fire, which he should suffer the next day should be of great heat unto his body, yet the comfort of God's spirit should cool it to his everlasting refreshing. At this word the said Thomas Bilney putting his hand toward the flame of the candle burning before them (as also he did divers times besides) and feeling the heat thereof, 'O', (said he), 'I feel by experience, and have known it long by philosophy,\* that fire by God's ordinance is naturally hot, but yet I am persuaded by God's holy word, and by the experience of some spoken of in the same, that in the flame they felt no heat, and in the fire they felt no consumption: and I constantly believe, that howsoever that stubble of this my body shall be wasted by it, yet my soul and spirit shall be purged thereby: a pain for the time, whereon notwithstanding followeth joy unspeakable'. And here he much entreated of this place of scripture: . . . 'Fear not, for I redeemed thee, and called thee by name; thou art mine own. When thou goest through the water, I will be with thee, and the strong floods shall not overflow thee. When thou walkest in the fire, it shall not burn thee, and the flame shall not kindle upon thee, for I am the Lord thy God, the holy one of Israel'.\* Which he did most comfortably entreat of, as well in respect of himself as applying it to the particular use of his friends there present, of whom, some took such sweet fruit therein, that they caused the whole said sentence to be fair written in tables,\* and some in their books. The comfort whereof (in diverse of them) was never taken from them to their dying day.

The Saturday next following, when the officers of execution (as the manner is) with their gleaves and halberds were ready

*The good courage of Bilney before his death.*

*Bilney tasted the fire with his finger.*

to receive him, and to lead him to the place of execution without the city gate, called Bishopsgate, in a low valley commonly called the Lollards' Pit,* under Saint Leonard's hill environed about with great hills (which place was chosen for the people's quiet sitting to see the execution) at the coming forth of the said Thomas Bilney out of the prison door, one of his friends came to him with few words, as he durst, spake to him and prayed him and in God's behalf, to be constant and to take his death as patiently as he could. Whereunto the said Bilney answered, with a quiet and mild countenance: 'Ye see when the mariner is entered his ship to sail on the troublous sea, how he for a while is tossed in the billows of the same but yet in hope that he shall once come to the quiet haven, he beareth in better comfort, the perils which he feeleth: so am I now toward this sailing, and whatsoever storms I shall feel, yet shortly after shall my ship be in the haven: as I doubt not thereof by the grace of God, desiring you to help me with your prayers to the same effect'. And so he, going forth in the streets, giving much alms by the way, by the hands of one of his friends, and accompanied with one Doctor Warner doctor of Divinity and parson of Winterton, whom he did choose as his old acquaintance, to be with him for his ghostly comfort: came at the last, to the place of execution, and ascended down from the hill to the same, apparelled in a layman's gown with his sleeves hanging down, and his arms out, his hair being piteously mangled at his degradation (a little single body in person, but always of a good upright countenance), and drew near to the stake prepared, and somewhat tarrying* the preparation of the fire, he desired that he might speak some words to the people, and there standing, thus he said:

*Constant Bilney exhorted to constancy.*

*Thomas Bilney going to his death.*

*The words of Thomas Bilney at the stake.*

'Good people, I am come hither to die, and born I was to live under that condition, naturally to die again, and that ye might testify that I depart out of this present life as a true Christian man in a right belief towards almighty God, I will rehearse unto you in a fast faith, the articles of my creed', and then began to rehearse them in order as they be in the common creed, with oft elevating his eyes and hands to almighty God, and at the article of Christ's incarnation having a little meditation in himself, and coming to the word 'crucified', he humbly bowed himself and made great reverence, and then proceeding in the articles and coming to these words, 'I believe the Catholic Church', there he paused and spake these words: 'Good people I must here confess to have offended the Church in preaching once against the prohibition of the same, at a poor cure belonging to Trinity Hall in Cambridge where I was fellow, earnestly entreated thereunto by the curate and other good people of the parish, showing that they had no sermon thereof long time before: and so in my conscience moved, I did make a poor collation* unto them, and thereby ran into the disobedience of certain authority in the church, by whom I was prohibited: howbeit I trust at the general day, charity that moved me to this act, shall bear me out at the judgement seat of God': And so he proceeded on, without any manner of words of recantation, or charging any man for procuring him to his death.

*Thomas Bilney put to death preaching, being thereunto desired.*

This once done, he put off his gown, and went to the stake, and, kneeling upon a little ledge coming out of the stake, whereon he should afterward stand to be better seen, he made his private prayer with such earnest elevation of his eyes and hands to heaven, and in so good quiet behaviour, that he seemed not much to consider the terror of his death; and ended at the last, his private prayers with the one hundred forty-third psalm . . . That is, 'Hear my prayer O Lord, consider my desire': and the next verse he repeated in deep meditation thrice . . . . : 'And enter not into judgement with thy servant, for in thy sight shall no man living be justified',* and so finishing that psalm he ended his private prayers.

*Master More proved a liar by witnes[ses] present at Bilney's death.*

*Thomas Bilney praying at the stake. Psalm 143.*

After that, he turned himself to the officers, asking them if they were ready, and they answered, 'Yea'. Whereupon he put off his jacket and doublet and stood in his hose and shirt, and went unto the stake, standing upon that ledge, and the chain was cast about him, and standing thereon, the said Doctor Warner came to him to bid him farewell, which spake but few words for* weeping. Upon whom the said Thomas Bilney did most gently smile, and inclined his body to speak to him a few words of thanks, and the last were these: 'O Master Doctor, . . . Feed your flock, feed your flock,* that when the Lord cometh, he may find you so doing, and farewell good Master Doctor, and pray for me', and so he departed without any answer, sobbing and weeping.

*Doctor Warner taking his farewell of Thomas Bilney.*

*The words of Thomas Bilney to Doctor Warner.*

And while he thus stood upon the ledge at the stake, certain friars, doctors and priors of their houses being there present (as they were uncharitably and maliciously present at his examination and degradation, et cetera) came to him and said: 'O Master Bilney the people be persuaded that we be the causers of your death, and that we have procured the same, and thereupon it is like that they will withdraw their charitable alms from us all, except you declare your charity towards us and discharge us of the matter'. Whereupon the said Thomas Bilney spake with a loud voice to the people, and said: 'I pray you good people be never the worse to these men for my sake, as though they should be the authors of my death. It was not they', and so he ended.

*The friars desire Bilney to speak for them.*

Then the officers put reed and faggots about his body and set fire on the reed, which made a very great flame which sparkled and deformed the visor* of his face, he holding up his hands and knocking upon his breast, crying sometimes 'Jesus', sometimes 'Credo.'* Which flame was blown away from him by the violence of the wind, which was that day and two or three days before notable great, in which it was said that the fields were marvellously plagued by the loss of corn: and so for a little pause, he stood without flame, the flame departing and recoursing thrice ere the wood took strength to be the sharper to consume him: and then he gave up the ghost, and his body being withered bowed downward upon the chain. Then one of the officers with his halberd smite out the staple in the stake behind him, and suffered his body to fall into the bottom of the fire, laying wood on it, and so he was consumed.

*The patient death and martyrdom of Master Bilney.*

Thus have ye (good readers) the true history, and martyrdom of this good man, that is, of blessed Saint Bilney (as Master Latimer doth call him) without any recantation, testified and ratified by the authority above said. By the which authority and party being there present and yet alive, it is furthermore constantly affirmed that Bilney not only did never recant, but also that he never had any such bill, or script or scroll in his hand to read, either softly, or apertly, as Master More *per licentiam Poeticam*,* would bear us down. Wherefore even as ye see Master More deal in this, so ye may trust him in the residue* of his other tales, if ye will.

*Saint Bilney.*

*Master More's false report refuted.*

# 2. WILLIAM TYNDALE

The life and story of the true servant and martyr of God, William Tyndale: Who for his notable pains and travail may well be called the apostle of England in this our latter age.

William Tyndale the faithful minister and constant martyr of Christ, was born about the borders of Wales and brought up from a child in the University of Oxford, where he by long continuance grew up, and increased as well in the knowledge of tongues, and other liberal arts, as especially in the knowledge of the scriptures: whereunto his mind was singularly addicted: in so much that he lying then in Magdalen Hall, read privily to certain students and fellows of Magdalen College, some parcel of Divinity: instructing them in the knowledge and truth of the scriptures. Whose manners also and conversation being correspondent to the same, were such, that all they which knew him, reputed and esteemed him to be a man of most virtuous disposition, and of life unspotted.

*W. Tyndale Martyr. {Anno 1536.}*

*The first taste of God's truth in Magdalen College, by the means of Master Tyndale.*

Thus he in the University of Oxford increasing more and more in learning and proceeding in degrees of the schools, spying his time, removed from thence to the University of Cambridge, where after he had likewise made his abode a certain space, being now further ripened in the knowledge of God's word, leaving that university also, he resorted to one Master Walsh a knight of Gloucestershire, and was there schoolmaster to his children, and in good favour with his master. This gentleman, as he kept a good ordinary commonly at his table, there resorted to him many times sundry abbots, deans, archdeacons, with other diverse doctors and great beneficed men: who there together with Master Tyndale sitting at the same table, did use many times to enter communication and talk of learned men, as of Luther and of Erasmus: also of diverse other controversies and questions upon the scripture.

Then Master Tyndale, as he was learned and well practised in God's matters, so he spared not to show unto them simply

*Tyndale disputing with the doctors.*

and plainly his judgement in matters, as he thought: and when as they at any time did vary from Tyndale in opinions and judgement, he would show them in the book and lay plainly before them the open and manifest places of the scriptures, to confute their errors, and to confirm his sayings. And thus continued they for a certain season, reasoning and contending together diverse and sundry times, till at length they waxed weary, and bare a secret grudge in their hearts against him.

Not long after this, it happened that certain of these great doctors had invited Master Walsh and his wife to a banquet: where they had talk at will and pleasure, uttering their blindness and ignorance without any resistance or gainsaying. Then Master Walsh and his wife coming home and calling for Master Tyndale, began to reason with him about those matters, whereof the priests had talked before at their banquet. Master Tyndale answering by scriptures, maintained the truth, and reproved their false opinions. Then said the Lady Walsh, a stout and a wise woman (as Tyndale reported). 'Well', (said she), 'there was such a doctor which may dispend a hundred pounds and another two hundred pounds and another three hundred pounds and what? Were it reason, think you, that we should believe you before them?' Master Tyndale gave her no answer at that time, nor also after that (because he saw it would not avail) he talked but little in those matters. At that time he was about the translation of a book called *Enchiridion militis Christiani*,* which being translated, he delivered to his master and lady. Who, after they had read and well perused the same, the doctorly* prelates were no more so often called to the house, neither had they the cheer and countenance when they came, as before they had. Which thing they marking and well perceiving, and supposing no less but it came by the means of Master Tyndale, refrained themselves, and at last utterly withdrew themselves, and came no more there.

As this grew on, the priests of the country clustering together, began to grudge and storm against Tyndale, railing against him in alehouses and other places. Of whom Tyndale* himself in his prologue before the first book of Moses, this testifieth in his own words, and reporteth that he suffered much in that country by a sort of unlearned priests, being full rule and ignorant

*Tyndale instructeth Master Walsh and his wife in the truth.*

*Enchiridion a book of Erasmus, translated by Tyndale.*

*The priests storm against Tyndale.*

(sayeth he) God knoweth: which have seen no more Latin than that only which they read in their portases and missals. . . .

It was not long after, but Master Tyndale happened to be in the company of a certain divine recounted for a learned man, and, in commoning and disputing with him, he drove him to that issue, that the said great doctor burst out into these blasphemous words, and said: 'we were better to be without God's law than the pope's'. Master Tyndale hearing this, full of godly zeal, and not bearing that blasphemous saying, replied again and said: 'I defy the pope and all his laws': and further added, that if God spared him life, ere many years he would cause a boy that driveth the plough to know more of the scripture, than he did.

*The rudeness of the country priests.*
*The blasphemy of a blind doctor.*
*The pope's law preferred before God's law.*

After this, the grudge of the priests increasing still more and more against Tyndale, they never ceased barking and rating at him, and laid many sore things to his charge, saying that he was an heretic in sophistry, an heretic in logic, an heretic in divinity: and said moreover to him, that he bare himself bold of the gentlemen there in that country: but notwithstanding, shortly he should be otherwise talked withal. To whom Master Tyndale answering again thus said, that he was contented they should bring him into any country in all England, giving him ten pounds a year to live with, and binding him to no more but to teach children and to preach.

To be short, Master Tyndale, being so molested and vexed in the country by the priests, was constrained to leave that country and to seek another place: and so coming to Master Walsh, he desired him of his good will, that he might depart from him, saying on this wise to him: 'Sir I perceive I shall not be suffered to tarry long here in this country, neither shall you be able though you would, to keep me out of the hands of the spirituality, and also what displeasure might grow thereby to you by keeping me, God knoweth: for the which I should be right sorry'. So that in fine, Master Tyndale with the good will of his master, departed, and eftsoons came up to London, and there preached a while, according as he had done in the country before, and specially about the town of Bristol, and also in the said town, in the common place called Saint Austin's Green. At length he bethinking himself of Cuthbert Tunstall, then

*Tyndale departeth from Master Walsh.*

*Tyndale cometh to London.*

Bishop of London, and especially for the great commendation of Erasmus, who in his annotations so extolleth him for his learning, thus cast with himself, that if he might attain unto his service he were a happy man. And so coming to Sir Henry Guildford the king's controller, and bringing with him an oration of Isocrates,* which he had then translated out of Greek into English, he desired him to speak to the said bishop of London for him. Which he also did, and willed him moreover to write an epistle to the bishop, and to go himself with him. Which he did likewise, and delivered his epistle to a servant of his, named William Hebilthwaite, a man of his old acquaintance. But God, who secretly disposeth the course of things, saw that was not the best for Tyndale's purpose, nor for the profit of his church, and therefore gave him to find little favour in the bishop's sight. The answer of whom was this, that his house was full, he had more than he could well find, and advised him to seek in London abroad, where he said he could lack no service. Et cetera. And so remained he in London the space almost of a year, beholding and marking with himself the course of the world, and especially the demeanour of the preachers, how they boasted themselves and set up their authority and kingdom: beholding also the pomp of the prelates, with other things more which greatly misliked him: Insomuch that he understood, not only there to be no room in the bishop's house for him to translate the New Testament: but also that there was no place to do it in all England. And therefore finding no place for his purpose within the realm, and having some aid and provision, by God's providence ministered unto him by Humphrey Monmouth* . . . and certain other good men, he took his leave of the realm, and departed into Germany. Where the good man being inflamed with a tender care and zeal of his country, refused no travail nor diligence how by all means possible, to reduce his brethren and countrymen of England to the same taste and understanding of God's holy word and verity, which the Lord had endued him withal.

Whereupon he considering in his mind, and partly also conferring with John Frith, thought with himself no way more to conduce thereunto, than if the scripture were turned into the vulgar speech, that the poor people might also read and see the

*An oration of Isocrates translated out of Greek into English by William Tyndale.*

*Tyndale sueth to bishop Tunstall to be his chaplain.*

*Tunstall refuseth Master Tyndale.*

*Tyndale departeth into Germany.*

*The causes moving Tyndale to translate the scripture into the English tongue.*

simple plain word of God. For first he wisely casting in his mind, perceived by experience, how that it was not possible to establish the lay people in any truth, except the scripture were so plainly laid before their eyes in their mother tongue, that they might see the process, order, and meaning of the text: for else what so ever truth should be taught them, these enemies of the truth would quench it again, either with apparent reasons of sophistry and traditions of their own making, founded without all ground of scripture: either else juggling with the text, expounding it in such a sense, as impossible it were to gather of the text, if the right process, order, and meaning thereof were seen.

Again, right well he perceived and considered this only, or most chiefly to be the cause of all mischief in the church, that the scriptures of God were hidden from the people's eyes: for so long the abominable doings and idolatries maintained by the Pharisaical clergy, could not be espied, and therefore all their labour was with might and main* to keep it down, so that either it should not be read at all, or if it were, they would darken the right sense with the mist of their sophistry, and so entangle them which rebuked or despised their abominations, with arguments of philosophy, and with worldly similitudes, and apparent reasons of natural wisdom: and with wresting the scripture unto their own purpose, contrary unto the process, order, and meaning of the text, would so delude them in descanting upon it with allegories, and amaze them, expounding it in many senses laid before the unlearned lay people, that though thou felt in thy heart, and were sure that all were false that they said yet couldest not thou solve their subtle riddles.*

*Hiding of scripture the cause of mischief.*

For these and such other considerations, this good man was moved (and no doubt stirred up of God) to translate the scripture into his mother tongue, for the public utility and profit of the simple vulgar people of the country: first, setting in hand with the New Testament, which he first translated about the year of our Lord 1527. After that he took in hand to translate the Old Testament, finishing the five books of Moses, with sundry most learned and godly prologues prefixed before every one, most worthy to be read and read again of all good Christians: as the like also he did upon the New Testament.

*The New Testament and the five books of Moses translated with Tyndale's prologues.*

He wrote also diverse other works under sundry titles, among the which is that most worthy monument of his, entitled: *The Obedience of a Christian Man*: wherein with singular dexterity he instructeth all men in the office and duty of Christian obedience, with diverse other treatises: as *The Wicked Mammon*: *The Practice of Prelates*, with expositions upon certain parts of the scripture, and other books also answering to Sir Thomas More and other adversaries of the truth, no less delectable, than also most fruitful to be read, which partly before being unknown unto many, partly also being almost abolished and worn out by time, the printer hereof (good Reader) for conserving and restoring such singular treasures, hath collected and set forth in print the same in one general volume, all and whole together, as also the works of John Frith, Barnes,* and other, as are to be seen most special and profitable for thy reading.

These books of William Tyndale being compiled, published and sent over into England, it cannot be spoken what a door of light they opened to the eyes of the whole English nation, which before were many years shut up in darkness.

At his first departing out of the realm, he took his journey *Tyndale went* into the further parts of Germany, as into Saxony, where he *into Saxony.* had conference with Luther and other learned men in those quarters. Where, after that he had continued a certain season, he came down from thence into the Netherlands, and had his *Tyndale came* most abiding in the town of Antwerp, unto the time of his appre-*to Antwerp.* hension: whereof more shall be said God willing hereafter.

Amongst his other books which he compiled, one work he made also for the declaration of the sacrament (as it was then called) of the altar: the which he kept by him, considering how the people were not as yet fully persuaded in other matters tending to superstitious ceremonies and gross idolatry. Wherefore he thought as yet time was not come, to put forth that work, but rather that it should hinder the people from other instructions, supposing that it would seem to them odious to hear any such thing spoken or set forth at that time, sounding against their great goddess Diana, that is, against their Mass, being had everywhere in great estimation, as was the goddess Diana amongst the Ephesians* whom they thought to come from heaven.

Wherefore Master Tyndale being a man both prudent in his doings, and no less zealous in the setting forth of God's holy truth, after such sort as it might take most effect with the people, did forbear the putting forth of that work, not doubting but by God's merciful grace, a time should come, to have that abomination openly declared, as it is at this present day: the Lord almighty be always praised therefore. Amen. *Tyndale bearing with time.*

These godly books of Tyndale, and specially the New Testament of his translation, after that they began to come into men's hands, and to spread abroad, as they wrought great and singular profit to the godly: so the ungodly envying and disdaining that the people should be anything wiser than they, and again fearing lest by the shining beams of truth, their false hypocrisy and works of darkness should be discerned: began to stir with no small ado, like as at the birth of Christ, Herod and all Jerusalem was troubled with him. But especially Satan the prince of darkness, maligning the happy course and success of the Gospel, set to his might also, how to impeach and hinder the blessed travails of that man: as by this, and also by sundry other ways may appear . . . *Darkness hateth light.* *Satan an enemy to all good purposes, especially to the Gospel.*

[*After publication of his translation of the New Testament, Tyndale migrated to Antwerp, where he lodged with Thomas Poyntz, a relative of Lady Anne Walsh, whom he had served as a tutor in Gloucestershire. Henry Phillips betrayed Tyndale to Imperial authorities.*]

Then said Phillips, 'Master Tyndale you shall be my guest here this day'. 'No', said Master Tyndale, 'I go forth this day to dinner, and you shall go with me and be my guest, where you shall be welcome'. So when it was dinnertime, Master Tyndale went forth with Phillips, and at the going forth of Poyntz's house, was a long narrow entry, so that two could not go in a front.* Master Tyndale would have put Phillips before him, but Phillips would in no wise, but put Master Tyndale afore, for that he pretended to show great humanity. So Master Tyndale being a man of no great stature, went before, and Phillips a tall comely person followed behind him, who had set officers on either side of the door upon two seats: which being there, might see who came in the entry, and coming through the same entry, Phillips pointed with his finger over Master *How Tyndale was betrayed into his enemies' hands.*

Tyndale's head down to him, that the officers which sat at the door, might see that it was he whom they should take, as the officers that took Master Tyndale, afterward told Poyntz, and said to Poyntz when they had laid him in prison, that they pitied to see his simplicity when they took him. Then they took him and brought him to the Emperor's attorney or Procurer General, where he dined. Then came the Procurer General to the house of Poyntz, and sent away all that was there of Master Tyndale's, as well his books as other things: and from thence *Tyndale had* Tyndale was had to the Castle of Vilvorde, eighteen English *to the Castle* miles from Antwerp, and there he remained until he was put to *of Vilvorde.* death . . .

*The* At last, after much reasoning, when no reason would serve, *condemnation* although he deserved no death, he was condemned by virtue of *of Master* the Emperor's decree made in the assembly at Augsburg . . . *Tyndale.* and upon the same, brought forth to the place of execution, *The* was there tied to the stake, and then strangled first by the hang-*martyrdom of* man, and afterward with fire consumed in the morning at the *William* *Tyndale.* town of Vilvorde, anno 1536, crying this at the stake with a {*Anno 1536*} fervent zeal, and a loud voice: 'Lord, open the king of England's *The prayer of* eyes'. *Master* *Tyndale.*

Such was the power of his doctrine, and sincerity of his life, that during the time of his imprisonment (which endured a *Master* year and a half) it is said, he converted his keeper, his daughter, *Tyndale* and other of his household.* Also the rest that were with him *converted his* conversant in the castle reported of him that if he were not a *keeper.* good Christian man, they could not tell whom to trust.

*Commendation* The Procurer General the Emperor's attorney being there, *of Master* left this testimony of him, that he was . . . a learned, a good, *Tyndale by* and a godly man. *them that were* *about him.*

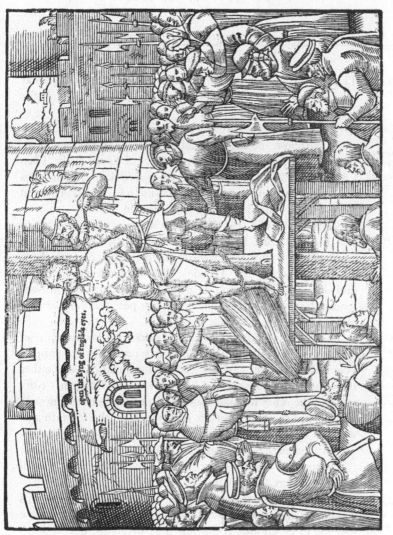

4. William Tyndale, at the stake at Vilvorde Castle, Flanders

# 3. ANNE ASKEW

## The first examination of Mistress Anne Askew before the inquisitors. 1545.

*The first examination of Anne Askew.*

To satisfy your expectation: good people (saith she) this was my first examination in the year of our Lord 1545 and in the month of March.

*Christopher Dare, inquisitor.*
*The first article against Anne Askew.*

First Christopher Dare examined me at Sadler's Hall, being one of the quest, and asked if I did not believe that the sacrament, hanging over the altar, was the very body of Christ really. Then I demanded this question of him: wherefore Saint Stephen was stoned to death, and he said, he could not tell. Then I answered that no more would I assoil his vain question.

*The second article.*

Secondly, he said that there was a woman, which did testify that I should read, how God was not in temples made with hands. Then I showed him the seventh and seventeenth chapters of the Acts of the Apostles, what Stephen and Paul had said therein.* Whereupon he asked me how I took those sentences? I answered, 'I would not throw pearls among swine,* for acorns were good enough.'

*The third article.*

Thirdly, he asked me wherefore I said that I had rather read five lines in the Bible, than to hear five masses in the temple? I confessed, that I had said no less: not for the dispraise of either the epistle or the gospel, but because the one did greatly edify me, and the other nothing at all. As Saint Paul doth witness in the fourteenth chapter of his first epistle to the Corinthians, whereas he saith, 'If the trumpet giveth an uncertain sound, who will prepare himself to the battle?'*

*1 Corinthians 14.*

*The fourth article.*

Fourthly: he laid unto my charge that I should say: 'If an ill priest ministered, it was the devil and not God'.

*Ill conditions of the ministers hurt not the faith of the receivers.*

My answer was, that I never spake any such thing. But this was my saying: that whosoever he were that ministered unto me, his ill conditions could not hurt my faith, but in spirit I received nevertheless, the body and blood of Christ.

*The fifth article.*

He asked me what I said concerning confession? I answered him my meaning, which was as Saint James saith, that every man ought to acknowledge his faults to other, and the one to pray for the other.*

Sixthly, he asked me what I said to the King's Book?* And I answered him, that I could say nothing to it, because I never saw it. *The sixth article.*

Seventhly, he asked me if I had the spirit of God in me? I answered, 'If I had not, I was but a reprobate or castaway'. Then he said he had sent for a priest to examine me, which was here at hand. *The seventh article.*

The priest asked me what I said to the sacrament of the altar, and required much to know therein my meaning. But I desired him again, to hold me excused concerning that matter. None other answer would I make him, because I perceived him to be a papist. *A priest brought to examine Anne Askew.*

Eighthly he asked me, if I did not think that private Masses* did help souls departed? I said it was great idolatry to believe more in them, than in the death which Christ died for us. *The eighth article. Private Masses' Idolatry.*

Then they had me thence unto my Lord Mayor, and he examined me, as they had before, and I answered him directly in all things as I answered the quest before. Besides this my Lord Mayor laid one thing to my charge, which was never spoken of me, but of them: and that was, whether a mouse eating the host, received God or no? This question did I never ask, but indeed they asked it of me, whereunto I made them no answer but smiled. *Anne Askew brought to the Lord Mayor.*

Then the bishop's chancellor rebuked me and said, that I was much to blame for uttering the scriptures. For Saint Paul (he said) forbade women to speak, or to talk of the word of God.* I answered him that I knew Paul's meaning as well as he, which is in 1 Corinthians 14, that a woman ought not to speak in the congregation by the way of teaching. And then I asked him, how many women he had seen go into the pulpit and preach? He said he never saw none. Then I said he ought to find no fault in poor women, except they had offended the law. *Women forbidden to speak in the congregation and how?*

Then the Lord Mayor commanded me to ward, I asked him if sureties would not serve me, and he made me short answer, that he would take none. Then was I had to the Counter, and there remained eleven days, no friend admitted to speak with me. But in the mean time there was a priest sent to me, which said that he *Anne Askew commanded to the Counter by the Lord Mayor.*

was commanded of the bishop to examine me, and to give me

*Talk between Anne Askew and a priest sent to her in prison.*

good counsel, which he did not. But first he asked me for what cause I was put in the Counter, and I told him, I could not tell. Then he said it was great pity that I should be there without cause, and concluded that he was very sorry for me.

Secondly he said, it was told him, that I should deny the sacrament of the altar. And I answered again that, that I have said, I have said.

Thirdly he asked me if I were shriven, I told him, so that I might have one of these three, that is to say, Doctor Crome, Sir Guillam, or Huntington. I was contented because I knew them to be men of wisdom, 'as for you or any other I will not dispraise, because I know you not.' Then he said, 'I would not have you think, but that I, or another that shall be brought to you, shall be as honest as they, for if we were not, you may be sure the king would not suffer us to preach.' Then I answered by the saying of Solomon: 'By communing with the wise, I may learn wisdom,

*Proverbs 1.*

but by talking with a fool, I shall take scathe.'* Pro.

Fourthly he asked, 'If the host should fall and a beast did eat

*Whether a mouse may eat Christ's body in the sacrament, or no.*

it, whether the beast did receive God or no?' I answered, 'Seeing you have taken the pains to ask the question, I desire you also to assoil it yourself: for I will not do it, because I perceive you come to tempt me.' And he said, 'It was against the order of schools that he which asked the question should answer it.' I told him [that] I was but a woman and knew not the course of schools.

Fifthly he asked me, if I intended to receive the sacrament at Easter,* or no? I answered, that else I were not Christian woman, and thereat I did rejoice, that the time was so near at hand, and then he departed thence with many fair words.

*Master Brittain seeketh to bail Anne Askew his cousin.*

The twenty-third day of March, my cousin Brittain came into the Counter unto me, and asked me whether I might be put to bail, or no? Then went he immediately unto my Lord Mayor, desiring of him to be so good unto me. That I might be bailed. My Lord answered him, and said that he would be glad to do the best that in him lay. Howbeit he could not bail me, without the consent of a spiritual officer: requiring him to go and speak with the chancellor of London.* For he said, like as he could not commit me to prison without the consent of a spiritual officer, no more could he bail me without the consent of the same.

So, upon that, he went to the chancellor, requiring of him as he did before of my Lord Mayor. He answered him that the matter was so heinous, that he durst not of himself do it, without my Lord of London were made privy thereunto. But he said he would speak unto my Lord in it, and bade him repair unto him the next morrow, and he should well know my Lord's pleasure: and upon the morrow after, he came thither, and spake both with the chancellor, and with the Bishop of London. The bishop declared unto him, that he was very well contented that I should come forth to a communication, and appointed me to appear before him the next day after, at three, of the clock at afternoon. Moreover, he said unto him, that he would, there should be at the examination such learned men as I was affectioned to,* that they might see, and also make report that I was handled with no rigour. He answered him that he knew no man that I had more affection to, than to other. Then said the bishop: 'Yes, as I understand, she is affectioned to Doctor Crome, Sir Guillam, Whitehead, and Huntington that they might hear the matter: for she did know them to be learned and of a godly judgement.' Also he required my cousin Brittain, that he should earnestly persuade me to utter even the very bottom of my heart: and he swore by his fidelity, that no man should take any advantage of my words: neither yet would he lay aught to my charge for anything that I should there speak: but if I said any manner of thing amiss, he with other more would be glad to reform me therein, with most godly counsel.

*Master Brittain for the bailing of Anne Askew, sent from the mayor, to the chancellor, from the chancellor, to the bishop.*

*Bonner's promise to Master Brittain.*

On the morrow after, the Bishop of London sent for me, at one of the clock, his hour being appointed at three, and as I came before him, he said he was very sorry of my trouble, and desired to know my opinion in such matters as were laid against me. He required me also in any wise boldly to utter the secrets of my heart, bidding me not to fear in any point, for whatsoever I did say in his house, no man should hurt me for it. I answered: 'Forsomuch as your lordship appointed three of the clock, and my friends shall not come till that hour, I desire you to pardon me of giving answer till they come.' Then said he, that he thought it meet to send for those four men which were afore named

*Anne Askew brought forth to communication before Bonner.*

and appointed. Then I desired him not to put them to the pain, for it should not need, because the two gentlemen which were my friends were able enough to testify that I should say. Anon after he went into his gallery with Master Spilman, and willed him in any wise that he should exhort me to utter all that I thought. In the mean while he commanded his archdeacon to common with

*Talk between the archdeacon and Anne Askew.*

me, who said unto me: 'Mistress wherefore are you accused and thus troubled here before the bishop?' To whom I answered again and said: 'Sir, ask I pray you my accusers, for I know not as yet.' Then took he my book out of my hand, and said: 'Such books as this, have brought you to the trouble you are in. Beware,' (saith he), 'beware, for he that made this book and was the author thereof, was an heretic I warrant you, and burnt in Smithfield.' Then I asked him, if he were certain and sure, that it was true that he had spoken. And he said he knew well the book was of John Frith's making. Then I asked him if he were not ashamed for to judge of the book before he saw it within, or yet knew the truth

*Rash judgement reproved.*

thereof. I said also, that such unadvised and hasty judgement is a token apparent of a very slender wit. Then I opened the book and showed it him. He said he thought it had been another, for he could find no fault therein. Then I desired him no more to be so unadvisedly rash and swift in judgement, till he thoroughly knew

*Good counsel giving to the archdeacon: Master Brittain. Edward Hall.*

the truth, and so he departed from me.

Immediately after came my cousin Brittain in with diverse other, as Master Hall of Gray's Inn,* and such other like. Then my Lord of London persuaded my cousin Brittain as he had done oft before, which was that I should utter the bottom of my heart

*Talk between Anne Askew and Bonner.*

in any wise. My Lord said after that unto me, that he would I should credit the counsel of such as were my friends and well willers* in this behalf, which was, that I should utter all things that burdened my conscience: for he ensured me that I should not need to stand in doubt to say anything. For like as he promised them (he said) he promised me and would perform it: which was that neither he nor any man for him, should take me at advantage of any word I should speak: and therefore he bade me say my mind without fear. I answered him that I had naught to say: for my conscience (I thanked God) was burdened with nothing.

*Bonner's similitude.*

Then brought he forth this unsavoury similitude: that if a man had a wound, no wise surgeon would minister help unto it before he had seen it uncovered. 'In like case,' saith he, 'can I give you no good counsel, unless I know wherewith your conscience is burdened.' I answered, that my conscience was clear in all things: and for to lay a plaster unto the whole skin, it might appear much folly.

'Then you drive me,' (saith he), 'to lay to your charge your own report, which is this: you did say, he that doth receive the sacrament by the hands of an ill priest, or a sinner, receiveth the devil and not God.' To that I answered, that I never spake such words. But as I said afore, both to the quest and to my Lord Mayor, so say I now again, that the wickedness of the priest should not hurt me, but in spirit and faith, I received no less than the body and blood of Christ. Then said the bishop unto me, 'What saying is this in spirit? I will not take you at the advantage.' Then I answered: 'My Lord without faith and spirit, I cannot receive him worthily.' *Bonner's first objection against Anne Askew.*

Then he laid unto me, that I should say that the sacrament remaining in the pyx, was but bread. I answered that I never said so, but indeed the quest asked me such a question, whereunto I would not answer (I said) till such time as they had assoiled me this question of mine: 'Wherefore Stephen was stoned to death?' They said they knew not. Then said I again, no more would I tell them, what it was. *Second article.*

Then said my Lord unto me, that I had alleged a certain text of the scripture. I answered that I alleged none other but Saint Paul's own saying to the Athenians in the eighteenth chapter in the Apostle's acts, that God dwelleth not in temples made with hands. Then asked he me what my faith and belief was in that matter? I answered him, 'I believe as the scripture doth teach me.' *Third article.*

Then enquired he of me, 'What if the scripture do say that it is the body of Christ?' 'I believe,' said I, 'as the scripture doth teach me.' Then asked he again, 'What if the scripture do say that it is not the body of Christ?' My answer was still, 'I believe as the scripture informeth me.' And upon this argument he tarried a great while, to have driven me to make him an answer to his mind. Howbeit I would not: but concluded this with him, that I believe therein and in all other things as Christ and his holy apostles did leave them. *Fourth article.*

*Anne Askew charged with few words.*

Then he asked me why I had so few words? And I answered, 'God hath given me the gift of knowledge, but not of utterance. And Solomon saith: "That a woman of few words is a gift of God."'* Proverbs nineteen.

*Fifth article.*

Fifthly, my Lord laid unto my charge, that I should say that the mass was superstitious, wicked, and no better than idolatry. I answered him, 'No: I said not so. Howbeit I say the quest did ask me whether private mass did relieve souls departed or no? Unto whom then I answered: "O Lord what idolatry is this, that we should rather believe in private masses, than in the healthsome death of the dear Son of God?"' Then said my Lord again: 'What an answer is that?' 'Though it be but mean,' (said I), 'yet it is good enough for the question.'

Then I told my Lord that there was a priest, which did hear what I said there before my Lord Mayor and them. With that the chancellor answered, which was the same priest. 'So she spake it in very deed,' (saith he), 'before my Lord Mayor and me.'

Then were there certain priests, as Doctor Standish and other, which tempted me much to know my mind. And I answered them always thus: that I said to my Lord of London, I have said. Then Doctor Standish desired my Lord to bid me say my mind concerning the same text of Saint Paul's learning, that I being a woman, should interpret the scriptures, specially, where so many wise learned men were.

*Doctor Standish's demand.*

Then my Lord of London said he was informed, that one should ask of me if I would receive the sacrament at Easter, and I made a mock of it. Then I desired that mine accuser might come forth, which my Lord would not. But he said again unto me, 'I sent one to give you good counsel, and at the first word you called him "papist."' That I denied not, for I perceived he was no less: yet made I him none answer unto it.

*Anne Askew could not have her accuser.*

Then he rebuked me, and said that I should report, that there were bent against me threescore priests at Lincoln. 'Indeed,' (quoth I), 'I said so. For my friends told me, if I did come to Lincoln, the priests would assault me and put me to great trouble, as thereof they had made their boast: and when I heart it, I went thither indeed, not being afraid, because I knew my matter to be good. Moreover, I remained there nine days to see what would be said unto me. And as I was in the minster

*The priests of Lincoln against Anne Askew.*

reading upon the Bible, they resorted unto me by two and by two, by five and by six minding to have spoken unto me, yet went they their ways again without words speaking.'

Then my Lord asked, if there were not one that did speak unto me. I told him yes, that there was one of them at the last, which did speak to me indeed. And my Lord then asked me what he said? And I told him his words were of small effect, so that I did not now remember them: then said my Lord, 'There are many that read and know the scripture, and yet follow it not, nor live thereafter.' I said again, 'My Lord I would wish that all men knew my conversation and living in all points, for I am sure of myself this hour that there are none able to prove any dishonesty by me. If you know any that can do it, I pray you bring them forth.'

*Anne Askew standeth upon her honesty.*

Then my Lord went away, and said he would entitle somewhat of my meaning, and so he wrote a great circumstance. But what it was, I have not all in memory, for he would not suffer me to have the copy thereof. Only do I remember this small portion of it.

'Be it known,' (saith he), 'of all men, that I Anne Askew do confess this to be my faith and belief, notwithstanding my reports made afore to the contrary. I believe that they which are houseled* at the hands of a priest, whether his conversation be good or not, do receive the body and blood of Christ in substance really. Also I do believe, that after the consecration, whether it be received or reserved, it is no less than the very body and blood of Christ in substance. Finally I do believe in this and in all other sacraments of holy church, in all points according to the old Catholic faith of the same. In witness whereof I the said Anne have subscribed my name.'

*Bonner's misreport of Anne Askew's confession.*

There was somewhat more in it, which because I had not the copy, I cannot now remember. Then he read it to me and asked me if I did agree to it. And I said again, 'I believe so much thereof, as the holy scripture doth agree unto: wherefore I desire you, that ye will add that thereunto.' Then he answered, that I should not teach him what he should write. With that, he went forth into his great chamber, and read the same bill before the audience, which inveigled and willed me to set to my hand, saying also, that I had favour showed me. Then said the Bishop, 'I might thank other, and not myself, of the favour that I found

*The tenor of Doctor Bonner's writing whereunto Anne Askew subscribed.*

at his hand,' for he considered (he said) that I had good friends, and also that I was come of a worshipful stock.

Then answered one Christopher, a servant to Master Denny: 'Rather ought you (my Lord) to have done it in such case for God's sake than for man's.' Then my Lord sat down, and took me the writing to set thereto my hand, and I writ after this manner: 'I Anne Askew do believe all manner things contained in the faith of the catholic church.'

And forasmuch as mention here is made of the writing of Bonner, which this godly woman said before she had not in memory, therefore I thought in this place to infer the same, both with the whole circumstance of Bonner, and with the title thereunto prefixed by the register, and also with her own *The words of* subscription: to the intent the reader seeing the same subscrip- *the registers.* tion, neither to agree with the time of the title above prefixed, nor with the subscription after the writing annexed, might the better understand thereby what credit is to be given hereafter to such bishops, and to such registers. Then tenor of Bonner's writing proceedeth thus.

*Ex Registrum.*    'The true copy of the confession and belief of Anne Askew, otherwise called Anne Kime, made before the Bishop of London, the twentieth day of March, in the year of our Lord God after the computation of the Church of England, 1545, and subscribed with her own hand, in the presence of the said bishop and other, whose names hereafter are recited, set forth and published at this present, to the intent the world may see what credence is now to be given unto the same woman, who in so short a time hath most damnably altered and changed her opinion and belief, and therefore rightfully in open court arraigned and condemned', *Ex. Registrum.**

*The copy of*    'Be it known to all faithful people, that as touching the *the bishops'* blessed sacrament of the altar, I do firmly and undoubtedly *report upon* believe, that after the words of consecration be spoken by *the confession* the priest, according to the common usage of this Church of *of Anne Askew* England, there is present really the body and blood of our *as it standeth* saviour Jesus Christ, whether the minister which doth conse- *in the registers.* crate, be a good man, or a bad man, and that also whensoever the said sacrament is received, whether the receiver be a good man or a bad man, he doth receive it really and corporally.

And moreover, I do believe, that whether the said sacrament then received of the minister, or else reserved to be put into the pix, or to be brought to any person that is impotent or sick, yet there is the very body and blood of our said saviour: so that whether the minister or the receiver be good or bad, yea whether the sacrament be received or reserved, always there is the blessed body of Christ really.

'And this thing with all other things touching the sacrament and other sacraments of the church, and all things else touching the Christian belief, which are taught and declared in the king's majesty's book lately set forth for the erudition of the Christian people, I Anne Askew, otherwise called Anne Kime, do truly and perfectly believe, and so here presently confess and knowledge. And here I do promise that henceforth I shall never say or do anything against the promises, or against any of them. In witness whereof, I the said Anne have subscribed my name unto these presents. Written the twentieth day of March, in the year of our Lord God 1545.' *Ex Registrum.*

By me Anne Askew, otherwise called Anne Kime. . . .

*Ex Registrum Londonium.*

Here mayest thou note gentle Reader in this confession, both in the bishop and his register: a double sleight of false conveyance. For although the confession purporteth the words of the bishop's writing, whereunto she did set her hand, yet by the title prefixed before, mayest thou see that both she was arraigned and condemned before this was registered, and also that she is falsely reported to have put to her hand, which indeed by this her own book appeareth not so to be, but after this manner and condition: 'I Anne Askew do believe all manner things contained in the faith of the Catholic Church, and not otherwise.' It followeth more in the story.

*Bonner and his register reproved with an untruth.*

Then because I did add unto it the Catholic Church he flang* into his chamber in a great fury. With that my cousin Brittain followed him, desiring him for God's sake to be good Lord unto me. He answered that I was a woman, and that he was nothing deceived in me. Then my cousin Brittain desired him to take me as a woman, and not to set my weak woman's wit to his lordship's great wisdom.

*Bonner Bishop of London in a chafe against Anne Askew.*

Then went in unto him Doctor Weston,* and said, that the cause why I did write there 'the Catholic Church', was that

*Doctor Weston.*

I understood not 'the church' written afore. So with much ado, they persuaded my Lord to come out again, and to take my name with the names of my sureties, which were my cousin Brittain, and Master Spilman of Gray's Inn.

This being done, we thought that I should have been put to bail immediately according to the order of the law. Howbeit, he would not suffer it, but committed me from thence to prison again, until the next morrow, and then he willed me to appear in the Guildhall, and so I did. Notwithstanding, they would not put me to bail there neither, but read the bishop['s] writing unto me, as before, and so commanded me again to prison.

*Anne Askew brought to the Guildhall.*

Then were my sureties appointed to come before them on the next morrow in Paul's Church: which did so indeed. Notwithstanding they would once again have broken off with them because they would not be bound also for another woman at their pleasure, whom they knew not nor yet what matter was laid unto her charge. Notwithstanding at the last, after much ado and reasoning to and fro, they took a bond of them of recognizance for my forthcoming. And thus I was at the last delivered.

*Anne Askew bailed at last under sureties with much ado.*

Written by me Anne Askew.

## The latter apprehension and examination of the worthy martyr of God, Mistress Anne Askew. Anno 1546.

[*Although church authorities released Anne Askew after her first examination for heresy in 1545, she underwent a second examination for heresy during the following year. After the prelates handed her over to civil authorities, she was racked until she could no longer stand upright and was condemned to death.*]

. . . Hitherto we have entreated of this good woman. Now it remaineth that we touch somewhat as concerning her end and martyrdom. After that she, being born of such stock and kindred, that she might have lived in great wealth and prosperity, if she would rather have followed the world, than Christ, now had been so tormented, that she could neither live long in so great distress, neither yet by her adversaries be suffered to die in secret: the day of her execution being appointed, she was brought into Smithfield in a chain, because she could not go on her feet, by

*Anne Askew brought unto the stake.*

5. Anne Askew, John Lacelles, John Adams, Nicholas Belenian, Smithfield

*Anne Askew lamed upon the rack.* means of her great torments. When she was brought unto the stake, she was tied by the middle with a chain that held up her body. When all things were thus prepared to the fire, Doctor

*Shaxton preached at Anne Askew's burning.* Shaxton* who was then appointed to preach, began his sermon. Anne Askew hearing, and answering again unto him, where he said well, confirmed the same: where he said amiss, there said she, 'He misseth, and speaketh without the book.'*

The sermon being finished, the martyrs standing there tied at three several stakes ready to their martyrdom, began their prayers. The multitude and concourse of the people was exceeding, the place where they stood being railed about to keep out the press. Upon the bench under Saint Bartholomew's Church, sat Wriothesley Chancellor of England, the old Duke of Norfolk,* the old Earl of Bedford, the Lord Mayor with diverse other more. Before the fire should be set unto them, one of the bench hearing that they had gunpowder about them, and being afraid lest the faggots by strength of the gunpowder would come flying about their ears, began to be afraid, but the Earl of Bedford declaring unto him how the gunpowder was not laid under the faggots, but only about their bodies to rid them out of their pain, which having vent, there was no danger to them of the faggots, so diminished that fear.

Then Wriothesley Lord Chancellor, sent to Anne Askew letters, offering to her the king's pardon, if she would recant. Who refusing once to look upon them, made this answer again:

*Anne Askew refuseth the king's pardon.* that she came not thither to deny her lord and master. Then were the letters likewise offered unto the other, who in like manner, following the constancy of the woman, denied not only to receive them, but also to look upon them. Whereupon the Lord Mayor commanding fire to be put unto them, cried

*Justitia injusta.* with a loud voice, '*Fiat justitia.*'*

And thus the good Anne Askew with these blessed martyrs, being troubled so many manner of ways, and having passed through so many torments, having now ended the long course of her agonies, being compassed in with flames of fire, as a blessed sacrifice unto God, she slept in the Lord, anno 1546, leaving behind her a singular example of Christian constancy for all men to follow.

# 4. JOHN ROGERS

## The Story, Life, and Martyrdom of Master John Rogers.

The fourth day of February [1555], suffered the constant martyr of God, Master John Rogers, concerning whose life, examinations, and suffering, here followeth in order set forth. And first touching his life and bringing up.

*February 4.*

John Rogers brought up in the University of Cambridge, where he profitably travailed in good learning, at the length was chosen and called by the Merchant Adventurers,* to be their chaplain at Antwerp in Brabant, whom he served to their good contentation many years. It chanced him there to fall in company with that worthy servant and martyr of God, William Tyndale, and with Miles Coverdale (which both for the hatred they have to popish superstition and idolatry, and love to true religion, had forsaken their native country.) In conferring with them the scriptures, he came to great knowledge in the gospel of God, insomuch that he cast off the heavy yoke of popery, perceiving it to be impure and filthy idolatry, and joined himself with them two in that painful and most profitable labour of translating the Bible into the English tongue, which is entitled: *The Translation of Thomas Matthew.** He knowing by the scriptures, that unlawful vows* may lawfully be broken, and that matrimony is both honest and honourable amongst all men, joined himself in lawful matrimony, and so went to Wittenberg in Saxony, where he with much soberness of living did not only greatly increase in all good and godly learning: but also so much profited in the knowledge of the Dutch tongue,* that the charge of a congregation was orderly committed to his cure.

*The life and story of Master John Rogers.*

*Master Rogers chaplain to the Merchant Adventurers at Antwerp.*

*Master Rogers brought to the gospel by Master William Tyndale, and Master Coverdale.*

*Of Master Rogers's doing in this translation read afore.*

*Master Rogers goeth to Wittenberg.*

In which ministry, he diligently and faithfully served many years, until such time as it pleased God, by the faithful travail of his chosen and dear servant King Edward the sixth, utterly to banish all popery forth of England, and to receive in true religion, setting God's gospel at liberty. He then being orderly called, having both a conscience and a ready good will to help

*Master Rogers returneth from Saxony into England in King Edward's time.*

forward the work of the Lord in his native country, left such honest and certain conditions as he had in Saxony, and came into England to preach the gospel, without certainty of any condition. In which office, after he had a space diligently and faithfully travailed, Nicholas Ridley then Bishop of London, gave him a prebend in the Cathedral Church of Paul's, and the Dean and the Chapter chose him to be the reader of the Divinity lesson there, wherein he diligently travailed, until such time as Queen Mary obtaining the crown, banished the gospel and true religion, and brought in the Antichrist of Rome, with his idolatry and superstition.

*Master Rogers, reader and prebendary in Paul's.*

After the queen was come to the Tower of London,* he being orderly called thereunto, made a godly and vehement sermon at Paul's Cross, confirming such true doctrine as he and other had there taught in King Edward's days, exhorting the people constantly to remain in the same, and to beware of all pestilent popery, idolatry, and superstition. The Council being then overmatched with popish and bloody bishops, called him to accompt for his sermon: to whom he made a stout, witty, and godly answer, and yet in such sort handled himself that at that time he was clearly dismissed. But after that, proclamation was set forth by the queen to prohibit true preaching, he was called again before the Council, (for the bishops thirsted after his blood). The Council quarrelled with him concerning his doctrine, and in conclusion commanded him as prisoner to keep his own house, and so he did: although by flying he might easily have escaped their cruel hands, and many things that were, which might have moved him thereunto. He did see the recovery of religion in England for that present, desperate: he knew he could not want a living in Germany, and he could not forget his wife and ten children, and to seek means to succour them. But all these things set apart, after he was called to answer in Christ's cause, he would not depart, but stoutly stood in defence of the same, and for the trial of that truth, was content to hazard his life.

*Master Rogers called to accompt for his sermon at Paul's Cross.*

*Master Rogers again called before the Council, and commanded to keep his house.*

Thus he remained in his own house as prisoner a long time, till at length through the uncharitable procurement of Bonner Bishop of London, who could not abide such honest neighbours to dwell by him, he was removed from his own house, to the prison called Newgate, where he was lodged among thieves and murderers, for a great space: during which time, *Master Rogers* what business he had with the adversaries of Christ, all is not *sent to Newgate.* known, neither yet any certainty of his examinations, further than he himself did leave in writing, which God would not to be lost, but to remain for a perpetual testimony in the cause of God's truth, as here followeth recorded and testified by his own writing. . . .

After that John Rogers (as ye have heard) had been long and *February 4.* straightly imprisoned, lodged in Newgate amongst thieves, often examined: and very uncharitably entreated and at length unjustly and most cruelly by wicked Winchester condemned the fourth of February, in the year of our Lord 1555, being *Master Rogers* Monday in the morning, he was warned suddenly by the keep- *warned to prepare to* er's wife of Newgate, to prepare himself to the fire: who then *death.* being sound asleep, scarce with much shoggling could be awaked. At length being raised and waked, and bid to make haste, 'Then,' said he, 'if it be so, I need not to tie my points':* and so was had down, first to Bonner to be disgraded. That *Master Rogers* done, he craved of Bonner but one petition. Bonner asking *disgraded.* what that should be: nothing said he: but that he might talk a *Master Rogers* few words with his wife, before his burning. But that could not *could not be suffered of* be obtained of him. 'Then,' said he, 'you declare your charity, *Bonner to* what it is': and so he was brought into Smithfield by Master *speak to his* Chester, and Master Woodruff, then Sheriffs of London, there *wife before his* to be burnt, where he showed most constant patience, not using *Master Rogers* many words, for he could not be permitted, but only exhorting *brought to* the people constantly to remain in that faith and true doctrine *Smithfield.* which he before had taught and they had learned, and for the confirmation whereof he was not only content patiently to suffer and bear all such bitterness and cruelty as had been showed him, but also most gladly to resign up his life, and to give his flesh to the consuming fire for the testimony of the same.

Briefly and in few words to comprehend the whole order of his life, doings, and martyrdom, first this godly Master Rogers was committed to prison (as is above said) and there continued a year and a half. In prison he was merry, and earnest in all he went about. He wrote much: his examinations he penned with his own hand, which else had never come to light.

Wherein is to be noted by the way a memorable working of God's providence. Ye heard a little above how Master Rogers craved of Bonner, going to his burning, that he might speak a few words before with his wife, which could not be granted. What these words were which he had to say to his wife, it is for no man certainly to define. Likely it may be supposed that his purpose was, amongst other things, to signify unto her of the book written of his examinations and answers which he had privily hid in a secret corner of the prison where he lay. But where man's power lacketh, see how God's providence work-

*The copy of Master Rogers's examinations by God's providence preserved.*

eth. For notwithstanding that during the time of his imprisonment straight search there was to take away his letters and writings: yet after his death, his wife and one of her sons called Daniel, coming into the place where he lay, to seek for his books and writings, and now ready to go away, it chanced her son aforenamed, casting his eye aside to spy a black thing (for it had a black cover belike because it should not be known) lying in a blind corner under a pair of stairs. Who willing his mother to see what it was, found it to be the book written with his own hand, containing these his examinations and answers with other matter above specified. In the latter end whereof this also was contained, which because it concerneth a prophetical forewarning of things pertaining to the church I thought to place the same his words, as they be there written, which

*Master Rogers seemeth to prophesy here of England, and that truly.*

are these. 'If God look not mercifully upon England, the seeds of utter destruction are sown in it already, by these hypocritical tyrants, and Antichristian prelates, popish papists, and double traitors to their natural country. And yet they speak of mercy, of blessing, of the Catholic Church, of unity, of power, and strengthening of the realm. This double dissimulation will show itself one day when the plague cometh, which will undoubtedly light upon these crown-shorn* captains, and that shortly, whatsoever the godly and the poor realm suffer in the meanwhile by God's sufferance and will.'

'Spite of Nebuchadnezzar's* beard, and maugre his heart, the captive, thrall, and miserable Jews must come home again, and have their city and temple builded up again by Zerubbabel, Esdras, and Nehemiah,* et cetera. And the whole kingdom of

Babylon must go to ruin and be taken of strangers, the Persians and Medes.* So shall the disparkled* English stock of Christ be brought again into their former estate, or to a better I trust in the Lord god, than it was in innocent King Edward's days, and our bloody Babylonical bishops, and the whole crown-shorn company, brought to utter shame: rebuke, ruin, decay, and destruction, for God cannot and undoubtedly will not suffer forever their abominable lying, false doctrine, their hypocrisy, blood thirst, whoredom, idleness, their pestilent life pampered in all kind of pleasure: their thrasonical* boasting, pride, their malicious, envious, and poisoned stomachs which they bear towards his poor and miserable Christians. Peter truly warneth that "if judgement beginneth in the house of god, what shall be the end of them that believe not the gospel? If the righteous shall scant be saved, where shall the ungodly and sinful appear?"* Some shall have their punishment here in this world and in the world to come, and they that do escape in this world, shall not escape everlasting damnation. This shall be your sauce O ye wicked papists, make ye merry here as long as ye may.'

*He meaneth here of the return of the exiles into England.*

*1 Peter 4.*

Furthermore, amongst other his words and sayings, which may seem prophetically to be spoken of him, this also may be added, and is notoriously to be marked, that he spake being then in prison, to the printer of this present book,* who then also was laid up for the like cause of religion: 'Thou,' said he, 'shalt live to see the alteration of this religion and the gospel to be freely preached again: And therefore have me commended to my brethren, as well in exile as others, and bid them be circumspect in displacing the papists, and putting good ministers into churches, or else their end will be worse than ours.'

*Master Rogers prophesieth of the return of the gospel.*

. . . To proceed now further in describing the doings of this man, during the time while he remained prisoner in Newgate, he was to the prisoners beneficial and liberal, for whom he had thus devised, that he with his fellows should have but one meal a day, they paying notwithstanding, for the charges of the whole: the other meal should be given to them that lacked on the other side of the prison. But Alexander their keeper, a straight man, and a right Alexander, a coppersmith* indeed,

*Provision by Master Rogers for the prisoners.*

of whose doings more shall be said God willing hereafter,
*Alexander* would in no case suffer that. The Sunday before he suffered,
*Andrew jailer* he drunk to Master Hooper (being then underneath him) and
*of Newgate* bade them commend him unto him, and tell him, there was
*compared to* never little fellow better would stick to a man than he would
*coppersmith.* stick to him, presupposing they should both be burned together,
although it happened otherwise, for Master Rogers was burnt
alone. And thus much briefly concerning the life and such acts
of Master Rogers as I thought worthy noting.

Now when the time came, that he being delivered to the
sheriffs, should be brought out of Newgate to Smithfield the
place of his execution, first came to him Master Woodruff
one of the foresaid sheriffs, and calling Master Rogers unto
him, asked him if he would revoke his abominable doctrine,
*The words of* and his evil opinion of the sacrament of the altar. Master
*Master* Rogers answered and said: 'That which I have preached, I will
*Woodruff to* seal with my blood.' Then, quoth Master Woodruff, 'Thou art
*Master* an heretic.' 'That shall be known,' quoth Rogers, 'at the Day
*Rogers.* of Judgement.'* 'Well,' quoth Master Woodruff, 'I will never
pray for thee.' 'But I will pray for you,' quoth Master Rogers,
and so was brought the same day, which was Monday the
fourth of February, by the sheriffs toward Smithfield, saying
the psalm *Miserere* by the way, all the people wonderfully
rejoicing at his constancy, with great praises and thanks to God
for the same: and there in the presence of Master Rochester,*
Comptroller of the queen's household, Sir Richard Southwell,*
both the sheriffs, and a wonderful number of people, he was
burned into ashes, washing his hands in the flame as he was
in burning. A little before his burning at the stake, his pardon
*Master Rogers* was brought if he would have recanted, but he utterly refused it.
*refuseth his* He was the first *protomartyr** of all that blessed company that
*pardon.* suffered in Queen Mary's time, that gave the first adventure
upon the fire. His wife and children, being eleven in number,
ten able to go, and one sucking on her breast, met him by the
way as he went towards Smithfield: this sorrowful sight of his
own flesh and blood could nothing move him, but that he constantly and cheerfully took his death with wonderful patience,
in the defence and quarrel of Christ's gospel.

Lorde receiue my spirite.

6. John Rogers, Vicar of St Pulchers and Reader of Paul's, London

# 5. LAWRENCE SAUNDERS

The history and martyrdom of Lawrence Saunders,
burned for the defence of the gospel at Coventry.
Anno 1555. February 8.

*February 8.
The story of
Lawrence
Saunders,
martyr.*
After that Queen Mary by public proclamation in the first year
of her reign, had inhibited the sincere preaching of God's holy
word, as is before declared, diverse godly ministers of the word
which had the cure and charge of souls committed to them, did
notwithstanding, according to their bounded duty, feed their
flock faithfully, not as preachers authorized by public authority
(as the godly order of the realm was in the happy days of
blessed King Edward) but as the private pastors of particular
flocks,* among whom Lawrence Saunders was one, a man of
worshipful parentage. His bringing up was in learning from his
youth, in places meet for that purpose, as namely in the school
*Scholars are
taken out of
Eton College
into the King's
College at
Cambridge.*
of Eton. From whence (according to the manner there used) he
was chosen to go to the King's College in Cambridge, where
he continued scholar of the College three whole years, and
there profited in knowledge, and learning very much for that
time: shortly after that, he did forsake the university, and went
to his parents, upon whose advice he minded to become a merchant, for that his mother was a gentlewoman of good estimation, being left a widow, and having a good portion for him
among his other brethren, she thought to set him up wealthily,
and so he coming up to London, was bound prentice with a
merchant, named Sir William Chester (who afterward chanced
to be Sheriff of London the same year that Saunders was
*Master
Saunders first
bound prentice
with Master
Chester.*
burned at Coventry). Thus by the mind of his friends
Lawrence should needs have been a merchant, but almighty
God which hath his secret working in all things, saw better for
his servant, as it fell out in the end, for although that Saunders
was bound by fast indenture to play the merchant, yet the Lord
so wrought inwardly in his heart, that he could find no liking
in that vocation: so that when his other fellows were busily
occupied about that kind of trade, he would secretly withdraw

himself into some privy corner, and there fall into his solitary lamentations, as one not liking with that kind and trade of life.

It happened that his master, being a good man, and hearing his prentice thus in his secret prayer inwardly to mourn by himself, called him unto him to know what the cause was of that his solitariness and lamentation, who then perceiving his mind nothing to fantasize* that kind of life, (for so Saunders declared unto him) and perceiving also his whole purpose to be bent to the study of his book, and spiritual contemplation, like a good man, directed his letters incontinently unto his friends, and giving him his indenture, so set him free. And thus Lawrence Saunders being ravished with the love of learning, and especially with the reading of God's word, tarried not long time in the traffic of merchandise, but shortly returned to Cambridge again to his study, where he began to couple to the knowledge of the Latin, the study of the Greek tongue, wherein he profited in small time very much: therewith also he joined the study of the Hebrew. Then gave he himself wholly to the study of the holy scripture, to furnish himself to the office of a preacher.

*Master Saunders, appointed to the trade of merchandise, could not away with that kind of life.*

*Master Saunders from merchandise returneth to his study.*

In study he was diligent and painful, in godly life he declared the fruits of a well-exercised* conscience, he prayed often and with great fervour, and in his prayers as also at other times, he had his part of spiritual exercises, which his hearty sighing to God declared. In which when any special assault did come, by prayer he felt present relief: then was his company marvellous comfortable.* For as his exercises were special teachings, so in the end they proved singular consolations: wherein he became so expert, that within short space he was able to comfort other which were in any affliction, by the consolation wherewith the Lord did comfort him. Thus continued he in the university, till he proceeded Master of Art, and a long space after.

In the beginning of King Edward's reign, when God's true religion was begun to be restored, after licence obtained, he began to preach, and was so well liked of them which then had authority, that they appointed him to read a Divinity lecture in the College at Fotheringhay,* where by doctrine and life he edified the godly, drew many ignorant to God's true knowledge,

*Master Saunders reader in the College of Fotheringay.*

and stopped the mouth of the adversaries. He married about that time, and in the married estate led a life unblameable before all men. The College of Fotheringhay being dissolved, he was placed to be reader in the minster at Litchfield: where *Saunders after* he so behaved himself in teaching and living, that the very *reader at* adversaries did give him a full report as well of learning, as of *Litchfield.* much godliness. After a certain space, he departed from Litchfield to a benefice in Leicestershire, called Churchlangton, whereupon he keeping residence, taught diligently, and kept a liberal house. From thence he was orderly called to take a benefice in the City of London, named All Hallows in Breadstreet. Then minded he to give over his cure in the country: and therefore after he had taken possession of his benefice in London, he departed from London into the country, clearly to discharge himself thereof. And even at that time began the broil about the claim that Queen Mary made to the crown, by reason whereof he could not accomplish his purpose.

In this trouble, and even among the beginners of it, (such *The constant* I mean as were for the queen) he preached at Northampton, *purpose of* nothing meddling with the estate,* but boldly uttered his con-
*Master*
*Saunders.* science against the popish doctrine and Antichrist's damnable errors, which were like to spring up again in England as a just plague for the little love which the English nation did bear to the blessed word of God, which had been so plentifully offered unto them.* The queen's men which were there and heard him, were highly displeased with him for his sermon, and for it kept him among them as prisoner. But partly for love of his brethren and friends, which were chief doers for the queen among them, partly because there was no law broken by his preaching, they dismissed him. He seeing the dreadful days at hand, inflamed with the fire of godly zeal, preached with diligence at both those benefices, as time could serve him, seeing he could resign neither of them now, but into the hand of a papist.

Thus passed he to and fro in preaching, until that proclamation was put forth, of which mention is made in the beginning. At which time he was at his benefice in the country, where he (notwithstanding the proclamation aforesaid) taught diligently God's truth, confirming the people therein, and arming them against false doctrine, until he was not only commanded to cease, but also with force resisted, so that he could not proceed there in preaching. Some of his friends perceiving such fearful menacings, counselled him to fly out of the realm, which he refused to do. But seeing he was with violence kept from doing good in that place, he returned towards London, to visit the flock, of which he had there the charge. *Master Saunders refuseth to fly the realm.*

On Saturday, the fourteenth of October, as he was coming nigh to the City of London, Sir John Mordant a Councillor to Queen Mary, did overtake him, and asked him whither he went. 'I have,' (said Saunders), 'a cure in London, and now I go to instruct my people according to my duty.' 'If you will follow my counsel,' quoth Master Mordant, 'let them alone, and come not at them.' To this Saunders answered: 'how shall I then be discharged before God, if any be sick and desire consolation, if any want good counsel and need instruction, or if any should slip into error and receive false doctrine?' *Master Mordant dissuadeth Lawrence Saunders from preaching.*

. . . Master Mordant of an uncharitable mind, went to give warning to Bonner Bishop of London, that Saunders would preach in his cure the next day. Saunders resorted to his lodging, with a mind bent to do his duty. Where because he seemed to be somewhat troubled, one which was there about him asked him how he did. 'In very deed,' (saith he), 'I am in prison till I be in prison': meaning that his mind was unquiet until he had preached, and that then he should have quietness of mind, though he were put in prison. *Master Saunders in prison, till he was in prison.*

The next day which was Sunday, in the forenoon he made a sermon in his parish, entreating that place which Paul writeth to the Corinthians: 'I have coupled you to one man, that ye should make of yourselves a chaste virgin unto Christ. But I fear lest it come to pass, that as the serpent beguiled Eve: even so your wits should be corrupt from the singleness which ye had towards Christ.' He recited a sum of that true Christian doctrine, through which they were coupled to Christ, to receive of him free justification through faith in his blood. The papistical doctrine he compared to the serpent's deceiving, and lest they should be deceived by it, he made a comparison between the voice of God, and the voice of the popish serpent: descending to more particular declaration thereof, as it were to *Master Saunders's sermon at All Hallows. 2 Corinthians 11[: 2-3].*

let them plainly see the difference that is between the order of the Church service set forth by King Edward in the English tongue: comparing it with the popish service then used in the Latin tongue.

The first he said was good, because it was according to the word of God. Corinthians 14. and the order of the primitive church. The other he said was evil, and though in that evil he intermingled some good Latin words: yet was it but as a little honey or milk mingled with a great deal of poison, to make them to drink up all. This was the sum of his sermon.

In the afternoon he was ready in his church to have given another exhortation to his people. But the Bishop of London *Master* interrupted him by sending an officer for him. This officer *Saunders* charged him upon the pain of disobedience and contumacy, *apprehended* forthwith to come to the bishop his master. Thus, as the apos- *by Bishop* tles were brought out of the Temple where they were teaching, *Bonner at his* unto the rulers of the priests,* so was Lawrence Saunders *sermon.* brought before this bishop in his Palace of London, who had in *Sir John* his company the aforenamed Sir John Mordant and some of *Mordant* his chaplains. The bishop laid no more to Lawrence Saunders's *accuser of* charge but treason for breaking the queen's proclamation, *Lawrence* heresy and sedition for his sermon. *Saunders.*

The treason and sedition, his charity was content to let slip, *Preaching of* until another time. But an heretic he would now prove him and *God's word* all those, he said, which did teach and believe that the admin- *made treason* istration of the sacraments and all orders of the church are *with Bishop* most pure, which do come most nigh to the order of the primi- *Bonner.* tive church. For the church was then but in her infancy, and could not abide that perfection which was afterward to be furnished with ceremonies. And for this cause Christ himself, and after him the apostles did in many things bear with the rudeness of the church. To this Lawrence Saunders answered with the authority of Saint Augustine, that ceremonies were even from the beginning invented and ordained for the rude *Ceremonies* infancy and weak infirmity of man, and therefore it was a token *invented only* of the more perfection of the primitive church, that it had few *for weak* ceremonies, and of the rudeness of the church papistical, *infirmity.* because it had so many ceremonies, partly blasphemous, partly unsavoury and unprofitable.

After much talk had concerning this matter, the bishop willed him to write what he believed of transubstantiation. Lawrence Saunders did so, saying: 'My Lord, ye do seek my blood, and ye shall have it: I pray God that ye may be so baptized in it, that ye may thereafter loathe bloodsucking, and become a better man.' This writing the bishop kept for his purpose, even to cut the writer's throat, as shall appear hereafter. *Bishop Bonner seeketh the blood of Master Saunders.*

The bishop when he had his will, sent Lawrence Saunders to the Lord Chancellor,* as Annas sent Christ to Caiaphas:* and like favour found Saunders as Christ his master did before him. But the Chancellor being not at home, Saunders was constrained to tarry for him by the space of four hours, in the utter* chamber, where he found a chaplain of the bishop's very merrily disposed with certain gentlemen playing at the tables,* with diverse other of the same family or house, occupied there in the same exercise. *Master Saunders sent from Annas to Caiaphas.*

All this time Saunders stood very modestly and soberly at the screen or cupboard, bareheaded, Sir John Mordant his guide or leader walking up and down by him: who (as I said before) was then one of the Council. At the last, the bishop returned from the court, whom, as soon as he was entered, a great many suitors met and received: so that, before he could get out of one house into another, half an hour was passed. At the last, he came into the chamber where Saunders was, and went through into another chamber: where in the mean way Saunders's leader gave him a writing containing the cause, or rather the accusation of the said Saunders, which when he had perused, 'Where is the man?' said the bishop. Then Saunders being brought forth to the place of examination, first, most lowly and meekly kneeled down, and made curtsy before the table where the bishop did sit: unto whom the bishop spake on this wise.

'How happeneth it,' (said he), 'that notwithstanding the queen's proclamation to the contrary, you have enterprised to preach?' *Winchester's talk with Master Saunders.*

Saunders denied that he did preach: saying, that forsomuch as he saw the perilous times now at hand, he did but (according as he was admonished, and warned by Ezekiel the prophet,*) exhort his flock and parishioners to persevere and stand steadfastly, *Master Saunders's answer to Master Winchester.*

in the doctrine which they had learned, saying also, that he was moved and pricked forward thereunto by that place of the apostle wherein he was commanded rather to obey God than man:* and moreover, that nothing more moved or stirred him thereunto, than his own conscience.

*Winchester.* 'A goodly conscience surely,' said the bishop. 'This your conscience could make our queen a bastard or misbegotten: would it not I pray you?'

*Master Saunders.* Then said Saunders, 'We,' (said he), 'do not declare or say that the queen is base or misbegotten, neither go about any such matter. But for that let them care whose writings are yet in the hands of men, witnessing the same, not without the great reproach and shame of the author': privily taunting the bishop

*A privy nip to Winchester.* himself, which had before (to get the favour of Henry the eighth) written and set forth in print a book of true obedience,*

*Winchester's book* De Vera Obedientia. wherein he had openly declared Queen Mary to be a bastard. Now Master Saunders going forwards in his purpose, said: 'We do only profess and teach the sincerity and purity of the word, the which albeit it be now forbidden us to preach with our mouths, yet notwithstanding I do not doubt, but that our blood hereafter shall manifest the same.' The bishop being in this sort prettily nipped and touched,* said: 'Carry away this

*Note how Winchester confuteth Master Saunders.* frenzy fool to prison.' Unto whom Master Saunders answered, that he did give God thanks which had given him at the last, a place of rest and quietness, whereas he might pray for the bishop's conversion.

Furthermore, he that did lie with him afterwards in prison in the same bed, reported that he heard him say that even in

*A notable example of the Lord comforting his servants in their troubles.* the time of his examination, he was wonderfully comforted, insomuch as not only in spirit, but also in body, he received a certain taste of that holy communion of saints, whilst a most pleasant refreshing did issue from every part and member of the body unto the seat and place of the heart, and from thence did ebb and flow to and fro, unto all the parts again.

*Master Saunders in prison a year and three months.* This Saunders continued in prison a whole year and three months. In all which space he sent diverse letters to diverse men: as one to Cranmer, Ridley, and Latimer: and other to his wife and also to others, certifying them both of the public calamity of the time, and also of his private afflictions, and of sundry his conflicts with his adversaries: As in writing to his friend, he speaketh of Weston* conferring with him in prison, whereof you shall hear anon (by the leave of the Lord) as followeth in the story. In the mean time the Chancellor, after this little talk with Master Saunders (as is aforesaid) sent him to the prison of the Marshalsea, et cetera. For the Caiaphas (Winchester, I mean) did nothing but bait him with some of his currish eloquence, and so committed him to the prison of the Marshalsea, where he was kept prisoner one whole year and a quarter. . . .

As the said Master Saunders was in prison, straight charge was given to the keeper, that no person should speak with him. His wife yet came to the prison gate with her young child in her arms, to visit her husband. The keeper, though for his charge, he durst not suffer her to come into the prison, yet did he take the little babe out of her arms, and brought him unto his father. Lawrence Saunders seeing him, rejoiced greatly, saying, that he rejoiced more to have such a boy, than he should if two thousand pound were given him. And unto the standers by, which praised the goodliness of the child, he said: 'What man fearing God would not lose this life present, rather than by prolonging it here, he should adjudge this boy to be a bastard, his wife a whore, and himself a whoremonger? Yea, if there were no other cause, for which a man of my estate should lose his life, yet who would not give it, to advouch this child to be legitimate, and his marriage to be lawful and holy?'

*Master Saunders's wife not suffered to speak with him in prison.*

I do (good reader) recite this saying, not only to let thee see what he thought of priest's marriage: but chiefly to let all married couples and parents learn to bear in their bosom true affections: natural, but yet seasoned with the true salt of the spirit, unfeignedly and thoroughly mortified to do the natural works and offices of married couples and parents, so long as with their doing they make keep Christ with a free confessing faith, in a conscience unsoiled: otherwise, both they and their own lives are so to be forsaken, as Christ required them to be denied, and given in his cause. . . .

[*Following formal examination for heresy, Saunders is deprived of his clerical office and sentenced to death.*]

The fourth day of February, the bishop of London did come to the prison where he was, to disgrade him: which when he had done, Lawrence Saunders said to him: 'I thank God I am none of your church.'

The day following in the morning, the Sheriff of London delivered him to certain of the queen's guard, which were appointed to carry him to the city of Coventry, there to be burned. The first night they came to Saint Albans, where Master Grimald* (a man who had more store of good gifts, than of great constancy*) did speak with him.

After Master Saunders had given him a lesson meet for his lightness, he took a cup into his hand, and asked him if he would pledge him of that cup, of which he would begin to him. Grimald by his shrugging and shrinking showing what it was, said: 'Of that cup which is in your hand, I will pledge you: but of that other which you mean I will not promise you.' 'Well,' said Master Saunders, 'my dear Lord Jesus Christ hath begone of a more bitter cup* than mine shall be, and shall I not pledge my most sweet saviour? Yes I hope.'

After they were come to Coventry, the same night a poor shoemaker, which was wont to serve him of shoes, came to him after his manner and said: 'Oh my good Master God strengthen and comfort you.' 'Gramercies good shoemaker,' quoth Master Saunders, 'and I pray thee to pray for me: for I am the unmeetest man for this high office, that ever was appointed to it: but my gracious God and dear father is able to make me strong enough.' That same night he was put into the common jail among other prisoners, where he slept little, but spent the night in prayer, and instructing of others.

The next day, which was the eighth of February he was led to the place of execution in the park without the city, going in an old gown, and a shirt, barefooted, and at times fell flat on the ground and prayed. When he was come nigh to the place, the officer appointed to see the execution done, said to Master Saunders, that he was one of them which marred the queen's realm with false doctrine and heresy: 'Wherefore thou hast deserved death' (quoth he), 'but yet, if thou wilt revoke thy heresies, the queen hath pardoned thee: if not, yonder fire is prepared for thee.' To whom Master Saunders answered: 'It is not I, nor my fellow preachers of God's truth, that have hurt the queen's realm, but it is yourself, and such as you are, which have always resisted God's holy word: it is you which have and do mar the queen's realm.* I do hold no heresies, but the doctrine of God, the blessed gospel of Christ: that hold I, that believe I, that have I taught, and that will I never revoke.' With that this tormentor cried, 'Away with him,' and away from him went Master Saunders with a merry courage towards the fire. He fell to the ground, and prayed: he rose up again, and took the stake to which he should be chained, in his arms and kissed it saying: 'Welcome the cross of Christ, welcome everlasting life': and being fastened to the stake, and fire put to him, full sweetly he slept in the Lord.*

*Ahab accuseth Elijah, for troubling Israel.*

And thus have ye the full history of Lawrence Saunders whom I may well compare to Saint Lawrence,* or any other of the old martyrs of Christ's church: both for the fervent zeal of the truth and gospel of Christ, and the most constant patience in his suffering: as also for the cruel torments that he in his patient body did sustain in the flame of fire. For so his cruel enemies handled him, that they burned him with green wood, and other smothering rather than burning fuel,* which put him to much more pain, but that the grace and most plentiful consolation of Christ, which never forsaketh his servants, and gave strength to Saint Lawrence gave also patience to this Lawrence, above all that his torments could work against: which well appeared by his quiet standing, and sweet sleeping in the fire, as is above declared.

*A comparison between Lawrence Saunders and Saint Lawrence.*

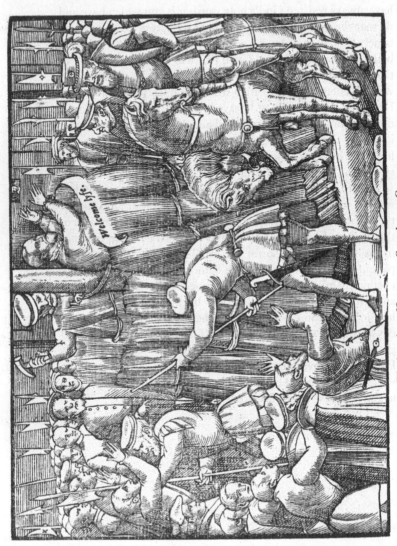

7. The burning of Lawrence Saunders at Coventry

# 6. JOHN HOOPER

The Life and Martyrdom of Master John Hooper,
Bishop of Worcester and Gloucester,
burnt for the defence of the gospel at Gloucester.
Anno 1555. February 9.

John Hooper student and graduate in the University of Oxford, *The story,* after the study of other sciences, wherein he had abundantly *life, and* profited and proceeded, through God's secret vocation was *martyrdom of* stirred with fervent desire to the love and knowledge of the *Hooper* scriptures. In the reading and searching whereof, as there *martyr.* lacked in him no diligence, joined with earnest prayer: so neither wanted unto him the grace of the Holy Ghost to satisfy his desire, and to open unto him the light of true divinity.

Thus Master Hooper growing more and more by God's grace, in ripeness of spiritual understanding, and showing withal some sparkles of his fervent spirit being then about the beginning of the Six Articles,* in the time of King Henry the eighth, fell eftsoons into displeasure and hatred of certain rabbis* in Oxford, who by and by began to stir coals against him, whereby, and especially by the procurement of Doctor Smith, he was compelled to void the University, and so removing from thence, was retained in the house of Sir Thomas Arundel,* and there was his steward, till the time that Sir Thomas Arundel having intelligence of his opinions and religion, which he in no case did favour, and yet exceedingly favouring the person and conditions of the man, found the means to send him in a message to the Bishop of Winchester, *Master* writing his letter privily to the bishop, by conference of learn- *Hooper sent to* ing to do some good upon him, but in any case requiring him *the Bishop of* to send home his servant to him again. *Winchester.*

Winchester after long conference with Master Hooper four or five days together, when he at length perceived that neither he could do that good, which he thought, to him, nor that he would take any good at his hand, according to Master Arundel's request, he sent home his servant again, right well condemning his learning and wit, but yet bearing in his breast a grudging stomach against Master Hooper still.

It followed not long after this (as malice is always working mischief) that intelligence was given to Master Hooper to provide for himself, for danger that was working against him. Whereupon Master Hooper leaving Master Arundel's house, and borrowing a horse of a certain friend (whose life he had saved a little before from the gallows) took his journey to the seaside, to go to France, sending back the horse again by one, which indeed did not deliver him to the owner. Master Hooper being at Paris tarried there not long, but in short time returned into England again, and was retained of Master Sentlow, till the time that he was again molested and laid for:* whereby he was compelled (under the pretence of being captain of a ship going to Ireland) to take the seas, and so escaped he (although not without extreme peril of drowning) through France, to the higher parts of Germany.* Where he entering acquaintance with the learned men, was of them friendly and lovingly entertained, both at Basle, and especially at Zurich of Master Bullinger, being his singular friend. Where also he married his wife, which was a Burgundian, and applied very studiously the Hebrew tongue.

At length when God saw it good to stay the bloody time of the Six Articles, and to give us King Edward to reign over this realm, with some peace and rest unto the gospel, amongst many other English exiles,* which then repaired homeward, Master Hooper also, moved in conscience, thought not to absent himself, seeing such a time and occasion offered to help forward the Lord's work, to the uttermost of his ability. And so coming to Master Bullinger, and other of his acquaintance in Zurich (as duty required) to give them thanks for their singular kindness and humanity toward him manifold ways declared, with like humanity again purposed to take his leave of them at this departing, and so did. . . .

To this also may be added another like prophetical demonstration, forshowing before the manner of his martyrdom wherewith he should glorify God, which was this. When Master Hooper being made Bishop of Worcester and Gloucester should have his arms given him by the herald, as the manner is

*Master Hooper forced to avoid the house of Sir Thomas Arundel.*

*Master Hooper flyeth again out of England.*

*Great friendship between Master Bullinger and Master Hooper.*

*A note of Master Hooper's arms presignifying his martyrdom.*

here in England, every bishop to have his arms assigned unto him (whether by the appointment of Master Hooper, or by the herald I have not certainly to say) but the arms which were to him allotted was this: a lamb in a fiery bush, and the sun beams from heaven descending down upon the lamb, rightly denoting (as it seemed) the order of his suffering, which afterward followed.

But now to the purpose of our story again: thus when Master Hooper had taken his farewell of Master Bullinger and his friends in Zurich, he made his repair again into England in the reign of King Edward VI, where he coming to London used continually to preach, most times twice, at least once every day, and never failed.

*Master Hooper returneth again into England.*

In his sermons, according to his accustomed manner, he corrected sin, and sharply inveighed against the iniquity of the world, and corrupt abuses of the church. The people in great flocks and companies, daily came to hear his voice, as the most melodious sound and tune of Orpheus's harp,* as the proverb saith: insomuch that oftentimes, when he was preaching, the church should be so full, that none could enter further than the doors thereof. In his doctrine he was earnest, in tongue eloquent, in the scriptures perfect, in pains indefatigable.

*The notable diligence of Master Hooper in preaching.*

Moreover, besides other his gifts and qualities, this is in him to be marvelled, that even as he began so he continued still unto his life's end. For neither could his labour and pain taking break him, neither promotion change him, neither dainty fare corrupt him. His life was so pure and good, that no kind of slander (although diverse went about to reprove it) could fasten any fault upon him. He was of body strong, his health whole and sound, his wit very pregnant, his invincible patience able to sustain whatsoever sinister fortune and adversity could do. He was constant of judgement, a good justicer, spare of diet, sparer of words, and sparest of time. In housekeeping very liberal,* and sometime more free than his living would extend unto. Briefly, of all those virtues and qualities required of Saint Paul in a good bishop in his epistle to Timothy,* I know not one in this good bishop lacking. He bare in countenance and talk always a certain severe and grave grace, which might peradventure be wished sometimes to have been a little

*The singular virtues of Master Hooper described.*

more popular and vulgar-like in him: but he knew what he had to do best himself.

This by the way I thought to note, for that there was once an honest citizen, and to me not unknown, which having in himself a certain conflict of conscience, came to his door for counsel: but being abashed at his austere behaviour durst not come in, but departed, seeking remedy of his troubled mind at other men's hands, which he afterward by the help of almighty God did find and obtain. Therefore in my judgement, such as are appointed and made governors over the flock of Christ, to teach and instruct them, ought so to frame their life, manners, countenance and external behaviour, as neither they show themselves too familiar and light whereby to be brought in contempt, nor in the other side again, that they appear more lofty and rigorous, than appertaineth to the edifying of the *Discretion how* simple flock of Christ. Nevertheless, as every man hath his *ministers and* peculiar gift wrought in him by nature, so this disposition of *preachers* fatherly gravity in this man neither was excessive, neither did *ought to* he bear that personage which was in him without great consid- *behave* *themselves.* eration. For it seemed to him peradventure, that this licentious and unbridled life of the common sort, ought to be chastened, not only with words and discipline, but also with the grave and severe countenance of good men.

After he had thus practised himself in this popular and common kind of preaching: at length, and that not without the great profit of many, he was called to preach before the king's majesty, and soon after, made Bishop of Gloucester by the *Master* king's commandment. In that office he continued two years, *Hooper made* and behaved himself so well, that his very enemies (except it *Bishop of* were for his good doings, and sharp correcting of sin) could *Gloucester and* find no fault with him: and after that he was made Bishop of *Worcester.* Worcester.

But I cannot tell what sinister and unlucky contention concerning the ordering and consecration of bishops, and of their apparel, with such other like trifles, began to disturb the good and lucky beginning of this godly bishop.* For notwithstanding that godly reformation of religion then begun in the church of England, besides other ceremonies more ambitious than profitable or tending to edification, they used to wear such garments and

apparel as the popish bishops were wont to do: first a chimere, *Popish attire.*
and under that a white rochet: then a mathematical cap with
four angles, dividing the whole world into four parts.* These
trifles tending more to superstition than otherwise, as he could
never abide, so in no wise could he be persuaded to wear them.
For this cause he made supplication to the king's majesty, most
humbly desiring his highness either to discharge him of the
bishopric, or else to dispense with him for such ceremonial
orders. Whose petition the king granted immediately, writing
his letter to the Archbishop.* . . .

Both this grant of the king, and also the Earl's letters aforesaid notwithstanding, the bishops still stood earnestly in the
defence of the foresaid ceremonies, saying it was but a small
matter, and that the fault was in the abuse of the things, and
not in the things themselves:* adding moreover, that he ought
not to be so stubborn in so light a matter, and that his wilful-
ness therein was not to be suffered. . . . *The king's request nor the Earl's could take effect.*

Master Hooper after all these tumults and vexations sustained about his investing and priestly vestures, at length
entering into his diocese, did there employ his time which the
Lord lent him under King Edward's reign, with such diligence, as may be a spectacle to all bishops, which shall ever
hereafter succeed him, not only in that place, but in whatsoever diocese through the whole realm of England, so careful
was he in his cure, that he left neither pains untaken, nor ways
unsought, how to train up the flock of Christ in the true word
of salvation, continually labouring in the same. Other men
commonly are wont for lucre or promotions' sake, to aspire to
bishoprics, some hunting for them, and some purchasing or
buying them, as men use to purchase lordships, and when they
have them, are loath to leave them, and thereupon also loath to
commit that thing by worldly laws, whereby to lose them.

To this sort of men Master Hooper was clean contrary, who
abhorred nothing more than gain, labouring always to save and
preserve the souls of his flock. Who being bishop of two dio- *The diligent care of Bishop Hooper in his diocese.*
ceses, so ruled and guided either of them, and both together, as
though he had in charge but one family. No father in his
household, no gardener in his garden, nor husbandman in his
vineyard, was more or better occupied, than he in his diocese

amongst his flock, going about his towns and villages in teaching and preaching to the people there.

That time that he had to spare from preaching, he bestowed either in hearing public causes, or else in private study, prayer, and visiting of schools, with his continual doctrine, he adjoined due and discrete correction, not so much severe to any, as to them which for abundance of riches, and wealthy state, thought *Master* they might do what they listed. And doubtless he spared no *Hooper bishop* kind of people, but was indifferent to all men, as well rich as *of two dioceses.* poor, to the great shame of no small number of men nowadays. *Master Hooper a light* Whereof many we do see so addicted to the pleasing of great *to all* and rich men, that in the mean time they have no regard to the *churchmen.* meaner sort of poor people, whom Christ hath bought as dearly as the other.

But now again we will return our talk to Master Hooper, all whose life in fine* was such, that to the church and all churchmen it might be a light and example, to the rest a perpetual lesson and sermon. Finally, how virtuous and good a bishop he was, ye may conceive and know evidently by this: that even as he was hated of none but of them which were evil, so yet the worst of them all could not reprove his life in any one jot.

I have now declared his usage and behaviour abroad in the public affairs of the church: and certainly there appeared in *The order and* him at home no less example of a worthy prelate's life. For *governance of* although he bestowed and converted the most part of his care *Master Hooper's* upon the public flock and congregation of Christ, for the which *house.* also he spent his blood: yet nevertheless there lacked no provision in him, and to bring up his own children in learning and good manners: even so much that ye could not discern whether he deserved more praise for his fatherly usage at home, or for *The care of* his bishoply doings abroad. For everywhere he kept one reli- *Master* gion in one uniform doctrine and integrity. So that if you *Hooper in* entered into the bishop's palace, you would suppose to have *instructing his* entered in to some church or temple. In every corner thereof, *family.* there was some smell of virtue, good example, honest conversation, and reading of holy scriptures. There was not to be seen in his house any courtly roisting or idleness: no pomp at all, no dishonest word, no swearing could there be heard.

As for the revenues of both his bishoprics, although they did not greatly exceed, as the matter was handled, yet if anything surmounted thereof, he pursed nothing, but bestowed it in hospitality. Twice I was (as I remember) in his house in Worcester, where in his common hall I saw a table spread with good store of meat, and beset full of beggars and poor folk: and I asking his servants what this meant, they told me that every day their Lord and master's manner was, to have customably to dinner a certain number of poor folk of the said city by course, who were served by four at a mess,* with hot and wholesome meats: and when they were served (being afore examined by him or his deputies of the Lord's Prayer, the articles of their faith, and Ten Commandments) then he himself sat down to dinner, and not before.

*The hospitality of Master Hooper.*

After this sort and manner Master Hooper executed the office of a most careful and vigilant pastor, by the space of two years and more, so long as the state of religion in King Edward's time did safely flourish and take place: and would God that all other bishops would use the like diligence, care, and observance in their function. After this, King Edward being dead, and Mary being crowned queen of England, religion being subverted and changed, this good bishop was one of the first that was sent for by a pursuivant to be at London, and that for two causes.

*Master Hooper called up to London at Queen Mary's coming in.*

First, to answer to Doctor Heath then appointed bishop of that diocese, who was before in King Edward's days deprived thereof for papistry.

*Two causes why Master Hooper was called up.*

Secondarily, to render account to Doctor Bonner Bishop of London, for that he in King Edward's time was one of his accusers, in that he showed himself not conformable to such ordinances as were prescribed to him by the king and his Council, openly at Paul's Cross. And although the said Master Hooper was not ignorant of the evils that should happen towards him (for he was admonished by certain of his friends to get him away and shift for himself) yet he would not prevent them, but tarried still, saying: 'Once I did flee and took me to my feet, but now, because I am called to this place and vocation, I am thoroughly persuaded to tarry, and to live and die with my sheep.'

And when at the day of his appearance (which was the first of September) he was come to London, before he could come to the foresaid Doctor Heath and Bonner, he was intercepted and commanded violently against his will to appear before the queen and her Council, to answer to certain bonds and obligations, wherein they said he was bound unto her. And when he came before them, Winchester by and by received him very opprobriously, and railing and rating of him, accused him of * religion. He again freely and boldly told his tale, and purged himself. But in fine it came to this conclusion, that by them he was commanded to ward (it being declared unto him by his departure, that the cause of his imprisonment was only for certain sums of money, for the which he was indebted to the queen, and not for religion.) This how false and untrue it was, shall hereafter in his place more plainly appear.

*Master Hooper refused to fly away.*
*Master Hooper cometh up to London.*

*Master Hooper charged to answer the queen for bonds of debt.*

*Master Hooper commanded to ward.*

The next year, being 1554 the nineteenth of March, he was called again to appear before Winchester and other the queen's commissioners: where, what for the bishop, and what for the unruly multitude, when he could not be permitted to plead his cause, he was deprived of his bishoprics. . . .

*Master Hooper deprived of his bishoprics.*

[*Following further interrogation, Hooper returned to prison, where he wrote the following account of his incarceration.*]

### The true report of Master Hooper's entertainment in the Fleet, written with his own hand, the seventh of January 1554.

*Master Hooper's report of his imprisonment in the Fleet*

The first of September, 1553. I was committed unto the Fleet, from Richmond, to have the liberty of the prison: and within six days after, I paid for my liberty five pounds sterling to the warden for fees: who immediately upon the payment thereof, complained unto Stephen Gardiner Bishop of Winchester, and so was I committed to close prison* one quarter of a year, in the tower chamber of the Fleet, used very extremely. Then by the means of a good gentlewoman, I had liberty to come down to dinner and supper, not suffered to speak with any of my friends: but as soon as dinner and supper was done, to repair to my chamber again. Notwithstanding whilst I came down thus to dinner and supper, the warden and his wife picked

*This good gentlewoman is thought to be Mistress Wilkinson.*

quarrels with me, and complained untruly of me, to their great friend the bishop of Winchester.

After one quarter of a year and somewhat more. Babington the Warden and his wife fell out with me for the wicked Mass: and thereupon the warden resorted to the bishop of Winchester and obtained to put me into the wards, where I have continued a long time, having nothing appointed to me for my bed, but a little pad of straw, and a rotten covering with a tick and a few feathers therein, the chamber being vile and stinking, until by God's means good people sent me bedding to lie in. Of the one side of which prison is the sink and filth of the house, and on the other side the town ditch, so that the stench of the house hath infected me with sundry diseases. *Babington warden of the Fleet a wicked tyrant to God's people.*

During which time I have been sick: and the doors, bars, hasps, and chains being all closed, and made fast upon me, I have mourned, called and cried for help. But the warden when he hath known me many times ready to die, and when the poor men of the wards have called to help me, hath commanded the doors to be kept fast, and charged that none of his men should come at me, saying: 'Let him alone, it were a good riddance of him.' And among many other times, he did thus the eighteenth of October, 1553, as many can witness. *The barbarous cruelty of the warden of the Fleet.*

I paid always like a baron to the said warden, as well in fees, as for my board, which was twenty shillings a week, besides my man's table,* until I was wrongfully deprived of my bishopric, and since that time I have paid him as the best gentleman doth in his house: yet hath he used me worse and more vilely, than the veriest slave* that ever came to the hall commons.

The said warden hath also imprisoned my man William Downton, and stripped him out of his clothes to search for letters, and could find none but only a little remembrance of good people's names, that gave me their alms to relieve me in prison: and to undo them also, the warden delivered the same bill unto the said Stephen Gardiner, God's enemy and mine. *William Downton Master Hooper's man.*

I have suffered imprisonment almost eighteen months, my goods, living, friends, and comfort taken from me, the queen owing me by just account eighty pounds or more. She hath put me in prison, and giveth nothing to find me, neither is there suffered any to come at me, whereby I might have relief. I am *Master Hooper eighteen months in prison. Queen Mary indebted to Master Hooper.*

with a wicked man and woman, so that I see no remedy (saving God's help) but I shall be cast away in prison before I come to judgement. But I commit my just cause to God, whose will be done, whether it be by life or death. Thus much wrote he himself of this matter. . . .

[*Following further examination concerning heresy, Hooper is deprived of his episcopal office in the following manner.*]

Here followeth the form and manner used in the disgrading of Bishop Hooper

*The form and manner of disgrading Bishop Hooper.*

The fourth day of February, the year above mentioned, in the chapel in Newgate, the Bishop of London there sitting with his notary and certain other witnesses, came Alexander Andrew the jailer, bringing with him Master Hooper and Master Rogers, being condemned before by the chancellor: where the said Bishop of London, at the request of the foresaid Winchester, proceeded to the degradation of the parties above mentioned, Master Hooper and Master Rogers, after this form and manner. First, he put upon them all the vestures and ornaments belonging to a priest, with all other things to the same order appertaining, as though (being re-vested) they should solemnly execute in their office. Thus they being apparelled and invested, the bishop beginneth to pluck off, first the uttermost vesture, and so by degree and order coming down to the lowest vesture, which they had only in taking benet and collet: and so being stripped and deposed, he deprived them of all order, benefit and privilege belonging to the clergy: and consequently, that being done, pronounced, degreed, and declared the said parties so disgraded, to be given personally to the secular power, as the sheriffs being for that year, Master Davy Woodruff, and Master William Chester: who, receiving first the said Master Rogers at the hands of the bishop had him away with them, bringing him to the place of execution where he suffered. . . .

*Alexander Andrew jailer of Newgate, a cruel enemy to God's people.*

*Master Hooper and Master Rogers disgraded together.*

*Davy Woodruff, William Chester sheriffs.*

The same Monday at night being the fourth of February, his keeper gave him an inkling that he should be sent to Gloucester to suffer death, whereat he rejoiced very much, lifting up his eyes and hands into heaven, and praising God that he saw it good to send him amongst the people, over whom he was pastor, there to confirm with his death the truth which he had before taught them: not doubting but the Lord would give him strength to perform the same to his glory: and immediately he sent to his servant's house for his boots, spurs, and cloak, that he might be in a readiness to ride when he should be called.

*Master Hooper glad that he should suffer amongst his own flock.*

The next day following, about four of the clock in the morning before day, the keeper with others came to him and searched him, and the bed wherein he lay, to see if he had written anything, and then he was led by the sheriffs of London and other their officers forth of Newgate, to a place appointed not far from Saint Dunstan's Church in Fleet Street, where six of the queen's guard were appointed to receive him and to carry him to Gloucester, there to be delivered unto the sheriff, who with the Lord Chandos,* Master Wickes, and other commissioners were appointed to see execution done. The which guard brought him to the Angel,* where he brake his fast with them, eating his meat at that time more liberally than he had used to do a good while before. About the break of the day he went to horse, and leapt cheerfully on horseback without help, having a hood upon his head under his hat that he should not be known, and so took his journey joyfully towards Gloucester, and always by the way the guard learned of him where he was accustomed to bait or lodge, and ever carried him to another inn.

*Master Hooper carried to Gloucester to be burned.*

Upon the Thursday following, he came to a town in his diocese, called Cirencester, fifteen miles from Gloucester, about eleven of the clock, and there dined at a woman's house which had always hated the truth, and spoken all evil she could of Master Hooper. This woman perceiving the cause of his coming, showed him all the friendship she could and lamented his case with tears, confessing that she before had often reported, that if he were put to the trial, he would not stand to his doctrine.

*A woman of Cirencester confirmed by the constancy of Master Hooper, which railed at him before.*

After dinner he rode forwards, and came to Gloucester about five of the clock, and a mile without the town was much people assembled which cried and lamented his estate: insomuch, that one of the guard rode post into the town, to require aid of the mayor and sheriffs, fearing lest he should have been taken from them.

*Master Hooper cometh to Gloucester.*

The officers and their retinue repaired to the gate with weapons, and commanded the people to keep their houses, et cetera, but there was no man that once gave any signification of any such rescue or violence. So was he lodged at one Ingram's house in Gloucester, and that night (as he had done all the way) he did eat his meat quietly, and slept his first sleep soundly, as it was reported by them of the guard and others. After his first sleep he continued all that night in prayer until the morning, and then he desired that he might go into the next chamber (for the guard were also in the chamber where he lay) that there being solitary, he might pray and talk with God: so that all that day, saving a little at meat, and when he talked at any time with such as the guard licensed to speak with him, he bestowed in prayer.

*The quiet mind of Master Hooper in his troubles.*

Amongst other that spake with him, Sir Anthony Kingston knight, was one. Who seeming in times past his very friend, was then appointed by the queen's letters, to be one of the commissioners, to see execution done upon him. Master Kingston being brought into the chamber, found him at his prayer, and as soon as he saw Master Hooper, he burst forth in tears. Master Hooper at the first blush knew him not. Then said Master Kingston, 'Why my Lord, do ye not know me an old friend of yours, Anthony Kingston?'

*Sir Anthony Kingston cometh to Master Hooper.*

. . . After these and many other words, the one took leave of the other, Master Kingston with bitter tears, Master Hooper with tears also trickling down his cheeks. At which departure Master Hooper told him that all the troubles he had sustained in prison, had not caused him to utter so much sorrow.

The same day in the afternoon, a blind boy, after long intercession made to the guard, obtained licence to be brought unto Master Hooper's speech. The same boy not long afore had suffered imprisonment at Gloucester for confessing of the truth. Master Hooper after he had examined him of his faith, and the cause of his imprisonment, beheld him steadfastly and (the water appearing in his eyes) said unto him: 'Ah poor boy, God hath taken from thee thy outward sight, for what consideration he best knoweth: but he hath given thee another sight much more precious: for he hath endued thy soul with the eye of knowledge and faith. God give thee grace

*A blind boy cometh to Master Hooper.*

*God's grace upon a blind boy at Gloucester.*

continually to pray unto him, that thou lose not that sight: for then shouldest thou be blind both in body and soul.'

After that another came to him, whom he knew to be a very papist and a wicked man, which appeared to be sorry for Master Hooper's trouble, saying: 'Sir, I am sorry to see you thus.' 'To see me? Why,' (said he) 'art thou sorry?' 'To see you,' (saith the other), 'in this case. For I hear say ye are come hither to die, for the which I am sorry.' 'Be sorry for thyself man,' (said Master Hooper), 'and lament thine own wickedness: for I am well, I thank God, and death to me for Christ's sake is welcome.'

The same night he was committed by the guard (their commission being then expired) unto the custody of the sheriffs of Gloucester. The name of the one was Jenkins, the other Bond, who with the Mayor and Aldermen repaired to Master Hooper's lodging, and at the first meeting saluted him, and took him by the hand. Unto whom Hooper spake on this manner. 'Master Mayor, I give most hearty thanks to you, and to the rest of your brethren, that you have vouchsafed to take me a prisoner and a condemned man by the hand: whereby to my rejoicing it is some deal apparent that your old love and friendship towards me, is not altogether extinguished: and I trust also, that all the things I have taught you in times past, are not utterly forgotten, when I was here by the godly king that dead is, appointed to be your bishop and pastor. For the which most true and sincere doctrine, because I will not now account it falsehood and heresy, as many other men do, I am sent hither (as I am sure you know) by the queen's commandment, to die, and am come to where I taught it, to confirm it with my blood. And now master sheriffs I understand by these good men, and my very friends, (meaning the guard) at whose hands I have found so much favour and gentleness by the way hitherward, as a prisoner could reasonably require (for the which also I most heartily thank them) that I am committed to your custody, as unto them that must see me brought tomorrow to the place of execution. My request therefore to you shall be only, that there may be a quick fire, shortly to make an end, and in the mean time I will be as obedient unto you, as yourselves would wish. If you think I do amiss in anything, hold up

*Master Hooper committed to the sheriffs of Gloucester.*

*The words of Master Hooper to the Mayor and sheriffs of Gloucester.*

*Master Hooper's petition to the sheriffs.*

your finger, and I have done. For I come not hither as one enforced or compelled to die (for it is well known, I might have had my life with worldly gain:) but as one willing to offer and give my life for the truth, rather than to consent to the wicked papistical religion of the Bishop of Rome, received and set forth by the magistrates in England, to God's high displeasure and dishonour: and I trust by God's grace tomorrow to die a faithful servant of God, and a true obedient subject to the queen.'

These and such like words in effect used Master Hooper to the mayor, sheriffs, and aldermen, whereat many of them mourned and lamented. Notwithstanding, the two sheriffs went aside to consult, and were determined to have lodged him in the common gaol of the town called Northgate, if the guard had not made earnest intercession for him: who declared at large how quietly, mildly, and patiently he had behaved himself in the way, adding thereto, that any child might keep him well enough, and that they themselves would rather take pains to watch with him, than that he should be sent to the common *The guard* prison. So it was determined at the length he should still *speaking for* remain in Robert Ingram's house, and the sheriffs and the ser- *Master* geants and other officers did appoint to watch with him that *Hooper.* night themselves. His desire was that he might go to bed that night betimes, saying that he had many things to remember: and so did at five of the clock, and slept one sleep soundly, and *Master* bestowed the rest of the night in prayer. After he gate up in the *Hooper* morning, he desired that no man should be suffered to come *spendeth the* into the chamber, that he might be solitary till the hour of *night in* execution. *prayer.*

About eight of the clock came Sir John Brydges Lord Chandos, with a great band of men, Sir Anthony Kingston, Sir Edmund Bridges, and other commissioners appointed to see *Sir John* execution done. At nine of the clock Master Hooper was willed *Bridges, Lord* to prepare himself to be in a readiness, for the time was at *Shandois, Sir* hand. Immediately he was brought down from his chamber by *Edmund* the sheriffs, who were accompanied with bills, glaives, and *Bridges, Sir* weapons. When he saw the multitude of weapons, he spake to *Anthony* the sheriffs on this wise: 'Master sheriffs,' (said he), 'I am no *Kingston,* traitor, neither needed you to have made such a business to *commissioners.*

bring me to the place where I must suffer: for if ye had willed me, I would have gone alone to the stake, and have troubled none of you all.' And afterward looking upon the multitude of people which were assembled, being by estimation to the number of seven thousand (for it was market day, and many also come to see his behaviour towards death) he spake unto those that were about him, saying: 'Alas, why be these people assembled and come together? Peradventure they think to hear something of me now, as they have in times past, but alas, speech is prohibited me. Notwithstanding the cause of my death is well known unto them. When I was appointed here to be their pastor, I preached unto them true and sincere doctrine, and that out of the word of God. Because I will not now accompt the same to be heresy and untruth, this kind of death is prepared for me.'

So he went forward led between the two sheriffs, (as it were a lamb to the place of slaughter) in a gown of his host's, his hat upon his head, and a staff in his hand to stay himself withal. For the grief of the sciatica, which he had taken in prison, caused him something to halt. All the way being straightly charged not to speak, he could not be perceived once to open his mouth, but beholding the people all the way which mourned bitterly for him, he would sometimes lift up his eyes towards heaven, and look very cheerfully upon such as he knew: and he was never known during the time of his being amongst them to look with so cheerful and ruddish a countenance as he did at that present. When he came to the place appointed where he should die, smilingly he beheld the stake and preparation made for him, which as near unto the great elm tree over against the college of priests, where he was wont to preach. The place round about the houses, and the bows of the tree were replenished with people, and in the chamber over the college gate stood the priests of the college. Then kneeled he down (forasmuch as he could not be suffered to speak unto the people) to prayer, and beckoned unto him six or seven times whom he knew well, to hear the said prayer, to make report thereof in time to come (pouring tears upon his shoulders and in his bosom), who gave attentive ears unto the same: the which prayer he made upon the whole creed, wherein he continued

*Master Hooper for preaching true doctrine put to death.*

*Master Hooper forbidden to speak to the people.*

*His cheerful going to death.*

*Master Hooper brought to the place of martyrdom.*

for the space of half an hour. Now after he was somewhat entered into his prayer, a box was brought and laid before him upon a stool, with his pardon (or at the leastwise it was feigned to be his pardon) from the queen, if he would turn. At the sight thereof he cried: 'If you love my soul, away with it, if you love my soul, away with it.' The box being taken away, the Lord Chandos said: 'Seeing there is no remedy, dispatch quickly.' Master Hooper said: 'Good my Lord, I trust your Lordship will give me leave to make an end of my prayers.'

*Master Hooper refuseth the queen's pardon.*

. . . Prayer being done, he prepared himself to the stake, and put off his host's gown, and delivered it to the sheriffs, requiring them to see it restored unto the owner, and put off the rest of his gear, unto his doublet and his hose, wherein he would have burned. But the sheriffs would not permit that, (such was their greediness) unto whose pleasures (good man) he very obediently submitted himself: and his doublet, hose, and petticoat were taken off. Then being in his shirt, he took a point from his hose himself, and trussed his shirt between his legs, where he had a pound of gunpowder in a bladder, and under each arm the like quantity delivered him by the guard. So desiring the people to say the Lord's prayer with him, and to pray for him, (who performed it with tears, during the time of his pains) he went up to the stake. Now when he was at the stake, three irons made to bind him to the stake, were brought: one for his neck, another for his middle, and the third for his legs. But he refusing them said: 'Ye have no need thus to trouble yourselves. For I doubt not but God will give strength sufficient to abide the extremity of the fire, without bands: notwithstanding, suspecting the frailty and weakness of the flesh, but having assured confidence in God's strength, I am content ye do as ye shall think good.'

*Master Hooper undresseth himself to the fire.*

So the hoop of iron prepared for his middle, was brought, which being made somewhat too short (for his belly was swollen by imprisonment) he shrank and put in his belly with his hand, until it was fastened: and when they offered to have bound his neck and his legs with the other two hoops of iron, he utterly refused them, and would have none, saying: 'I am well assured I shall not trouble you.'

*Master Hooper bound to the stake.*

Thus being ready, he looked upon the people, of whom he might be well seen (for he was both tall, and stood also on an high stool) and beheld round about him: and in every corner there was nothing to be seen but weeping and sorrowful people. Then lifting up his eyes and hands unto heaven, he prayed to himself. By and by he that was appointed to make the fire, came to him, and did ask him forgiveness. Of whom he asked why he should forgive him, saying: that he knew never any offence he had committed against him. 'Oh sir,' (said the man), 'I am appointed to make the fire.' 'Therein,' (said Master Hooper), 'thou doest nothing offend me: God forgive thee thy sins and do thine office, I pray thee.' Then the reeds were cast up, and he received two bundles of them in his own hands, embraced them, kissed them, and put under either arm one of them, and showed with his hand how the rest should be bestowed, and pointed to the place where any did lack.

*The weeping of the people at Master Hooper's burning.*

*He forgiveth his executioner.*

Anon commandment was given that fire should be set to, and so it was. But because there were put to no fewer green faggots than two horses could carry upon their backs, it kindled not by and by, and was a pretty while also before it took the reeds upon the faggots. At length it burned about him, but the wind having full strength in that place (it was also a lowering and a cold morning) it blew the same from him, so that he was in a manner no more but touched by the fire.

*Fire put to Master Hooper.*

Within a space after, a few dry faggots were brought, and a new fire kindled with faggots, (for there were no more reeds:) and that burned at the nether parts, but had small power above, because of the wind, saving that it did burn his hair and scorch his skin a little. In the time of which fire, even as at the first flame, he prayed, saying mildly and not very loud (but as one without pains:) 'O Jesus the son of David have mercy upon me, and receive my soul.' After the second was spent, he did wipe both his eyes with his hands, and beholding the people, he said with an indifferent loud voice: 'For God's love (good people) let me have more fire.' And all this while his nether parts did burn: for the faggots were so few, that the flame did not burn strongly at his upper parts.

*A new fire made to Master Hooper.*

*Master Hooper calleth for more fire.*

The third fire was kindled within a while after, which was more extreme than the other two: and then the bladders of gunpowder brake, which did him small good, they were so placed, and the wind had such power. In the which fire he prayed with somewhat a loud voice: 'Lord Jesu have mercy upon me: Lord Jesu have mercy upon me: Lord Jesus receive my spirit.' And these were the last words he was heard to utter. But when he was black in the mouth, and his tongue swollen, that he could not speak, yet his lips went till they were shrunk to the gums: and he knocked his breast with his hands, until one of his arms fell off, and then knocked still with the other, what time the fat, water, and blood dropped out at his fingers' ends, until by renewing of the fire, his strength was gone, and his hand did cleave fast in knocking to the iron upon his breast. So immediately bowing forwards, he yielded up his spirit. . . .

*The last words of Master Hooper.*

*The blessed martyr long tormented in the fire.*

Thus was he three quarters of an hour or more in the fire. Even as a lamb, patiently he abode the extremity thereof, neither moving forwards, backwards, or to any side, but having his nether parts burned, and his bowels fallen out, he died as quietly as a child in his bed: and he now reigneth as a blessed martyr in the joys of heaven prepared for the faithful in Christ, before the foundations of the world: for whose constancy all Christians are bound to praise God.

*The patient end of this holy martyr.*

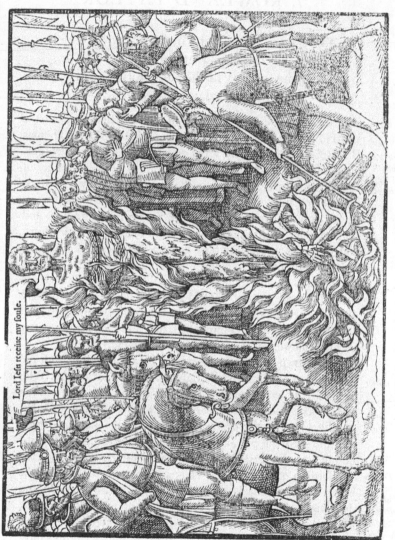

Lord Iesu receiue my soule.

8. The burning of John Hooper, Bishop of Gloucester

# 7. ROWLAND TAYLOR

The history of Doctor Rowland Taylor, which
suffered for the truth of God's word,
under the tyranny of the Roman Bishop. 1555.
the ninth day of February.

The town of Hadleigh* was one of the first that received the word of God in all England at the preaching of Master Thomas Bilney:* by whose industry the gospel of Christ had such gracious success, and took such root there, that a great number of that parish became exceeding well learned in the holy scriptures, as well woman as men: so that a man might have found among them many that had often read the whole Bible through, and that could have said a great part of Saint Paul's epistles by heart, and very well and readily have given a godly learned sentence* in any matter of controversy. Their children and servants were also brought up and trained so diligently in the right knowledge of God's word, that the whole town seemed rather an university of the learned, than a town of cloth-making or labouring people: and that most is to be commended, they were for the more part faithful followers of God's word in their living.

*Hadleigh town commended. Thomas Bilney.*

In this town was Doctor Rowland Taylor, doctor in both the civil and canon laws,* and a right perfect divine, parson. Who at his first entering into his benefice, did not, as the common sort of beneficed men do, let out his benefice to a farmer,* that should gather up the profits, and set in an ignorant unlearned priest to serve the cure, and so they may have the fleece, little or nothing care for feeding the flock: but contrarily he forsook the Archbishop of Canterbury Thomas Cranmer, with whom he before was in household, and made his personal abode and dwelling in Hadleigh among the people committed to his charge. Where he as a good shepherd, abiding and dwelling among his sheep, gave himself wholly to the study of holy scriptures most faithful endeavouring himself to fulfil that charge, which the Lord gave unto Peter, saying, 'Peter lovest thou me? Feed my lambs, feed my sheep, feed my sheep.'* This love of Christ so

*Doctor Taylor, a doctor in both laws and a divine.*

*Thomas Cranmer, Archbishop of Canterbury.*

*A good shepherd and his conditions.*

*John 2. Feed with word.*

wrought in him, that no Sunday nor holy day passed, nor other time when he might get the people together, but he preached to them the word of God, the doctrine of their salvation.

Not only was his word a preaching unto them, but all his life and conversation was an example of unfeigned Christian life, and true holiness. He was void of all pride, humble, and meek as any child: so that none were so poor, but they might boldly as unto their father, resort unto him, neither was his lowliness childish or fearful, but as occasion, time and place required, he would be stout in rebuking the sinful and evil doers, so that none was so rich but he would tell him plainly his fault, with such earnest and grave rebukes as became a good curate and pastor. He was a man very mild, void of all rancour, grudge or evil will, ready to do good to all men, readily forgiving his enemies, and never sought to do evil to any. *Feed with example.*

To the poor that were blind, lame, sick, bedridden, or that had many children, he was a very father, a careful patron, and diligent provider, insomuch that he caused the parishioners to make a general provision for them: and he himself (beside the continual relief that they always found at his house) gave an honest portion yearly, to the common alms box. His wife also was an honest, discreet, and sober matron, and his children well nurtured, brought up in the fear of God and good learning. *Feed with alms.*

*Commendation of Doctor Taylor's wife and his children.*

To conclude, he was a right and lively image or pattern of all those virtuous qualities described by Saint Paul in a true bishop,* a good salt of the earth savoury biting the corrupt manners of evil men, a light in God's house set upon a candlestick* for all good men to imitate and follow.

Thus continued this good shepherd among his flock, governing and leading them through this wilderness of the wicked world, all the days of the most innocent and holy king of blessed memory, Edward the sixth. But after it pleased God to take King Edward from this vale of misery unto his most blessed rest, the papists, who ever sembled and dissembled, both with King Henry the eighth, and King Edward his son, now seeing the time convenient for their purpose, uttered their false hypocrisy, openly refusing all good reformation made by the said two most godly kings,* and contrary to that, they had all these two kings' days preached, taught, written, and sworn, *The papists and their natural works.*

they violently overthrew the true doctrine of the gospel, and persecuted with sword and fire all those that would not agree to receive again the Roman bishop as supreme head of the universal Church, and allow all the errors, superstitions, and idolatries, that before by God's word were disproved and justly condemned, as though now they were good doctrine, virtuous, and true religion.

In the beginning of this rage of Antichrist, a certain petty gentleman after the sort of a lawyer, called Foster, being steward and keeper of courts, a man of no great skill, but a bitter persecutor in those days, with one John Clerk of Hadleigh, which Foster had ever been a secret favourer of all Romish idolatry, conspired with the said Clerk to bring in the pope and his mammetry again into Hadleigh church. For as yet Doctor Taylor, as a good shepherd, had retained and kept in his church, the godly church service and reformation made by King Edward, and most faithfully and earnestly preached against the popish corruptions, which had infected the whole country round about.

*Foster a lawyer, and John Clerk of Hadleigh, two notorious papists.*

Therefore the foresaid Foster and Clerk hired one John Averth, parson of Aldham, a very money Mammonist,* a blind leader of the blind, a popish idolater, and an open advouterer and whoremonger, a very fit minister for their purpose, to come to Hadleigh, and there to give the onset to begin again the popish Mass.

*John Averth, a right popish priest.*

To this purpose they built up with all haste possible the altar, intending to bring in their Mass again, about the Palm Monday.* But this their device took none effect: for in the night the altar was beaten down. Wherefore they built it up again the second time, and laid diligent watch, lest any should again break it down.

*Mark how unwillingly the people were to receive the papacy again.*

On the day following came Foster and John Clerk, bringing with them their popish sacrificer, who brought with him all his implements and garments, to play his popish pageant, whom they and their men guarded with swords and bucklers, lest any man should disturb him in his missal sacrifice.*

*Doctor Taylor's custom to study.*

When Doctor Taylor, who (according to his custom) sat at his book studying the word of God, heard the bells ring, he arose and went into the church, supposing something had been there to be done, according to his pastoral office: and coming to the church, he found the church doors shut and fast barred, saving the chancel door, which was only latched: where he entering in, and coming into the chancel, saw a popish sacrificer in his robes, with a broad new shaven crown, ready to begin his popish sacrifice, beset round about with drawn swords and bucklers, lest any man should approach to disturb him.

*Mass brought into Hadley with swords and bucklers.*

Then said Doctor Taylor: 'Thou devil, who made thee so bold to enter into this church of Christ, to profane and defile it with this abominable idolatry?' With that start up Foster, and with an ireful and furious countenance, said to Doctor Taylor: 'Thou traitor, what doest thou here, to let and disturb the queen's proceedings?'* Doctor Taylor answered: 'I am no traitor, but I am the shepherd that God and my Lord Christ hath appointed to feed this his flock: wherefore I have good authority to be here: and I command thee, thou popish wolf, in the name of God to avoid hence, and not to presume here with such a popish idolatry, to poison Christ's flock.'

*Doctor Taylor rebuked the devil.*

*The papists call all their trumpery the queen's proceedings. For you must remember that Antichrist reigneth by another's arm, and not by his own power. Read Daniel, of the king of faces, the eighth chapter. Doctor Taylor here playeth a right Elijah. 3 Regum 18.*

Then said Foster: 'Wilt thou traitorly heretic make a commotion, and resist violently the queen's proceedings?'

Doctor Taylor answered: 'I make no commotion, but it is you papists that maketh commotions and tumults.* I resist only with God's word, against your popish idolatries, which are against God's word, the queen's honour, and tend to the utter subversion of this realm of England. And further thou doest against the canon law, which commandeth that no Mass be said, but at a consecrated altar.'

When the parson of Aldham heard that, he began to shrink back, and would have left his saying of Mass. Then start up John Clerk, and said: 'Master Averth, be not afraid, ye have a super-altar.* Go forth with your business, man.'

Then Foster with his armed men, took Doctor Taylor, and led him with strong hand out of the church, and the popish prelate proceeded in his Romish idolatry. Doctor Taylor's wife, who followed her husband into the church, when she saw her husband thus violently thrust out of his church, she kneeled down, and held up her hands, and with loud voice said: 'I beseech God the righteous judge to avenge this injury, that this popish idolater this day doth to the blood of Christ.' Then they thrust her out of the church also, and shut to the doors: for they feared

*Super-altar is a stone consecrated by the bishops, commonly of a foot long which the papists carry instead of an altar, when they Mass for money in gentlemen's houses.*

that the people would have rent their sacrificer in pieces. Notwithstanding, one or two threw in great stones at the windows, and missed very little the popish Masser.*

*The papists' arguments wherewith they maintain their doctrine. Sapientia 2.*

Thus you see how without consent of the people, the popish Mass was again set up, with battle array, with swords and bucklers, with violence and tyranny: which practice the papists have ever yet used. As for reason, law, or scripture, they have none on their part. Therefore they are the same that saith: 'The law of unrighteousness is our strength: come, let us oppress the righteous without any fear,'* et cetera.

Within a day or two after, with all haste possible, this Foster and Clerk made a complaint of Doctor Taylor, by a letter written to Stephen Gardiner Bishop of Winchester, and Lord Chancellor.

When the bishop heard this, he sent a letter missive to Doctor Taylor, commanding him within certain days, to come and to appear before him upon his allegiance, to answer such complaints as were made against him.

*Doctor Taylor cited by a letter missive.*

When Doctor Taylor's friends heard of this, they were exceeding sorry and aggrieved in mind: which then foreseeing to what end the same matter would come, seeing also all truth and justice were trodden under foot, and falsehood with cruel tyranny were set aloft and ruled all the whole rout: his friends I say came to him, and earnestly counselled him to depart and fly, alleging and declaring unto him, that he could neither be indifferently heard to speak his conscience and mind, nor yet look for justice or favour at the said Chancellor's hands, who as it was well known, was most fierce and cruel: but must needs (if he went up to him) wait for imprisonment and cruel death at his hands.

*Doctor Taylor's friends would have him to fly.*

*The valiant courage of Doctor Taylor in Christ's cause.*

Then said Doctor Taylor to his friends: 'Dear friends, I most heartily thank you, for that ye have so tender a care over me. And although I know, that there is neither justice nor truth to be looked for at my adversary's hands, but rather imprisonment and cruel death: yet know I my cause to be so good and righteous, and the truth so strong upon my side, that I will by God's grace go and appear before them and to their beards* resist their false doings.'

Then said his friends: 'Master Doctor, we think it not best so to do. You have sufficiently done your duty, and testified the truth, both by your godly sermons, and also in resisting the parson of Aldham, with other that came hither to bring in again the popish Mass. And forasmuch as our Saviour Christ willeth and biddeth us, that when they persecute us in one city, we should fly into another:* we think in flying at this time ye should *Matthew 10.* do best, keeping yourself against another time when the church shall have great need of such diligent teachers, and godly pastors.'

'Oh,' (quoth Doctor Taylor), 'what will ye have me to do? I am now old, and have already lived too long to see these terrible and most wicked days. Fly you, and do as your conscience leadeth you. I am fully determined (with God's grace) to go to the bishop, and to his beard to tell him that he doth naught, God shall well *Doctor Taylor* hereafter raise up teachers of his people, which shall with much *refuseth to fly.* more diligence and fruit teach them, than I have done. For God will not forsake his church, though now for a time he trieth and correcteth us, and not without a just cause.

'As for me, I believe before God, I shall never be able to do God so good service, as I may do now: nor I shall never have so glorious a calling, as I now have, nor so great mercy of God proffered me, as is now at this present. For what Christian man would not gladly die against the pope and his adherents? I know that the papacy is the kingdom of Antichrist, altogether full of lies, altogether full of falsehood: so that all their doctrine, even from Christ's cross be my speed and Saint Nicholas's,* unto the end of their Apocalypse, is nothing but idolatry, superstition, errors, hypocrisy and lies.

'Wherefore I beseech you, and all other my friends, to pray for *The papacy a* me, and I doubt not, but God will give me strength and his holy *kingdom of lies.* spirit, that all mine adversaries shall have shame of their doings.' *Sir Richard Yeoman*

When his friends saw him so constant, and fully determined *Doctor Taylor's* to go, they with weeping eyes commended him unto God: and *curate, and* he within a day or two prepared himself to his journey, leaving *martyr of Christ.* his cure with a godly old priest, named Sir Richard Yeoman, *John Alcock of Hadleigh* who afterward for God's truth, was burnt at Norwich. *troubled for*

There was also in Hadleigh one Alcock, a very godly man, well *God's truth,* learned in the holy scriptures, who (after Sir Richard Yeoman was *and died in* driven away) used daily to read a chapter, and to say the English *prison.* litany in Hadleigh church. But him they fetched up to London, and cast him in prison in Newgate: where after a year imprisonment, he died.

But let us return to Doctor Taylor again, who being accompanied with a servant of his own, named John Hull,* took his journey towards London. By the way this John Hull laboured to counsel and persuade him very earnestly to fly, and not to come to the bishop, and proffered himself to go with him to serve him, and in all perils to venture his life for him, and with him.

*Doctor Taylor's journey.*

*John Hull a faithful servant to Doctor Taylor.*

But in no wise would Doctor Taylor consent or agree thereunto, but said: 'Oh John, shall I give place to this thy counsel and worldly persuasion, and leave my flock in this danger? Remember the good shepherd Christ, which not only fed his flock, but also died for his flock. Him must I follow, and with God's grace will do.

'Therefore good John pray for me: and if thou seest me weak at any time, comfort me, and discourage me not in this my godly enterprise and purpose.' Thus they came up to London, and shortly after Doctor Taylor presented himself to the Bishop of Winchester Stephen Gardiner, then Lord Chancellor of England. . . .

*Doctor Taylor again advised to fly but he refused so to do.*

Now when Gardiner saw Doctor Taylor, he according to his common custom, all reviled him, calling him knave, traitor, heretic, with many other villainous reproaches: which all Doctor Taylor heard patiently, and, at the last, said unto him:

*The first meeting between Winchester and Doctor Taylor.*

'My Lord,' (quoth he), 'I am neither traitor nor heretic, but a true subject, and a faithful Christian man, and am come according to your commandment, to know what is the cause that your Lordship hath sent for me.'

*Doctor Taylor's patience and magnanimity.*

Then said the bishop, 'Art thou come, thou villain? How darest thou look me in the face for shame? Knowest thou not who I am?'

'Yes,' (quoth Doctor Taylor), 'I know who ye are. Ye are Doctor Stephen Gardiner Bishop of Winchester, and Lord Chancellor, and yet but a mortal man I trow. But if I should be afraid of your lordly looks, why fear you not God, the Lord of us all? How dare ye for shame look any Christian man in the face, seeing ye have forsaken the truth, denied our saviour Christ and his word, and done contrary to your own oath and writing?

*Stephen Gardiner's lordly looks.*

With what countenance will ye appear before the Judgement Seat of Christ, and answer to your oath made, first unto that blessed King Henry the eighth of famous memory, and afterward unto that blessed King Edward the sixth, his son?'

*The notable answer of Doctor Taylor to the Bishop of Winchester.*

The bishop answered: 'Tush, tush, that was Herod's oath, unlawful and therefore worthy to be broken.* I have done well in breaking it: and (I thank God) I am come home again to our mother to the Catholic Church of Rome, and so I would thou shouldest do.'

*Herod's oath. Here the bishop confesseth unlawful oaths ought not to be kept.*

Doctor Taylor answered: 'Should I forsake that Church of Christ, which is founded upon the true foundation of the apostles and prophets, to approve those lies: errors, superstitions and idolatries, that the popes and their company at this day so blasphemously do approve? Nay God forbid.

'Let the pope and his return to our saviour Christ, and his word, and thrust out of the churches such abominable idolatries as he maintaineth, and then will Christian men turn unto him. You wrote truly against him, and were sworn against him.'

*The true church of Christ whereunto all men ought to turn.*

'I tell thee,' (quoth the Bishop of Winchester), 'it was Herod's oath, unlawful, and therefore ought to be broken and not kept, and our holy father the pope hath discharged me of it.'

Then said Doctor Taylor: 'But you shall not so be discharged before Christ, who doubtless will require it at your hands, as a lawful oath made to your liege and sovereign lord the king, from whose obedience no man can assoil you, neither the pope nor none of his.'

*Christ will require lawful oaths and promises.*

'I see,' (quoth the bishop), 'thou art an arrogant knave, and a very fool.'

*Gardiner again railing.*

'My Lord,' (quoth Doctor Taylor), 'leave your unseemly railing at me, which is not seemly for such a one in authority as you are. For I am a Christian man, and you know that "He that sayeth to his brother Racha is in danger of a counsel, and he that saith thou fool is in danger of hell fire."'

*Railing words become not a magistrate.*

*Matthew 5[: 22].*

The bishop answered, 'Ye are all false, and liars all the sort of you.' 'Nay,' (quoth Doctor Taylor), 'we are true men, and know that it is written . . . "The mouth that lieth slayeth the soul".* And again, "Lord God, thou shalt destroy all that speak lies".* And therefore we abide by the truth of God's word which ye contrary to your own conscience deny and forsake.'

*Marriage objected to Doctor Taylor.* 'Thou art married?' (quoth the bishop.) 'Yea,' (quoth Doctor Taylor), 'that I thank God I am, and have had nine children, and all in lawful matrimony, and blessed be God that ordained matrimony, and commanded that every man that hath not the gift of continency should marry a wife of his own, *Marriage defended.* and not live in adultery, or whoredom.'*

Then said the bishop: 'Thou hast resisted the queen's proceedings, and wouldst not suffer the parson of Aldham a very *One idolater holdeth with another.* virtuous and devout priest, to say Mass in Hadleigh.' Doctor Taylor answered, 'My Lord, I am parson of Hadleigh, and it is against all right, conscience and laws, that any man shall come into my charge and presume to infect the flock committed unto *The Mass.* me, with venom of the popish idolatrous Mass.'

With that the bishop waxed very angry, and said, 'Thou art a blasphemous heretic indeed, that blasphemest the blessed sacrament,' (and put off his cap), 'and speakest against the holy Mass, which is made a sacrifice for the quick and the dead.' Doctor Taylor answered, 'Nay I blaspheme not the blessed sacrament which Christ instituted, but I reverence it as a true Christian ought to do, and confess that Christ ordained the holy commu- *The communion.* nion in the remembrance of his death and passion, which: when we keep according to his ordinance, we (through faith) eat the body of Christ, and drink his blood giving thanks for our redemp- *The true sacrifice for the quick and the dead, what it is.* tion, and this is our sacrifice for the quick and the dead, to give God thanks for his merciful goodness showed to us, in that he gave his son Christ unto the death for us.'

'Thou sayest well,' (quoth the bishop). 'It is all that thou hast said, and more too, for it is a propitiatory sacrifice for the quick *Propitiatory sacrifice offered never more than once.* and the dead.' Then answered Doctor Taylor, 'Christ gave himself to die for our redemption upon the cross, whose body there offered, was the propitiatory sacrifice, full, perfect, and sufficient unto salvation, for all them that believe in him. And this sacrifice did our saviour Christ offer in his own person himself once for all, neither can any priest any more offer him, nor we need no more propitiatory sacrifice, and therefore I say with *Our sacrifice is only memorative.* Chrysostom, and all the doctors: "Our sacrifice is only memorative, in the remembrance of Christ's death and passion, a sacrifice of thanksgiving and therefore fathers called it 'Eucharistia': and other sacrifice hath the church of God none." '*

'It is true,' (quoth the bishop), 'the sacrament is called "Eucharistia," a thanksgiving, because we there give thanks for our redemption, and it is also a sacrifice propitiatory for the quick and the dead, which thou shalt confess ere thou and I have done.' Then called the bishop his men, and said: 'Have this fellow hence, and carry him to the King's Bench, and charge the keeper he be straitly kept.'

Then kneeled Doctor Taylor down and held up both his hands, and said: 'Good Lord, I thank thee, and from the tyranny of the Bishop of Rome, and all his detestable errors, idolatries, and abominations, good Lord deliver us: and God be praised for good King Edward.' So they carried him to prison, to the King's Bench, where he lay prisoner almost two years.

☞ This is the sum of that first talk, as I saw it mentioned in a letter that Doctor Taylor wrote to a friend of his, thanking God for his grace, that he had confessed his truth, and was found worthy for truth to suffer prison and bands, beseeching his friends to pray for him, that he might persevere constant unto the end.

Being in prison, Doctor Taylor spent all his time in prayer, reading the holy scriptures, and writing, and preaching, and exhorting the prisoners and such as resorted to him, to repentance and amendment of life.

Within a few days after, were diverse other learned and godly men in sundry counties of England committed to prison for religion, so that almost all the prisons in England were become right Christian schools and churches, so that there was no greater comfort for Christian hearts, than to come to the prisons, to behold their virtuous conversation, and to hear their prayers, preachings, most godly exhortations, and consolations.

Now were placed in churches, blind and ignorant Mass mongers, with their Latin babblings and apish ceremonies: who like cruel wolves spared not to murder all such, as anything at all, but once whispered against their popery. As for the godly preachers which were in King Edward's time, they were either fled the realm, or else, as the prophets did in King Ahab's days, they were privily kept in corners.* As for as many as the papists could

*Winchester's strong argument carry him to prison.*

*Doctor Taylor's prayer against the pope and his detestable enormities.*

*The godly behaviour and conversation of Doctor Taylor in the prison.*

*Prisons turned into churches, and churches into dens of thieves.*

*The lamentable distress of God's true worshippers in those days.*

lay hold on, they were sent into prison, there as lambs waiting when the butchers would call them to the slaughter.

When Doctor Taylor was come into the prison called the King's Bench, he found therein the virtuous and vigilant preacher of God's word, Master Bradford: which man, for his innocent and godly living, his devout, and virtuous preaching, was worthily counted a miracle of our time, as even his adver-

*John Bradford and Doctor Taylor prison fellows in the King's Bench.*

saries must needs confess. Finding this man in prison, he began to exhort him to faith, strength, and patience, and to persevere constant unto the end. Master Bradford hearing this, thanked God that he had provided him such a comfortable prison fellow: and so they both together lauded God, and continued in prayer, reading, and exhorting one the other: insomuch that Doctor Taylor told his friends that came to visit him, that God had most graciously provided for him, to send him to that prison where he found such an angel of God, to be in his company to comfort him. . . .

[*Further examinations ensue until Rowland Taylor is summoned before the bishops for a final time in the company of John Bradford and Lawrence Saunders.*]

Upon which day and year aforesaid, Doctor Taylor and Master Bradford, and Master Saunders were again called to appear before the Bishop of Winchester, the Bishop of Norwich,

*Gardiner. Hopton. Bonner. Capon. Tunstall.*

of London, of Salisbury, and of Durham, and there were charged again with heresy and schism, and therefore a determinate answer was required: whether they would submit themselves to the Roman bishop and abjure their errors or else they would according to their laws proceed to their condemnation.

When Doctor Taylor and his fellows, Master Bradford and Master Saunders heard this, they answered stoutly and boldly, that they would not depart from the truth which they had preached in King Edward's days, neither would they submit themselves to the Romish Antichrist but they thanked God for

*The constancy of these men.*

so great mercy, that he would call them to be worthy to suffer for his word and truth.

*Sentence of death given upon innocents.*

When the bishops saw them so boldly, constantly, and unmoveably fixed in the truth, they read the sentence of death upon them, which when they had heard, they most joyfully gave God thanks, and stoutly said unto the bishops: 'We doubt not but God the righteous judge, will require our blood at your hands, and the proudest of you all shall repent this receiving again of Antichrist, and your tyranny that ye now show against the flock of Christ.'

So was Doctor Taylor now condemned, committed to the Clink,* and the keepers charged straitly to keep him: 'For ye have now another manner of charge,' (quoth the Lord Chancellor), 'than ye had before: therefore look ye take heed to it.'

*Doctor Taylor condemned.*

When the keeper brought him toward the prison, the people flocked about to gaze upon him: unto whom he said: 'God be praised (good people). I am come away from them undefiled, and will confirm the truth with my blood.' So was he bestowed in the Clink till it was toward night, and then he was removed to the Counter by the Poultry.

*Doctor Taylor removed from the Clink to the Counter by night.*

When Doctor Taylor had lain in the said Counter in the Poultry a seven-night or thereabouts prisoner, the fourth day of February, anno 1555, Edmund Bonner Bishop of London with others, came to the said Counter to disgrade him, bringing with them such ornaments, as do appertain to their massing mummery. Now being come, he called for the said Doctor Taylor to be brought unto him (the bishop being then in the chamber, where the keeper of the Counter and his wife lay.) So Doctor Taylor was brought down from the chamber above that, to the said Bonner. And at his coming, the bishop said: 'Master Doctor, I would you would remember yourself, and turn to your mother holy Church: so may you do well enough, and I will sue for your pardon.' Whereunto Master Taylor answered: 'I would you and your fellows would turn to Christ. As for me I will not turn to Antichrist.' 'Well,' (quoth the bishop), 'I am come to disgrade you: wherefore put on these vestures.' 'No,' (quoth Doctor Taylor), 'I will not.' 'Wilt thou not?' said the bishop. 'I shall make thee, ere I go.' Quoth Doctor Taylor, 'You shall not by the grace of God.' Then he charged him upon his obedience to do it: but he would not do it for him.

*Bonner cometh to the Counter to disgrade Doctor Taylor.*

*Bonner persuading Doctor Taylor to turn.*

*Doctor Taylor refuseth to turn from Christ to Antichrist.*

So he willed another to put them on his back: and when he was thoroughly furnished therewith, he set his hands by his side, walking up and down, and said: 'How say you my Lord, am I not a goodly fool? How say you my masters? If I were in

*Doctor Taylor and Bonner striving for putting on the Massing garments.*

cheap,* should I not have boys enough to laugh at these apish

Doctor Taylor
derideth the
pope's Massing
toys.

toys, and toying trumpery?' So the bishop scraped his fingers thumbs, and the crown of his head, and did the rest of such like devilish observances.

At the last, when he should have given Doctor Taylor a stroke on the breast with his crosier staff,* the bishop's chaplain said: 'My Lord strike him not, for he will sure strike again.' 'Yea by Saint Peter will I,'* quoth Doctor Taylor. 'The cause is Christ's: and I were no good Christian if I would not fight in my master's quarrel.' So the bishop laid his curse upon him, but stroke him not. Then Doctor Taylor said: 'Though you do curse me, yet God doth bless me. I have the witness of my conscience, that ye have done me wrong and violence: and yet I pray God (if it be his will) forgive you. But from the tyranny

Doctor Taylor
prayeth again
against the
pope and his
detestable
enormities.

Bonner afeard
of Doctor
Taylor.

of the Bishop of Rome, and his detestable enormities, good Lord deliver us.' And in going up to his chamber, he still said: 'God deliver me from you, God deliver me from you.' And when he came up, he told Master Bradford (for they both lay in one chamber) that he had made the Bishop of London afeard: 'For,' (saith he, laughingly) 'his chaplain gave him counsel not to strike me with his crosier staff, for that I would strike again: and by my troth,' (said he rubbing his hands), 'I made him believe I would do so indeed.'

The night after that he was disgraded, his wife and his son Thomas resorted to him, and were by the gentleness of the

Keepers of
prison.

keepers permitted to sup with him. For this difference was ever found between the keepers of the bishop's prisons, and the keepers of the king's prisons: that the bishop's keepers were ever cruel, blasphemous, and tyrannous, like their masters: but the keepers of the king's prisons showed for the most part, as much favour, as they possibly might. . . .

On the next morrow, after that Doctor Taylor had supped with his wife in the Counter (as is before expressed) which was the fifth day of February, the Sheriff of London, with his officers came to the Counter by two of the clock in the morning,

Doctor Taylor
led from the
Counter by
night toward
Hadleigh.

and so brought forth Doctor Taylor, and without any light led him to the Woolsack, an Inn without Aldgate. Doctor Taylor's wife suspecting that her husband should that night be carried away, watched all night within Saint Botolph's Church porch beside Aldgate, having with her two children, the one named Elizabeth of fourteen years of age (whom being left without father or mother, Doctor Taylor had brought up of alms from three years old) the other named Mary, Doctor Taylor's own daughter.

Now, when the Sheriff and his company came against* Saint Botolph's church, Elizabeth cried saying: 'O my dear father. Mother, mother, here is my father led away.' Then cried his wife: 'Rowland, Rowland, where art thou?' For it was a very dark morning, that the one could not see the other. Doctor Taylor answered: 'Dear wife, I am here,' and stayed. The Sheriff's men would have led him forth, but the Sheriff said: 'Stay a little masters, I pray you, and let him speak with his wife,' and so they stayed.

*The last meeting and leave-taking with his wife and children.*

Then came she to him, and he took his daughter Mary in his arms, and he, his wife, and Elizabeth kneeled down and said the Lord's Prayer. At which sight the Sheriff wept apace, and so did diverse other of the company. After they had prayed, he rose up and kissed his wife, and shook her by the hand, and said: 'Farewell my dear wife, be of good comfort, for I am quiet in my conscience. God shall stir up a father for my children.' And then he kissed his daughter Mary and said: 'God bless thee, and make thee his servant': and kissing Elizabeth, he said: 'God bless thee. I pray you all stand strong and steadfast unto Christ and his word, and keep you from idolatry.' Then said his wife: 'God be with thee dear Rowland. I will with God's grace meet thee at Hadleigh.'

*This Sheriff was Master Chester.*

And so was he led forth to the Woolsack, and his wife followed him. As soon as they came to the Woolsack, he was put into a chamber, wherein he was kept with four yeomen of the guard, and the Sheriff's men. Doctor Taylor, as soon as he was come into the chamber, fell down on his knees and gave himself wholly to prayer. The Sheriff then seeing Doctor Taylor's wife there, would in no case grant her to speak any more with her husband, but gently desired her to go to his house and take it as her own, and promised her she should lack nothing, and sent two officers to conduct her thither. Notwithstanding, she desired to go to her mother's, whither the officers led her, and charged her mother to keep her there, till they came again.

*The Sheriff's gentleness showed to the woman.*

Thus remained Doctor Taylor in the Woolsack, kept by the Sheriff and his company, till eleven of the clock. At which time the Sheriff of Essex was ready to receive him: and so they set him on horseback within the Inn, the gates being shut.

*Doctor Taylor brought to the sign of the Woolsack.*

At the coming out of the gates, John Hull (before spoken of) stood at the rails with Thomas Doctor Taylor's son. When Doctor Taylor saw them, he called them, saying: 'Come hither my son Thomas.' And John Hull lifted the child up, and set him on the horse before his father. And Doctor Taylor put off his hat and said to the people that stood there looking on him: 'Good people, this is mine own son, begotten of my body in lawful matrimony: and God be blessed for lawful matrimony.' Then lift he his cries towards heaven, and prayed for his son, laid his hat upon the child's head, and blessed him, and so delivered the child to John Hull, whom he took by the hand: and said: 'Farewell John Hull, the faithfullest servant that ever man had.' And so they rode forth, the Sheriff of Essex with four yeomen of the guard, and the Sheriff's men leading him.

*Doctor Taylor taketh his leave of his son Thomas and John Hull.*

*A good testimony for all servants to make.*

When they were come almost at Brentwood, one Arthur Faysie, a man of Hadleigh, who before time had been Doctor Taylor's servant, met with them, and he, supposing him to have been at liberty, said: 'Master Doctor I am glad to see you again at liberty,' and came to him and took him by the hand. 'Soft, sir,' (quoth the Sheriff), 'he is a prisoner: what hast thou to do with him?' 'I cry you mercy,' (said Arthur), 'I knew not so much, and I thought it none offence to talk to a true man.' The Sheriff was very angry with this, and threatened to carry Arthur with him to prison: notwithstanding, he bade him get him quickly away and so they rode forth to Burntwood: where they caused to be made for Doctor Taylor a close hood, with two holes for his eyes to look out at and a slit for his mouth to breathe at. This they did, that no man should know him, nor he speak to any man. Which practice they used also with others. Their own consciences told them, that they led innocent lambs to the slaughter. Wherefore they feared, lest if the people should have heard them speak, or have seen them, they might have been much more strengthened by their godly exhortations, to stand steadfast in God's word, and to fly the superstitions and idolatries of the papacy.

*Arthur Faysie.*

*A close hood made for Doctor Taylor that no man should know him.*

*Christ's adversaries work all by darkness.*

All the way Doctor Taylor was joyful and merry, as one that accounted himself going to a most pleasant banquet or bridal. He spake many notable things to the Sheriff and yeomen of the guard that conducted him, and often moved them to weep through his much earnest calling upon them to repent, and to amend their evil and wicked living. Oftentimes also he caused them to wonder and rejoice, to see him so constant and steadfast, void of all fear, joyful in heart, and glad to dye. Of these yeomen of the guard, three used Doctor Taylor friendly, but the fourth (whose name was Homes) used him very homely, unkindly, and churlishly.

*Doctor Taylor is joyful in his way.*

*Homes a notorious adversary to Doctor Taylor.*

At Chelmsford met them the Sheriff of Suffolk, there to receive him, and to carry him forth into Suffolk. And being at supper, the Sheriff of Essex very earnestly laboured him to return to the popish religion, thinking with fair words to persuade him, and said, 'Good Master Doctor, we are right sorry for you, considering what loss is of such one as ye might be if ye would: God hath given you great learning and wisdom, wherefore ye have been in great favour and reputation in times past with the Council and highest of this realm. Besides this, ye are a man of goodly personage, in your best strength, and by nature like to live many years, and without doubt, ye should in time to come be in as good reputation as ever ye were, or rather better. For ye are well beloved of all men, as well for your virtues as for your learning: and me think it were great pity you should cast away yourself willingly, and so come to such a painful and shameful death. Ye should do much better to revoke your opinions, and return to the Catholic Church of Rome, acknowledge the pope's holiness to be the supreme head of the universal church, and reconcile yourself to him. You may do well yet, if you will: doubt ye not but ye shall find favour at the queen's hands, I and all these your friends will be suitors for your pardon: which, no doubt, ye shall obtain. This counsel I give you, good Master Doctor, of a good heart, a good will toward you: and thereupon I drink to you.' In like manner said all the yeomen of the guard: 'Upon that condition, Master Doctor, we will all drink to you.'

*The Sheriff of Essex laboreth Doctor Taylor to return to papism.*

*The Sheriff's words to Doctor Taylor.*

When they had all drunk to him, and the cup was come to him, he stayed a little, as one studying what answer he might give.

At the last, thus he answered and said: 'Master Sheriff, and my masters all, I heartily thank you of your good will. I have hearkened to your words and marked well your counsels. And to be plain with you, I do perceive that I have been deceived myself, and am like to deceive a great many of Hadleigh, of their expectation.' With that word they all rejoiced. 'Yea good Master Doctor,' (quoth the Sheriff), 'God's blessing on your heart: hold you there still. It is the comfortablest word, that we heard you speak yet. What? Should ye cast away yourself in vain? Play a wise man's part, and I dare warrant it, ye shall find favour.' Thus they rejoiced very much at the word, and were very merry.

*Doctor Taylor maketh a jest of death, with a meet answer for such Doctors and Counsellors.*

At the last: 'Good Master Doctor,' (quoth the Sheriff), 'what meant ye by this, that ye said ye think ye have been deceived yourself, and think ye shall deceive many one in Hadleigh?' 'Would you know my meaning plainly?' quoth he. 'Yea,' (quoth the Sheriff), 'good Master Doctor, tell it us plainly.'

Then said Doctor Taylor, 'I will tell you how I have been deceived, and as I think, I shall deceive a great many. I am as you see, a man that hath a very great carcass, which I thought should have been buried in Hadleigh Churchyard if I had died in my bed, as I well hoped I should have done: but herein I see I was deceived: and there are a great number of worms in Hadleigh Churchyard, which should have had jolly feeding upon this carrion, which they have looked for many a day. But now I know we be deceived, both I and they: for this carcass must be burnt to ashes and so shall they lose their bait and feeding, that they looked to have had of it.'

*Apothegm of Doctor Taylor.*

When the Sheriff and his company heard him say so, they were amazed, and looked one on another, marvelling at the man's constant mind, that thus without all fear, made but a jest at the cruel torment, and death now at hand prepared for him. Thus was their expectation clean disappointed. And in this appeareth what was his meditation in his chiefest wealth and prosperity: namely, that he should shortly die and feed worms in his grave: which meditation if all our bishops, and spiritual men had used, they had not for a little worldly glory forsaken the word of God, and truth, which they in King Edward's days had preached and set forth, nor yet to maintain the Bishop of Rome's authority, have committed so many to the fire as they did.

*A good meditation.*

But let us return to Doctor Taylor, who at Chelmsford was delivered to the Sheriff of Suffolk, and by him conducted to Hadleigh, where he suffered. When they were come to Lanham, the Sheriff stayed there two days: and thither came to him a great number of gentlemen and justices upon great horses, which all were appointed to aid the Sheriff. These gentlemen laboured Doctor Taylor very sore, to reduce him to the Romish religion, promising him his pardon, which said they, 'we have here for you.' They promised him great promotions, yea a bishopric if he would take it: but all their labour and flattering words were in vain. For he had not built his house upon the sand in peril of falling at every puff of wind, but upon the sure and unmovable rock Christ.* Wherefore he abode constant and unmovable unto the end.

*Lanham is a town in Suffolk.*

After two days, the Sheriff and his company led Doctor Taylor towards Hadleigh, and coming within a two mile of Hadleigh, he desired to light off his horse to make water: which done, he leapt, and set a frisk or twain, as men commonly do in dancing. 'Why Master Doctor,' (quoth the Sheriff), 'how do you now?' He answered: 'Well God be praised, good Master Sheriff. Never better: for now I know I am almost at home. I lack not past two stiles to go over, and I am even at my father's house.* But Master Sheriff,' (said he), 'shall not we go through Hadleigh?' 'Yes,' said the Sheriff, 'you shall go through Hadleigh.' Then said he: 'O good Lord, I thank thee. I shall yet once ere I die see my flock, whom thou Lord knowest I have most heartily loved, and truly taught. Good Lord bless them and keep them steadfast in thy word and truth.'

*Doctor Taylor rejoiceth that he is nigh home.*

*Another apothegm of Doctor Taylor.*

*Doctor Taylor desirous to see his flock.*

When they were now come to Hadleigh, and came riding over the bridge, at the bridge-foot waited a poor man with five small children: who when he saw Doctor Taylor, he and his children fell down upon their knees, and held up their hands, and cried with a loud voice, and said: 'O dear father, and good shepherd, Doctor Taylor: God help and succour thee, as thou hast many a time succoured me, and my poor children.' Such witness had the servant of God of his virtuous and charitable alms given in his lifetime. For God would now the poor should testify of his good deeds, to his singular comfort, to the example of others, and confusion of his persecutors and tyrannous adversaries. For the

*A poor man with five children comforted Doctor Taylor.*

Sheriff and other that lead him to death, were wonderfully astonied at this: and the Sheriff sore rebuked the poor man for so crying. The streets of Hadleigh were beset on both sides the way with men and women of the town and country, who waited to see him: whom when they beheld so led to death, with weeping eyes and lamentable voices they cried, saying one to another: 'Ah good Lord, there goeth our good shepherd from us, that so faithfully hath taught us, so fatherly hath cared for us, and so godly hath governed us. O merciful God: what shall we poor scattered lambs do? What shall come of this most wicked world? Good Lord, strengthen him and comfort him': with such other most lam-

*The people lament Doctor Taylor.*

entable and piteous voices. Wherefore the people were sore rebuked by the sheriff and the catchpoles his men, that led him. And Doctor Taylor evermore said to the people: 'I have preached to you God's word and truth, and am come this day to seal it with my blood.'

*Doctor Taylor confesseth the truth, and confirmeth the same with his blood.*

Coming against the alms houses, which he well knew, he cast to the poor people money, which remained of that good people had given him in time of his imprisonment. As for his living, they took it from him at his first going to prison, so that he was sustained all the time of his imprisonment by the char-

*Doctor Taylor lived of alms and gave alms.*

itable alms of good people that visited him.

Therefore the money that now remained, he put in a glove ready for the same purpose, and (as is said) gave it to the poor almsmen standing at their doors to see him. And coming to the last of the alms houses, and not seeing the poor that there dwelt ready in their doors, as the other were, he asked: 'Is the blind man and blind woman, that dwelt here, alive?' It was answered, 'Yea: they are there within.' Then threw he glove and all in at the window, and so rode forth.

*Note this custom.*

Thus this good father and provider for the poor, now took his leave of those, for whom all his life he had a singular care and study. For this was his custom, once in a fortnight at the least, to call upon Sir Henry Doyle, and others the rich cloth makers, to go with him to the alms houses and there to see how the poor lived: what they lacked in meat, drink, clothing, bedding, or any other necessaries. The like did he also to other poor men that had many children, or were sick. Then would he exhort and comfort them, and where he found cause, rebuke the unruly, and what they lacked, that gave he after his power: and what he was not able, he caused the rich and wealthy men to minister unto them. Thus showed he himself in all things an example to his flock, worthy to be followed: and taught by his deed, what a great treasure alms is to all such, as cheerfully for Christ's sake do it.

At the last, coming to Aldham Common, the place assigned where he should suffer, and seeing a great multitude of people gathered thither, he asked what place is this, and what meaneth it that so much people are gathered hither? It was answered: 'It is Aldham Common, the place where you must suffer: and the people are come to look upon you.' Then said he: 'Thanked be God, I am even at home,' and so light from his horse, and with both his hands, rent the hood from his head.

*Aldham Common.*

*Doctor Taylor is come home.*

Now was his head notted evil-favouredly, and clipped much like as a man would clip a fool's head: which cost the good bishop Bonner had bestowed upon him when he disgraded him. But when the people saw his reverend and ancient face, with a long white beard, they burst out with weeping tears, and cried saying: 'God save thee good Doctor Taylor. Jesus Christ strengthen thee, and help thee. The holy ghost comfort thee': with such other like godly wishes. Then would he have spoken to the people: but the yeomen of the guard were so busy about him, that as soon as he opened his mouth, one or other thrust a tipstaff into his mouth, and would in no wise permit him to speak.

*Bishop Bonner's cost and liberality upon Doctor Taylor.*

*The people wisheth God to help him.*

Then desired he licence of the Sheriff to speak: but the Sheriff denied it to him, and bade him remember his promise to the Council.

'Well,' (quoth Doctor Taylor), 'promise must be kept.' What this promise was, it is unknown: but the common fame,* was that after he and others were condemned, the Council sent for them, and threatened them, they would cut their tongues out of their heads, except they would promise, that at their deaths they would keep silence, and not speak to the people: wherefore they desirous to have the use of their tongues, to call upon God as long as they might live, promised silence. For the papists feared much, lest this mutation of religion, from truth to lies, from Christ's ordinances to the popish traditions, should not so quietly have been received, as it was, especially this burning of the preachers: but they measuring others' minds by their own, feared lest the tumult

*Doctor Taylor could not be suffered to speak to the people.*

or uproar might have been stirred, the people having so just a cause not to be contented with their doings, or else (that they most feared) the people should more have been confirmed by their godly exhortations to stand steadfast against their vain popish doctrine, and idolatry. But thanks to God, which gave to his witnesses faith and patience, with stout and manly hearts to despise all torments: neither was their so much as any one man *The gospellers* that once showed any sign of disobedience toward the magistrates. *are not* They shed their blood gladly in the defence of the truth, so leav- *seditious, as* ing example unto all men of true and perfect obedience: which is *the papists* *commonly be.* to obey God more than men, and if need require it, to shed their own blood rather than to depart from God's truth.

Doctor Taylor perceiving that he could not be suffered to *Soyce pulleth* speak, sat down, and seeing one named Soyce, he called him and *off his boots.* said: 'Soyce, I pray thee come and pull off my boots and take them for thy labour. Thou hast long looked for them, now take them.' Then rose he up, and put off his clothes unto his shirt, and gave them away. Which done, he said with loud voice: 'Good people, I have taught you nothing but God's holy word, and *Doctor Taylor* those lessons that I have taken out of God's blessed book, the holy *confesseth the* Bible: and I come hither this day to seal it with my blood.' With *truth.* that word Homes, yeoman of the guard, aforesaid, who had used *Homes a cruel* Doctor Taylor very cruelly all the way, gave him a great stroke *tyrant.* upon the head with a waster,* and said: 'Is that the keeping of thy promise, thou heretic?' Then he seeing they would not permit *Doctor Taylor* him to speak, kneeled down and prayed, and a poor woman *prayeth.* that was among the people, stepped in and prayed with him: but her they thrust away, and threatened to tread her down with *A good woman* horses: notwithstanding she would not remove, but abode and *coming to pray* prayed with him. When he had prayed, he went to the stake and *with him could* *not be suffered.* kissed it, and set himself into a pitch barrel, which they had set for him to stand in, and so stood with his back upright against the stake, with his hands folded together, and his eyes toward heaven, and so he continually prayed.

Then they bound him with chains: and the Sheriff called *Richard* one Richard Doningham a butcher, and commanded him to set *Doningham.* up faggots: but he refused to do it, and said: 'I am lame Sir, and not able to lift a faggot.' The Sheriff threatened to send him to prison: notwithstanding he would not do it.

Then appointed he one Mulleine of Kersey, a man for his virtues fit to be a hangman, and Soyce a very drunkard, and Warwick, who in the commotion time in King Edward's days, lost one of his ears for his seditious talk, amongst whom was also one Robert King a deviser of interludes, who albeit was there present and had doing there with the gunpowder, what he meant and did therein (he himself saith he did it for the best, and for quick dispatch) the Lord knoweth which shall judge all, more of this I have not to say. *The tormentors. Warwick a cruel tormentor. This King was also one of them which went with his halberd to bring them to death which were burned at Bury.*

These four were appointed to set up the faggots and to make the fire, which they most diligently did: and this Warwick cruelly cast a faggot at him, which lit upon his head, and brake his face, that the blood ran down his visage. Then said Doctor Taylor: 'Oh friend, I have harm enough, what needed that?' *Doctor Taylor is patient.*

Furthermore, Sir John Shelton there standing as Doctor Taylor was speaking and saying the psalm *Miserere* in English, struck him on the lips: 'Ye knave,' said he, 'speak Latin,* I will make thee.' At the last they set to fire: and Doctor Taylor holding up both his hands, called upon God, and said: 'Merciful father of heaven, for Jesus Christ my Saviour's sake, receive my soul into thy hands.' So stood he still without either crying or moving, with his hands folded together, till Soyce with a halberd struck him on the head that the brains fell out, and the dead corpse fell down into the fire. *Sir John Shelton. Doctor Taylor's last words. Soyce striketh him down with an halberd.*

Thus rendered the man of God his blessed soul into the hands of his merciful father, and to his most dear and certain saviour Jesus Christ, whom he most entirely loved, faithfully and earnestly preached obediently followed in living, and constantly glorified in death.

They that were present and familiarly conversant with this Doctor Taylor, reported of him, that they never did see in him any fear of death, but especially and above all the rest which besides him suffered at the same time, always showed himself merry and cheerful in time of his imprisonment, as well before his condemnation as after: he kept one countenance and like behaviour. Whereunto he was the rather confirmed by the company and presence of Master John Bradford, who then was in prison and chamber with him. *An example of singular courage in Doctor Taylor.*

Merciful father for Iesus
sake, receiue my soule.

9. Doctor Taylor, burning at Hadleigh for the testimony of the Gospel

# 8. THOMAS TOMKINS

The history of Thomas Tomkins, having first his
hand burned, after was burned himself by
Bishop Bonner, for the constant testimony of
Christ's true profession.

[When six alleged heretics were] brought and examined before
Bishop Bonner, the eighth of February, . . . [all] received their
condemnation together the next day after, yet because the time
of their execution was then driven off from February till the
next month of March, I did therefore refer the story of them to
this present month of March aforesaid, wherein now remaineth
severally to entreat of the martyrdom of these six persons, as
the order and time of their sufferings severally do require. Of
the which six aforenamed martyrs, the first was Thomas
Tomkins burned in Smithfield, the sixteenth day of March,
anno 1555.

This Thomas Tomkins a weaver by his occupation, dwelling
in Shoreditch, and of the diocese of London, was of such conversation and disposition so godly, that if any woman had come
unto him with her web,* as sometime they did three or four in
a day, he would always begin with prayer. Or if any other had
come to talk of any matter, he would likewise first begin with
prayer. And if any had sought unto him to borrow money, he
would show him such money as he had in his purse, and bid
him take it.

And when they came to repay it again, so far off was he from
seeking any usury at their hand, or from straight exaction of his
due, that he would bid them keep it longer, while they were
better able. And these were the conditions of Thomas Tomkins,
testified yet to this present day by the most part of all his
neighbours, and almost of all his parish which knew him, as
Master Skinner, Master Leeke, and other more. Of whom
more than half a dozen at once came to me discreet and substantial men, reporting the same unto me, recording moreover
as followeth: that Doctor Bonner Bishop of London kept the

*The godly life
and disposition
of Thomas
Tomkins.*

said Tomkins with him in prison half a year. During which time the said bishop was so rigorous unto him, that he beat him bitterly about the face, whereby his face was swelled. Whereupon the bishop caused his beard to be shaven, and gave the barber twelve pence.

Touching which shaving of Thomas Tomkins's beard, this is more to be added: Bishop Bonner having Tomkins with him prisoner at Fulham, in the month of July, did set him with his *Tomkins* other work folks, to make hay. And seeing him to labour so *maketh the* well, the bishop sitting him down, said: 'Well, I like thee well, *bishop's hay.* for thou labourest well: I trust thou wilt be a good Catholic.' 'My lord,' said he, 'Saint Paul saith: "He that doth not labour, is not worthy to eat." '* Bonner said: 'Ah, Saint Paul is a great *And so should* man with thee.' And so after such other talk, the bishop infer- *he be with* ring moreover, wished his beard off, saying, that so he would *you, if ye were* look like a Catholic. 'My Lord,' said Tomkins, 'before my *a right bishop.* beard grew, I was, I trust a good Christian, and so I trust to be my beard being on.' But Bonner in fine sent for the barber, and caused his beard to be shaven off. The very cause was for that Bonner had plucked off a piece of his beard before.

The rage of this bishop was not so great against him, but the constancy of the party was much greater with patience to bear *The notable* it: who although he had not the learning as other have, yet he *constancy in a* was so endued with God's mighty spirit, and so constantly *true Christian* *soldier.* planted in the perfect knowledge of God's truth, that by no means he could be removed from the confession of truth, to impiety and error. Whereupon Bonner the Bishop being greatly vexed against the poor man, when he saw that by no persuasions he could prevail with him, devised another practice not so strange as cruel, further to try his constancy, to the intent, that seeing he could not otherwise convince him by doctrine of the scriptures, yet he might overthrow him by some forefeeling and terror of death. So having with him Master Harpsfield, Master Pendleton, Doctor Chedsey, Master Willerton, and other standing by, he called for Thomas Tomkins, who coming before the bishop, and standing as he was wont in defence of his faith, the bishop fell from beating to burning. Who, having there a taper or wax candle of three or four wicks standing upon the table, thought there to represent

10. The burning of Thomas Tomkins's hand by Bishop Bonner

unto us, as it were, the old image of King Porsenna. For as he
burned the hand of Scaevola, so this Catholic bishop took
Tomkins by the fingers, and held his hand directly over the
flame, supposing that by the smart and pain of the fire being
terrified, he would leave off the defence of his doctrine, which
he had received.

*Bishop Bonner playeth King Porsenna in burning the hand of Scaevola.*

Tomkins thinking no otherwise, but there presently to die,
began to commend himself unto the Lord, saying: 'O Lord
into thy hands I commend my spirit,' et cetera. In the time that
his hand was in burning, the said Tomkins afterward reported
to one James Hinse, that his spirit was so rapt up, that he felt
no pain. In the which burning he never shrunk, till the veins
shrunk, and the sinews burst, and the water did spurt into
Master Harpsfield's face: insomuch that the said Master Harpsfield moved with pity, desired the bishop to stay, saying, that he
had tried him enough. This burning was in the hall at Fulham.

*Tomkins compared to Scaevola. Bonner more cruel than Porsenna the Etruscan.*

And where the bishop thought by that means to drive him
from his opinions, it proved much otherwise: for this Christian
Scaevola, so valiantly did despise, abide, and endure that burning, that we have less cause hereafter to marvel at the manful-
ness of that Roman Scaevola: I would to God the other had as
well followed the example of that Etruscan tyrant. For he, after
the left hand of Scaevola was half burned, either satisfied with
his punishment, or overcome by his manhood, or driven away
by fear, sent him home safe unto his people: whereas Bonner
hitherto not contented with the burning of his hand, rested not
until he had consumed his whole body into ashes, at London
in Smithfield.*

But before we come to his suffering, we will first entreat of
some part of his examination and articles, with his answers and
confession thereunto annexed, as it is credibly in register
recorded.

## The first examination of Thomas Tomkins

This faithful and valiant soldier of God Thomas Tomkins,
after he had remained the space (as is said) of half a year in
prison, about the eighth day of February, was brought with
certain other before Bonner sitting in his consistory, to be
examined. To whom first was brought forth a certain bill or

*The first examination of Thomas Tomkins before Bonner, Bishop of London.*

schedule subscribed (as it appeared) with his own hand, the fifth day of the same month last before, containing these words following.

Thomas Tomkins of Shoreditch, and of the diocese of London, hath believed and doth believe, that in the sacrament of the altar, under the forms of bread and wine, there is not the very body and blood of our saviour Jesus Christ in substance, but only a token and remembrance thereof, the very body and blood of Christ only being in heaven and nowhere else.

*The confession of Tomkins subscribed with his own hand.*

By me Thomas Tomkins

Whereupon he was asked whether he did acknowledge the same subscription to be of his own hand. To the which he granted, confessing it so to be. This being done, the bishop went about to persuade him, (with words, rather than with reasons) to relinquish his opinions, and to return again to the unity of the catholic church, promising if he would so do, to remit all that was past: but he constantly denied so to do. When the bishop saw he could not so convince him, he brought forth and read to him another writing containing articles and inter-rogatories whereunto he should come the next day and answer: in the mean time he should deliberate unto himself what to do, and so the next day, being the ninth day of March, at eight of the clock in the morning, to be present in the same place again, to give his determinate answer what he would do in the prem-ises, and then either to revoke and reclaim himself, or else in the afternoon the same day to come again and have justice (as he called it) ministered unto him: the copy of which articles here followeth. . . .

*Tomkins constant in his faith.*

The bishop repeateth again the confession of Thomas Tomkins written before by the said Bishop of London, and subscribed by the said Tomkins, the twenty-sixth day [of] September, anno 1554, which is this.

I Thomas Tomkins of the parish of Shoreditch, in the diocese of London, having confessed and declared openly heretofore to Edmund Bishop of London mine ordinary, that my belief hath been many years past, and is at this present: that the body of our saviour Jesus Christ is not truly and in very deed in the sacrament of the altar, but only in heaven, and so in heaven, that it cannot now indeed be really and truly in the sacrament of the altar.

*The first confession of Tomkins offered to Bishop Bonner, and now here again repeated.*

And moreover, having likewise confessed and declared to my said ordinary openly many times, that although the church, called the Catholic church, hath allowed and doeth allow the Mass and sacrifice made and done therein, as a wholesome, profitable, and a godly thing: yet my belief hath been many years past, and is at this present, that the said Mass is full of *The Mass full* superstition, plain idolatry, and unprofitable for my soul, and *of superstition* so have I called it many times, and take it at this present.

*The Mass full of superstition and idolatry.*

Having also likewise confessed and declared to my said ordinary, that the sacrament of baptism ought to be only in the *Baptism ought* vulgar tongue, and not otherwise ministered, and also without *to be* any such ceremonies, as customably are used in the Latin *ministered in* church, and otherwise not to be allowed.*

*Baptism ought to be ministered in the vulgar tongue.*

Finally, being many times and often called openly before my said ordinary, and talked withal touching all my said confessions and declarations, both by the said mine ordinary and diverse other learned men, as well his chaplains as other, and counselled by all them to embrace the truth, and to recant mine error in the premises, which they told me was plain heresy and *Tomkins* manifest error: do testify and declare hereby, that I do and will *constantly* continually stand to my said confession, declaration, and belief, *standeth to the* in all the premises and every part thereof, and in no wise recant *truth of the* or go from any part of the same. In witness whereof I have *gospel.* subscribed, and passed this writing the twenty-sixth day of September the year aforesaid.

*Tomkins constantly standeth to the truth of the gospel.*

By me Thomas Tomkins aforesaid

The names of them that sat upon Thomas Tomkins at this session, were these, Edmund Bonner, John Feckenham Dean of Paul's, John Harpsfield Archdeacon of London, John Morwen Master of Art, Thomas Morton parson of Fulham, Tristram Swadell, Thomas More, Thomas Beckinsaw, James Cline, clerks.

## The last appearance of Thomas Tomkins before Bonner and the commissioners.

*The last appearance and condemnation of Thomas Tomkins, martyr.*

The same day and place, at two of the clock in the afternoon, he was (the last time) brought forth before the bishops of London, Bath, and Saint David's, with others: where he was earnestly exhorted by the said Bishop of Bath, to revoke and leave off his opinions. Unto whom he answered: 'My Lord, I was born and brought up in ignorance unto now of late years. And now I know the truth, wherein I will continue unto the death.'

Then Bonner caused all his articles and confession to be again openly read, and so in his accustomed manner persuaded with him to recant. To whom he finally said: 'My Lord, I cannot see but that you would have me to forsake the truth, and to fall into error and heresy.' The bishop seeing he would not recant, did proceed in his law, and so gave sentence of condemnation upon him.

Then he delivered him to the sheriff of London, who carried him straight unto Newgate, where he remained most joyous and constant, unto the sixteenth day of March next after: on which day, he was by the said sheriff conveyed into Smithfield, and there sealed up his faith in the flaming fire, to the glory of God's holy name, and confirmation of the weak.

*Sentence read against Thomas Tomkins. March 16.*

# 9. WILLIAM HUNTER

A notable history of William Hunter, a young man
of nineteen years, pursued to death by Justice Brown
for the gospel's sake, worthy of all young men and
parents to be read.

*William Hunter prentice and martyr. March 26.* [On] the twenty-sixth day of the said month of March [1555] . . . followed the martyrdom of William Hunter, a right godly young man of the age of nineteen years, and born of like godly parents: by whom he was not only instructed in true religion and godliness, but also confirmed by them unto death, after a rare and strange example, worthy to be noted and had in admiration of all parents. Wherein may appear a singular spectacle, not only of a marvellous fortitude in the party so young: but also in his parents, to behold nature in them striving with religion, and overcome of the same. Whereby Christian parents may learn what is to be done not only in their children, but also in themselves, if need at any time do require, or godliness should demand the duty of a Christian man against natural affection. Example whereof in the sequel of this history* we have here present before our eyes. Which history as it was faithfully drawn out by Robert Hunter his own brother (who being present with his brother William, and never left him till his death, sent the true report unto us) we have here with like faithfulness placed and recorded the same, as followeth.

*William Hunter prentice in Coleman Street with Thomas Taylor.*

*William Hunter threatened for not receiving at a Mass. William Hunter willed of his master to depart.* William Hunter being a prentice in London, in the first year of Queen Mary, was commanded at the Easter next following, to receive the communion at a Mass,* by the priest of the parish where he dwelt, called Coleman Street: which, because he refused to do, he was very much threatened that he should be therefore brought before the Bishop of London. Wherefore William Hunter's master, one Thomas Taylor, a silk weaver, required William Hunter, to go and depart from him, lest that he should come in danger, because of him, if he continued in his house. For the which causes, William Hunter took leave of his said master, and thence came to Brentwood where his father dwelt, with whom he remained afterward, about the space of half a quarter of a year.

After this it happened, within five or six weeks, that William going into the chapel of Brentwood, and finding there a Bible lying on a desk, did read therein. In the meantime there came in one Father Atwell a summoner, which hearing William read in the Bible, said to him, 'What meddlest thou with the Bible? Knowest thou what thou readest, and canst thou expound the scriptures?'

*William Hunter cometh to his father to Brentwood.*

*Father Atwell a summoner or promoter.*

To whom William answered and said: 'Father Atwell, I take not upon me to expound the scriptures, except I were dispensed withal, but I finding the Bible here when I came, read in it to my comfort.' To whom father Atwell said: 'It was never merry since the Bible came abroad in English.'*

To the which words William answered, saying: 'Father Atwell, say not so for God's sake, for it is God's book, out of the which every one that hath, grace may learn to know what things both please God, and also what displeaseth him.' Then said Father Atwell: 'Could we not tell before this time, as well as now, how God was served?' William answered: 'No, father Atwell, nothing so well, as we may now, if that we might have his blessed word amongst us still as we have had.' 'It is true,' said father Atwell, 'if it be as you say.'

*Talk between Atwell and William Hunter concerning the Bible.*

'Well,' said William Hunter, 'it liketh me very well, and I pray God that we may have the blessed Bible amongst us continually.' To the which words Father Atwell said, 'I perceive your mind well enough, you are one of them that misliketh the queen's laws, and therefore you came from London, I hear say. You learned these ways at London, but for all that,' said father Atwell, 'you must turn another leaf, or else you and a great sort more heretics will broil for this gear, I warrant you.' To the which words William said: 'God give me grace that I may believe his word, and confess his name, whatsoever come thereof.' 'Confess his name?' quoth old Atwell.

*The Catholics cannot abide the Bible.*

'No, no, ye will go to the devil all of you, and confess his name.'

'What?' said William. 'You say not well Father Atwell.' At the which words he went out of the chapel in a great fury, saying: 'I am not able to reason with thee, but I will fetch one straight way which shall talk with thee, I warrant thee thou

*Atwell not able to reason, but he is able to accuse the innocent.*

heretic.' And he, leaving William Hunter reading in the Bible, straight ways brought one Thomas Wood, who was then vicar of South Weald, which was at an alehouse even over against the said chapel: who hearing old Atwell say, that William Hunter was reading of the Bible in the chapel, came by and by to him, and finding him reading in the Bible, took the matter very heinously, saying: 'Sirrah, who gave thee leave to read in the Bible and to expound it?'

*The vicar of South Weald angry with William Hunter for reading in the Bible.*

Then William answered: 'I expound not the scriptures Sir, but read them for my comfort.' 'What meddlest thou with them at all?' said the vicar. 'It becometh not thee, nor none such to meddle with the scriptures.' But William answered: 'I will read the scriptures God willing, while I live, and you ought, Master Vicar, not to discourage any man for that matter, but rather exhort men diligently to read the scriptures for your discharge and their own.'

Unto the which the vicar answered: 'It becometh thee well to tell me what I have to do. I see thou art a heretic, by thy words.' William said, 'I am no heretic for speaking the truth.' But the vicar said, 'It is a merry world when such as thou art,

*The Catholics in no wise will be controlled.*

shall teach us what is the truth. Thou art meddling Father Atwell tells me with the sixth chapter of John, wherein thou mayst perceive, how Christ saith: "Except that ye eat the flesh of Christ and drink his blood, ye have no life in you." '* William said, 'I read the sixth chapter of John, indeed: howbeit, I made no exposition on it.'

Then said father Atwell, 'When you read it I said, that you there might understand how that in the sacrament of the altar is Christ's very natural body and blood: unto the which you answered, how that you would take the scriptures as they are, and that you would meddle with no great exposition, except that ye were dispensed withal.'

'Ah,' said the vicar. 'What say you to the blessed sacrament of the altar? Believest thou not in it, and that the bread

*William Hunter examined of the sacrament.*

and wine is transubstantiated into the very body and blood of Christ?' William answered, 'I learn no such thing in the sixth chapter of John, as you speak of.' 'Why,' said the vicar, 'doest thou not believe in the sacrament of the altar?'

'I believe,' said William Hunter, 'all that God's word teacheth.' 'Why,' said the vicar, 'thou mayest learn this which I say plainly in the sixth chapter of John.'

Then said William, 'You understand Christ's words much like the carnal Capernaites,* which thought that Christ would have given them his flesh to feed upon, which opinion our saviour Christ corrected, when he said, "The words which I speak to you, are spirit and life." '*

*The Catholics like to the Capernaites.*

'Now,' quoth the vicar, 'I have found you out: now I see that thou art a heretic indeed, and that thou doest not believe in the sacrament of the altar.'

Then said William Hunter, 'Whereas you doubt my belief, I would it were tried whether that you or I would stand faster in our faith.' 'Yea, thou heretic,' (said the vicar), 'wouldest thou have it so tried?' William Hunter answered, 'That which you call heresy, I serve my Lord God withal.'

*Heresy mistaken with the papists.*

Then said the vicar: 'Canst thou serve God with heresy?' But William answered, 'I would that you and I were even now fast tied to a stake, to prove whether that you or I would stand strongest to our faith.' But the vicar answered: 'It shall not so be tried.' 'No,' quoth William, 'I think so: for if I might, I think I know who would soonest recant, for I durst set my foot against yours even to the death.' 'That we shall see,' quoth the vicar, and so they departed, the vicar threatening William much, how that he would complain of him: with other much communication which they had together.

Immediately after, this vicar of Weald* told Master Brown of the communication which William Hunter and he had together. Which when Master Brown understood, immediately he sent for William's father and the constable, one Robert Salmon. For immediately after William Hunter and the vicar had reasoned together, he took his leave of his father and fled, because Wood the vicar threatened him. Now when the constable and William's father were come, and were before Master Brown, he asked where William Hunter was. His father answered, saying: 'If it please you Sir, I know not where he is become.' 'No?' quoth Master Brown. 'I will make thee tell where he is, and fetch him forth also ere I have done with thee.'

*The vicar complaineth to Justice Brown of William Hunter.*

*Justice Brown sendeth for Hunter's father.*

'Sir,' said William's father, 'I know not where he is become, nor where to seek for him.'

Then said Master Brown, 'Why didst thou not bring him when thou hadst him? I promise thee if thou wilt not fetch him, I will send thee to prison till I shall get him. Wherefore see that thou promise me to fetch him, or else it is not best to look me in the face any more, nor yet to rest in Brentwood. Well,' quoth Master Brown to William's father, 'see that thou seek him forth, and bring him to me.'

*The fruit of the pope's doctrine to set the father against the son.*

*An unreasonable request of Justice Brown.*

William's father answered: 'Sir, would you have me seek out my son to be burned?' 'If thou bring him to me,' quoth Master Brown, 'I will deal well enough for that matter: thou shalt not need to care for the matter. Fetch him, and thou shalt see what I will do for him.

'Moreover, if thou lackest money,' quoth he, 'thou shalt have some,' and bade the constable Master Salmon to give him a crown, but William's father took none of him. Howbeit Master Brown would never rest, till William's father had promised him to seek out his son. And thus Master Brown sent the constable home again, and William's father, commanding him to seek out William Hunter, and then to come again and bring him to him.

*The father pretended to seek the son.*

*The son meeteth with him in the way.*

After that old father Hunter had ridden a two or three days' journey to satisfy Master Brown's expectation, it happened that William met with his father in the highway as he travelled, and first he seeing his father, came to him, and spake to him, and told him how that he thought he sought for him: and then his father confessing it, wept sore and said, that Master Brown charged him to seek him, and bring him to him: 'Howbeit,' said he, 'I will return home again, and say I cannot find you.' But William said: 'Father, I will go home with you and save you harmless, whatsoever cometh of it.'

*The working of nature between the father and the son.*

And thus they came home together: but William as soon as he was come home, was taken by the said constable, and laid in the stocks till the day. Master Brown hearing that William Hunter was come home, sent for him to the constable, who brought him immediately to Master Brown.

*William Hunter brought before Justice Brown.*

Now when William was come, Master Brown said to him, 'Ah sirrah, are ye come?' And then by and by he commanded the Bible to be brought, and opened it, and then began to reason with William on this manner, saying: 'I hear say you are a scripture man, you: and can reason much of the sixth chapter of John, and expound as pleaseth you,' and turned the Bible to the sixth chapter of Saint John, and then he laid to his charge, what an exposition he made, when the vicar and he talked together. And William said, 'He urged me to say so much as I did.'

'Well,' quoth Master Brown, 'because you can expound that place so well, how say you to another place, turning to the twenty-second chapter of Saint Luke?' And Master Brown said, 'Look here,' (quoth he), 'for Christ saith, that the bread is his body.'*

*Talk between William Hunter and Justice Brown about the sacrament.*

To the which William answered, 'The text saying, how Christ took bread, but not that he changed it, into another substance, but gave that which he took, and brake that which he gave, which was bread, as is evident by the text. For else he should have had two bodies, which to affirm I see no reason,' said William.

*Bread broken but not changed.*

At the which answer Master Brown was very angry, and took up the Bible and turned the leaves, and then flung it down again in such a fury, that William could not well find the place again whereof they reasoned.

Then Master Brown said, 'Thou naughty boy, wilt thou not take things as they are, but expound them as thou wilt? Doth not Christ call the bread his body plainly, and thou wilt not believe that the bread is his body after the consecration?* Thou goest about to make Christ a liar.'

*Master Brown in a pelting chafe.*

But William Hunter answered: 'I mean not so sir, but rather more earnestly to search what the mind of Christ is in that holy institution, wherein he commendeth unto us the remembrance of his death, passion, resurrection and coming again, saying: "This do in the remembrance of me."* And also though Christ call the bread his body, as he doeth also say, that he is a vine, a door,* et cetera. Yet is not his body turned into bread, nor more than he is turned into a door, or vine. Wherefore Christ called the bread his body by a figure.'

*How Christ called bread his body.*

At that word Master Brown said, 'Thou art a villain indeed. Wilt thou make Christ a liar yet still?' And [he] was in such a

fury with William, and so raged, that William could not speak
a word, but he crossed him, and scoffed at every word.
Wherefore William seeing him in such fury, desired him that
he would either hear him quietly, and suffer him to answer for
himself, or else send him away. To the which Master Brown
answered: 'Indeed I will send thee tomorrow to my Lord of
London, and he shall have thee under examination,' and thus
left off the talk, and made a letter immediately, and sent William
Hunter with the constable to Bonner Bishop of London, who
received William.

After that he had read the letter, and the constable returned
home again, the bishop caused William to be brought into a
chamber, where he began to reason with him in this manner:
'I understand William Hunter,' (quoth he), 'by Master Brown's
letter, how that you have had certain communication with the
vicar of Weald, about the blessed sacrament of the altar, and
how that ye could not agree, whereupon Master Brown sent for
thee to bring thee to the Catholic faith, from the which he
saith, that thou art gone. Howbeit, if thou wilt be ruled by me,
thou shalt have no harm, for anything that thou hast said or
done in this matter.'

William answered, saying: 'I am not fallen from the Catholic
faith of Christ, I am sure, but do believe it, and confess it with
all my heart.'

'Why,' quoth the bishop, 'how sayest thou to the blessed
sacrament of the altar? Wilt thou not recant thy saying, which
thou confessedst before Master Brown, how that Christ's body
is not in the sacrament of the altar, the same that was born of
the Virgin Mary?'

To the which William answered, saying: 'My Lord I understand, that Master Brown hath certified you of the talk, which
he and I had together, and thereby ye know what I said to
him, the which I will not recant by God's help.' Then said
the bishop, 'I think thou art ashamed to bear a faggot and
recant openly, but if thou wilt recant thy sayings, I will promise thee, that thou shalt not be put to open shame: but speak
the word here now between me and thee, and I will promise
thee, it shall go no further, and thou shalt go home again
without any hurt.'

*Master Brown in a rage.*

*Master Brown sendeth up William Hunter to Bishop Bonner.*

*Bonner's words to William Hunter.*

*Talk between William Hunter and the bishop about the sacrament.*

*Bonner's fair promise to William Hunter.*

William answered and said, 'My Lord: if you will let me alone and leave me to my conscience, I will go to my father and dwell with him, or else with my master again, and so if nobody will disquiet nor trouble my conscience, I will keep my conscience to myself.'

Then said the bishop, 'I am content, so that thou wilt go to the church and receive and be shriven, and so continue a good Catholic Christian.' 'No,' quoth William, 'I will not do so for all the good in the world.'

*William Hunter not suffered to have his conscience free.*

'Then,' quoth the bishop, 'if you will not do so, I will make you sure enough, I warrant you.' 'Well,' quoth William, 'you can do no more than God will permit you.'* 'Well,' quoth the bishop, 'wilt thou not recant indeed by no means?' 'No,' quoth William, 'never while I live, God willing.'

*William Hunter denieth to recant.*

Then the bishop (this talk ended) commanded his men to put William in the stocks in his gatehouse, where he sat two days and nights, only with a crust of brown bread and a cup of water.

At the two days' end the bishop came to him, and finding the cup of water and the crust of bread still by him upon the stocks, said to his men: 'Take him out of the stocks, and let him break his fast with you.' Then they let him forth of the stocks, but would not suffer him to eat with them, but called him heretic. And he said he was as loath to be in their company, as they were, to be in his.

*Bonner commandeth William Hunter to the stocks. William Hunter two days and two nights in the stocks, with a crust of bread, and a cup of water.*

After breakfast the bishop sent for William, and demanded whether he would recant or no. But William made him answer, how that he would never recant that which he had confessed before men, as concerning his faith in Christ.

*Hunter again refuseth to recant his faith in Christ.*

Then the bishop said that he was no Christian, but denied the faith in which he was baptized. But William answered: 'I was baptized in the faith of the holy Trinity, the which I will not go from, God assisting me with his grace.'

Then the bishop sent him to the convict prison, and commanded the keeper to lay irons on him as many as he could bear, and moreover asked him, how old he was: and William said, that he was nineteen years old.

*William Hunter laid in the convict prison with as many irons as he could bear.*

'Well,' said the bishop, 'you will be burned ere you be twenty years old, if you will not yield yourself better than you

*Hunter allowed an halfpenny a day to live on.*

have done yet.' William answered, 'God strengthen me in his truth': and then he parted, the bishop allowing him a halfpenny a day to live on in bread, or drink.

Thus he continued in prison three quarters of a year. In the which time he had been before the bishop five times, besides the time when he was condemned in the consistory in Paul's, the ninth day of February: at the which time I his brother Robert Hunter was present, when and where I heard the bishop condemn him, and five other more.

*These five were Tomkins, Pigot, Knight, Haukes, and Laurence.*

And then the bishop calling William, asked him if he would not recant, and so read to him his examination and confession, as is above rehearsed, and then rehearsed how that William confessed that he did believe that he received Christ's body spiritually, when he did receive the communion. 'Dost thou mean,' quoth the bishop, 'that the bread is Christ's body spiritually?'

William answered: 'I mean not so, but rather when I receive the holy communion rightly and worthily, I do feed upon Christ spiritually through faith in my soul, and made partaker of all the benefits which Christ hath brought unto all faithful believers through his precious death, passion, and resurrection, and not that the bread is his body, either spiritually or corporally.'

*The bread is Christ's body neither spiritually nor bodily, but in receiving the communion we feed on Christ spiritually in our soul.*

Then said the bishop to William, 'Doest thou not think,' (holding up his cap), 'that for example here of my cap, thou mayest see the squareness and colour of it, and yet not to be the substance, which thou judgest by the accidences.'\*

William answered: 'If you can separate the accidences from the substance, and show me the substance without the accidences, I could believe.' Then said the bishop: 'Thou wilt not believe that God can do anything above man's capacity.' 'Yes,' said William, 'I must needs believe that: for daily experience teacheth all men that thing plainly: but our question is not what God can do, but what he will have us to learn in his holy supper.'

*The question is not what God can do, but what he would have us to believe in his holy supper.*

Then the bishop said, 'I always have found thee at this point, and I see no hope in thee to reclaim thee unto the Catholic faith, but thou wilt continue a corrupt member,' and then pronounced sentence upon him, how that he should go from that place to Newgate for a time, and so from thence to Brentwood, 'Where,' said he, 'thou shalt be burned.'

*A sentence pronounced against William Hunter.*

Then the bishop called for another, and so when he had condemned them all, he called for William Hunter, and persuaded with him, saying: 'If thou wilt yet recant, I will make thee a freeman in the City, and give thee forty pounds in good money to set up thine occupation withal: or I will make thee steward of my house and set thee in office, for I like thee well, thou hast wit enough, and I will prefer thee, if thou recant.'

But William answered, 'I thank you for your great offers: notwithstanding, my Lord,' said he, 'if you cannot persuade my conscience with scriptures, I cannot find in my heart to turn from God for the love of the world: for I count all things worldly, but loss and dung, in respect of the love of Christ.'*

*The large offers of Bishop Bonner to William Hunter.*

Then said the bishop, 'If thou diest in this mind, thou art condemned forever.' William answered: 'God judgeth righteously, and justifieth them whom man condemneth unjustly.'

*William Hunter refuseth to come from Christ for the love of the world.*

Thus William and the bishop departed, William and the rest to Newgate, where they remained about a month, which afterward were sent down, William to Brentwood, and the others into diverse places of the country. Now, when William was come down to Brentwood which was the Saturday before the Annunciation of the Virgin Mary that followed on the Monday after, William remained till the Tuesday after, because they would not put him to death, then for the holiness of the day.

*William Hunter sent down to Brentwood to be burnt.*

In the mean time William's father and mother came to him, and desired heartily of God that he might continue to the end in that good way which God had begon, and his mother said to him, that she was glad that ever she was so happy to bear such a child, which could find in his heart to lose his life for Christ's name's sake.

*His father and mother come to comfort him.*

Then William said to his mother: 'For my little pain which I shall suffer, which is but a short braid, Christ hath promised me mother,' said he, 'a crown of joy:* may you not be glad of that, mother?' With that, his mother kneeled down on her knees, saying: 'I pray God strengthen thee my son, to the end.

Yea, I think thee as well bestowed as any child that ever I

*His father and mother exhort him to be constant.*
bare.'

... William's father said: 'I was afraid of nothing, but that my son should have been killed in the prison for hunger and cold, the bishop was so hard to him.' But William confessed, after a month that his father was charged with his board, that he lacked nothing, but had meat and clothing enough, yea, even out of the court, both money, meat, clothes, wood and coals, and all things necessary.

*Mark here whether Bonner did nothing but by the law.*
Thus they continued in their inn, being the Swan in Brentwood, in a parlour, whither resorted many people of the country to see those good men which were there: and many of William's acquaintance came to him, and reasoned with him, and he with them, exhorting them to come away from the abomination of popish superstition and idolatry.

Thus passing away Saturday, Sunday, and Monday, on Monday at night it happened that William had a dream about

*A notable thing concerning William Hunter's dream.*
two of the clock in the morning, which was this: how that he was at the place where the stake was pitched, where he should be burned, which (as he thought in his dream) was at the town's end where the butts stood: which was so indeed. And also he dreamed that he met with his father as he went to the stake, and also that there was a priest at the stake, which went about to have him recant.

To whom he said (as he thought in his dream) how that he bade him, 'Away false prophet,' and how that he exhorted the people to beware of him, and such as he was: which things came to pass indeed. It happened that William made a noise to himself in his dream, which caused Master Higbed* and the others to awake him out of his sleep, to know what he lacked. When he awaked, he told them his dream in order,

*William Hunter led to the place of martyrdom.*
as is said.

Now when it was day, the sheriff Master Brocket called on to set forward to the burning of William Hunter. Then came the sheriff's son to William Hunter, and embraced him in

*The sheriff's son giveth comfortable words to William Hunter.*
his right arm, saying: 'William, be not afraid of these men which are here present with bows, bills, and weapons ready prepared to bring you to the place where you shall be burned.' To whom William answered: 'I thank God I am not afraid, for

I have cast my [ac]count what it will cost me already.' Then the sheriff's son could speak no more to him for weeping.

Then William Hunter plucked up his gown, and stepped over the parlour groundsel,* and went forward cheerfully, the sheriff's servant taking him by the arm, and I his brother by another, and thus going in the way, met with his father according to his dream, and he spake to his son, weeping and saying, 'God be with thee son William,' and William said, 'God be with you father, and be of a good comfort, for I hope we shall meet again when we shall be merry.' His father said, 'I hope so William,' and so departed. So William went to the place where the stake stood, even according to his dream, whereas all things were very unready. Then William took a wet broom faggot, and kneeled down thereon, and read the fifty-first Psalm, till he came to these words, 'the sacrifice of God is a contrite spirit, a contrite and a broken heart, O God, thou wilt not despise.'*

*William Hunter's dream verified.*

*His words to his father.*

Then said Master Tyrrell of the Beaches, called William Tyrrell, 'Thou liest,' (said he), 'thou readest false, for the words are "an humble spirit."'* But William said, 'The translation saith "a contrite heart."' 'Yea,' quoth Master Tyrrell, 'the translation is false, ye translate books as ye list yourselves, like heretics.' 'Well,' quoth William, 'there is no great difference in those words.' Then said the sheriff, 'Here is a letter from the queen. If thou wilt recant thou shalt live, if not thou shalt be burned.' 'No,' quoth William, 'I will not recant, God willing.' Then William rose and went to the stake, and stood upright to it. Then came one Richard Ponde, a bailiff, and made fast the chain about William. . . .

*Master William Tyrrell of the Beaches carpeth where he hath no cause.*

*William Hunter refuseth the queen's pardon.*

Then said Master Brown, 'Here is not wood enough to burn a leg of him.' Then said William: 'Good people pray for me: and make speed and dispatch quickly: and pray for me while ye see me alive, good people, and I pray for you likewise.'

'Now,' quoth Master Brown, 'pray for thee? I will pray no more for thee, than I will pray for a dog.' To whom William answered Master Brown: 'Now you have that which you sought for, and I pray God it be not laid to your charge in the last day: howbeit I forgive you.' Then said Master Brown, 'I ask no forgiveness of thee.' 'Well,' said William, 'if God forgive you no, I shall require my blood at your hands.'

*A dogged saying of Master Brown.*

Then said William, 'Son of God shine upon me,' and immediately the sun in the element* shone out of a dark cloud, so *An external* full in his face that he was constrained to look another way: *show of* whereat the people mused, because it was so dark a little time *Christ's favour* *upon William* afore. Then William took up a faggot of broom, and embraced *Hunter.* it in his arms.

Then this priest which William dreamed of, came to his brother Robert with a popish book to carry to William, that he might recant, which book his brother would not meddle *William's* withal.
*dream verified.*

Then William seeing the priest, and perceiving how he would have showed him the book, said: 'Away, thou false prophet. Beware of them good people, and come away from *Hunter's* their abominations, lest that you be partakers of their plagues.' *words to a* 'Then,' quoth the priest, 'look how thou burnest here, so shalt *popish priest.* thou burn in hell.' William answered, 'Thou liest, thou false prophet: away thou false prophet, away.'

Then was there a gentleman which said, 'I pray God have mercy upon his soul.' The people said: 'Amen, Amen.' Immediately fire was made.

Then William cast his Psalter right into his brother's hand, who said: 'William, think on the holy passion of Christ, and be *Hunter* not afraid of death.'
*comforted by* And William answered: 'I am not afraid.' Then lift[ed] he *his brother* up his hands to heaven, and said, 'Lord, Lord, Lord, receive *Robert.* my spirit,' and casting down his head again into the smothering smoke, he yielded up his life for the truth, sealing it with his blood, to the praise of God.

# 10. RAWLINS WHITE

The history of one Rawlins White, burned at
Cardiff in Wales, about the month of March, for the
testimony of Christ's gospel, reported by John Dane
being yet alive, who was almost continually with him
during his trouble, unto his death.

This Rawlins was by his calling or occupation a fisherman, living and continuing in the said trade by the space of twenty
years at the least, in the town of Cardiff, being (as a man of
his vocation might be) one of a very good name, and well
accompted among his neighbours. As touching his religion at
the first, it cannot otherwise be known but that he was a great
partaker of the superstition and idolatry that then was used,
I mean in the reign of King Henry the eighth. But after that
God of his mercy had raised up the light* of his gospel through
the blessed government of King Edward the sixth here in this
realm of England, this Rawlins began partly to mislike that
which before he had embraced, and to have some good opinion
of that which before by the iniquity of the time had been concealed from him: and the rather to bring this good purpose and
intent of his to pass, he began to be a diligent hearer, and a
great searcher out of the truth.

But because the good man was altogether unlearned, and
withal very simple, he knew no ready way how he might satisfy
his great desire: At length it came in his mind to take a special
remedy to supply his necessity, which was this: He had a little
boy which was his own son, which child he set to school to
learn to read English. Now after the little boy could read indifferently well, his father every night after supper, summer and
winter, would have the boy to read a piece of the holy scripture, and now and then of some other good book. In which
kind of virtuous exercise, the old man had such a delight and
pleasure, that as it seemed, he rather practised himself in the
study of scripture, than in the trade or science which before-
time he had used: so that Rawlins within few years in the said

*The desirous
mind of
Rawlins to
search for
truth.*

*The godly
intent of
Rawlins in
setting his son
to school.*

time of King Edward, through the help of his little son, as a
special minister appointed by God (no doubt) for that purpose,
and through much conscience besides, profited and went forward in such sort, that he was able not only to resolve himself
touching his own former blindness and ignorance, but was also
able to admonish and instruct other: and therefore when occasion served, he would go from one place to another, visiting
such as he had best hope in. By which his doing, he became in
that country both a notable and open professor of the truth,
being at all times and in all such places, not without the company of his little boy, whom (as I have said) he used as an
assistance to this his good purpose. And to this his great industry and endeavour in holy scripture, God did also add in him a
singular gift of memory, so that by the benefit thereof he would
and could do that in vouching* and rehearsing of the text,
which men of riper and more profound knowledge, by their
notes and other helps of memory, could very hardly accomplish. Insomuch that he upon the alleging of scripture, very
often would cite the book, the leaf, yea and the very sentence:*
such was the wonderful working of God in this simple and
unlearned father.

*The means whereby Rawlins first came to knowledge.*

*Rawlins by the means of his young son came to the knowledge of the scripture.*

*The gift of memory in Rawlins.*

Now when he had thus continued in his profession the space
of five years, King Edward died, upon whose decease Queen
Mary succeeded, and with her all kind of superstition and
papistry crept in. Which thing being once perceived, Rawlins
did not altogether use open instruction and admonition (as
before he was wont) and therefore oftentimes in some private
place or other, he would call his trusty friends together, and
with earnest prayer and great lamentation pass away the time,
so that by his virtuous instructions, being without any blemish of error, he converted a great number, which number
(no doubt) had greatly increased, had not the cruel storm of
persecution been.

The extremity and force whereof, at the last so pursued this
good father Rawlins, that he looked every hour to go to prison:
whereupon many of those which had received comfort by his
instructions, did resort unto him, and by all means possible
began to persuade him to shift for himself, and to dispose of his

goods by some reasonable order to the use of his wife and children, and by that means he should escape that danger which was imminent over his head.

But Rawlins nothing abashed for his own part, through the iniquity of the time, and at all nothing moved with these their fleshly persuasions, thanked them most heartily for their good will, and told them plainly, that he had learned one good lesson touching the confessing and denial of Christ, advertising them, that if he upon their persuasions should presume to deny his master Christ, Christ in the last day would deny and utterly condemn him: 'And therefore,' (quoth he), 'I will by his favourable grace confess and bear witness of him before men, that I may find him in everlasting life.'*

Notwithstanding which answer, his friends were very importunate with him. Howbeit, Father Rawlins continued still in his good purpose, so long till at the last he was taken by the officers of the town as a man suspected of heresy: upon which apprehension he was convented before the Bishop of Llandaff that then was, the said bishop lying then at his house besides Chepstow: by whom, after diverse combats and conflicts with him and his chaplains, this good Father Rawlins was committed to prison in Chepstow. But this his keeping, whether it were by the bishop's means, because he would rid his hands of him, or through the favour of his keeper, was not so severe and extreme, but that (if he had so listed) he might have escaped oftentimes.

But that notwithstanding, he continued still, insomuch, that at the last he by the aforenamed bishop was removed from Chepstow to the castle of Cardiff, where he continued by the space of one whole year. During which time, this reporter* resorted to him very often, with money and other relief from this reporter's mother (who was a great favourer of those that were in affliction in those days) and other of his friends: which he received not without great thanks and praises given to the name of God. And albeit that he was thus troubled and imprisoned, as ye have heard, to his own undoing in this world, and to the utter decay of his poor wife and children: yet was his heart so set to the instruction and furtherance of other[s] in the

*Rawlins exhorted to shift for himself.*

*Rawlins promiseth to be constant to the death.*

*Rawlins apprehended and convented before the Bishop of Llandaff named Anthony Kitchin.*

*Rawlins might escape and would not.*

*Rawlins a whole year in prison.*

*A godly woman stirred up to relieve Rawlins.*

way of salvation, that he was never in quiet,* but when he was persuading or exhorting such of his familiar friends as commonly came unto him. Insomuch that on the Sundays and

*Exhortation of
Rawlins to his
friends.*

other times of leisure, when his friends came to visit him, he would pass away the time in prayer and exhortations, admonishing them always to beware of false prophets which come in sheep's clothing.*

Now when he had continued in Cardiff Castle by the space of one whole year (as I have said) the time of his further trial was at hand. Whereupon, the aforenamed Bishop of Llandaff caused him to be brought again from the castle of Cardiff unto his own house besides Chepstow, and whilst he continued there, the bishop assayed many ways how to reduce him to some conformity. But when all means either by their threaten-

*Rawlins by no
means could be
reduced to
return to
popery.*

ing words or flattering promises, were to no purpose: the bishop willed him to advise and be at a full point with himself, either to recant his opinions, or else to abide the rigour of the law, and thereupon gave him a day of determination.

Which day being come, the bishop with his chaplains went into his chapel, not without a great number of other by-dwellers,* that came to behold the manner of their doings. When the bishop with his retinue were placed in order, poor Rawlins was

*Rawlins
brought before
the Bishop of
Llandaff in
open
judgement.*

brought before them. The bishop after great deliberation in addressing himself (as it seemed) and silence forewarned to the rest that were there present, used a long kind of talk to him, declaring the cause of his sending for, which was, for that he was a man well known to hold heretical opinions, and that through his instruction many were led into blind error. In the end he exhorted him to consider his own estate wherein he stood: 'For,' (said the bishop), 'Rawlins, you have been oftentimes since your first trouble, both here in my house, and elsewhere been travailed withal touching your opinions, and that

*The words of
the bishop to
Rawlins.*

notwithstanding ye seem altogether obstinate and wilful.

'Now hereupon we thought good to send for you, to see if there were any conformity in you: so that the matter is come to this point, that if you shall show yourself repentant for that which you have done, both against God and the prince's law, we are ready to use favour towards you: but if by no means we can persuade with you touching your reformation, we are minded at this time to minister the law unto you, and therefore advise yourself what you will do.'

When the bishop had made an end of his long tale, this good father Rawlins spake very boldly to him, and said: 'My Lord, I thank God I am a Christian man, and I hold no opinions contrary to the word of God, and if I do, I desire to be reformed out of the word of God, as a Christian man ought to be': many more words in like sort were between the bishop and Rawlins which this reporter doth not well remember. But in the end when Rawlins would in no wise recant his opinions, the bishop told him plainly, that he must proceed against him by the law, and condemn him as a heretic.

*Rawlins answereth to the bishop.*

'Proceed in your law, in God's name,' said Rawlins, 'but for a heretic you shall never condemn me while the world standeth.' 'But,' (said the bishop to his company), 'before we proceed any further with him, let us pray unto God that he would send some spark of grace upon him,' (meaning Rawlins), 'and it may so chance that God through our prayer will here turn and convert his heart.' When Rawlins heard the bishop say so, 'Ah, my Lord,' quoth he, 'now you deal well and like a godly bishop, and I thank you most heartily for your great charity and gentleness. Christ saith: "Whereas two or three be gathered in my name, I will be in the midst of them,"* and there be more than two or three of you. Now if it be so that your request be godly and lawful, and that that you pray as ye should pray, without doubt God will hear you. And therefore my Lord, go to, do you pray to your God, and I will pray to my God, I know that my God will both hear my prayer, and perform my desire.'*

*The Bishop of Llandaff proceedeth with prayer in condemnation of Rawlins, which commonly the popish persecutors are not wont to do.*

By and by the bishop with his company fell to prayer. And Rawlins turning himself to a pew that stood somewhat near him, fell down upon his knees, covering his face with his hands: and when they had prayed a while, the bishop with his company arose from prayer. And then also arose Rawlins, and came before the bishop.

*The bishop prayeth to his God, and Rawlins to his.*

Then said the bishop. 'Now Rawlins, how is it with thee? Wilt thou revoke thy opinions, or no?' 'Surely,' (said Rawlins), 'my Lord, Rawlins you left me, and Rawlins you find me, and by God's grace Rawlins I will continue. Certainly if your petitions had been just and lawful, God would have heard them: but you honour a false god and pray not as ye should pray, and therefore hath not God granted your desire: But I am one poor simple man as you see, and God hath heard my complaint, and I trust he will strengthen me in his own cause.'

. . . Whereupon the bishop caused the definitive sentence to be read. Which being ended, Rawlins was dismissed, and from thence was by the bishop's commandment carried again to Cardiff, there to be put into the prison of the town, called Cockmarel, a very dark loathsome, and most vile prison.

Rawlins in the mean while passed away the time in prayer, and chiefly in singing of Psalms: which kind of godly exercises he always used, both at Cardiff Castle and in all other places.

Now, after he had thus continued as prisoner in Cockmarel prison at Cardiff (as is aforesaid) a good space, about three weeks before the day wherein he suffered, the head officers of the town that had the charge of his execution, were determined to burn him. . . . Now, when he perceived his time no less near then it was reported unto him, he sent forthwith to his wife and willed her by the messenger that in any wise she should make ready, and send unto him his wedding garment, meaning a

shirt, which afterward he was burned in. Which request or rather commandment of his, his wife with great sorrow and grief of heart did perform, and early in the morning did send it him, which he received most gladly and joyfully.

Now when the hour of his execution was come, this good and constant father Rawlins was brought out of prison, having on his body the long shirt, which (as you heard before) he called his wedding garment, and an old russet coat which he was wont to wear. Besides this, he had upon his legs an old pair of leather buskins which he had used long afore. And thus being brought out of the prison (as I have said) he was accompanied or rather guarded with a great company of bills and

glaives: which sight when he beheld: 'Alas,' (quoth he), 'what meaneth all this? All this needed not. By God's grace I will not start away: but I with all my heart and mind give unto God most hearty thanks that he hath made me worthy to abide all this for his holy name's sake.'

So he came to a place in his way whereas his poor wife and children stood weeping and making great lamentation: the sudden sight of whom so pierced his heart, that the very tears trickled down his face. But he soon after, as though he had misliked this infirmity of his flesh, began to be as it were altogether angry with himself: insomuch that in striking his breast with his hand, he used these words: 'Ah, flesh, stayest thou me so? Wouldst thou fain prevail? Well, I tell thee do what thou canst, thou shalt not, by God's grace, have the victory.' By this time this poor innocent came to the very altar of his sacrifice (I mean the place appointed for his death) and there found a stake ready set up, with some wood toward the making of the fire. Which when he beheld, he set forward himself very boldly: but in going toward the stake he fell down upon his knees and kissed the ground, and in rising again, the earth a little sticking on his nose, he said these words: 'Earth unto earth, and dust unto dust, thou art my mother, and unto thee I shall return.' Then went he cheerfully and very joyfully, and set his back close unto the stake, and when he had stood there a while, he cast his eye upon this reporter, and called unto him, and said: 'I feel a great fighting between the flesh and the spirit, and the flesh would very fain have his swing,* and therefore, I pray you, when you see me anything tempted, hold your finger up to me, and I trust I shall remember myself.'

As he was thus standing with his back close unto the stake, a smith came with a great chain of iron: whom when he saw, he cast up his hand with a loud voice and gave God great thanks. Then the smith cast the chain about him, and as he was making it fast on the other side, Rawlins said unto him, 'I pray you good friend knock in the chain fast, for it may be that the flesh would strive mightily: but God of thy great mercy give me strength and patience to abide the extremity.'

Now when the smith had made him sure to the stake, the officers began to lay on more wood, with a little straw and reed: wherein the good old man was no less occupied than the best:* for as far as he could reach his hands, he would pluck the straw and reed, and lay it about him in places most convenient for his speedy dispatch. Which thing he did with such a cheerful

*Rawlins somewhat moved at the sight of his wife and children.*

*Rawlins wrestleth against his flesh.*

*The agony and fight of this Christian warrior.*

*Rawlins fastened to the stake.*

countenance and familiar gesture, that all men there present
were in a manner astonied.

*The
cheerfulness of
father Rawlins
at his death.*

Thus when all things were ready, so that there lacked nothing but the putting to of the fire, directly over against the stake
in the face of Rawlins, there was a standing erected, whereon

*A popish
sermon
preached at
Rawlins's
martyrdom.*

stepped up a priest addressing himself to speak to the people,
which were many in number, because it was market day. When
Rawlins perceived him, and considered the cause of his coming, he reached a little straw unto him, and made two little stays,
and set them under his elbows. Then went the priest forward
in his sermon, wherein he spake of many things touching the
authority of the Church of Rome. In the mean time Rawlins
gave such good ear and attention that he seemed nothing at all
moved or disquieted. At the last the priest came to the sacrament
of the altar, and there he began to inveigh against Rawlins's
opinions: in which his invection* he cited the common place of
scripture, and thereupon made a clerkly* interpretation.

Now when Rawlins perceived that he went about not only to
preach and teach the people false doctrine, but also to confirm
it by scripture, he suddenly started up and beckoned his hands
to the people, saying twice: 'Come hither good people, and
hear not a false prophet preaching': and then said unto the
preacher: 'Ah thou naughty hypocrite, doest thou presume to
prove thy false doctrine by scripture? Look in the text what
followeth: did not Christ say: "Do this in the remembrance of

*Rawlins's
words to the
false prophet.*

me"?'* After which words the priest being rather amazed than
interrupted, forthwith held his peace.

Then some that stood by cried out, 'Put fire, set to fire':
which being set to, the straw and reed by and by cast up both
a great and sudden flame. In the which flame this good and
blessed man bathed his hands so long, until such time as the
sinews shrunk, and the fat dropped away, saving that once he
did, as it were, wipe his face with one of them. All this while,
which was somewhat long, he cried with a loud voice: 'O Lord
receive my soul: O Lord receive my spirit,' until he could not
open his mouth. At the last the extremity of the fire was so
vehement against his legs, that they were consumed almost
before the rest of his body was burned: which made the whole

body fall over the chain into the fire sooner than it would have done. During which time of his burning it cannot be said that he suffered or felt any great pain, considering that not without his perfect memory he abided both quietly and patiently, even unto the departing of his life. Thus died this godly and old man Rawlins for the testimony of God's truth, being now rewarded, no doubt, with the crown of everlasting life.

*The constant patience of Rawlins at his burning.*

It is recorded furthermore of the said good father Rawlins by this reporter, that as he was going to his death, and standing at the stake, he seemed in a manner to be altered in nature. For whereas before he was wont to go stooping, or rather crooked, through the infirmity of age, having a sad countenance and a very feeble complexion, and withal very soft in speech and gesture.

*A sudden alteration of nature marvellous in Rawlins before his death.*

Now he went and stretched up himself, not only bolt upright, but also bore withal a most pleasant and comfortable countenance, not without great courage and audacity both in speech and behaviour. He had (of which thing I should have spoken before) about his head a kerchief. The hairs of his head (somewhat appearing beneath his kerchief) and also of his beard were more inclined to white than to grey: which gave such a show and countenance to his whole person, that he seemed to be altogether angelical.

It is also said by this reporter, that a little before the fire flashed up to his body (as ye have heard) many of his friends came to him, and took him by the hand, amongst whom, the reporter of this story held him so long by the hand, till the flame of the fire rose, and forced them to sunder. In the mean time the priest of whom I spake afore, cried out, and said, that it was not lawful for any man to take him by the hand, because he was a heretic, and condemned by the Church. The chief cause of his trouble, was his opinion touching the sacrament of the altar. He was at the time of his death, of the age of threescore years or thereabouts.

*The reporter of this story one Master Dane.*

# 11. GEORGE MARSH

A declaration of the life, examination, and burning of
George Marsh, who suffered most constant
martyrdom for the profession of the gospel of
Christ, at Winchester, the twenty-fourth day of
April, anno 1555.

*April 24.
George
Marsh,
martyr.* The said George Marsh was born in the parish of Dean, in the county of Lancaster, and was well brought up in learning and honest trade of living by his parents, who afterwards about the twenty-fifth year of his age, took to wife an honest maiden of the country, with whom he continued, earning their living *George Marsh
first a farmer.* upon a farm, having children between them lawfully begotten: and then God taking his wife out of this world, he being most desirous of godly studies, (leaving his household and children in good order) went unto the University of Cambridge, where he studied, and much increased in learning and godly virtues, and was a minister of God's holy word and sacraments, and for a while was curate to Lawrence Saunders, as he himself *George Marsh
made minister.* reporteth. In which condition of life, he continued for a space, earnestly setting forth God's true religion, to the defacing of Antichrist's false doctrine, by his godly readings and sermons, as well there and in the parish of Dean, or elsewhere in Lancashire.

Whereupon at length, by detection of certain adversaries he was apprehended, and kept in close prison by George Cotes then Bishop of Chester, in straight prison in Chester, within the precinct of the bishop's house, about the space of four months, being not permitted to have relief and comfort of *Doctor Cotes
Bishop of
Chester, a
persecutor.
George Marsh
detected.* his friends: but charge being given unto the porter, to mark who they were that asked for him, and to signify their names unto the bishop, as by the particular description of his story, testified and recorded with his own pen, more evidently may appear in the process hereunder following.

## The handling, entreating, and examination of George Marsh, being sent first by the Earl of Derby to Doctor Cotes Bishop of Chester

On the Monday before Palm Sunday, which was the twelfth day of March, it was told me at my mother's house that Roger Wrinstone, with other of Master Barton's servants did make diligent search for me in Bolton, and when they perceived that I was not there, they gave straight charge to Roger Ward and Robert Marsh, to find and bring me to Master Barton the day next following, with others, to be brought before the honourable Earl of Derby, to be examined in matters of religion, et cetera.

I knowing by this relation of diverse of my friends, was diversely affected, my mother, and other my friends advertising me to flee and to avoid the peril, which thing I had intended afore after a week then next ensuing, if this in the mean while had not chanced, seeing, that if I were taken, and would not recant in matters of religion (as they thought I would not, and as God strengthening and assisting me with his holy spirit I never will) it would not only have put them to great sorrow, heaviness, and losses, with costs and charges, to their shame and rebuke in this world, but also mine own self after troubles and painful imprisonment, unto shameful death.

This considered, they advised me and counselled me to depart and fly the country, as I had intended to have done, if this had not happened. To whose counsel my weak flesh would gladly have consented, but my spirit did not fully agree: thinking and saying thus to myself, that if I fled so away, it would be thought, reported, and said, that I did not only fly the country and my nearest and dearest friends: but much rather from Christ's holy word, according as these years past I had with my heart, or at least with mine outward living professed, and with my mouth and word taught, according to the small talent given me of the Lord. I being thus with their advice and counsel, and the cogitations and counsels of my own mind drawn, as it were diverse ways, went from my mother's house, saying, I would come again at evening.

In the mean time I ceased not by earnest prayer to ask and seek counsel of God (who is the giver of all good gifts) and of

*The examination of George Marsh, written with his own hand.*

*Master Barton Gentleman, and persecutor.*

*George Marsh advertised by his friends to fly.*

*George Marsh in a perplexity whether to fly or to tarry.*

*George Marsh consulteth with God.*

other my friends, whose godly judgements and knowledge I much trusted unto. After this, I met with one of my said friends on Dean Moor, about sun going down: and after we had consulted together of my business, not without hearty prayer kneeling on our knees, we departed, I not fully determining what to do, but taking my leave with my friend said I doubted not but God (according as our prayer and trust was) would give me such wisdom and counsel, as should be most to his honour and glory, the profit of my neighbours and brethren in the world, and obtaining of mine eternal salvation by Christ in heaven.

This done, I returned to my mother's house again, where had been diverse of Master Barton's servants seeking after me: who when they could not find me, straightly charged my brother and William Marsh to seek me that night, and to bring me to Smethehilles the next day: who being so charged were gone to *Marsh's* seek me in Adderton, or elsewhere I know not. Thus intending *brethren* afore to have been all night with my mother, but then consider- *charged to seek* ing that my tarrying there would disquiet her with her house- *him.* hold, I departed from thence, and went beyond Dean Church, and there tarried all night with an old friend of mine, taking ill rest, and consulting much with myself of my trouble.

So at my first awaking, one came to me from a faithful friend of mine with letters, which I never read, nor yet looked on, who said this: my friend's advice was that I should in no wise fly, but abide and boldly confess the faith of Jesus Christ. At whose words I was so confirmed and established in my conscience, that from thenceforth I consulted no more, whether was better to fly or to tarry, but was at a point with myself, that I would not fly, but go to Master Barton, who did seek for me, and there present myself, and patiently bear such cross, as it should please God to lay upon my shoulders. Whereupon my mind and conscience afore being much unquieted* and *The* troubled, was now merry and in quiet estate. *marvellous*

*providence of* So betimes in the morning I arose, and after I had said the *God in* English litany (as my custom was) with other prayers kneeling *resolving* on my knees by my friend's bedside, I prepared myself to go *George Marsh* toward Smethehilles: and as I was going thitherward, I went *not to fly, but* into the houses of Harry Widdows, of my mother-in-law, of *to tarry.* Rafe Yeton, and of the wife of Thomas Richardson, desiring them to pray for me, and have me commended to all my friends, and to comfort my mother, and be good to my little children, for (as I supposed) they should not see my face any more, before the last day: and so took my leave of them not without tears shed on both parties, and came to Smethehilles about nine of the clock, and presented myself afore Master Barton: who showed me a letter from the Earl of Derby, wherein he was commanded to send me with others to Latham.

*George Marsh took his leave of his friends.*

Whereupon he charged my brother and William Marsh, to bring and deliver me the next day, by ten of the clock before the said Earl or his council. I made earnest suit with other special friends, which I had there at the same time, to Master Barton, that he would take some one of them or them all bound by recognizance or otherwise for mine appearing before the said Earl or his said council, that my brother and William Marsh might be at home, because it was the chiefest time of seeding, and their ploughs could not go if they were not at home: but nothing could be obtained.

*George Marsh of his own voluntary mind offereth himself to his enemies.*

So we went to my mother's, and there I dined and shifted part of my clothes, and so praying, took my leave of my mother, the wife of Richard Marsh, and both their households, they and I both weeping, and so departed from them and went toward Latham, and were all night a mile and a half on this side [of] Latham. So the next day which was Wednesday, we arose, prayed, and came to Latham betimes, and tarried there till four of the clock at afternoon.

*George Marsh taketh his leave of his mother.*

Then was I called by Roger Mekinson, to come to my Lord and his council, and so I was brought into the chamber of presence, where was present Sir William Norris, Sir Pierce Alee, Master Sherburn the parson of Grappenhall, Master More, with others. Where when I had tarried a little while, my Lord turned him toward me, and asked what was my name. I answered, 'Marsh.'

*George Marsh brought before the Earl of Derby.*

Then he asked whether I was one of those that sowed evil seed and dissension amongst the people. Which thing I denied, desiring to know mine accusers, and what could be laid against me: but that I could not know.

*George Marsh examined before the Earl of Derby.*

Then said he, he would with his council examine me themselves, and asked me whether I was a priest. I said, 'No.' Then he asked me, what had been my living? I answered, 'I was a minister, served a cure, and taught a school.' Then said my Lord to his council, 'This is a wonderful thing. Afore he said he was no priest, and now he confesseth himself to be one.' I answered, 'By the laws now used in this realm (as far as I do know) I am none.'

Then they asked me who gave me orders, or whether I had taken any at all? I answered, 'I received orders of the Bishops of London and Lincoln.'*

Then said they one to another, 'Those be of these new heretics,' and asked me what acquaintance I had with them? I answered, 'I never saw them, but at the time when I received orders.'

They asked me how long I had been curate, and whether I had ministered with a good conscience? I answered [that] I had been curate but one year, and had ministered with a good conscience, I thanked God, and if the laws of the realm, would have suffered me, I would have ministered still: and if the laws at any time hereafter would suffer me to minister after that sort, I would minister again.

*This blasphemous mouth of the parson of Grappenhall.*

Whereat they murmured: and the parson of Grappenhall said: 'This last communion was the most devilish thing that ever was devised.' Then they asked me what my belief was.

I answered, [that] I believed in God the Father, the Son and the holy Ghost, according as the scriptures of the Old and New Testament do teach and according as the four symbols, or creeds,* that is to wit, the creed commonly called *Apostolorum*,* the creed of Nice Council, of Athanasius and of Austen,* and Ambrose do teach.

And after a few words, the parson of Grappenhall said: 'But what is thy belief in the sacrament of the altar?'

I answered, [that] I believed that whosoever, according to Christ's institution, did receive the holy sacrament of Christ's body and blood, did eat and drink Christ's body and blood with all the benefits of his death and resurrection to their eternal salvation. 'For Christ,' (said I), 'is ever present with his sacrament.'

*George Marsh's belief in the sacrament.*

Then asked they me, whether the bread and wine, by the virtue of the words pronounced of the priest, were changed into the flesh and blood of Christ, and that the sacrament, whether it were received or reserved, was the very body of Christ?

Whereunto I made answer, [that] I knew no further than I had showed already. 'For my knowledge is unperfect,' (said I), desiring them not to ask me, such hard and unprofitable questions, whereby to bring my body into danger of death, and to suck my blood. Whereat they were not a little offended, saying they were no bloodsuckers, and intended nothing to me but to make me a good Christian man.

So after many other questions, which I avoided as well as I could, remembering the saying of Paul: 'Foolish and unlearned questions avoid, knowing they do but engender strife':* my Lord commanded me to come to the board, and gave me pen and ink in my hand and commanded me to write mine answers to the questions of the sacrament above named: and I wrote as I had answered before. Whereat he being much offended, commanded me to write a more direct answer, saying, I should not choose but do it.

Then I took the pen and wrote, that further I knew not. Whereat he being sore grieved, after many threatenings, said I should be put to shameful death like a traitor, with such other like words, and sometimes giving me fair words, if I would turn and be conformable as other were, how glad he would be.

In conclusion, after much ado, he commanded me to ward in a cold windy stone house, where was little room where I lay two nights without any bed, saving a few great canvas tent cloths, and that done, I had a pair of sheets, but no woollen clothes, and so continued till Palm Sunday, occupying myself as well as I could in meditation, prayer, and study, for no man could be suffered to come to me but my keeper twice a day when he brought me meat and drink. . . .

[*After a sequence of additional examinations, Bishop Cotes condemned George Marsh to death as an unregenerate heretic.*]

So the bishop read out his sentence unto the end and straight after said unto him, 'Now will I no more pray for thee, than I will for a dog.' And Marsh answered, that notwithstanding, he would pray for his Lordship: and after this the bishop delivered him unto the sheriffs of the city. Then his late keeper bade him, 'Farewell good George,' with weeping tears, which caused the officers to carry him to a prison at the Northgate,

*George Marsh loath to answer to the question of transubstantiation.*

*George Marsh commanded by the Earl of Derby to write his answers.*

*The Earl of Derby commandeth George Marsh into prison.*

*George Marsh exhorted to recant but could not be turned. The bishop readeth out the sentence.*

*A dogged saying of the bishop.*

*George Marsh delivered to the sheriffs.*

where he was very straitly kept unto the time he went to his
death, during which time he had small comfort or relief of any
worldly creature.

For being in the dungeon or dark prison, none that would
him good, could speak with him, or at least durst enterprise*
*The strait* so to do for fear of accusation: and some of the citizens which
*keeping of* loved him in God for the gospel sake (whereof they were but a
*Marsh in* few) although they were never acquainted with him, would some-
*prison.* time in the evening at a hole upon the wall of the city (that went
*The brotherly* into the said dark prison) call to him, and ask him how he did.
*zeal of good* He would answer them most cheerfully, that he did well, and
*men in* thanked God most highly that he would vouchsafe of his mercy
*comforting* to appoint him to be a witness of his truth, and to suffer for
*George Marsh.* the same, wherein he did most rejoice, beseeching him that he
would give him grace not to faint under the cross, but patiently
bear the same to his glory and comfort of his church: with many
other like godly sayings at sundry times, as one that most
desired to be with Christ. Once or twice he had money cast him
in at the same hole, about ten pence at one time, and two shillings at another time: for which he gave God thanks, and used
the same to his necessity.

When the time and day appointed came that he should suffer:
*Amry and* the sheriffs of the city (whose names were Amry and Cooper)
*Cooper sheriffs* with their officers and a great number of poor simple barbers,
*of Chester.* with rusty bills and pole-axes, went to the Northgate, and there
took out the said George Marsh, who came with them most
*Marsh led to* humbly and meekly, with a lock upon his feet.* And as he came
*his martyrdom.* upon the way towards the place of execution, some folks proffered him money, and looked that he should have gone with a
little purse in his hand (as the manner of felons was, accustomed
in that city in times past, at their going to execution) to the end
to gather money to give unto a priest to say trentals or Masses
*The old use in* for them after their death, whereby they might (as they thought)
*Lancashire to* be saved: but Marsh said he would not as then be troubled with
*give money to* meddling with money, but willed some good man to take the
*buy trentals.* money, if the people were disposed to give any, and to give it unto
*George Marsh* the prisoners or poor people. So he went all the way unto his
*refuseth to* death, with his book* in his hand, looking upon the same, and
*receive money* many of the people said: 'This man goeth not unto his death as a
*going to his* thief, or as one that deserveth to die.'
*death.*

Now when he came to the place of execution without the city, near unto the Spittle-Boughton, one Vawdrey, being then deputy chamberlain of Chester, showed Marsh a writing under a great seal, saying, that it was a pardon for him if he would recant. Whereat Marsh answered, that he would gladly accept the same (and said further, that he loved the queen) but forasmuch as it tended to pluck him from God, he would not receive it upon that condition.

*George Marsh refuseth the queen's pardon.*

After that, he began to speak to the people showing the cause of his death, and would have exhorted them to stick unto Christ. Whereupon one of the sheriffs said: 'George Marsh, we must have no sermoning now.' To whom he said, 'Master, I cry you mercy': and so kneeling down made his prayers, and then put off his clothes unto his shirt, and then was he chained unto the post, having a number of faggots under him, and a

*George Marsh not suffered to speak to the people.*

11. The cruel burning of George Marsh, Martyr

thing made like a firkin, with pitch and tar in the same over his head: and by reason the fire was unskilfully made, and that the wind did drive the flame to and fro, he suffered great extremity in his death, which notwithstanding he abode very patiently.

Wherein this in him is to be noted, that when as he had been a long time tormented in the fire without moving having his flesh so broiled and puffed up that they which stood before him unneath could see the chain wherewith he was fastened, and therefore supposed no less but he had been dead, notwithstanding suddenly he spread abroad his arms, saying: 'Father of heaven have mercy upon me,' and so yielded his spirit into the hands of the Lord.

*The patience of George Marsh, the blessed martyr.* Upon this, many of the people said that he was a martyr, and died marvellous patiently and godly. Which thing caused the bishop shortly after to make a sermon in the cathedral church, and therein affirmed, that the said Marsh was an heretic, burnt like an heretic, and was a firebrand in hell.

# 12. THOMAS HAUKES

Here followeth the history and martyrdom of the
worthy servant of Christ, Thomas Haukes gentleman,
with his examinations and answers had with Bishop
Bonner, recorded and penned with his own hand.

Immediately after the story of Doctor Taylor ... mention before *The story of*
was made of six men brought and convented before Bishop *Master*
Bonner upon the eighth day of February [1555]. The names of *Haukes,*
which martyrs were Steven Knight, William Pigot, Thomas *martyr.*
Tomkins, John Laurence, William Hunter. In which number was
also Thomas Haukes, and condemned likewise with them the
ninth day of the foresaid month of February. But because his execution did not so shortly follow with theirs, but was prolonged to
this present tenth day of the month of June, wherewith we are
now in hand, it followeth therefore now consequently to enter
tractation thereof,* first beginning briefly with his godly conversation and institution of life, then showing of his troubles, also of his
examinations and conflicts with the bishop and other adversaries
according as the order of his story doth require.

As touching therefore his education and order of life, first he
was of the country of Essex, born of an honest stock, in calling
and profession a courtier, brought up daintily from his childhood,
and like a gentleman. Besides that, he was of such comeliness and *The life and*
stature, so well endued with excellent qualities, that he might *conversation of*
seem on every side a man (as it were) made for the purpose. But *Haukes.*
his gentle behaviour toward other, and especially his fervent
study and singular love unto true religion and godliness did sur-
mount all the rest. Wherein as God did singularly adorn him:
even so he being such a valiant martyr of God, may seem to
nobilitate* the whole company of other holy martyrs, and as a
bright star, to make the church of God and his truth, of themselves bright and clear, more gloriously to shine by his example. *The victory of*

For if the conquests of martyrs are the triumphs of Christ (as *martyrs, is the*
Saint Ambrose doth notably and truly write*) undoubtedly Christ *triumph of*
in few men hath either conquered more notably, or triumphed *Christ.*
*Ambrose.*

more gloriously, than in this young man: he stood so wisely in his cause, so godly in his life, and so constantly in his death.

But to the declaration of the matter: first this Haukes following the guise of the court, as he grew in years, entered service with the Lord of Oxford,* where he remained a good space, being there right well esteemed and loved of all the household, so long as Edward the sixth lived. But he dying, all things began to go backward, religion to decay, godliness not only to wax cold, but also to be in danger everywhere and chiefly in the houses of great men. Haukes misliking the state of things, and especially in such men's houses rather than he would change the profession of true godliness which he had tasted, thought to change the place: and so forsaking the nobleman's house, departed home to his own home, where more freely he might give himself to God, and use his own conscience.

*Thomas Haukes first in service with the Earl of Oxford.*

*Haukes compelled to leave the Earl of Oxford's house.*

But what place in this world shall a man find so secret for himself, whither that old wicked Serpent* cannot creep, whereby he may have some matter to overthrow the quietness of the godly? Now in the mean season (as it happened) Haukes keeping his house at home, had born unto him a young son, whose baptism was deferred to the third week, for that he would not suffer him to be baptized after the papistical manner, which thing the adversaries not able to suffer, laying hands upon him did bring him, to the Earl of Oxford, there to be reasoned with, as not sound in religion, in that he seemed to condemn the sacraments of the church.

*Haukes's child three weeks unchristened.*

*Haukes brought before the Earl.*

The Earl either intending not to trouble himself in such matters, or else seeing himself not able to weigh with him in such cases of religion, sent him up to London with a messenger and letters, and so willing to clear his own hands, put him in the hands of Bonner, Bishop of London. . . .

*Haukes sent up by the Earl to Bishop Bonner.*

[*After recurrent examinations by Edmund Bonner, William Chedsey, John Feckenham, or John Harpsfield, Haukes and his colleagues appeared before the consistory of the diocese of London.*]

## The public examination of Thomas Haukes

After all these private conferences, persuasions, and long debatings had with Thomas Haukes in the bishop's house, as hitherto have been declared, the bishop, seeing no hope to win him to his wicked ways, was fully set to proceed openly against him after the ordinary course of his popish law. Whereupon Thomas Haukes shortly after was cited with the rest of his other fellows, above specified, to wit, Thomas Tomkins, Stephen Knight, William Pygot, John Laurence, and William Hunter, to appear in the bishop's consistory, the eighth day of February, this present year, videlicet 1555. Upon which appearance was laid against him, in like order, as to the other, first the bill of his confession, written with Bonner's hand, to the which bill . . . the blessed servant of God denied to subscribe.

*Thomas Haukes cited to the bishop's consistory.*

After which bill of confession being read, and he constantly standing to the said confession, the bishop then assigned him with the other five the next day following, which was the ninth of February, to appear before him again, to give a resolute answer what they would stick unto. Which day being come, and these foresaid six prisoners being severally called before the bishop, at the coming of Thomas Haukes, the bishop willed him to remember what was said to him yesterday, and now while he had time and space, to advise with himself, what he would answer: for he stood upon life and death. 'Well,' quoth Master Haukes again, 'I will willingly receive whatsoever shall be put unto me.'

*Ex Registro. The first day's sessions against Thomas Haukes.*

*The second day's sessions against Thomas Haukes.*

Then were certain other interrogatories or articles commenced against him by the said bishop (in like manner as to the other) to the number of four: with another bill also, which Bonner brought out of his bosom containing private matters against the said Thomas Haukes, which the bishop called heresies and errors, but we may better call them Christian verities. To the which matter being read, the said Haukes answered openly again saying that it was true, and that he was glad it was so true, as it was: with more words to the like effect. And this was on the forenoon, the ninth day of February.

*The answer of Thomas Haukes.*

In the afternoon again the said Haukes appearing and hearing the foresaid bill of his confession, with the articles and interrogatories read unto him, with like constancy in answering again to the bishop: 'My Lord,' (said he), 'as you being my friend have caused these my sayings to be written: so do you cause them to be read: and yet I will never go from them.'

*The words of Thomas Haukes at his judgement.*

And then being exhorted by the bishop with many fair words, to return again to the bosom of the mother Church: 'No, my Lord,' (said he), 'that will I not: for if I had an hundredth bodies, I would suffer them all to be torn in pieces, rather than I will abjure or recant.'

*The invincible constancy of Thomas Haukes.*

And so continuing still in the same song, notwithstanding that the doctors and lawyers were ever calling upon him to come again to the unity of the church he ever kept them off with this answer, that he would never go from the belief he was in, so long as he lived. Whereupon Bonner, at last read the sentence of death upon him, and so was he condemned the same day with the residue of his fellows which was the ninth of February.

*Thomas Haukes condemned by Bishop Bonner.*

Nevertheless his execution was prolonged, and he remained in prison till the tenth day of June.

*The death of Haukes deferred.*

Then was he committed to the hands and charge of the Lord Rich,* who being assisted with power sufficient of the worshipful of the shire, had the foresaid Thomas Haukes down into Essex . . . to suffer martyrdom. . . .

*Thomas Haukes brought down to Essex by the Lord Rich.*

Thomas Haukes by the way used much exhortation to his friends, and whensoever opportunity served to talk with them, he would familiarly admonish them.

A little before his death certain there were of his familiar acquaintance and friends, who frequenting his company more familiarly, which seemed not a little to be confirmed both by the example of his constancy, and by his talk: yet notwithstanding the same again being feared with the sharpness of the punishment, which he was going to, privily desired that in the midst of the flame he would show them some token if he could, whereby they might be more certain whether the pain of such burning were so great, that a man might not therein keep his mind quiet and patient. Which thing he promised them to do, and so secretly between them it was agreed, that if the rage of the pain were tolerable and might be suffered, then he should lift up his hands above his head toward heaven before he gave up the ghost.

*Agreed between Thomas Haukes and his friends to give them a token in the fire, whether the pain of the burning were so grievous as it seemeth or no.*

Not long after, when the hour was come Thomas Haukes was led away to the place appointed for the slaughter, by the Lord Rich and his assistance, who, being now come unto the stake, there mildly and patiently addressed himself to the fire, having a strait chain cast about his middle, with no small

*Thomas Haukes carried to the place of execution.*

multitude of people on every side compassing him about. Unto whom after he had spoken many things, but especially unto the Lord Rich, reasoning with him of the innocent blood of saints, at length after his fervent prayers first made, and poured out unto God, the fire was set unto him.

*Thomas Haukes standing at the stake reasoneth with the Lord Rich.*

In the which when he continued long, and when his speech was taken away by violence of the flame, his skin also drawn together, and his fingers consumed with the fire, so that now all men thought certainly he had been gone, suddenly and contrary to all expectation, the blessed servant of God, being mindful of his promise afore made, reached up his hands burning on a light fire (which was marvellous to behold) over his head to the living God, and with great rejoicing, as seemed, struck or clapped them three times together. At the sight whereof there followed such applause and outcry of the people, and especially of them which understood the matter, that the like hath not commonly been heard: and so the blessed martyr of Christ, straightway sinking down into the fire, gave up his spirit, anno 1555, June 10. And thus have you plainly and expressly described unto you the whole story, as well of the life, as of the death of Thomas Haukes, a most constant and faithful witness of Christ's holy gospel.

*A token given in the fire that burning is not so intolerable a pain as it was thought.*

*The end and martyrdom of Thomas Haukes at Coxehall.*

O Lord receiue my spirite.

12. The martyrdom of Thomas Haukes, Coggeshall, Essex

# 13. JOHN BRADFORD AND JOHN LEAF

The history of the worthy martyr and servant of God, Master John Bradford, with his life and acts, and sundry conflicts, with his adversaries, and martyrdom at length most constantly suffered for the testimony of Christ and his truth.

As touching first the country and education of John Bradford, he was born at Manchester in Lancashire. His parents did bring him up in learning from his infancy, until he attained such knowledge in the Latin tongue, and skill in writing, that he was able to gain his own living in some honest condition. Then he became servant to Sir John Harington* knight, who in the great affairs of King Henry the eighth and King Edward the sixth which he had in hand when he was Treasurer of the King's camps and building, at diverse times in Boulogne, had such experience of Bradford's activity in writing, of expertness in the art of auditors, and also of his faithful trustiness, that not only in those affairs, but in many other of his private business he trusted Bradford, in such sort that above all other he used his faithful service.

Thus continued Bradford certain years in a right honest and good trade of life, after the course of this world, like to come forward (as they say) if his mind could so have liked, or had been given to the world as many other be. But the Lord which had elected him unto a better function, and preordained him to preach the gospel of Christ in that hour of grace which in his secret counsel he had appointed, called this his chosen child, to the understanding and partaking of the same gospel of life. In which call, he was so truly taught, that forthwith his effectual call was perceived by the fruits. For then Bradford did forsake his worldly affairs and forwardness in worldly wealth, and after the just accompt given to his master of all his doings, he departed from him, and with marvellous favour to further the kingdom of God by the ministry of his holy word, he gave

*July 1. The history of Master John Bradford, martyr.*

*Sir John Harington, knight.*

*The trusty service of John Bradford under Master Harington.*

*Bradford called to the gospel.*

*Bradford
giveth himself
to the study of
scripture.* himself wholly to the study of the holy scriptures. The which his purpose to accomplish the better, he departed from the Temple at London, where the temporal law is studied, and went to the University of Cambridge, to learn by God's law how to further the building of the Lord's Temple. In Cambridge his diligence in study, his profiting in knowledge and godly conversation so pleased all men, that within one whole year after that he had been there, the University did give him the degree of a Master of Art.

Immediately after the Master and Fellows of Pembroke Hall *Bradford
Master of Art
and Fellow in
Pembroke
Hall.* did give him a fellowship in their College with them: yea that man of God Martin Bucer* so liked him, that he had him not only most dear unto him, but also often times exhorted him to bestow his talent in preaching. Unto which Bradford answered *Master
Bucer's
saying.* always, that he was unable to serve in that office through want of learning. To the which Bucer was wont to reply, saying: 'If thou have not fine manchet bread, yet give the poor people barley bread, or whatsoever else the Lord hath committed unto thee.' And whiles Bradford was thus persuaded to enter into the ministry, Doctor Ridley that worthy Bishop of London and glorious martyr of Christ, according to the order that then was in the Church of England called him to take the degree of deacon. Which order because it was not without some such abuse *John Bradford
made deacon
by Bishop
Ridley without
any
superstitious
abuse therein.* as to the which Bradford would not consent, the bishop, yet perceiving that Bradford was willing to enter into the ministry, was content to order him deacon without any abuse, even as he desired. This being done, he obtained for him a licence to preach, and did give him a prebend in his cathedral church of *John Bradford
made
prebendary in
Paul's and
licensed to
preach.* Saint Paul's.

In this preaching office by the space of three years, how faithfully Bradford walked, how diligently he laboured, many parts of England can testify. Sharply he opened and reproved sin, sweetly he preached Christ crucified, pithily he impugned heresies and errors, earnestly he persuaded to godly life. After the death of blessed young King Edward the sixth, when *Bradford
unjustly
deprived of his
living and
preaching.* Queen Mary had gotten the crown, still continued Bradford diligent in preaching until he was unjustly deprived both of his office and liberty by the queen and her Council. To the doing whereof, because they had no just cause, they took occasion to

do this injury for such an act, as among Turks and infidels would have been with thankfulness rewarded, and with great favour accepted, as indeed it did no less deserve.

The fact was this. The thirteenth day of August, in the first year of the reign of Queen Mary, Master Bourn, then Bishop of Bath, made a seditious sermon at Paul's Cross in London . . . to set popery abroad, in such sort that it moved the people to no small indignation, being almost ready to pull him out of the pulpit. Neither could the reverence of the place, nor the presence of the Bishop Bonner, who then was his master, nor yet the commandment of the Mayor of London, whom the people ought to have obeyed, stay their rage: but the more they spake, the more the people were incensed. At length Bourn seeing the people in such a mood, and himself in such peril (whereof he was sufficiently warned by the hurling of a drawn dagger at him as he stood in the pulpit) and that he was put from ending his sermon, fearing lest against his will, he should there end his wretched life, desired Bradford who stood in the pulpit behind him, to come forth and to stand in his place and speak to the people. Good Bradford at his request was content, and there spake to the people of godly and quiet obedience. Whom as soon as the people saw to begin to speak unto them, so glad they were to hear him, that they cried with a great shout: 'Bradford, Bradford, God save thy life Bradford': well declaring not only what affection they bare unto him, but also what regard they gave to his words. For after that he had entered a little to preach unto them, and to exhort them to quiet and patience, eftsoons all the raging ceased, and they in the end quietly departed each man to his house. Yet in the mean season (for it was a long time before that so great a multitude could all depart), Bourn thought (and truly) himself not yet full sure of his life till he were safely housed, notwithstanding, that the Mayor and sheriffs of London were there at hand to help him. Wherefore he desired Bradford not to depart from him till he were in safety: which Bradford according to his promise performed. For while the Mayor and Sheriffs did lead Bourn to the schoolmaster's house, which is next to the pulpit, Bradford went at his back, shadowing him from the people with his gown, and so to set him safe.

*Bradford appeaseth the rage of the people, and guardeth the papistical preacher.*

*The reverent regard and affection of the people to Master Bradford.*

*Master Bradford procureth Master Bourn's safety.*

Let the reader now consider the peril of Bourn, the charity of Bradford, and the headiness of the multitude, and also the grudging minds of certain, which yet still there remained behind, grieved not a little their minds, to see that so good a man should save the life of such a popish priest, so impudently and openly railing against King Edward. Among whom, one gentleman said these words: 'Ah, Bradford, Bradford, thou savest him that will help to burn thee. I give thee his life: if it were not for thee, I would (I assure thee) run him through with my sword.' Thus Bourn for that time, through Bradford's means escaped bodily death: but God hath his judgement to be showed in the time appointed.

The same Sunday in the afternoon Bradford preached at the Bow church in Cheapside, and reproved the people sharply for their seditious misdemeanour. After this he did abide still in London with an innocent conscience, to try what should become of his just doing.*

*Bradford rebuketh the people for the tumult at Paul's Cross.*

Within three days after he was sent for to the Tower of London, where the queen then was, to appear there before the Council. There was he charged with this act of saving of Bourn, which act they there called seditious, and also objected against him for preaching, and so by them he was committed first to the Tower, then unto other prisons, out of the which neither his innocency, godliness, nor charitable dealing could purchase him liberty of body, till by death (which he suffered for Christ's cause) he obtained the heavenly liberty, of which neither pope nor papist shall ever deprive him. From the Tower he came to the King's Bench in Southwark: and after his condemnation, he was sent to the Counter in the Poultry in London: in the which two places for the time he did remain prisoner, he preached twice a day continually, unless sickness hindered him: where also the sacrament was often ministered, and through his means (the keepers so well did bear with him) such resort of good folks was daily to his lecture, and to the ministration of the sacrament, that commonly his chamber was well nigh filled therewith. Preaching, reading and praying was all his whole life. He did not eat above one meal a day: which was but very little when he took it: and his continual study was upon his knees. In the midst of dinner he used often to muse

*Bradford charged with sedition, for saving the preacher.*

*Bradford committed to the Tower most unjustly.*

*Bradford in the King's Bench.*

*Bradford in the Counter.*

*Bradford preacheth and ministereth the sacrament in prison.*

with himself, having his hat over his eyes, from whence came commonly plenty of tears dropping on his trencher. Very gentle he was to man and child, and in so good credit with his keeper, that at his desire, in an evening (being prisoner in the King's Bench in Southwark) he had licence upon his promise to return again that night, to go into London without any keeper, to visit one that was sick, lying by the Steelyard. Neither did he fail his promise, but returned unto his prison again, rather preventing his hour,* than breaking his fidelity: so constant was he in word and deed.

*Bradford came into London without his keeper, and returned that night to prison again.*

Of personage he was somewhat tall and slender, spare of body, of a faint sanguine colour, with an auburn beard. He slept not commonly above four hours in the night: and in his bed till sleep came, his book went not out of his hand. His chief recreation was in no gaming or other pastime, but only in honest company, and comely talk, wherein he would spend a little time after dinner at the board, and so to prayer and his book again. He counted that hour not well spent, wherein he did not some good, either with his pen, study, or in exhorting of others, et cetera. He was no niggard of his purse, but would liberally participate that he had to his fellow prisoners. And commonly once a week, he visited the thieves, pick-purses, and such others that were with him in the prison where he lay, on the other side: unto whom he would give godly exhortation to learn the amendment of their lives by their troubles, and after that so done, distribute among them some portion of money to their comfort.

*The description of Bradford.*

*Bradford content with a little sleep.*

*Bradford's recreation.*

*The holy life of Bradford.*

*Bradford visited the thieves, pick-purses, et cetera.*

By the way this I thought not to conceal. While he was in the King's Bench, and Master Saunders in the Marshalsea, both prisoners, on the backside* of those two prisons they met many times, and conferred together when they would: so mercifully did the Lord work for them, even in the midst of their troubles: and the said Bradford was so trusted with his keeper, and had such liberty in the backside, that there was no day but that he might have easily escaped away, if he would, but that the Lord had another work to do for him. In the summertime, while he was in the said King's Bench, he had liberty of his keeper, to ride into Oxfordshire, to a merchant's house of his acquaintance, and horse and all things prepared for him

*The meeting and conference between Lawrence Saunders and John Bradford.*

*Bradford refusing to escape out of prison, though he might.*

for that journey, and the party in a readiness that should ride with him: but God prevented him by sickness that he went not at all.

One of his old friends and acquaintance came unto him *Bradford* whilst he was prisoner, and asked him, if he sued to get him *would not fly* out, what then he would do, or whither he would go? Unto *out of England* whom he made answer, as not caring whether he went out or *though he* no: but if he did, he said he would marry, and abide still *might.* in England secretly, teaching the people as the time would suffer him, and occupy himself that way. He was had in so great reverence and admiration with all good men, that a multitude which never knew him but by fame, greatly lamented *Bradford* his death: yea, and a number also of the papists themselves *believed.* wished heartily his life. There were few days in which he was *Bradford's* thought not to spend some tears before he went to bed, neither *tears.* was there ever any prisoner with him but by his company he greatly profited, as all they will yet witness, and have confessed of him no less, to the glory of God, whose society he frequented, as among many, one special thing I thought to note, which is this.

Bishop Farrar being in the King's Bench prisoner . . . was travailed withal of the papists in the end of Lent, to receive the sacrament at Easter in one kind,* who after much persuading, yielded to them, and promised so to do. Then (so it happened by God's providence) the Easter even, the day before he should have done it, was Bradford brought to the King's Bench prisoner, where the Lord making him his instrument, Bradford only was the mean that the said Bishop Farrar revoked his promise and word, and would never after *Bishop Farrar* yield to be spotted with that papistical pitch: so effectually the *confirmed in* Lord wrought by this worthy servant of his. Such an instru- *the truth, by* ment was he in God's church, that few or none there were that *John* knew him, but esteemed him as a precious jewel and God's *Bradford.* true messenger.

The night before he was had to Newgate, which was the Saturday night, he was sore troubled diverse times in his sleep by dreams, how the chain for his burning was brought to the Counter gate, and how the next day being Sunday, he should be had to Newgate, and on the Monday after burned in

Smithfield, as indeed it came to pass accordingly, which here-after shall be showed. Now he being vexed so often times in this sort with these dreams, about three of the clock in the morning, he waked him that lay with him, and told him his unquiet sleep, and what he was troubled withal. Then after a little talk, Master Bradford rose out of the bed, and gave himself to his old exercise of reading and prayer, as always he had used before: and at dinner according to his accustomed manner, he did eat his meat, and was very merry, nobody being with him from morning till night, but he that lay with him, with whom he had many times on that day communication of death, of the kingdom of heaven, and of the ripeness of sin in that time.

*Bradford dreameth of his burning according as it came to pass.*

In the afternoon they two walking together in the keeper's chamber, suddenly the keeper's wife came up, as one half amazed, and seeming much troubled, being almost windless said: 'Oh Master Bradford, I come to bring you heavy news.' 'What is that?' said he. 'Marry,' quoth she, 'tomorrow you must be burned, and your chain is now a-buying,* and soon you must go to Newgate.' With that Master Bradford put off his cap, and lifting up his eyes to heaven, said: 'I thank God for it: I have looked for the same a long time, and therefore it cometh not now to me suddenly, but as a thing waited for every day and hour, the Lord make me worthy thereof': and so thanking her for her gentleness, departed up into his chamber, and called his friend with him, who when he came thither, he went secretly himself, alone a long time and prayed. Which done, he came again to him that was in his chamber, and took him diverse writings and papers, and showed him his mind in those things what he would have done, and after they had spent the afternoon till night in many and sundry such things, at last came to him half a dozen of his friends more, with whom all the evening he spent the time in prayer and other good exercises, so wonderfully, that it was marvellous to hear and see his doings.

*Bradford hath word of his burning.*

A little before he went out of the Counter, he made a notable prayer of his farewell, with such plenty of tears, and abundant spirit of prayer, that it ravished the minds of the hearers. Also, when he shifted himself* with a clean shirt that was made for

*Bradford maketh his prayer taking his farewell at the Counter.*

his burning (by one Master Walter Marlar's wife, who was a good nurse* unto him, and his very good friend) he made such a prayer of the wedding garment,* that some of those that were present, were in such great admiration, that their eyes were as thoroughly occupied in looking on him, as their ears gave place to hear his prayer. At his departing out of the chamber, he made likewise a prayer, and gave money to every servant and officer of the house, with exhortation to them to fear and serve God, continually labouring to eschew all manner of evil. That done, he turned him to the wall and prayed vehemently, that his words might not be spoken in vain, but that the Lord would work the same in them effectually, for his Christ's sake. Then being beneath in the court, all the prisoners cried out to him and bid him farewell, as the rest of the house had done before with weeping tears.

*Bradford's going from the Counter.*

*The prisoners take their leave of Bradford with tears.*

The time they carried him to Newgate, was about eleven or twelve o' clock in the night, when it was thought none would be stirring abroad: and yet contrary to their expectation in that behalf, was there in Cheapside and other places (between the Counter and Newgate) a great multitude of people that came to see him, which most gently bade him farewell, praying for him with most lamentable and pitiful tears, and he again as gently bade them farewell, praying most heartily for them and their welfare. Now, whether it were a commandment from the queen and her Council, or from Bonner and his adherents, or whether it were merrily devised of the Lord Mayor, Aldermen, and Sheriffs of London, or no, I cannot tell: but a great noise there was overnight about the city by diverse, that Bradford should be burnt the next day in Smithfield, by four of the clock in the morning, before it should be greatly known to any. In which rumour many heads had diverse minds: some thinking the fear of the people to be the cause thereof. Other thought nay, that it was rather because the papists judged, his death would convert many to the truth, and give a great overthrow to their kingdom. So some thought one thing, and some another, that no just conjecture of the cause could be known that ever I heard yet. But this was certain, the people prevented the device suspected: for the next day, at the said hour of four o' clock in the morning, there was

*Bradford was carried to Newgate at midnight.*

*The people in Cheapside bade Bradford farewell.*

*A noise of Bradford's early burning.*

in Smithfield such a multitude of men and women, that many being in admiration thereof, thought it was not possible that they could have warning of his death, being so great a number in so short a time, unless it were by the singular providence of almighty God.

*A multitude in Smithfield by four o' clock.*

Well, this took not effect as the people thought: for that morning it was nine o' clock of the day, before Master Bradford was brought into Smithfield: which in going through Newgate thitherward, spied a friend of his whom he loved, standing on the one side the way to the keeper's houseward, unto whom he reached his hand over the people, and plucked him to him, and delivered to him from his head, his velvet nightcap, and also his handkerchief, with other things besides. Which after a little secret talk with him, and each of them parting from other, immediately came to him a brother-in-law of his, called Roger Beswick, which as soon as he had taken the said Bradford by the hand, one of the sheriffs of London called Woodruff, came with his staff and brake the said Roger's head, that the blood ran about his shoulders. Which sight Bradford beholding with grief, bade his brother farewell, willing to commend him to his mother, and the rest of his friends and to get him to some surgeon betimes: and so they departing, had little or no talk at all together. Then was he led forth to Smithfield with a great company of weaponed men, to conduct him thither, as the like was not seen at no man's burning: for in every corner of Smithfield there were some, besides those which stood about the stake. Bradford then being come to the place, fell flat to the ground, secretly making his prayers to almighty God. Then rising again and putting off his clothes unto his shirt, he went to the stake, and there suffered with a young man of twenty years of age, joyfully and constantly, whose name was John Leaf. . . .

*Bradford going to Smithfield.*

*Bradford gave his nightcap away.*

*Woodruff breaketh the head of Bradford's brother-in-law.*

[*An apprentice to a tallow chandler, this youth underwent examination for heresy by Bishop Edmund Bonner.*]

Then the bishop after many words to and fro, at last asked him, if he had been Master Rogers's scholar?* To whom the foresaid John Leaf answered again, granting him so to be: and that he the same John did believe in the doctrine of the said

*John Leaf Master Rogers's scholar.*

Rogers, and in the doctrine of Bishop Hooper, Cardmaker,* and other of their opinion, which of late were burned for the testimony of Christ, and that he would die in that doctrine that they died for: and after other replications again of the bishop, moving him to return to the unity of the church, he with a great courage of spirit answered again in these words: 'My Lord,' quoth he, 'you call mine opinion heresy: it is the true light of the word of God': and again repeating the same, he professed that he would never forsake his staid and well grounded opinion, while that breath should be in his body. Whereupon the bishop being too weak, either to refute his sentence, or to remove his constancy, proceeded consequently *Sentence read* to read the popish sentence of cruel condemnation, whereby *against John* this godly and constant young man being committed to the *Leaf.* secular power of the sheriffs there present, was then adjudged, and not long after suffered the same day with Master Bradford, confirming with his death that which he had spoken and professed in his life.

It is reported of the said John Leaf, by one that was in the Counter the same time, and saw the thing, that after his examinations before the bishop, when two bills were sent unto him in the Counter in Breadstreet, the one containing a recantation, the other his confessions, to know to which of them he would put to his hand, first hearing the bill of recantation read unto him (because he could not read nor write himself) that he *John Leaf* refused. And when the other was read unto him, which he well *sealed the bill* liked of, instead of a pen he took a pin, and so pricking his *of his* hand, sprinkled the blood upon the said bill, willing the reader *confessions* thereof, to show the bishop that he had sealed the same bill *with his blood.* with his blood already.

### The behaviour of Master John Bradford preacher, and the young man that suffered with him in Smithfield, named John Leaf, a prentice, which both suffered for the testimony of Christ.

First, when they came to the stake in Smithfield to be burned, Master Bradford lying prostrate on the one side of the stake, and the young man John Leaf on the other side, they lay flat on their faces, praying to themselves the space of a minute of an hour. Then one of the sheriffs said to Master Bradford: 'Arise and make an end, for the press of the people is great.'

*Bradford and John Leaf at the stake how they behaved themselves.*

At that word they both stood up upon their feet: and then Master Bradford took a faggot in his hand, and kissed it, and so likewise the stake. And when he had so done, he desired of the sheriffs that his servant might have his raiment. 'For,' (said he), 'I have nothing else to give him: and besides that, he is a poor man.' And the sheriff said, 'He should have it.' And so forthwith Master Bradford did put off his raiment, and went to the stake: and holding up his hands and casting his countenance to heaven, he said thus: 'O England, England, repent thee of thy sins, repent thee of thy sins. Beware of idolatry, beware of false Antichrists take heed they do not deceive you.' And as he was speaking these words, the sheriff bade tie his hands, if he would not be quiet. 'O Master Sheriff,' (said Master Bradford), 'I am quiet: God forgive you this, Master Sheriff.' And one of the officers which made the fire, hearing Master Bradford so speaking to the sheriff, said: 'If you have no better learning than that, you are but a fool, and were best to hold your peace.' To the which words Master Bradford gave no answer: but asked all the world forgiveness, and forgave all the world, and prayed the people to pray for him, and turned his head unto the young man that suffered with him, and said: 'Be of good comfort Brother, for we shall have a merry supper with the Lord this night': and so spake no more words that any man did hear, but embracing the reeds, said thus: 'Strait is the way, and narrow is the gate that leadeth to eternal salvation, and few there be that find it.'*

*The words of Master Bradford to England.*

*The saying of Master Bradford at his death.*

And thus they both ended their mortal lives, most likest two lambs, without any alteration of their countenance, being void of all fear, hoping to obtain the price of the game that they had long run at: to the which I beseech almighty God happily to conduct us, through the merits of Jesus Christ our Lord and saviour. Amen.

13. John Bradford and John Leaf

# 14. HUGH LATIMER AND NICHOLAS RIDLEY

The Behaviour of Doctor Ridley and Master Latimer, at the time of their death, which was the sixteenth of October. Anno 1555.

Upon the north side of the town, in the ditch over against Balliol College, the place of execution was appointed: and for fear of any tumult that might arise, to let the burning of them, the Lord Williams* was commanded by the queen's letters, and the householders of the city to be there assistant, sufficiently appointed, and when everything was in a readiness, the prisoners were brought forth by the mayor and bailiffs.

*The order and manner of Bishop Ridley and Master Latimer going to the stake.*

Master Ridley had a fair black gown furred, and faced with foins, such as he was wont to wear being bishop, and a tippet of velvet furred likewise about his neck, a velvet nightcap upon his head, and a corner cap upon the same, going in a pair of slippers to the stake, and going between the Mayor and an Alderman, et cetera.

After him came Master Latimer in a poor Bristol frieze frock all worn, with his buttoned cap, and a kerchief on his head, all ready to* the fire, a new long shroud hanging over his hose down to the feet, which at the first sight, stirred men's hearts to rue upon them, beholding on the one side, the honor they sometime had, on the other, the calamity whereunto they were fallen.

Master Doctor Ridley, as he passed toward Bocardo,* looking up where Master Cranmer did lie, hoping belike to have seen him at the glass window, and to have spoken unto him. But then Master Cranmer was busy with Friar Soto* and his fellows disputing together, so that he could not see him through that occasion. Then Master Ridley looking back, espied Master Latimer coming after. Unto whom he said: 'Oh be ye there?' 'Yea,' said Master Latimer, 'have after as fast as I can follow.' So he following a pretty way* off, at length they came both to the stake, one after the other, where first Doctor Ridley entering the place,

*Doctor Ridley and Master Latimer brought together to the stake.*

marvellous earnestly holding up both his hands, looked towards heaven: then shortly after espying Master Latimer, with a wonderous cheerful look, ran to him, embraced, and kissed him, and as they that stood near reported, comforted him, saying: 'Be of good heart brother, for God will either assuage the fury of the flame, or else strengthen us to abide it.'

*The behaviour of Doctor Ridley and Master Latimer at the stake.*

With that went he to the stake, kneeled down by it, kissed it, most effectuously prayed, and behind him Master Latimer kneeled, as earnestly calling upon God as he. After they arose, the one talked with the other a little while, till they which were appointed to see the execution removed themselves out of the sun. What they said, I can learn of* no man.

*Doctor Smith preaching at the burning of Bishop Ridley and Master Latimer.*

Then Doctor Smith,* of whose recantation in King Edward's time, ye heard before, began his sermon to them, upon this text of Saint Paul, in the thirteenth chapter of the first epistle to the Corinthians: . . . That is, if I yield my body to the fire to be burnt and have not charity, I shall gain nothing thereby.* Wherein he alleged, that the goodness of the cause, and not the order of death: maketh the holiness of the person:* which he confirmed by the examples of Judas, and of a woman in Oxford that of late hanged herself, for that they and such like as he recited, might then be adjudged righteous, which desperately sundered their lives from their bodies, as he feared that those men that stood before him would do. But he cried still to the people to beware of them, for they were heretics, and died out of the Church. And on the other side, he declared their diversities in opinions, as Lutherans, Oecolampadians,* Zwinglians, of which sect they were, (he said) and that was the worst: but the old Church of Christ, and the Catholic faith* believed far otherwise. At which place they lifted up both their hands and eyes to heaven, as it were calling God to witness of the truth. The which countenance they made in many other places of his sermon, whereas they thought he spake amiss. He ended with a very short exhortation to them to recant and come home again to the Church, and save their lives and souls, which else were condemned. His sermon was scant in all a quarter of an hour.

*Doctor Smith raileth against the martyrs.*

*Christ's congregation burdened with diversity of opinions.*

Doctor Ridley said to Master Latimer, 'Will you begin to answer the sermon, or shall I?' Master Latimer said, 'Begin you first, I pray you.' 'I will,' said Master Ridley.

Then the wicked sermon being ended, Doctor Ridley and Master Latimer kneeled down upon their knees towards my Lord Williams of Thame, the Vice Chancellor of Oxford,* and diverse other commissioners appointed for that purpose, which sat upon a form* thereby. Unto whom Master Ridley said: 'I beseech you my lord even for Christ's sake, that I may speak but two or three words,' and whilst my lord bent his head to the Mayor and Vice Chancellor, to know (as it appeared) whether he might give him leave to speak, the bailiffs and Doctor Marshall* Vice Chancellor ran hastily unto him, and with their hands stopped his mouth and said: 'Master Ridley, if you will revoke your erroneous opinions, and recant the same, you shall not only have liberty so to do, but also the benefit of a subject, that is, have your life.' 'Not otherwise?' said Master Ridley. 'No,' quoth Doctor Marshall. 'Therefore if you will not do so, then there is no remedy but you must suffer for your deserts.' 'Well,' quoth Master Ridley, 'so long as the breath is in my body, I will never deny my Lord Christ, and his known truth: God's will be done in me.' And with that he rose up, and said with a loud voice: 'Well, then I commit our cause to Almighty God, which shall indifferently judge all.'

To whose saying, Master Latimer added his old poesy.* 'Well, there is nothing hid but it shall be opened':* and he said he could answer Smith well enough if he might be suffered.* Incontinently they were commanded to make them* ready, which they with all meekness obeyed. Master Ridley took his gown and his tippet, and gave it to his brother-in-law Master Shipside, who all his time of imprisonment, although he might not be suffered to come to him, lay there at his own charges to provide him necessaries, which from time to time, he sent him by the sergeant that kept him. Some other of his apparel that was little worth, he gave away, other the bailiffs took.

He gave away besides, diverse other small things to gentlemen standing by, and diverse of them pitifully weeping, as to Sir Henry Lee,* he gave a new groat, and to diverse of my Lord Williams's gentlemen, some napkins, some nutmegs, and races* of ginger, his dial, and such other things as he had about him, to everyone that stood next him. Some plucked the points off his hose. Happy was he that might get any rag of him.

*Doctor Ridley ready to answer Doctor Smith's sermon, but could not be suffered.*

*Doctor Marshall Vice Chancellor of Oxford, stoppeth Doctor Ridley's mouth.*

*Bishop Ridley committeth his cause to God.*

*Master Latimer's words when he could not be suffered to answer Doctor Smith. This was no Popish tippet, but made only to keep his neck warm.*

*Doctor Ridley giveth away his apparel and other gifts to the people about him.*

Master Latimer gave nothing, but very quietly suffered his
*Master
Latimer
standing at the
stake in his
shirt.* keeper to pull off his hose, and his other array, which to look
unto was very simple: and being stripped into his shroud, he
seemed as comely a person to them that were there present, as
one should lightly* see: and whereas in his clothes, he appeared
a withered and crooked silly old man, he now stood bolt
upright, as comely a father as one might lightly behold.

Then Master Ridley standing as yet in his truss,* said to his
brother: 'It were best for me to go in my truss still.' 'No,' quoth
his brother, 'it will put you to more pain: and the truss will do
a poor man good.' Whereunto Master Ridley said: 'Be it, in the
name of God,' and so unlaced himself. Then being in his shirt,
he stood upon the foresaid stone, and held up his hands and
*Bishop Ridley
thanketh God
for his
martyrdom,
and prayeth
for England.* said: 'Oh heavenly Father, I give unto thee most hearty thanks,
for that thou hast called me to be a professor of thee, even unto
death. I beseech thee Lord God take mercy upon this realm of
England, and deliver the same from all her enemies.'

Then the smith took a chain of iron, and brought the same
about both Doctor Ridley's, and Master Latimer's middles:
and as he was knocking in a staple, Doctor Ridley took
the chain in his hand, and shaked the same, for it did gird in
his belly, and, looking aside to the smith, said: 'Good fellow
knock it in hard, for the flesh will have his course.' Then his
brother did bring him gunpowder in a bag,* and would have
*Gunpowder
given to the
martyrs.* tied the same about his neck. Master Ridley asked what it was.
His brother said, 'Gunpowder.' Then said he, 'I take it to be
sent of God, therefore I will receive it as sent of him.' 'And
have you any,' said he, 'for my brother?' meaning Master
Latimer. 'Yea sir, that I have,' quoth his brother. 'Then give it
unto him,' said he, 'betime, lest you come too late.' So his
brother went, and carried of the same gunpowder unto Master
Latimer. . . .

Then brought they a faggot kindled with fire, and laid the
same down at Doctor Ridley's feet. To whom Master Latimer
spake in this manner: 'Be of good comfort Master Ridley, and
play the man:* we shall this day light such a candle by God's
*The church
lightened by
the martyrdom
of saints.** grace in England, as (I trust) shall never be put out.'*

And so the fire being given unto them, when Doctor Ridley
saw the fire flaming up toward him, he cried with a wonderful

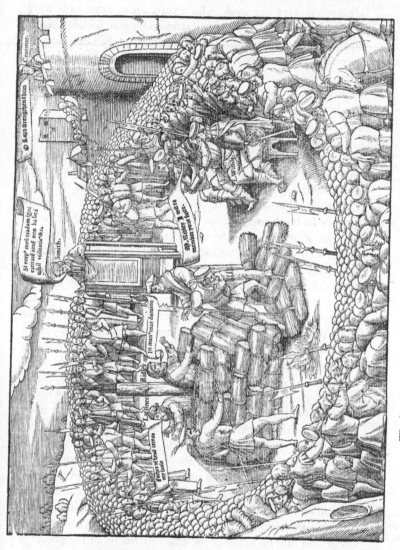

14. The burning of Latimer and Ridley at Oxford, Doctor Smith preaching

*Master Latimer's prayer and martyrdom.*

loud voice: . . . 'Lord, Lord, receive my spirit.'* Master Latimer crying as vehemently on the other side: 'Oh Father of Heaven, receive my soul,' who received the flame as it were embracing of it. After, as he had stroked his face with his hands and (as it were) bathed them a little in the fire, he soon died (as it appeared) with very little pain or none. And thus much concerning the end of this old and blessed servant of God, Master Latimer, for whole laborious travails, fruitful life, and constant death, the whole realm hath cause to give great thanks to almighty God.

*The order of Bishop Ridley's burning.*

But Master Ridley by reason of the evil* making of the fire unto him, because the wooden faggots were laid about the goss,* and over-high built, the fire burned first beneath, being kept down by the wood.* Which when he felt, he desired them for Christ's sake to let the fire come unto him. Which when his brother-in-law heard, but not well understood, intending to rid him out of his pain (for the which cause he gave attendance) as one in such sorrow, not well advised what he did, heaped faggots upon him, so that he clean covered him, which made the fire more vehement beneath, that it burned clean all his nether parts before it once touched the upper, and that made him leap up and down under the faggots, and often desire them to let the fire come unto him, saying, 'I cannot burn,' which indeed appeared well: for after his legs were consumed by reason of his stringling through the pain (whereof he had no release, but only his contentation in God) he showed that side toward us clean, shirt and all untouched with flame. Yet in all this torment he forgot not to call unto God still, having in his mouth, 'Lord have mercy upon me,' intermeddling this cry, 'Let the fire come unto me; I cannot burn.' In which pains he laboured, till one of the standers-by with his bill, pulled off the faggots above, and where he saw the fire flame up, he wrested himself unto that side. And when the flame touched the gunpowder, he was seen [to] stir no more, but burned on the other side, falling down at Master Latimer's feet. Which some said happened, by reason that the chain loosed: other said that he fell over the chain by reason of the poise* of his body, and the weakness of the nether limbs.

*Doctor Ridley long in burning.*

*The death and martyrdom of Doctor Ridley.*

Some say that before he was like to fall from the stake he desired them to hold him to it with their bills. Howsoever it was, surely it moved hundreds to tears, in beholding the horrible sight. For I think there was none that had not clean exiled all humanity and mercy, which would not have lamented to behold the fury of the fire so to rage upon their bodies. Signs there were of sorrow on every side. Some took it grievously to see their deaths, whose lives they held full dear. Some pitied their persons that thought their souls had no need thereof. His brother moved many men, seeing his miserable case: seeing (I say) him compelled to such infelicity, that he thought then to do him best service, when he hastened his end. Some cried out of the luck, to see his endeavour, who most dearly loved him, and sought his release, turn to his greater vexation, and increase of pain. But whoso considered their preferments in time past, the places of honour that they sometime occupied in this commonwealth, the favour they were in with their princes, and the opinion of learning they had, could not choose but sorrow with tears, to see so great dignity, honour, and estimation, so necessary members sometime accounted, so many godly virtues, the study of so many years, such excellent learning, to be put into the fire, and consumed in one moment. Well, dead they are, and the reward of this world they have already. What reward remaineth for them in Heaven, the day of the Lord's glory when he cometh with his Saints, shall shortly I trust declare.

*The lamenting hearts of the people, at the martyrdom of these two saints.*

# 15. STEPHEN GARDINER

## The death and end of Stephen Gardiner Bishop of Winchester.

Notwithstanding, here by the way touching the death of this foresaid bishop, I thought not to overpass a certain hearsay, which not long since came to me by information of a certain worthy and credible gentlewoman, and another gentleman of the same name and kindred: which Mistress Munday, being the wife of one Master Munday secretary sometime to the old Lord Thomas Duke of Norfolk, a present witness of this that is testified, thus openly reported in the house of a worshipful citizen, bearing yet office in this city, in words and effect as followeth. The same day, when as Bishop Ridley, and Master Latimer suffered at Oxford, being about the nineteenth day of October,* there came to the house of Stephen Gardiner, the old Duke of Norfolk with the foresaid Master Munday his secretary above named, reporter hereof. The old aged Duke, there waiting and tarrying for his dinner, the bishop being not yet disposed to dine, deferred the time to three or four of the clock at afternoon. At length, about four of the clock cometh his servant posting in all possible speed from Oxford, bringing intelligence to the bishop what he had heard and seen: of whom the said bishop diligently enquiring the truth of the matter, and hearing by his man, that fire, most certainly was set unto them, cometh out rejoicing to the Duke: 'Now,' saith he, 'let us go to dinner.' Whereupon, they being set down, meat immediately was brought, and the bishop began merrily to eat: but what followed? The bloody tyrant had not eaten a few bites, but the sudden stroke of God, his terrible hand fell upon him in such sort, as immediately he was taken from the table, and so brought to his bed, where he continued the space of fifteen days in such intolerable anguish and torments, that all that mean while, during those fifteen days, he could not avoid by order of urine, or otherwise, anything that he received: whereby, his body being miserably inflamed within (who had inflamed so many good martyrs before) was brought to a wretched end. And thereof no doubt, as most like* it is, came the thrusting out of his tongue from his mouth so swollen and black, with the inflammation of his body. A spectacle worthy to be noted and beholden of all such bloody burning persecutors.

# 16. JOHN PHILPOT

The process and history of Master John Philpot,
examined, condemned, and martyred for the
maintenance and defence of the gospel's cause,
against the Antichristian See of Rome.

*December 20.*
*The history of*
*Master John*
*Philpot,*
*martyr.*
Next followeth the constant martyrdom of Master John
Philpot. . . . He was of a worshipful house, a knight's son born
in Hampshire, brought up in the New College in Oxford,
where he studied the civil law, the space of six or seven years,

*John Philpot a*
*knight's son,*
*student of law*
*in New*
*College in*
*Oxford.*
besides the study of other liberal arts, especially of the tongues,
wherein very forwardly he profited, namely in the knowledge
of the Hebrew tongue, et cetera. In wit he was pregnant and
happy, of a singular courage, in spirit fervent, in religion zealous and also well practised and exercised in the same (which is
no small matter in a true divine) of nature and condition plain
and apert, far from all flattery, farther from all hypocrisy and
deceitful dissimulation. What his learning was, his own examinations penned of his own hand can declare.

*John Philpot*
*went over to*
*Italy.*

*John Philpot*
*in danger by*
*an Italian*
*friar.*

*The return of*
*John Philpot*
*into England.*
From Oxford desirous to see other countries as occasion
served thereunto, he went over into Italy, and places thereabouts, where he coming upon a time from Venice to Padua, was
in danger through a certain Franciscan friar, accompanying
him in his journey, who coming to Padua, sought to accuse him
of heresy. At length returning to England his country again, as
the time ministered more boldness to him in the days of King
Edward, he had diverse conflicts with Gardiner the bishop, in
the city of Winchester. . . .

*John Philpot*
*Archdeacon of*
*Winchester.*

*This Doctor*
*Ponet Bishop*
*of Winchester*
*fled afterward*
*into Germany,*
*and there*
*deceased.*
*Anno 1557.*
After that, having an advowson* by the said bishop, he was
made there Archdeacon of Winchester, under Doctor Ponet,*
who then succeeded Gardiner in that bishopric. Thus during
the time of King Edward, he continued to no small profit of
those parties thereabout. When that blessed king was taken
away, and Mary his sister came in place, whose study was wholly
bent to alter the state of religion in the woeful realm of England:
first she caused a convocation of the prelates and learned men
to be congregated, to the accomplishment of her desire.

In the which convocation, Master Philpot being present according to his room and degree,* with a few other sustained the cause of the gospel manfully against the adversary part (as is above recited) for the which cause, notwithstanding the liberty of the house promised before, he was called to accompt before Bishop Gardiner the Chancellor, then being his ordinary, by whom he was first examined, although that examination came not yet to our hands. From thence again he was removed to Bonner and other commissioners, with whom he had diverse and sundry conflicts. . . .

*John Philpot sent from Gardiner to Bonner.*

[*At this point the text shifts from third-person narrative concerning Philpot to his own first-person account of his experience after the accession of Mary I.*]

After this, I with four other more were brought to the keeper's house in Paternoster Row, where we supped, and after supper I was called up to a chamber by the Archdeacon of London's servant,* and that in his master's name, who offered me a bed for that night. To whom I gave thanks, saying: that it should be a grief to me to lie well one night, and the next worse: 'Wherefore I will begin,' (said I), 'as I am like to continue, to take such part as my fellows do.' And with that we were brought through Paternoster Row, to my Lord of London's coal house: unto the which is joined a little blind* house, with a great pair of stocks appointed both for hand and foot, but thanks be to God we have not played of those organs yet, although some before us had tried them; and there we found a minister of Essex a married priest, a man of godly zeal, with one other poor man. And this minister (at my coming) desired to speak with me, and did greatly lament his own infirmity, for that through extremity of imprisonment, he was constrained by writing to yield to the Bishop of London: whereupon he was once set at liberty, and afterward felt such a hell in his conscience, that he could scarce refrain from destroying himself, and never could be at quiet until he had gone unto the bishop's register, desiring to see his bill again, the which as soon as he had received, he tore it in pieces: and after he was as joyful as any man might be. Of the which when my Lord of London had understanding, he sent for him, and fell upon him like a lion, and like a manly bishop buffeted him well, so that he made his

*Master Philpot laid in Bishop Bonner's coal house.*

*This godly man was Thomas Whittle, whose story followeth.*

*Example what an unquiet conscience doth.*

*Thomas Whittle after his recantation repenteth and tore his subscription.*

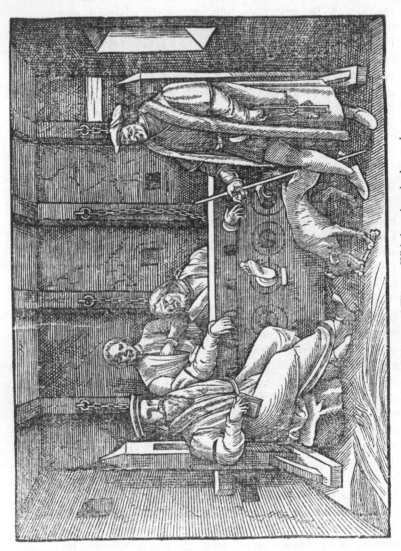

15. Master Philpot and Thomas Whittle, priest, in the stocks

face black and blue, and plucked away a great piece of his beard: but now thanks be to God, he is as joyful under the cross as any of us, and very sorry of his former infirmity. I write this because I would all men to take heed how they do contrary to their conscience: which is to fall into the pains of hell. And here an end. . . .

*Bishop Bonner plucked away a great part of Whittle's beard, and made his face black and blue.*

[*After undergoing seven formal examinations for heresy before Edmund Bonner, Bishop of London, other bishops, Queen's Commissioners, and others, Philpot recorded the following informal interrogation at his ad hoc prison at the palace of the Bishop of London.*]

## Another private conference between the bishop and Master Philpot in the coal house.

*Philpot.* The Sunday after, the bishop came into the coal house at night with the keeper, and viewed the house, saying that he was never here afore: whereby a man may guess how he hath kept God's commandment in visiting the prisoners,* seeing he was never with them that have been so nigh his nose: and he came not then for any good zeal, but to view the place, and thought it too good for me, and therefore after supper between eight and nine he sent for me, saying

*Another private talk or conference between him and the bishop.*

*Bishop Bonner viewing his coal house.*

[*Bishop of*] *London.* 'Sir, I have great displeasure of the queen and the Council for keeping you so long, and letting you have so much liberty. And besides that, you be yonder, and strengthen the other prisoners in their errors, as I have laid wait for your doings, and am certified of you well enough: I will sequester you therefore from them, and you shall hurt no more as you have done, and I will out of hand dispatch you, as I am commanded, unless you will be a conformable man.'

*Philpot.* 'My Lord, you have my body in your custody: you may transport it whither it please you: I am content. And I would you would make as quick expedition in my judgement, as you say, I long therefore; and as for conformity, I am ready to yield to all truth, if any can bring better than I.'. . .

[*Seven more examinations and private conversations preceded Philpot's condemnation and death sentence.*]

## The condemnation of the worthy martyr of God, John Philpot

These books, letters, supplications and other matters being thus read, the bishop demanded of him, if the book entitled *The true report of the disputation,** et cetera, were of his penning or not? Whereunto Philpot answered, that it was a good and true book, and of his own penning and setting forth.

*Of this book of disputation in the Convocation. . . .*

The bishops waxing now weary, and being not able by any sufficient ground, either of God's word or of the true ancient Catholic fathers,* to convince and overcome him, fell by fair and flattering speech, to persuade with him, promising that if he would revoke his opinions, and come home again to their Romish and Babylonical church, he should not only be pardoned that which was past, but also they would with all favour and cheerfulness of heart, receive him again as a true member thereof. Which words when Bonner saw would take no place: he demandeth of Master Philpot (and that with a charitable affection, I warrant you) whether he had any just cause to allege, why he should not condemn him as a heretic. 'Well,' quoth Master Philpot: 'your idolatrous sacrament which you have found out, ye would fain defend, but ye cannot, nor never shall.'

*Ah my Lord what needed this question when no reasonable answer could be allowed.*

In the end, the bishop seeing his unmovable steadfastness in the truth, did pronounce openly the sentence of condemnation against him. In the reading whereof . . . Master Philpot said, 'I thank God that I am a heretic out of your cursed church: I am no heretic before God. But God bless you and give you once grace to repent your wicked doings: and let all men beware of your bloody church.'

*Sentence of condemnation read against Master Philpot.*

Moreover, whiles Bonner was about the midst of the sentence, the Bishop of Bath* pulled him by the sleeve, and said: 'My Lord, my Lord, know of him first whether he will recant or no?' Then Bonner said (full like himself), 'Oh let me alone': and so read forth the sentence.

*Master Philpot's words in reading the sentence.*

And when he had done, he delivered him to the sheriffs: and so two officers brought him through the bishop's house into Paternoster Row, and there his servant met him, and when he saw him, he said: 'Ah dear master.'

*Master Philpot delivered to the sheriffs.*

Then Master Philpot said to his man: 'Content thyself, I shall do well enough: for thou shalt see me again.'

And so the officers thrust him away, and had his master to Newgate: and as he went, he said to the people: 'Ah good people, blessed be God for this day': and so the officers delivered him to the keeper. Then his man thrust to go in after his master, and one of the officers said unto him: 'Hence fellow what shouldst thou have?' And he said, 'I would go speak with my master.' Master Philpot then turned him about, and said to him, 'Tomorrow you shall speak with me.'

Then the under-keeper said to Master Philpot: 'Is this your man?' And he said, 'Yea.' So he did license his man to go in with him, and Master Philpot and his man were turned into a little chamber on the right hand, and there remained a little time, until Alexander the chief keeper did come unto him: who at his entering, greeted him with these words. 'Ah,' said he, 'hast not thou done well to bring thy self hither?' 'Well,' said Master Philpot, 'I must be content, for it is God's appointment: and I shall desire you to let me have your gentle favour: for you and I have been of old acquaintance.' 'Well,' said Alexander, 'I will show thee gentleness and favour, so you wilt be ruled by me.' Then said Master Philpot: 'I pray you show me what you would have me to do.'

He said, 'If you would recant, I will show you any pleasure I can.' 'Nay,' said Master Philpot. 'I will never recant whilst I have my life, that which I have spoken, for it is a most certain truth, and in witness hereof, I will seal it with my blood.' Then Alexander said: 'This is the saying of all the whole pack of you heretics.' Whereupon he commanded him to be set upon the block, and as many irons upon his legs as he might bear, for that he would not follow his wicked mind.

Then the clerk told Alexander in his ear that Master Philpot had given his man money. And Alexander said to his man: 'What money hath thy master given thee?' His man said: 'My master hath given me none.' 'No?' said Alexander. 'Hath he given thee none? That will I know for I will search thee.' 'Do with me what you list, and search me all that you can,' quoth his servant. 'He hath given me a token or two, to send to his friends, as to his brother and sister.' 'Ah,' said Alexander to

Master Philpot: 'Thou art a maintainer of heretics. Thy man should have gone to some of thine affinity: but he shall be known well enough.' 'Nay,' said Master Philpot: 'I do send it to my friends. There he is: let him make answer to it. But good Master Alexander, be so much my friend, that these irons may be taken off.' 'Well,' said Alexander, 'give me my fees, and I will take them off: if not, thou shalt wear them still.'

*Alexander taketh Philpot's tokens from his man.*

Then said Master Philpot, 'Sir, what is your fees?' He said, four pound was his fees. 'Ah,' said Master Philpot. 'I have not so much: I am but a poor man, and I have been long in prison.' 'What wilt thou give me then?' said Alexander. 'Sir,' (said he), 'I will give you twenty shillings, and that I will send my man for, or else I will lay my gown to gage:* for the time is not long (I am sure) that I shall be with you: for the bishop said unto me that I should be soon dispatched.'

*Alexander the cruel keeper requireth four pounds of Master Philpot for his irons.*

Then said Alexander unto him, 'What is that to me?' and with that he departed from him, and commanded him to be had into limbo,* and so his commandment was fulfilled: but before he could be taken from the block, the clerk would have a groat.

*Master Philpot had into limbo.*

Then one Wittrence, steward of the house, took him on his back, and carried him down, his man knew not whither. Wherefore Master Philpot said to his man: 'Go to Master Sheriff and show him how I am used, and desire Master Sheriff to be good unto me.' And so his servant went straightway, and took an honest man with him.

And when they came to Master Sheriff (which was Master Macham) and showed him how Master Philpot was handled in Newgate. The Sheriff hearing this, took his ring off from his finger, and delivered it unto that honest man which came with Master Philpot's man, and bade him go unto Alexander the keeper, and commanded him to take off his irons, and to handle him more gently, and to give his man again that which he had taken from him. And when they came again to the said Alexander, and told their message from the Sheriff, Alexander took the ring, and said: 'Ah, I perceive that Master Sheriff is a bearer with him, and all such heretics as he is: therefore tomorrow I will show it to his betters': Yet at ten of the clock he went into Master Philpot where he lay, and took off his

*Master Macham Sheriff, a good man, sendeth his ring to take off Master Philpot's irons, and to restore the man's tokens.*

*Note the spitefulness of this keeper.*

irons, and gave him such things as he had taken before from his servant.

*Master Philpot with much ado released of his irons.*

Upon Tuesday at supper, being the seventeenth day of December there came a messenger from the sheriffs, and bade Master Philpot make him ready, for the next day he should suffer, and be burned at a stake with fire. Master Philpot answered and said, 'I am ready: God grant me strength, and a joyful resurrection.' And so he went unto his chamber, and poured out his spirit unto the Lord God, giving him most hearty thanks that he of his mercy had made him worthy to suffer for his truth.

*December 17. Master Philpot warned by the sheriffs to prepare him against the next day to the fire.*

In the morning the sheriffs came according to the order, about eight of the clock, and calleth for him, and he most joyfully came down with them. And there his man did meet him, and said: 'Ah dear master, farewell.' His master said unto him, 'Serve God and he will help thee.' And so he went with the sheriffs unto the place of execution: and when he was entering into Smithfield, the way was foul, and two officers took him up to bear him to the stake. Then he said, merrily, 'What? Will you make me a pope? I am content to go to my journey's end on foot.' But first coming into Smithfield, he kneeled down there saying these words: 'I will pay my vows in thee O Smithfield.'

*December 18.*

*Master Philpot brought to the place of martyrdom.*

*Master Philpot's words going to the stake.*

And when he was come to the place of suffering, he kissed the stake and said: 'Shall I disdain to suffer at this stake seeing my redeemer did not refuse to suffer most vile death upon the cross for me?' And then with an obedient heart full meekly he said the one-hundred-sixth, one-hundred-seventh, and one-hundred-eighth psalms: and when he had made an end of all his prayers, he said to the officers: 'What have you done for me?' and every one of them declared what they had done: and he gave to every of them money.

*Master Philpot's prayers.*

*John Philpot giveth the officers money.*

Then they bound him unto the stake, and set fire unto that constant martyr: who the eighteenth day of December, in the midst of the fiery flames, yielded his soul into the hands of the almighty God, and full like a lamb gave up his breath his body being consumed into ashes.

Thus hast thou (gentle reader) the life and doings of this learned and worthy soldier of the Lord, John Philpot: with all his examinations that came to our hands:* first penned and written with his own hand, being marvellously reserved from the sight and hands of his enemies: who by all manner means sought not only to stop him from all writing, but also to spoil and deprive him of that which he had written. For the which cause he was many times stripped and searched in the prison of his keeper:* but yet so happily these his writings were conveyed and hid in places about him or else his keeper's eyes so blinded that notwithstanding all this malicious purpose of the bishops, they are yet remaining and come to light. . . .

*The writings and examinations of Master John Philpot by the providence of almighty God preserved.*

[*Foxe then appends a variety of letters written by Philpot, including these excerpts.*]

## To his dear friend in the Lord John Careless*
## prisoner in the King's Bench

My dearly beloved brother Careless, I have received your loving letters full of love and compassion, insomuch that they made my hard heart to weep, to see you so careful for one that hath been so unprofitable a member as I have been and am in Christ's church. God make me worthy of that I am called unto, and I pray you, cease not to pray for me but cease to weep for him who hath not deserved such gentle tears: and praise God with me, for that I now approach to the company of them, whose want you may worthily lament: God give your pitiful heart, his inward consolation. Indeed my dear Careless, I am in this world in hell, and in the shadow of death: but he that hath brought me for my deserts down unto hell, shall shortly lift me up to heaven, where I shall look continually for your coming and others my faithful brethren in the King's Bench. And though I tell you that I am in hell in the judgement of this world, yet assuredly I feel in the same the consolation of heaven, I praise God: and this loathsome and horrible prison is as pleasant to me, as the walk in the garden of the King's Bench.

*Good conscience. Another letter of Master Philpot to John Careless.*

*Experience of the Lord's comfort in trouble.*

You know brother Careless, that the way to heaven out of this life, is very narrow, and we must strive to enter in at a narrow gate.* If God do mitigate the ugliness of mine imprisonment, what will he do in the rage of the fire whereunto I am appointed? And this hath happened unto me that I might be

*Example of Christ's comfort to be taken by Master Philpot.*

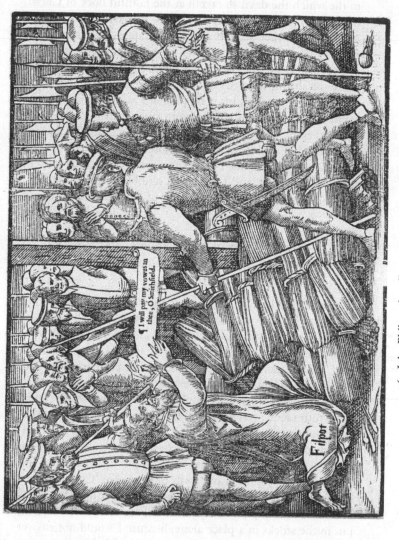

16. John Philpot, kneeling and praying at the stake

hereafter an example of comfort, if the like happen unto you or to any other of my dear brethren with you in these cruel days, in the which the devil so rageth at the faithful flock of Christ, but in vain (I trust) against any of us, who be persuaded that neither life neither death is able to separate us from the love of Christ's gospel,* which is God's high treasure committed to your brittle vessels to glorify us by the same. God of his mercy make us faithful stewards to the end, and give us grace to fear nothing whatsoever in his good pleasure we shall suffer for the same. That I have not written unto you erst, the cause is our strait keeping and the want of light by night, for the day serveth us but a while in our dark closet. This is the first letter that I have written since I came to prison, besides the report of mine examinations: and I am fain to scribble it out in haste. . . .

Out of the coal house by your
brother John Philpot

## Another letter to John Careless, profitable to be read of all them which mourn in repentance for their sins.

*True Christians how they ought to be careless in their careful estate.*

. . . Since God hath willed you at your baptism in Christ to be careless, why do you make yourself careful:* cast all your care on him. Set the Lord before your eyes always, for he is on your right side, that you shall not be moved. Behold the goodness of God toward me. I am careless, being fast closed in a pair of stocks, which pinch me for very straitness: and will you be careful? I will not have that unseemly addition to your name. Be as your name pretendeth, for doubtless you have none other cause but so to be. Pray, I beseech you, that I may be still careless in my careful estate, as you have cause to be careless in your easier condition. Be thankful and put away all care, and then I shall be joyful in my strait present care. Commend me to all our brethren, and desire them to pray for me, that I may overcome my temptations: for the devil rageth against me, I am put in the stocks in a place alone, because I would not answer to such articles, as they would charge me withal in a corner at the bishop's appointment, and because I did not come to Mass when the bishop sent for me, I will lie all the days of my life in the stocks (by God's grace) rather than I will consent to the wicked generation. Praise God and be joyful, that it hath pleased him to make us worthy to suffer somewhat for his name's sake. The Devil must rage for ten days.* Commend me to Master F.* and thank him for his law books, but law, neither equity will take any place among these blood-thirsty. I would for your sake their unjust dealing were noted unto the parliament house, if it might avail. God shorten these evil days, I have answered the bishop meetly plain already, and I said to him, if he will call me in open judgement, I will answer him as plainly as he will require: otherwise I have refused, because I fear they will condemn me in hugger mugger. The peace of God be with you my dear brother. I can write no more for lack of light, and that I have written I cannot read myself, and God knoweth it is written far uneasily. I pray God you may pick out some understanding of my mind towards you. Written in a coal house of darkness, out of a pair of painful stocks, by thine own in Christ.

John Philpot.

# 17. BARTLETT GREEN

## The story of Master Bartlett Green, gentleman and lawyer, martyr.

*The story of Master Bartlett Green gentleman and martyr. January 27.*

After the martyrdom of Thomas Whittle,* next followeth in order to speak of Bartlett Green, who the next day after the foresaid Whittle, was likewise condemned. This Green was of a good house, and having such parents, as both favoured learning, and were also willing to bring up this their child in the same. Who after some entrance in other inferior schools, was *Bartlett Green, student at Oxford.* by them sent unto the University of Oxford: where through exercise and diligent study, he so profited, that within short time he attained, as well to the knowledge of sundry profane sciences, and also now in his last years, unto the godly understanding of Divinity. Whereunto through ignorance (in which he was trained up from his youth) he was at the first an utter enemy, until such time as God of his mercy had opened his eyes, by his often repairing unto the common lectures of Peter *Master Green converted by the lecture of Peter Martyr.* Martyr, reader of the Divinity lecture in the same University: so that thereby (as by God's instrument) he saw the true light of Christ's gospel.

Whereof when he had once tasted, it became unto him as the fountain of lively water, that our saviour Christ spake of unto the woman of Samaria,* so as he never thirsted any more, but *John 4.* had a well springing unto everlasting life. Insomuch as when he was called by his friends from the university, and was placed in the Temple at London, there to attain to the knowledge of *Master Green student in the Temple at London.* the common laws of the realm, he yet continued still in his former study, and earnest profession of the gospel: wherein also he did not a little profit. Howbeit (such is the frailty of our corrupt nature, without the special assistance of God's holy spirit) through the continual accompanying, and fellowship of such worldly (I will not say too much youthful) young gentlemen as are commonly in that and the like houses, he became by little and little, a compartner* of their fond follies, and youthful vanities, as well in his apparel, as also in banquetings, and other superfluous excesses, which he afterward (being again called by God's merciful correction) did sore lament and bewail: as appeareth by his one testimony,* notified and left in a book of a certain friend of his, a little before his death, written with his own hand, in manner as followeth.

## This did Master Bartlett Green write in Master Bartram Calthrop's book

Two things have very much troubled me whilst I was in the Temple, pride, and gluttony, which under the colour of glory and good fellowship, drew me almost from God. Against both there is one remedy, by prayer earnest, and without ceasing. And forasmuch as vainglory is so subtle an adversary, that almost it woundeth deadly, ere ever a man can perceive himself to be smitten, therefore we ought so much the rather by continual prayer, to labour for humbleness of mind. Truly gluttony beginneth under a charitable pretence, of mutual love and society, and hath in it most uncharitableness. When we seek to refresh our bodies, that they may be the more apt to serve God, and perform our duties towards our neighbours, then stealeth it in as a privy thief, and murdereth both body and soul, that now it is not apt to pray, or serve God, nor apt to study, or labour for our neighbours. Let us therefore watch and be sober: for our adversary* the devil walketh about like a roaring lion seeking whom he may devour.* And remember what Solomon saith: . . . A patient man is better than a strong warrior, and he that conquereth his own stomach, is better than he that conquereth towns and cities.*

*A good note or lesson for young lawyers to mark and follow.*

*What lewd company doeth.*

Bartlett Green . . .

Thus we see the fatherly kindness of our most gracious and merciful God, who never suffereth his elect children so to fall, that they lie still in security of sin, but oftentimes quickeneth them up by some such means, as perhaps they think least of, as he did here this his strayed sheep. And now therefore to return to our history: for the better maintenance of himself in these his studies, and other his affairs he had a large exhibition of his grandfather Master Doctor Bartlett, who during the time of Green's imprisonment made unto him

*Large gifts offered to Master Green by Doctor Bartlett to return to the Church of Rome.*

large offers of great livings, if he would recant, and (forsake the truth, and gospel of Christ) come home again to the church and synagogue of Rome.\* But these his persuasions (the Lord be therefore praised) took small effect in this faithful heart, as the sequel did declare. He was a man beloved of all men (except of the papists, who love none that love the truth) and so he well deserved: for he was of a meek, humble, discreet, and most gentle behaviour to all. Injurious he was to none, beneficial to many, especially those that were of the household of faith: as appeared (amongst other) by his friendly dealing with Master Christopher Goodman,\* being at that present a poor exile beyond the seas. With whom this Bartlett Green (as well for his toward learning, as also for his sober and godly behaviour) had often society in Oxford, in the days of good King Edward: which now, notwithstanding his friend's misery and banishment, he did not lightly forget, and that turned, as it chanced (not without the providence of almighty God) to the great grief of both, the one of heart for the loss of his friend, and the other of body in suffering the cruel and murdering rage of papists.

*Friendship between Christopher Goodman and Master Green.*

The cause hereof was a letter which Green did write unto the said Goodman, containing as well the report of certain demands or questions, which were cast abroad in London (as appeareth hereafter in a letter of his own penning, which he meant to have sent unto Master Philpot, wherein he declareth his full usage before the Bishop of London and others) as also an answer to a question made by the said Christopher Goodman, in a letter written unto him, in which he required to have the certainty of the report, which was spread amongst them on the other side of the seas, that the queen was dead. Whereunto Master Green answered simply, and as the truth then was, that she was not dead.

*Occasion of apprehending of Master Green, came by letters intercepted.*

These letters with many other, written to diverse of the godly exiles, by their friends here in England, being delivered to a messenger to carry over, came by the apprehension of the said bearer, unto the hands of the King and Queen's Council, who at their convenient leisure, (which in those days by some of them was quickly found out for such matters) perused the whole number of the said letters, and amongst them espied this letter of Master Green's, written unto his friend Christopher

Goodman, in the contents whereof (amongst other news and private matters) they found these words: the queen is not yet dead.* Which words were only written as an answer, to certify Master Goodman of the truth of his former demand. Howbeit (to some of the council) they seemed very heinous words, yea, treason they would have made them, if the law would have suffered. Which when they could not do (and being yet very loath to let any such depart freely, whom they suspected to be a favourer of the gospel) they then examined him upon his faith in religion, but upon what points, it is not certainly known. *Master Green examined by the counsel of his faith.*

Nevertheless (as it seemeth) his answers were such, as little pleased them (especially the anointed sort*) and therefore after they had long detained him in prison, as well in the Tower of London, as elsewhere, they sent him at last unto Bonner Bishop of London, to be ordered according to his ecclesiastical law: as appeareth by their letters sent unto the bishop, with the said prisoner also: wherein it may appear that Sir John Bourne* (then secretary to the queen) was a chief stirrer in such cases, yea, and an enticer of others of the council: who otherwise (if for fear they durst) would have been content to have let such matters alone. The Lord forgive them their weakness (if it be his good pleasure) and give them true repentance. Amen. . . . *John Bourne a stirrer of persecution.*

## The last examination and condemnation of Master Green.

Thus (as it seemeth) for this time they left off. But not long after the bishop perceiving Green's learning, and constancy to be such, as neither he, nor any of his doctors and chaplains, could by the scriptures refel, began then to object and put in practice his chief, and strongest argument against him: which was the rigour of the law, and cruelty of execution: an argument I ensure you, which without the special grace of our God, to flesh is importable.* And therefore using law as a cloak of his tyranny, the twenty-eighth day of November, the said bishop examined him upon certain points of Christian religion. Whereunto, when he had answered, the bishop appointed the register (as their most common manner is) to draw there out an *The last examination of Master Green.*

order of confession. Which being afterwards read unto Green, was also subscribed by him, as a confirmation of his former assertions: the tenor whereof here ensueth.

## The confession and saying of Bartlett Green.

Bartlett Green born in the City of London, in the parish of Bassingshall of the diocese of London, and of the age of twenty-five years, being examined in the bishop's palace, the twenty-eighth day of November, anno 1555, upon certain articles answered as followeth. Videlicet, that neither in the time of King Edward, after that the Mass by him was put down, neither in the time of Queen Mary after that the Mass was restored again, he hath heard any Mass at all: but he saith that in the reign of the said queen's majesty he the said Bartlett two times, to wit, at two Eastertides or days, in the chamber of John Pullain, one of the preachers in King Edward's time, within the parish of Saint Michael's in Cornhill, of the diocese of London, did receive the communion with the said Pullain and Christopher Goodman, sometime reader of the Divinity Lecture in Oxford, now gone beyond the sea, and the second time with the said Polline with one Runneger, Master of Art of Magdalen College in Oxford and this examinate also saith, that at both the said communions he, and the other before named did take, and receive bread and wine, which bread and wine he called sacramental bread, and sacramental wine, which he saith were used there by them, Pullain only reading the words of the institution, expressed in the book of communion.

In which receiving and using, this examinate saith, that the other aforenamed, did receive the sacrament of the Lord's supper, and that they received material bread, and material wine, no substance thereof changed and so no real presence of the body and blood of Christ there being, but only grace added thereto.* And further this examinate saith, that he had heretofore, during the reign of the queen's majesty aforesaid, refused, and so now doth refuse to come and hear Mass, and to receive the sacrament of the altar, as they are now used and ministered in this Church, of England, because he saith that concerning the Mass, he cannot be persuaded, in his conscience, that the sacrifice pretended to be in the same, is agreeable to God's word, or maintainable by the same: or that without deadly offence, he cannot worship the body and blood of Christ, that is pretended to be there. And as concerning the sacrament of the altar, this examinate saith, that he heretofore during the said reign hath refused, and now doth refuse to receive the same, as is now used in this Church of England, because it is not used, according to the institution of Christ but both in a strange tongue, and also not ministered in both kinds,* and besides that, contrary to God's word it is there taught, that the thing there ministered is to be adored, as the real and true body of Christ. And furthermore this examinate saith, that during the said reign, he hath not been confessed to the priest, nor received absolution at his hands, because he is not bound by God's word, to make auricular confession.

*Sacrifice of the Mass not maintainable by God's word.*

*Master Green against the sacrament of the altar.*

*Auricular confession refused.*

Bartlett Green.

Many other sundry conferences, and public examinations they brought him unto. But in the end, seeing his steadfastness of faith to be such, as against the which, neither the threatenings, nor yet their flattering promises could prevail, the fifteenth day of January, the bishop caused him with the rest above named,* to be brought into the consistory in Paul's: where, being set in his judgement seat, accompanied with Feckenham, then Dean of the same church, and other his chaplains, after he had condemned the other six he then called for Bartlett Green [and] began with these or the like words.

*Master Green with the other six martyrs brought to the consistory.*

'Honourable audience, I think it best to open unto you, the conversation of this man, called Bartlett Green. And because you shall not charge me, that I go about to seek any man's blood, here you shall hear the council's letters, which they sent with him unto me. The effect whereof is: that where he had been of long time in the Tower of London for heresy, they have now sent him unto me to be ordered, according to the laws therefore provided. . . .'

*Bishop Bonner's words to the audience.*

[*Green then underwent interrogation concerning his understanding of patristic commentary on Eucharistic theology and whether he accepted the Church of Rome as the universal Christian church.*]

*Feckenham.* At last Feckenham demanded of him, how long he had been of his opinion? 'For Master Green,' (said he), 'you confessed once to me, that when you were at Oxford at school, you were called the rankest papist in that house, and being compelled to go to the lecture of Peter Martyr, you were converted from your old doctrine.'

*Master Green first a rank papist.*

*Green.* And Green confessed the same.

*Feckenham.* Then again he said, that Green told him that the said Peter Martyr was a papist in his first coming to Oxford. Whereupon he made an exclamation, and praised the people to consider, how vain his doctrine that he professed was, which was grounded upon one man and that upon so unconstant a man as Peter Martyr, which perceiving the wicked intent of the Council, was content to please them, and forsake the true and Catholic faith.

*Untrue report of Peter Martyr.*

*Green.* Green said that he grounded not his faith upon Martyr, nor any other, nor did believe so because Martyr believed the same, but because that he had heard the scriptures, and the doctors of the church truly and wholesomely expounded by him: neither had he any regard of the man, but of the word which he spake. And further he said, that he heard the said Master Peter say often, that he had not as yet, while he was a papist, read Chrysostom* upon the tenth chapter to the Corinthians, nor many other places of the doctors: but when he had read them, and well considered them, he was content to yield to the doctors having first humbled himself in prayer, desiring God to illuminate him, and bring him to the true understanding of the scripture. 'Which thing,' (said Green), 'if you my Lord would do, I do not doubt, but God would open your eyes, and show you his truth, no more than I do doubt his words be true: that saith: "Ask, and it shall be given to you, knock, and it shall be opened unto you."* Et cetera. . . .

*Peter Martyr first turned from popery to the truth, by prayer and reading the doctors.*

*Feckenham.* Then Feckenham desired him that he would not so wilfully cast himself away, but to be rather conformable to reason, and that my Lord bishop there present, would be good unto him, and would grant him respite (if he would demand it) for a fortnight, or three weeks and that he should choose any learned man whom he would and should go with him home to his house and that he whom he would choose, would willingly take the pains to read and confer the doctors with him, and open the doctors' minds and meanings unto him.

*Bonner*. Then Bonner said, that he was proud and an obstinate boy, and therefore he bade Feckenham to hold his peace, and to call him no more Master Green: 'For,' (said he), 'you ought not to call an heretic, "Master."'

... This talk ended, he asked Green if he would recant and return to their Romish mother. Which when he denied, the bishop pronounced the sentence definitive against him, and so committed him to the sheriffs of London, who caused him to be carried to Newgate.

And as he was going thither, there met with him two gentlemen, being both his special friends, minding belike to comfort this their persecuted brother. But at their meeting, their loving and friendly hearts (not able any longer to hide themselves) were manifested by the abundance of their pitiful tears. To whom, when Green saw them, he said in these or like words: 'Ah my friends is this your comfort you are come to give me, in this my occasion of heaviness? Must I, who needed to have comfort ministered to me, become now a comforter of you?' And thus declaring his most quiet and peaceable mind and conscience, he cheerfully spake to them and others, until he came to the prison door, into the which he joyfully entered, and there remained always either in prayer (whereunto he much gave himself) or else in some other godly meditations and exercises, unto the twenty-eighth day of January, when he with his other above mentioned brethren went most cheerfully unto the place of their torments often repeating, as well by the way, as also at the stake, these [verses]. . . .

> O Christ my God, sure hope of health.
>   besides thee have I none:
> The truth I love, and falsehood hate,
>   by thee my guide alone.

During the time of his imprisonment in Newgate, diverse of his friends had access unto him, to whom he gave sundry godly exhortations: wherewith they were not only well contented, but for better remembrance, as well of the same his instructions, as also of his own good and godly person, they desired

*Bonner forbiddeth Master Green to be called, 'Master.'*

*Sentence given against Master Green.*

*The words of Master Green to his friends by the way going to Newgate.*

*Verses of Master Green written in his friend's book.*

him to write somewhat in their books, which request he willingly granted, as in manner here ensueth.

These verses were written in a book of Master Hussey of the Temple.

Behold thyself by me, such one was I, as thou:
And thou in time shalt be, even dust as I am now.

Bartlett Green.

These verses were also written in a book of Master William Fleetwood, of the same house.

My resting rood is found, vain hope and hap adieu.
Love whom you list with change, death shall me rid from you.

Bartlett Green.

Among other diverse and singular good virtues of this good man, especially in him was to be noted such a modest nature, so humbly thinking of himself, as in few men is to be found, ever dejecting himself under that was in him, and ever seeming to be less than he was so that nothing less he could abide, than *The singular* to hear of his praise or commendation: as well declareth not *modesty, and* only his letter written to Master Philpot, wherein he doth earn-*humble nature* estly expostulate with him, for slandering him with praise of *of Master* his wit and learning, and other manifold virtues of great excel-*Green.* lency, but also by his own speech and answers in his examination wherein he casteth from him all knowledge of learning and cunning, when notwithstanding he had more in him, than to any men's eyes did appear.

So great and admirable was this gift of modesty grafted in the nature of him, so far abhorring from all pride and arrogancy, that as he could not abide anything that was spoken to his advancement or praise: so neither did there appear in him any show or brag in those things wherein he might justly glory, which were his punishments and sufferings for the cause and quarrel of Christ. For when he was beaten and scourged with rods by Bishop Bonner (which scarce any man would believe, nor I neither, but that I heard it of him, which heard it of his mouth) and he greatly rejoiced in the same, yet his shamefast* modesty was such, that never he would express any mention thereof, lest he should seem to glory too much in himself, save that only he opened the same to one Master Cotton of the Temple a friend of his, a little before his death.

Moreover, to this rare and maidenly modesty in him was also adjoined the like nature of mercy and pitiful\* compassion: which affection though it seemed to be little regarded of some, yet in my mind is there no other thing wrought in nature, wherein man resembleth more truly the image of the high majesty of almighty God than this. And as in this respect of merciful tenderness, man only excelleth all other beasts: so almost no less may this man seem to pass many other men, whose customable property and exercise was to visit the poor prisoners with him in prison, both with bodily relief, and also with spiritual comfort: and finding many of them (I mean such as were there for theft, and other naughty facts) very penitent and sorry for their evil demeanours, in hope of their amendment, did not only by mouth, but also by his letters require, yea, as it were of duty in love, did charge his friends, to travail for their deliverances: such was the pity and charitable mercy of this godly and most true member of Christ's church. . . .

*The pitiful nature of Master Green.*

# 18. THOMAS CRANMER

The life, state,* and story of the reverend pastor and
prelate, Thomas Cranmer Archbishop of Canterbury,
martyr, burned at Oxford, for the confession of
Christ's true doctrine, under Queen Mary.
Anno 1556. March 21.

*March 21.*
*Thomas
Cranmer
Archbishop of
Canterbury
and martyr.* As concerning the life and estate of that most reverend father
in God, and worthy prelate of godly memory, Thomas
Cranmer late Archbishop of Canterbury, and of the original
cause and occasion of his preferment unto his archepiscopal
dignity, who of many hath been thought to have procured
the same by friendship only, and of some other esteemed
unworthy of so high a vocation: It is first therefore to be noted
and considered, that the same Thomas Cranmer coming of an
ancient parentage, from the conquest to be deducted,* and
continuing sithens in the name and family of a gentleman, was
*Thomas
Cranmer a
gentleman
born.* born in a village called Arselacton in Nottinghamshire. Of
whose said name and family there remaineth at these days one
manor and mansion house in Lincolnshire, called Cranmer
Hall, et cetera, sometimes of heritage of the said stock and
*Thomas
Cranmer first
coming to
Cambridge.* family. Who being from his infancy kept at school, and brought
up not without much good civility, came in process of time
unto the University of Cambridge, and there prospering in
right good knowledge amongst the better sort of students, was
*Thomas
Cranmer,
fellow of Jesus
College.
Cranmer
married.* chosen fellow of Jesus College in Cambridge. And so being
Master of Art, and fellow of the same college, it chanced him
to marry a gentleman's daughter: by means whereof he lost
and gave over his fellowship there,* and became the reader in
*Cranmer
reader in
Buckingham
College.* Buckingham College:* and for that he would with more
diligence apply that his office of reading, placed his said wife in
an Inn, called the Dolphin in Cambridge, the wife of the
house being of affinity unto her. By reason whereof, and for
that his often resort unto his wife, in that Inn he was much
marked of some popish merchants: whereupon rose the slan-
derous noise and report against him, after he was preferred to

the Archbishopric of Canterbury, raised up by the malicious disdain of certain malignant adversaries to Christ and his truth, bruiting abroad everywhere, that he was but an hostler, and therefore without all good learning. Of whose malicious reports, one of their practices in that behalf shall hereafter be declared, as place and time shall serve.

But in the mean time to return to the matter present. Whist this said Master Cranmer continued as reader in Buckingham College, his wife died in childbed. After whose death, the masters and fellows of Jesus College desirous again of their old companion, namely for his towardness in learning, chose him again fellow of the same college. Where he remaining at his study, became in few years after, the Reader of Divinity lecture* in the same college, and in such special estimation and reputation with the whole university, that being Doctor of Divinity, he was commonly appointed one of the heads (which are two or three of the chiefest learned men) to examine such as yearly profess in commencement, either bachelors, or doctors of divinity, by whose approbation the whole university licenseth them to proceed unto their degree: and again by whose disallowance the university also rejecteth them for a time to proceed, until they be better furnished with more knowledge.

*Thomas Cranmer after the decease of his wife, chosen fellow into Jesus College.*

*Thomas Cranmer made reader in Jesus College, and Doctor of Divinity.*

Now, Doctor Cranmer ever much favouring the knowledge of the scripture, would never admit any to proceed in divinity, unless they were substantially seen in the story of the Bible: by means whereof certain friars and other religious persons, who were principally brought up in the study of school authors without regard had to the authority of scriptures, were commonly rejected by him,* so that he was greatly for that his severe examination of the religious sort, much hated, and had in great indignation: and yet it came to pass in the end, that diverse of them being thus compelled to study the scriptures, became afterwards very well learned and well affected, insomuch, that when they proceeded doctors of divinity, could not overmuch extol and commend Master Doctor Cranmer's goodness towards them, who had for a time put them back, to aspire unto better knowledge and perfection. Among whom Doctor Barret a white friar,* who afterwards dwelt at Norwich,

*Doctor Cranmer public examiner in Cambridge of them that were to proceed.*

*Friars in hatred with Doctor Cranmer.*

was after that sort handled, giving him no less commendation for his happy rejecting of him for a better amendment. Thus much I repeat that our apish and popish sort of ignorant priests may well understand that this his exercise, kind of life, and vocation was not altogether hostler-like.

Well, to go forwards: like as he was neither in fame unknown, nor in knowledge obscure, so was he greatly solicited by Doctor Capon, to have been one of the fellows in the foundation of Cardinal Wolsey's college in Oxford* (which he utterly refused, not without danger of indignation). . . . For whiles he thus continued in Cambridge, the great and weighty cause of King Henry the eighth, his divorce with the Lady Catherine Dowager of Spain,* came into question, which being many

ways by the space of two or three years amongst the canonists, civilians,* and other learned men diversely disputed and debated, it came to pass that this said Doctor Cranmer, by reason that the plague was in Cambridge, resorted to Waltham Abbey,* to one Master Cressy's house there, whose wife was of kin to the said Master Cranmer. And for that he had two sons of the said Cressy with him at Cambridge as his pupils, he rested at Waltham Cross, at the house of the said Master Cressy, with the said two children, during that summer time whiles the plague reigned.

In this summer time Cardinal Campeius* and Cardinal Wolsey, being in commission from the pope, to hear and determine that great cause in controversy between the king and the queen his pretended wife,* dallied and delayed all the summer time until the month of August [1529] came in, hearing the said cause in controversy debated. When August was come, the said Cardinals little minding to proceed to sentence giving, took occasion to finish their commission, and not further to determine therein, pretending not to be permitted by the laws to keep courts of ecclesiastical matters in harvest time, which sudden stay and giving over of the said commission by both the cardinals, being unknown to the king, it so much moved him that he taking it as a mock at the cardinals' hands, commanded the Dukes of Norfolk and Suffolk* to dispatch forthwith Cardinal Campeius home again to Rome, and so in haste removed himself from London to Waltham, for a night or twain whiles his household removed to Greenwich:* by means whereof it chanced that the harbingers* lodged Doctor Stephens secretary,* and Doctor Foxe almoner (who were the chief furtherers, preferers and defenders on the king's behalf of the said cause) in the house of the said Master Cressy, where the said Doctor Cranmer was also lodged and resident. When suppertime came, they all three doctors met together, Doctor Stephens and Doctor Foxe, much marvelling of Doctor Cranmer's being there. Who declared to them the cause of his there being, namely, for that the plague was in Cambridge. And as they were of old acquaintance, so the secretary and the almoner right well entertained Doctor Cranmer, minding to understand part of his opinion touching their great business they had in hand. And so as good occasion served, whiles they were at supper, they conferred with Doctor Cranmer concerning the king's cause, requesting him of his opinion what he thought therein.

*Stephen Gardiner and Doctor Foxe, chief stirrers of the king's divorce.*

*Doctor Stephens, Doctor Foxe, Doctor Cranmer conferring together in the king's cause.*

Whereunto Doctor Cranmer answered, that he could say little to the matter, for that he had not studied nor looked for it. Notwithstanding he said to them, that in his opinion they made more ado in prosecuting the law ecclesiastical, than needed. 'It were better as I suppose,' (quod Doctor Cranmer), 'that the question, whether a man may marry his brother's wife or no, were decided and discussed by the divines, and by the authority of the word of God,* whereby the conscience of the prince might be better satisfied and quieted, than thus from year to year by frustratory* delays to prolong the time, leaving the very truth of the matter unbolted out by* the word of God. There is but one truth in it, which the scripture will soon declare, make open and manifest, being by learned men well handled, and that may be as well done in England in the universities here, as at Rome or elsewhere in any foreign nation, the authority whereof will compel any judge soon to come to a definitive sentence: and therefore as I take it, you might this way have made an end of this matter long sithens.' When Doctor Cranmer had thus ended his tale, the other two well liked of his device, and wished that they had so proceeded aforetime, and thereupon conceived some matter of that device to instruct the king withal, who then was minded to send to Rome again for a new commission.

*Doctor Cranmer's answer in the question of the king's divorce.*

*Doctor Cranmer's device well liked of.*

Now, the next day when the king removed to Greenwich, like as he took himself not well handled by the cardinals in thus deferring his cause, so his mind being unquieted and desirous of an end of his long and tedious suit he called to him these his two principal doers of his said cause, namely the said Doctor Stephens and Doctor Foxe, saying unto them: 'What now my masters,' (quoth the king), 'shall we do in this infinite cause of mine? I see by it there must be a new commission procured from Rome, and when we shall have an end, God knoweth and not I.' When the king had said somewhat his mind herein, the almoner Doctor Foxe said unto the king again: 'We trust that there shall be better ways devised for your majesty, than to make travail so far as to Rome any more in your highness's cause, which by chance was put into our heads this other night being at Waltham.' The king being very desirous to understand his meaning, said: 'Who hath taken in hand to instruct you by any better or shorter way to proceed in our said cause?' Then said Doctor Foxe: 'It chanced us to be lodged at Waltham in Master Cressy's house this other night, your highness being there, where we met with an old acquaintance of ours, named Doctor Cranmer, with whom having conference concerning your highness's cause, he thought that the next way were, first to instruct and quiet your majesty's conscience by trying your highness's question out by the authority of the word of God, and thereupon to proceed to a final sentence.' With this report the secretary was not content with the almoner, for that he did not utter this device as of their own invention. And when the secretary would have seemed by colourable* words to make it appear to the king, that they of themselves had devised that means: the king then said, 'Where is that Doctor Cranmer? Is he still at Waltham?' They answered that they left him there. 'Marry,' said the king, 'I will surely speak with him, and therefore let him be sent for out of hand. I perceive,' quoth the king, 'that that man hath the sow by the right ear.* And if I had known this device but two year ago, it had been in my way a great piece of money, and had also rid me out of much disquietness.'

Whereupon Doctor Cranmer was sent for, and being removed from Waltham to Cambridge, and so towards his

*The king troubled about the divorce.*

*Doctor Cranmer's device reported to the king.*

*Note the glorious head of Doctor Stephens.*

*Doctor Cranmer sent for to the king.*

friends in Nottinghamshire, a post went for him. But when he came to London, he began to quarrel with these two his acquaintances, that he by their means was thus troubled and brought thither to be encumbered in a matter wherein he had nothing at all travailed in study, and therefore most instantly entreated them, that they would make his excuse in such sort, that he might be dispatched away from coming in the king's presence. They promised and took the matter upon them so to do, if by any means they might compass it. But all was in vain, for the more they began to excuse Doctor Cranmer's absence, the more the king chid with them, for that they brought him not out of hand to his presence, so that no excuse serving, he was fain undelayedly to come to the court unto the king, whom the gentle prince benignly accepting, demanded his name, and said unto him: 'Were you not at Waltham such a time, in the company of my secretary and my almoner?' Doctor Cranmer affirming the same, the king said again: 'Had you not conference with them concerning our matter of divorce now in question after this sort, repeating the manner and order thereof?' 'That is right true, if it please your highness,' quod Doctor Cranmer. 'Well,' said the king, 'I well perceive that you have the right scope of this matter. You must understand,' quoth the king, 'that I have been long troubled in conscience, and now I perceive that by this means I might have been long ago relieved one way or other from the same, if we had this way proceeded. And therefore master Doctor I pray you, and nevertheless because you are a subject, I charge and command you (all your other business and affairs set apart) to take some pains to see this my cause to be furthered according to your device, as much as it may lie in you, so that I may shortly understand whereunto I may trust. For this I protest before God and the world, that I seek not to be divorced from the queen, if by any means I were justly persuaded that our matrimony were inviolable, and not against the laws of God: for otherwise there was never cause to move me to seek any such extremity. Neither there was ever prince had a more gentler, a more obedient and loving companion and wife than the queen is, nor I never fancied woman in all respects better, if this doubt had not risen: assuring you that for the singular virtues wherewith

*Doctor Cranmer seeketh excuses loth to come unto the king's presence.*

*Doctor Cranmer brought to the king.*

*Talk between the king and Doctor Cranmer.*

*The king troubled in conscience.*

*Mark this you papists, which so rashly judge the king's divorce, and the pope's overthrow to have sprung of light causes.*

she is endued, besides the consideration of her noble stock, I could be right well contented still to remain with her, if so it would stand with the will and pleasure of almighty God.' And thus greatly commending her many and singular qualities, the king said: 'I therefore pray you with an indifferent eye, and with as much dexterity as lieth in you, that you for your part do handle the matter for the discharging of both our consciences.'

Doctor Cranmer much disabling himself to meddle in so weighty a matter, besought the king's highness to commit the trial and examining of this matter by the word of God, unto the best learned men of both his universities, Cambridge and Oxford. 'You say well,' said the king, 'and I am content therewith. But yet nevertheless, I will have you specially to write your mind therein.' And so calling the Earl of Wiltshire* to him, said: 'I pray you my Lord, let Doctor Cranmer have entertainment in your house at Durham Place for a time, to the intent he may be there quiet to accomplish my request, and let him lack neither books, nay anything requisite for his study.' And thus after the king's departure, Doctor Cranmer went with my Lord of Wiltshire unto his house, where he incontinent wrote his mind concerning the king's question: adding to the same besides the authorities of the scriptures: of general councils, and of ancient writers: also his opinion which was this: that the Bishop of Rome had no such authority, as whereby he might dispense with the word of God and the scripture.* When Doctor Cranmer had made this book, and committed it to the king, the king said to him: 'Will you abide by this, that you have here written before the Bishop of Rome': 'That will I do, by God's grace,' quoth Doctor Cranmer, 'if your majesty do send me thither.' 'Marry,' quoth the king, 'I will send you even to him in a sure ambassage.'*

And thus by means of Doctor Cranmer's handling of this matter with the king, not only certain learned men were sent abroad to the most part of the universities in Christendom, to dispute the question, but also the same being by commission disputed by the divines in both the Universities of Cambridge and Oxford, it was there concluded that no such matrimony was by the word of God lawful. Whereupon a solemn ambassage was then prepared and sent to the Bishop of

*Doctor Cranmer excusing and disabling himself to the king.*

*Doctor Cranmer assigned by the king to search the scriptures in the cause of his divorce.*

*The king first given to understand that the pope hath no authority to dispense with the word of God.*

*The king's matter removed from the pope's canon law to the trial of the scriptures. The king's marriage found by God's word unlawful.*

Rome, then being at Bologna, wherein went the Earl of Wiltshire, Doctor Cranmer, Doctor Stokesley, Doctor Carne, Doctor Benet, and diverse other learned men and gentlemen. And when the time came that they should come before the Bishop of Rome to declare the cause of their ambassage, the bishop sitting on high in his cloth of estate, and in his rich apparel, with his sandals on his feet, offering as it were, his foot to be kissed of the ambassadors, the Earl of Wiltshire disdaining thereat, stood still, and made no countenance thereunto, so that all the rest kept themselves from that idolatry.*

*Doctor Cranmer with other sent to Rome ambassador to the pope.*

Howbeit, one thing is not here to be omitted, as a prognosticate of our separation from the See of Rome,* which then chanced by a spaniel of the Earl of Wiltshire. For he having there a great spaniel which came out of England with him, stood directly between the Earl and the Bishop of Rome. When the said bishop had advanced forth his foot to be kissed, now whether the spaniel perceived the bishop's foot of another nature than it ought to be, and so taking it to be some kind of repast, or whether it was the will of God to show some token by the dog unto the bishop of his inordinate pride, that his feet were more meet to be bitten of dogs, than kissed of Christian men: the spaniel (I say) when the bishop extended his foot to be kissed, no man regarding the same, straight way (as though he had been of purpose appointed thereunto) went directly to the pope's feet, and not only kissed the same unmannerly, but as some plainly reported and affirmed, took fast with his mouth the great toe of the pope, so that in haste he pulled in his glorious feet from the spaniel. Whereat our men smiling in their sleeves,* what they thought, God knoweth. But in fine, the pontifical bishop after that sought no more at that present for kissing his feet, but without any further ceremony gave ear to the ambassadors what they had to say.

*The English ambassadors not hasty to kiss the pope's foot.*

*The unmannerly nature of a dog presuming to kiss the pope's foot.*

Who entering there before the bishop, offered on the king's behalf to be defended,* that no man *Jure divino*,* could or ought to marry his brother's wife, and that the Bishop of Rome by no means ought to dispense to the contrary. Diverse promises were made, and sundry days appointed, wherein the question should have been disputed, and when our part was ready to answer, no man there appeared to dispute in that behalf.

*Arguing to the pope's face, that contrary to the word of God he had no power to dispense.*

So in the end the bishop, making to our ambassadors good countenance, and gratifying Doctor Cranmer with the office of the penitentiaryship,* dismissed them undisputed withal.

*Doctor Cranmer made the pope's Penitentiary.*

Whereupon the Earl of Wiltshire and other commissioners, saving Doctor Cranmer, returned home again into England. And forthwith Doctor Cranmer went to the Emperor* being in his journey towards Vienna, in expedition against the Turk, there to answer such learned men of the Emperor's council, as would or could say anything to the contrary part. Where amongst the rest, at the same time was Cornelius Agrippa,* an high officer in the Emperor's court, who having private conference with Doctor Cranmer in the question, was so fully resolved and satisfied in the matter, that afterwards there was never disputation openly offered to Doctor Cranmer in that behalf. For through the persuasion of Agrippa, all other learned men there were much discouraged: insomuch that after Doctor Cranmer was returned into England, Agrippa fell into such displeasure with the Emperor, as some men thought, that because of the hindering and discouraging so much the contrary part, he was committed to prison, where he for sorrow ended his life, as it was reported.* In the mean space while the Emperor returned home from Vienna through Germany, Doctor Cranmer in that voyage had conference with diverse learned men of Germany concerning the said question, who very ambiguously heretofore conceiving the cause, were fully resolved and satisfied by him.

*Doctor Cranmer ambassador to the Emperor. Conference between Bishop Cranmer and Cornelius Agrippa.*

This matter thus prospering on Doctor Cranmer's behalf, as well touching the king's question, as concerning the invalidity of the Bishop of Rome's authority, Bishop Warham* then Archbishop of Canterbury, departed this transitory life, whereby that dignity then being in the king's gift and disposition, was immediately given to Doctor Cranmer as worthy for his travail, of such a promotion. Thus much touching the preferment of Doctor Cranmer unto his dignity, and by what means he achieved unto the same: not by flattery, not by bribes, nor by none other unlawful means: which thing I have more at large discoursed, to stop the railing mouths of such, who being themselves obscure and unlearned, shame not so to detract a learned man most ignominiously with the

*Doctor Cranmer made Archbishop of Canterbury.*

surname of a hostler, whom for his godly zeal unto sincere religion, they ought with much humility to have had in regard and reputation. . . .

[*This narrative continues with a laudatory account of Cranmer's career, during which he retained the confidence of Henry and Edward VI. After falling from grace following the accession of Mary I, he was incarcerated at the Bocardo prison in Oxford and underwent examination for heresy at the University church of St Mary the Virgin. Following his degradation from archiepiscopal office, he recanted and then was made to attend his own funeral sermon prior to execution. When it was over, he delivered the address that follows.*]

'Every man (good people) desireth at that time of their death to give some good exhortation, that other may remember the same before their death, and be the better thereby: so I beseech God grant me grace, that I may speak something at this my departing, whereby God may be glorified, and you edified. *The last words of exhortation of the Archbishop to the people.*

'First, it is an heavy case to see that so many folk be so much doted upon the love of this false world, and so careful for it, that of the love of God, or the world to come, they seem to care very little or nothing. Therefore this shall be my first exhortation, that you set not your minds over much upon this glozing world, but upon God and upon the world to come: and to learn to know what this lesson meaneth, which Saint John teacheth, "that the love of this world is hatred against God."* *Exhortation to contempt of the world.*

'The second exhortation is, that next under God you obey your king and queen willingly and gladly, without murmuring or grudging: not for fear of them only, but much more for the fear of God: knowing that they be God's ministers, appointed by God to rule and govern you: and therefore whosoever resisteth them, resisteth the ordinance of God. *Exhortation to obedience.*

'The third exhortation is, that you love altogether like brethren and sisters. For alas, pity it is to see what contention and hatred one Christian man beareth to another, not taking each other as brother and sister, but rather as strangers and mortal enemies. But I pray you learn and bear well away this one lesson, *Exhortation to brotherly love.*

to do good unto all men, as much as in you lieth, and to hurt no man, no more than you would hurt your own natural loving brother or sister. For this you may be sure of, that whosoever hateth any person, and goeth about maliciously to hinder or hurt him, surely, and without all doubt God is not with that man, although he think himself never so much in God's favour.

*Exhortation to rich men of this world moving them to charitable alms. Luke 18. I John 3.* 'The fourth exhortation shall be to them that have great substance and riches of this world, that they will well consider and weigh three sayings of the scripture. One is of our saviour Christ himself, who sayeth: "It is hard for a rich man to enter into the kingdom of heaven."* A sore saying, and yet spoken of him that knoweth the truth.

'The second is of Saint John, whose saying is this: "He that hath the substance of this world, and seeth his brother in necessity, and shutteth up his mercy from him, how can he say that he loveth God?"*

'The third is of Saint James, who speaketh to the covetous rich man after this manner: "Weep you and howl for the misery that shall come upon you: your riches do rot, your clothes be moth eaten, your gold and silver doth canker and rust, and their rust shall bear witness against you, and consume you like fire: you gather a hoard or treasure of God's indignation against the last day."* Let them that be rich, ponder well these three sentences: for if they had occasion to show their charity, they have it now at this present, the poor people being so many, and victuals so dear.

'And now, for as much as I am come to the last end of my life, whereupon hangeth all my life past, and all my life to come, either to live with my master Christ forever in joy, or else to be in pain forever, with wicked devils in hell, and I see before mine eyes presently either heaven ready to receive me, or else hell ready to swallow me up: I shall therefore declare *The Archbishop declareth the true confession of his faith without all colour or dissembling.* unto you my very faith how I believe, without any colour* or dissimulation: for now is no time to dissemble, whatsoever I have said or written in time past.

'First, I believe in God the father almighty, maker of heaven and earth,* et cetera. And I believe every Article of the catholic faith,* every word and sentence taught by our saviour

Jesus Christ, his apostles and prophets, in the new and old Testament.

'And now I come to the great thing, that so much troubleth my conscience more than anything that ever I did or said in my whole life, and that is the setting abroad of a writing contrary to the truth: which now here I renounce and refuse as things written with my hand, contrary to the truth which I thought in my heart, and written for fear of death, and to save my life if it might be, and that is, all such bills and papers which I have written or signed with my hand since my degradation: wherein I have written many things untrue. And forasmuch as my hand offended, writing contrary to my heart, my hand shall first be punished therefore: for may I come to the fire, it shall be first burned.

'And as for the pope, I refuse him as Christ's enemy and Antichrist, with all his false doctrine.

'And as for the sacrament, I believe as I have taught in my book against the Bishop of Winchester,* the which my book teacheth so true a doctrine of the sacrament, that it shall stand at the last day before the judgement of God, where the papistical doctrine contrary thereto, shall be ashamed to show her face.'

Here the standers-by were all astonied, marvelled, were amazed, did look one upon another, whose expectation he had so notably deceived. Some began to admonish him of his recantation, and to accuse him of falsehood.

Briefly, it was a world to see the doctors beguiled of so great an hope. I think there was never cruelty more notably or better in time deluded and deceived. For it is not to be doubted but they looked for a glorious victory, and a perpetual triumph by this man's retractation.

Who as soon as they heard these things, began to let down their ears, to rage, fret, and fume: and so much the more, because they could not revenge their grief: for they could now no longer threaten or hurt him. For the most miserable man in the world can die but once: and whereas of necessity he must needs die that day, though the papists had been never so well pleased: now being never so much offended with him, yet could he not be twice killed of them. And so when they

*The Archbishop revoketh his former recantation and repenteth the same.*

*The Archbishop refuseth the pope as Christ's enemy and Antichrist.*

*The Archbishop standeth to his book written against Winchester.*

*The expectation of the papists deceived.*

*The papists in a great chafe against the Archbishop.*

could do nothing else unto him, yet lest they should say nothing, they ceased not to object unto him his falsehood and dissimulation.

*Cranmer's answer to the papists.*

Unto which accusation he answered: 'Ah my masters,' (quoth he), 'do not you take it so. Always since I lived hitherto, I have been a hater of falsehood, and a lover of simplicity, and never before this time have I dissembled': and in saying this, all the tears that remained in his body, appeared in his eyes. And when he began to speak more of the sacrament and of the papacy, some of them began to cry out, yelp, and bawl, and specially Cole cried out upon him: 'Stop the heretic's mouth, and take him away.'

*Cranmer pulled down from the stage.*

And then Cranmer being pulled down from the stage, was led to the fire, accompanied with those friars, vexing, troubling, and threatening him most cruelly. 'What madness,' (say they), 'hath brought thee again into this error, by which thou wilt draw innumerable souls with thee into hell?' To whom he answered nothing, but directed all his talk to the people, saving that to one troubling him in the way, he spake and exhorted him to get him home to his study, and apply his book diligently, saying if he did diligently call upon God, by reading more he should get knowledge.

*Cranmer led to the fire.*

But the other Spanish barker,* raging and foaming, was almost out of his wits, always having this in his mouth: . . . 'Diddest thou it not?'

But when he came to the place where the holy bishops and martyrs of God, Hugh Latimer and Ridley were burnt before him for the confession of the truth, kneeling down, he prayed to God, and not long tarrying in his prayers, putting off his garments to his shirt, he prepared himself to death. His shirt was made long down to his feet. His feet were bare. Likewise his head, when both his caps were off, was so bare, that one hair could not be seen upon it. His beard was long and thick, covering his face with marvellous gravity. Such a countenance of gravity moved the hearts both of his friends and of his enemies.

*The Archbishop brought to the place of execution.*

Then the Spanish friars John and Richard . . . began to exhort him and play their parts with him afresh, but with vain and lost labour, Cranmer with steadfast purpose abiding in the

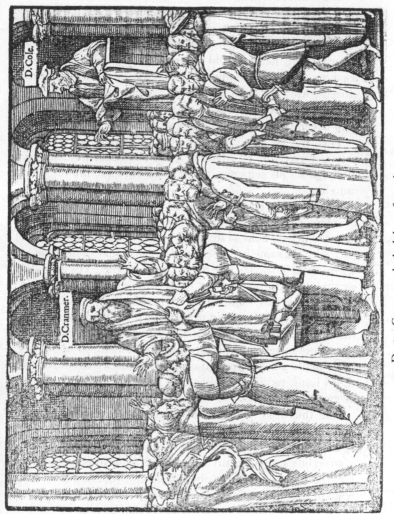

17. Doctor Cranmer, plucked down from the stage

profession of his doctrine, gave his hand to certain old men, and other that stood by, bidding them farewell.

And when he had thought to have done so likewise to Ely,* the said Ely drew back his hand and refused, saying: it was not lawful to salute heretics, and specially such a one as falsely *Master Ely* returned unto the opinions that he had forsworn. And if he had *refuseth to* known before that he would have done so, he would never have *give his hand* used his company so familiarly, and chid those sergeants and *to the* citizens, which had not refused to give him their hands. This *Archbishop.* Ely was a priest lately made, and student in divinity, being then one of the fellows of Brasenose [College].

*The* Then was an iron chain tied about Cranmer, whom when *Archbishop* they perceived to be more steadfast than that he could be *tied to the* moved from his sentence, they commanded the fire to be set *stake.* unto him.

And when the wood was kindled, and the fire began to burn near him, stretching out his arm, he put his right hand into the *Cranmer* flame: which he held so steadfast and immoveable (saving that *putteth his* once with the same hand he wiped his face) that all men might *right hand* see his hand burned before his body was touched. His body did *which* *subscribed first* so abide the burning of the flame with such constancy and *into the fire.* steadfastness, that standing always in one place without moving of his body, he seemed to move no more than the stake to which he was bound: his eyes were lifted up into heaven, and *The last words* oftentimes he repeated his unworthy right hand, so long as his *of Cranmer at* voice would suffer him: and using often the words of Steven, *his death.* 'Lord Jesus, receive my spirit,'* in the greatness of the flame, he gave up the ghost. . . .

And thus have you the full story concerning the life and death of this reverend Archbishop and martyr of God, Thomas *Archbishop* Cranmer, and also of diverse other the learned sort of Christ's *Cranmer the* martyrs burned in Queen Mary's time, of whom this Archbishop *middle martyr* was the last, being burnt about the very middle time of the *of all the* reign of that Queen, and almost the very middle man of all the *martyrs burnt* *in Queen* martyrs which were burned in all her reign besides. *Mary's time.*

Lord receiue my spirit

Frier Iohn.

18. Cranmer, in the town ditch at Oxford, with his hand first thrust into the fire

# 19. THE GUERNSEY MARTYRS

A tragical, lamentable, and pitiful history, full of
most cruel and tyrannical murder, done by the
pretenced Catholics, upon three women and an
infant: to wit, the mother, her two daughters, and the
child, in the Isle of Guernsey, for Christ's true
religion, the year of our Lord 1556. July 18.

Among all and singular histories touched in this book before, as
there be many pitiful, diverse lamentable, some horrible and
tragical: so is there none almost either in cruelty to be compared
or so far off from all compassion and sense of humanity, as this
merciless fact* of the papists, done in the Isle of Guernsey, upon
three women and an infant, whose names be these as follow.

*The martyrdom of three women with a young infant, burned in the Isle of Guernsey. July 18.*

{ Katherine Cawches, the mother. }
{ Guillemine Gilbert, the daughter. }
Perotine Massey, the other daughter.
An infant, the son of Perotine.

But before I come to the purpose of this story, it shall be
necessary, for the better explaining of the matter, to begin first
with the circumstances, whereupon the first original and occasion did rise of this tragical cruelty. The case was this.

*The first occasion of the trouble of these women.*

The twenty-seventh day of May, anno 1556, in the Isle of
Guernsey, which is a member* of England, in a town there called
Saint Peter's Port, was a naughty woman named Vincent Gosset,
who being evil disposed, went (the day aforesaid) to the house of
one Nicholas le Conronney, dwelling in the town of the said Saint
Peter's Port, about ten of the clock at night, and there taking the
key of the house (lying under the door) entered into a chamber
toward the street, where she espying a cup of silver within a cupboard, took it away, and so conveyed herself out of the house
again. Who immediately after this fact done (whether by counsel
or by what occasion else, I have not to say) brought the said cup
to one Perotine Massey, an honest woman, dwelling in the said
town, desiring her to lend her sixpence upon the same.

Perotine seeing the cup or goblet, and suspecting (as truth was) the same to be stolen, answered that she would not take it: yet nevertheless having knowledge of the owner thereof, took it, to restore it again to whom it did appertain, and to the end she should not carry it to another, gave her then presently sixpence. Where moreover is to be noted, that Thomas Effart saith and testifieth, that knowledge as given by the said Perotine to Conronney touching the stealing of his piece, who eftsoons upon the misliking thereof attached* the said Vincent Gosset, of the trespass. Who being apprehended and examined upon the same, immediately confessed the fact, desiring to have one sent with her (which was Collas de Loutre) with sixpence to fetch again the goblet, where it was: and so did.

The next day following, the king's officers being informed of the premises by one Nicholas Cary of the said town constable, assembled the justices there to inquire and examine further, as well upon that fact of Vincent Gosset, as upon other griefs and things there amiss. So that after declaration made by the officers and constable before the justice, for that the said constable did report to have found certain vessel of pewter in the house of the foresaid Perotine Massey (who then dwelt with her mother Katherine Cawches, and her sister Guillemine Gilbert) the which vessel did bear no mark, and especially for that there was a pewter dish, whereof the name was scraped out, their bodies upon the same were attached, and put in prison, and their moveable goods taken by inventory.* Within a few days after these things this done and past, these three silly women abiding thus in durance* in the castle, made their supplication to the justices to have justice ministered unto them, videlicet: If they had offended the law, then to let them have the law: if not, beseeching to grant them the benefit of subjects, et cetera. Which supplication put up, thereupon were they appointed to come to their answer the first day of June, in the year aforesaid. Upon which day, after straight examining of the matter, and the honest answering of the cause by the said good woman, at the last they submitted them to the report of their neighbours, that they were no thieves, nor evil disposed persons, but lived truly and honestly, as became Christian women to do, the false and untrue report of their accusers notwithstanding.

*Nicholas Cary constable, accuser.*

*Katherine with her two daughters, imprisoned in the castle.*

*Katherine with her two daughters, stand to the judgement of their neighbours.*

So the cause being thus debated, after the inquiry made by the king's officers, they were found by their said neighbours not guilty of that they were charged with, but had lived always as *The three* honest women among them: saving only that to the command- *women quit of* ments of holy church, they had not been obedient, et cetera. *theft and* *dishonesty.* Upon this trial, and verdict of the neighbours, it was in fine adjudged, first that the said Vincent Gosset, being attained of felony and condemned for the same should be whipped, and after her ear being nailed to the pillory, should so be banished out of *New trouble* the isle without further punishment. And as touching the other *against the* *three women,* three women, the mother with her two daughters, for their not *for not coming* coming to the church, they were returned prisoners again into the *to the church.* castle the first of July. And thus far concerning the true discourse of this matter, with all the circumstances and appurtenance of the same in every point as the case stood, according to the faithful tenor and testimony of the Guernsey men written with their own hands both in French and English tongue. Wherein you see what false surmised matter was pretended against these women, and nothing proved, and how by the attestation of their neighbours they were fully cleared of that fact, and should by the temporal court have been dismissed, had not the spiritual clergymen pick- ing matter of religion against them, exercised such extremity in persecuting these miserable prisoners, that in no case they could escape their bloody hands, till at length they had brought them (as you shall hear) to their final end. For after the time of this declaration above mentioned made by the neighbours, whereby they were purged of all other things, and being then known of their not coming to the church, the bailiff's lieutenant and the justice, thinking the matter not to pertain to them, but to the *Jacques Amy* clergy, forthwith wrote their letters or mandate under their signs *Dean of* to the dean,* whose name was Jacques Amy, and curates of the *Guernsey* *persecutor.* said isle: the contents whereof here followeth.

A letter sent from the bailiff's lieutenant, and jurats of Saint Peter's Port, to the dean and curates of the Isle of Guernsey.

*A letter of the* Master Dean and justices in your court and jurisdiction, after *bailiffs to the* *Dean of* all amiable recommendations, pleaseth you to know that we are *Guernsey.* informed by the deposition of certain honest men, past before us in manner of an inquiry: in the which inquiry Katherine Cawches and her two daughters have submitted themselves in a certain matter criminal. Wherein we be informed that they have been disobedient to the commandments, and ordinances of the church, in containing and forsaking the Mass and the ordinances of the same, against the will and commandment of our sovereign lord the king and the queen. Whereof we send you the said matter, for as much as the matter is spiritual, to the end you may proceed therein after your good discretions, and as briefly as you can possible, and also that it pertained to your office, recommending you to God, the which give you grace to do that pertaineth to right and justice. Written the first day of the month of July, the year of our Lord 1556.

After these letters, and information thus addressed to Jacques Amy dean, and to other of the clergy, the said women were again commenced before the justice aforesaid with his assistances. In the presence of whom they being examined of their faith, concerning the ordinances of the Romish church, made their answer that they would obey and keep the ordinances of the king and queen, and the commandments of the church, notwithstanding that they had said and done the contrary in the time of King Edward the sixth in showing obedience to his ordinances and commandments before. After which answer taken, they were returned again to prison, until the other had an answer of their letter from the dean and his complices.* During which time, the dean and curates gave their information touching the said women, and delivered the same to the bailiff and jurats,* condemning and reputing them for heretics, the women neither hearing of any information, neither yet being ever examined at any time before of their faith and religion. Whereupon when the said bailiff and jurats understood that the said dean and curates had not examined the women of their faith, would not sit in judgement on that day, but ordained the women to come first before the dean and curates to be examined of their faith. And so the officers at the commandment of the justices, did fetch and present them before the said dean and curates. The which being accomplished and done, they were examined apart severally one from another: after which examination they incontinently were returned again into prison.

*Rash information given, before the cause was heard.*

*Katherine Cawches, Perotine Massey, Guillemine Gilbert, examined before the dean and his fellows.*

*The names of the persecutors which sat upon\* the death of the three women.*

Then the fourteenth day of the said month of July, in the year aforesaid, after the examination above specified before Helier Gosselin bailiff, in the presence of Thomas Devicke, Pierres Martin, Nicholas Cary, John Blondel, Nicholas de Lisle, John Laverchaunt, John le Fever, Pierres Bonnamy, Nicholas Martin, John de la March jurates, Sir Jacques Amy dean, and the curates, did deliver before the justice under the seal of the dean, and under the signs of the curates, a certain act and sentence, the sum whereof was that Katherine Cawches and her two daughters were found heretics, and such they reputed them, and have delivered them to justice, to do execution, according to the sentence. . . .

When this was done, commandment was given to the king's officers, to go to the castle to fetch the said women, to hear the sentence against them in the presence aforesaid. And they appearing before them, said in the ears of all the auditory, that they would see their accusers, and know them that have deposed\* against them, because they might make answers to their sayings and personages and to have their libel accordingly: for they knew not to have offended the majesties of the king and queen, nor of the church, but entirely would obey, observe and keep the ordinances of the king and queen, and of the church, as all good and true subjects are bound to do. And for any breach of the

19. Three women, with the infant bursting from the mother's womb

king and queen's laws that they had done, they required justice. *The three women willing to be conformed to the queen's ordinances, were notwithstanding condemned.* All which their reasons and allegations notwithstanding, the said poor women were condemned, and adjudged to be burnt, until they were consumed into ashes, according to a sentence given by Helier Gosselin bailiff. . . .

After which sentence pronounced, the said women did appeal unto the king and the queen, and their honourable council, saying that against reason and right they were condemned, and for that cause they made their appeal: notwithstanding they could not be heard, but were delivered by the said bailiff, to the king and queen's officers, to see the execution done on them, according to the said sentence. *The mother and the two daughters made their appeal to the king and queen but could not be heard.*

The time then being come, when these three good servants and holy saints of God, the innocent mother with her two daughters should suffer, in the place where they should consummate their martyrdom, were three stakes set up. At the middle post was the mother, the eldest daughter on the right hand, the youngest on the other. They were first strangled, but the rope break before they were dead, and so the poor women fell in the fire. Perotine, who was then great with child, did fall on her side, where happened a rueful sight, not only to the eyes of all that there stood, but also to the ears of all true hearted Christians, that shall read this history: For as the belly of the woman burst asunder by vehemency of the flame, the infant being a fair man child, fell into the fire, and eftsoons being taken out of the fire by one William House, was laid upon the grass.

Then was the child had to the provost, and from him to the bailiff, who gave censure, that it should be carried back again and cast into the fire. And so the infant baptized in his own blood, to fill up the number of God's innocent saints, was both born, and died a martyr, leaving behind to the world, which it never saw, a spectacle wherein the whole world may see the Herodian cruelty* of this graceless generation of Catholic tormentors.

# 20. JOAN WASTE

## The martyrdom of Joan Waste, a blind woman in the town of Derby.

*August 1. Joan Waste a blind woman and martyr.*

The first day of August [1556] . . . suffered likewise at the town of Derby, a certain poor honest godly woman: being blind from her birth, and unmarried, about the age of twenty-two, named Joan Waste, of the parish of All Hallows. Of them that sat upon this innocent woman's blood, the chiefest was Ralph Bayne bishop of the diocese, Doctor Draycot his chancellor, Sir John Port knight; Henry Vernon esquire, Peter Finch official of Derby, with the assistance also of diverse other, Richard Ward, and William Bainbridge, the same time being bailiffs of the town of Derby, et cetera. First after the above-named bishop, and Doctor Draycot had caused the said Joan Waste to be apprehended in the town of Derby, suspecting her to be guilty of certain heresies, she was diverse times privily examined, as well in prison as out of prison: by Finch the official aforesaid: after that brought to public examination before the bishop, at last was there burnt in Derby. . . . Touching whose life, bringing up, and conversation, somewhat more amply we mind to discourse as by faithful relation hath come to my hands.

*The life and conversation of Joan Waste.*

First, this Joan Waste was the daughter of one William Waste, an honest poor man, and by his science a barber: who sometime also used to make ropes. His wife had the same Joan and one other at one birth, and she was born blind. And when she was about twelve or fourteen years old, she learned to knit hosen and sleeves, and other things, which in time she could do very well. Furthermore as time served she would help her father to turn ropes, and do such other things as she was able, and in no case would be idle. Thus continued she with her father and mother

*Joan Waste drawn by the spirit of God, to the love of religion.*

during their lives: after whose departure then kept she with one Roger Waste her brother, who in the time of King Edward the sixth of blessed memory, gave herself daily to go to the church to hear divine service read in the vulgar tongue. And thus by hearing homilies and sermons, she became marvellously well affected to the religion then taught. So at length having by her labour gotten and saved so much money as would buy her a New Testament, she caused one to be provided for her. And though she was of herself unlearned and by reason of her blindness unable to read, yet for the great desire she had to understand and have printed in her memory the sayings of holy scriptures contained in the New Testament, she acquainted herself chiefly with one John Hurt, then prisoner in the Common Hall of Derby, for debts.

The same John Hurt being a sober grave man of the age of three score and ten years, by her earnest entreaty, and being prisoner, and many times idle and without company, did for his exercise daily read unto her some one chapter of the New Testament. And if at any time he were otherwise occupied or letted through sickness: she would repair unto one John Pemerton clerk of the parish church of All Saints in the same town of Derby, or to some other person which could read, and sometimes she would give a penny or two (as she might spare) to such persons as would not freely read unto her, appointing unto them afore hand how many chapters of the New Testament they should read, or how often they should repeat one chapter upon a price.*

*The earnest desire of Joan Waste to learn the scriptures.*

*John Hurt and John Pemerton readers to Joan Waste.*

Moreover in the said Joan Waste, this was notorious* that she being utterly blind, could notwithstanding without a guide, go to any church within the said town of Derby, or to any other place or person, with whom she had any such exercise. By which exercise she so profited, that she was able not only to recite many chapters of the New Testament without book, but also could aptly impugn, by diverse places of scriptures, as well sin, as such abuses in religion, as then were too much in use, in diverse and sundry persons.

*A notable gift of God in a blind woman.*

*Joan Waste both blind and unlearned, yet was perfect in the scriptures.*

As this godly woman thus daily increased in the knowledge of God's holy word and no less in her life expressed the virtuous fruits and exercise of the same: not long after, through the fatal death of blessed King Edward followed the woeful ruin of religion, in the reign of Queen Mary his sister. In which alteration, notwithstanding the general backsliding of the greatest part and multitude of the whole realm into the old papism again, yet this poor blind woman continuing in a constant conscience, proceeded still in her former exercise, both being zealous in that she had learned, and also refusing to communicate in religion with those which taught contrary doctrine to that she before had learned in King Edward's time. . . .

For the which she was called and convented before the foresaid bishop and Doctor Draycot, with diverse other called in to bear witness. . . .

*The answer of Joan Waste to the articles.*

Whereunto she answered, that she believed therein so much as the holy scriptures taught her, and according to that she had heard preached unto her by diverse learned men whereof some suffered imprisonment, and other some suffered death for the same doctrine. Amongst whom she named, beside other, Doctor Taylor, whom she said took it of his conscience, that that doctrine which he taught was true, and asked of them, if they would do so in like case for their doctrine, which if they would not, she desired them for God's sake not to trouble her being a blind, poor, and unlearned woman, with any further talk, saying (by God's assistance) that she was ready to yield up her life in that faith, in such sort as they should appoint.

And yet notwithstanding being pressed by the said bishop and Doctor Draycot, with many arguments of Christ's omnipotency, as, why was not Christ able as well to make the bread his body, as to turn water into wine,* raise Lazarus from

*Well argued: Because Christ is omnipotent. Ergo, there is no bread in the sacrament.*

death,* and such other like arguments: and many times being threatened with grievous imprisonments, torments, and death. The poor woman thus being, as it were, half astonied through their terrors and threats, and desirous (as it seemed) to prolong her life, offered unto the bishop then present, that if he would before that company, take it upon his conscience, that the doctrine which he would have her to believe concerning the sacrament, was true, and that he would at the dreadful day of judgement answer for her therein (as the said Doctor Taylor,

*The offer of Joan Waste to the bishop, if he would take upon his conscience, to answer before God for his doctrine.*

in diverse of his sermons did offer) she would then further answer them.

Whereunto the bishop answered, he would. But Doctor Draycot his chancellor, hearing that, said: 'My Lord, you know not what you do, you may in no case answer for an heretic.' And immediately he asked the poor woman whether she would recant or no, and said she should answer for herself. Unto whose sayings the bishop also reformed himself.

The poor woman perceiving this, answered again that if they refused to take of their conscience that it was true they would have her to believe, she would answer no further, but desired them to do their pleasure, and so after certain circumstances, they pronounced sentence against her, and delivered her unto the bailiffs of the said town of Derby aforenamed. Who after they had kept her about a month or five weeks, at length there came unto them a writ *De haeretico comburendo*:* by virtue whereof they were appointed by the said bishop to bring her to the parish church of All Saints at a day appointed where Doctor Draycot should make a sermon.

When the day and time was come that this innocent martyr should suffer, first cometh to the church Doctor Draycot accompanied with diverse gentlemen, as Master Thomas Powthread, Master Henry Vernon, Master Dethick of Newhall, and diverse others. This done, and all things now in a readiness, at last the poor blind creature and servant of God was brought and set before the pulpit, where the said Doctor being entered into his sermon, and there inveighing against diverse matters, which he called heresies, declared unto the people that that woman was condemned for denying the blessed sacrament of the altar to be the very body and blood of Christ really and substantially, and was thereby cut off from the body of the Catholic church and said, that she was not only blind of her bodily eyes but also blind in the eyes of her soul. And he said, that as her body should be presently consumed with material fire: so her soul should be burned in hell with everlasting fire, as soon as it should be separated from the body, and there to remain world without end, and said it was not lawful for the people to pray for her: and so with many terrible threats he made an end of his sermon, and commanded the bailiffs and those gentlemen to see her executed. And the sermon thus ended, eftsoons the blessed servant of God was carried away from the said church, to a place called the windmill pit, near unto the said town, and holding the foresaid Roger Waste her brother by the hand she prepared herself, and desired the people to pray with her, and said such prayers as she before

*Note here the difference between the conscience of the Protestant, and of the Papist. The bishop and his chancellor durst not take upon their conscience, to answer before God for their doctrine.*

*Sentence pronounced against Joan Waste.*

*The writ brought down for the burning of Joan Waste.*

*Doctor Draycot appointed to preach at the burning of Joan Waste.*

*Doctor Draycot's railing sermon against Joan Waste.*

*Blessed are you when men shall revile you, and say all evil against you, for my name's sake. Matthew 5.*

*Joan Waste brought to the place of execution.*

had learned, and cried upon Christ to have mercy upon her as
long as life served. In this mean season, the said Doctor
Draycot went to his inn, for great sorrow of her death, and
there laid him down, and slept during all the time of her execution and thus much of Joan Waste.

*The*
*martyrdom of*
*Joan Waste.*

# 21. WILLIAM DANGERFIELD

A pitiful story concerning the unmerciful handling of
William Dangerfield, and Joan his wife being in
childbed, taken out of her house, with her sucking
infant of fourteen days old, and laid in the common
jail amongst thieves and murderers.

When I had written and finished the story of the Guernsey *The cruel*
women, with the young infant there with them burned, and also *handling of*
had passed the burning of the poor blind woman Joan Waste at *Dangerfield*
Derby,* I well hoped I should have found no more such stories *and Joan his*
of unmerciful cruelty showed upon silly women with their chil- *wife in prison.*
dren and young infants: but now coming to the persecution of
Gloucestershire about the parts of Bristol, I find another story of
such unmercifulness showed against a woman in childbed, as far
from all charity and humanity, as hath been any other story yet
hitherto rehearsed, as by the sequel hereof may appear.

In the parish of Wotton-under-Edge, not far from Bristol,
was dwelling one William Dangerfield a right honest and godly
poor man, who by Joan Dangerfield his wife had nine children,
and she now lying in childbed of the tenth. This William, after
he had been abroad from his house a certain space, for fear of
persecution, hearing that his wife was brought to bed, repaired*
home to visit her, as natural duty required, and to see his children, she being now delivered four days before.

The return of this man was not so soon known to some of his
unkind and uncharitable neighbours, but they incensed with the
spirit of papistry, eftsoons beset the house about, and there took *No charity in*
the said William Dangerfield, and carried him to prison, and so *popery to be*
at length he was brought to the bishop, being then Doctor *noted.*
Brooks:* in whose cruel handling he remained a certain space, so *William*
long till his legs almost were fretted off* with irons. *Dangerfield*

After the apprehension, of the husband, the wife likewise was *apprehended*
taken, with her young born child, being but fourteen days old *in his own*
(as is said) out of her childbed, and carried into the common *house.*

Joan the wife
of William
Dangerfield
taken with her
young infant
out of
childbed, and
had to prison.
jail, and there placed amongst thieves and murderers, where both she and her poor innocent found so small charity amongst the Catholic men, that she never could come to any fire, but was driven to warm the clothes that she should put about the child, in her bosom.

In the mean season while they lay thus enclosed in several prisons, the husband and the wife, the bishop beginneth to practise not with the woman first, as the serpent did with Eve,* but with the man, craftily deceiving his simplicity, with fair glozing words, falsely persuading him that his wife had recanted, and asking him, wherefore he should more stand in his own conceit, than she being as well learned as he, and so subtly drew out a form of recantation, wherewith he deceived the simple soul. Whereunto after that he had once granted that he would consent, although he had not yet recanted, they suffered him to go to his wife, where she lay in the common jail.

Dangerfield
made to
believe falsely,
that his wife
had recanted.

Dangerfield
upon hope of
his wife's
recantation,
consented to
the bishop.

Then they with melting hearts opening their minds one to another, when he saw his wife not released, and perceiving that he had not done well, he declared unto her the whole matter, how falsely he was circumvented by the subtle flatterings of the bishop, bearing him in hand that certainly she had recanted: 'And thus deceiving me,' (said he), 'brought this unto me,' and so plucked out of his bosom the copy of the recantation, whereunto he had granted his promise. At the sight whereof the wife hearing what her husband had done, her heart clave asunder, saying: 'Alack, thus long have we continued one, and hath Satan so prevailed, to cause you to break your first vow made to Christ in baptism?'* And so departed the said William and Joan his wife, with what hearts the Lord knoweth. Then began he not a little to bewail his promise made to the bishop, and to make his prayer to almighty God, desiring him that he might not live so long as to call evil good, and good evil: or light darkness, or darkness light, and so departed he home toward his house: where by the way homeward (as it is affirmed) he took his death and shortly after departed according to his prayer, after he had endured in prison twelve weeks.

The wife
lamented the
fall of her
husband.

Dangerfield
lamenteth his
promise made
to the bishop.
The prayer of
Dangerfield to
God.

The death of
the husband.

After this, Joan his wife continued still in prison with her tender infant, till at last she was brought before that bishop to be examined. Whereunto what her answers were, it is not certainly known. Howbeit most like it is whatsoever they were, they pleased not the bishop, as appeared by his ire increased against the poor woman and her long continuance in the prison, together with her tender babe, which also remained with her in the jail, partaker of her martyrdom, so long as her milk would serve to give it suck, till at length the child being starved for cold and famine, was sent away when it was past all remedy, and so shortly after died. And not long after the mother also followed, besides the old woman, which was mother of the husband, of the age of eighty years and upward. Who being left in the house after their apprehension for lack of comfort there perished also.

*The young infant famished in prison.*

*The martyrdom of the mother.*

And thus have ye in one story the death of four together: first of the old woman, then of the husband, after that of the innocent child, and lastly of the mother. What became of the other nine children, I am not perfectly sure, but that I partly understand, that they were all undone by the same.

*The death of the old woman.*

This story is reported and testified as well by other as namely by Mistress Bridges, dwelling in the same town, and partaker then of the like afflictions, and hardly escaped with her life.

*Mistress Bridges persecuted the same time for God's word, and witness of this story.*

# 22. RICHARD WOODMAN

The history of ten true godly disciples, and martyrs
of Christ, burnt together in one fire at Lewes.
Anno. 1557. June 22.

*June 22.* In the town of Lewes were ten faithful servants of God put in one fire, the twenty-second day of June. . . . Of the which number Richard Woodman was the first. Concerning whose apprehension first by his enemies, and of his deliverance out of Bishop Bonner's hands, then of his second taking again by the procurement of his father, brother, kinsfolks and friends, also of his sundry examinations and courageous answers before the bishops, and lastly of his condemnation, and of his letters sent to his faithful friends, here followeth to be declared by his own *The life and* words, and relation reported. Which Richard Woodman, by *story of* his occupation was an ironmaker,* dwelling in the parish of *Richard* Warbleton, in the county of Sussex, and diocese of Chichester, *Woodman.* of the age of thirty years, and somewhat more. The occasion of his first apprehension was this.

*Fairbank* There was one Fairbank, who sometimes had been a married *preaching* priest, and served the cure of Warbleton, where he had often *contrary to* persuaded the people not to credit any other doctrine, but *himself.* that which he then preached, taught, and set forth in King Edward's days. And afterward in the beginning of Queen Mary's reign, the said Fairbank turning head to tail,* preached clean contrary to that which he had before taught.

Whereupon Richard Woodman hearing him in the church of Warbleton so to preach contrary to himself, admonished him of his inconstancy, how before time he had taught them one thing, and now another, and desired him to teach them the *Justices of* truth. For the which words he was apprehended* and brought *Sussex* before Master John Ashbornham, Master Toston, Master *troublers of* Culpepper, and Master Roberts, Justices of Peace in the county *Richard* of Sussex, and by them committed to the King's Bench, where *Woodman,* he continued from June, the space almost of a year and a half: *and what were* and from thence was transferred by Doctor Story* into Bonner's *their names.*

coal house, where he remained the space of a month before he came to examination.

At length, the same day when Master Philpot was burned, which was the eighteenth of December, he with four other prisoners was delivered and set at liberty by Bonner himself. Notwithstanding, shortly after he was sought for again, and at last found out and taken by means of his father, brother, and certain other his acquainted friends, and so was sent up again to London to Bishop Bonner, where he remained in the coal house eight weeks. He was there six times examined, and twenty-six times before, so that his examinations in all were thirty-two from his first apprehension, to his condemnation. Touching the whole discourse whereof, for so much as the matter is something strange, and will peradventure scarce find credit upon my narration, with them which deny all things, that like them not to believe, ye shall hear himself speak, and testify both of the manner of his troubles, and also his own examinations by himself recorded, in order as followeth.

Richard Woodman delivered out of his first trouble.

Richard Woodman again apprehended, and by whose means.

Thirty-two examinations of Richard Woodman.

A true certificate written by Richard Woodman, of his taking, and how he was brought to the sheriffs the twenty-fifth of March, 1556, and how long he was in prison, and how he was there used, till he was brought before the Bishop of Chichester at Blackfriars in London, with the order of his examinations following after the same.

Gentle reader, here you shall perceive how the scriptures be partly fulfilled on me, being one of the least of his poor lambs. First, you shall understand that since I was delivered out of the Bishop of London's hands, which was in the year of our Lord, 1555, and the same day that Master Philpot was burned, (which was the eighteenth of December) I lay in his coal house eight weeks lacking but one day. And before that, I was a year and a half almost, in the King's Bench after my first apprehension, for reproving a preacher in the pulpit, in the parish of Warbleton where I dwelt. Wherefore I was at two sessions before I was sent to prison, and carried to two more sessions while I was in prison, twice before the Bishop of Chichester, and five times before the commissioners, and then sent to

The certificate of Richard Woodman concerning the truth of his own story and troubles.

The first apprehension of Richard Woodman.

London's coal house, and many times called before him, as it appeareth by my examinations which I wrote, the which examinations, the Bishop of Chichester now hath, for they were found in my house when I was taken, wherein is contained all the talk, which I had before them aforenamed. Also there be in London [those] that had copies of the same of me, when I was in the coal house.

*Richard Woodman delivered out of Bonner's hands, with four more. What the Bishop required at their deliverance.*

And it pleased God to deliver me, with four or more, out of the butcher's hands, requiring nothing else of us but that we should be honest men, and members of the true Catholic Church that was builded upon the prophets and apostles, Christ being the head of the true Church, the which all we affirmed that we were members of the true Church, and purposed by God's help therein to die. And hereupon we were delivered, but he willed us many times to speak good of him.

*Bishop Bonner bloodthirsty.*

And no doubt he was worthy to be praised, because he had been so faithful an aid in his master the devil's business. For he had burnt good Master Philpot the same morning, in whose blood his heart was so drunken (as I supposed) that he could not tell what he did, as it appeared to us, both before and after. For but two days before he promised us that we should be condemned that same day that we were delivered: yea and the morrow after that he had delivered us, he sought for some of us again, yea and that earnestly. He waxed dry after his great drunkenness, wherefore he is like to have blood to drink in hell as he is worthy, if he repent it not with speed. The Lord turn all their hearts if it be his will.

*Woodman purgeth himself of false slander.*

This have I written, chiefly to certify all people how we were delivered, because many carnal gospellers* and papists have said, that it was prescribed that we should be so delivered, because they think that God is subject to man, and not man to God. For if they did, they would not blaspheme him as they do, or if they thought they should give account for it. Have not many of them read, how God delivered Israel out of Egypt? Daniel out of the Lion's Den? Shadrach, Meshach, and Abednago out of the burning oven?* With diverse other such like examples, yea, God is the same God that he was then. He is no older, nor less in power, as some count him in wondering at his works. Now to the matter.

After I was delivered, the papists said that I had consented to them, whereof they made themselves glad: the which was the least part of my thought (I praise God therefore) as they well perceived, and knew the contrary within a while. For I went from parish to parish, and talked with them, to the number of thirteen or fourteen, and that of the chiefest in all the country: and I angered them so, that they with the commissioners complained on me to my Lord Chamberlain that was then to the queen, Sir John Gage showing him that I baptized children, and married folks, with many such lies, to bring me into their hands again. Then the commissioners sent out certain citations to bring me to the court. My Lord Chamberlain had directed out four or five warrants for me, that if I had come there, I should have been attached and sent to prison straightway. Which was not God's will: for I had warning of their laying await for me, and came not there, but sent my deputy, and he brought me word that the bailiffs waited for me there, but they missed of their prey for that time, whereupon they were displeased.

Then, within three days after, my Lord sent three of his men to take me, whose names were Dean, Jeffrey, and Francis. I being at plough with my folks, right in the way as they were coming to my house, least mistrusting them of all other, came to them and spake to them, asking them how they did. And they said, they arrested me in the king* and queen's name, and that I must go with them to their master the Lord Chamberlain. Which words made my flesh to tremble and quake because of that sudden. But I answered them that I would go with them. Yet I desired them that they would go to my house with me, that I might break my fast, and put on some other gear, and they said I should. Then I remembered myself, saying in my heart: 'Why am I thus afraid? They can lay no evil to my charge. If they kill me for well doing, I may think myself happy.' I remembered how I was contented gladly before to die in that quarrel, and so had continued ever since: and should I now fear to die? God forbid that I should, for then were all my labour in vain.

So by and by I was persuaded, I praise God, considering it was but the frailty of my flesh, which was loath to forgo my

*Marginal notes:*

*False surmises against Richard Woodman.*

*Woodman complained of to Sir John Gage Lord Chamberlain.*

*Warrants sent out to attach Woodman.*

*Lord Chamberlain sendeth to take Woodman at his plough.*

*Woodman arrested.*

*Fear coming upon Woodman at his first taking.*

*Woodman comforted in his spirit after his fear.*

wife and children and goods: for I saw nothing but present death before mine eyes. And as soon as I was persuaded in my mind to die, I had no regard of nothing in this world, but was as merry and glad and joyful, I praise God, as ever I was. This battle* lasted not a quarter of an hour, but it was sharper than death itself for the time, I dare say.

*Woodman asketh for their warrant.*

So when I had my breakfast, I desired them to show me their warrant, thinking thereby I should have seen wherefore I was arrested, to the intent I might the better answer for myself when I came before their master. And one of them answered, they had not their warrant there. Which words made me astonied,

*How God worketh for his servants.*

and it was put in my mind by God, that I need not to go with them, unless they had their warrant. . . .

*God's great work, how the persecutors which came to take Woodman, went away without him.*

When I saw that, I knew it was God's doing to set me at liberty once again. Yet I was compelled to speak to them, and said: 'If you have a warrant, I desire you for God's sake to show it me, and I will go with you, with all my heart: if not, I desire you to depart in God's peace and the king's: for surely I will not go with you without the order of the law: for I have been too simple in such things already. For before I was sent to prison first, I went to the justices to two sessions, without any warrant or commandment, but had word by one of their men, and I went gently to them, and they sent me to prison, and kept me there almost a year and three quarters, without all right or equity, as it is openly known, not hearing my cause justly debated. And it seemeth to me that I should be thus evil handled, and therefore I will not go to none of them all henceforth without the extremity of the law.'

Then one of them answered me, and said: 'We have not the warrant here, but it is at home at my house: the worst is you can but make us fetch it.' Then I said: 'Fetch it, if you will, but if you come in my house before you have it, at your own adventure.' So I shut my door, and went my way out of the other

*Woodman escapeth the hands of his takers. Woodman's house again searched for him.*

door. So they got help to watch my house, while one of them set the constable and many more, thinking to have had me in my house, and to have taken me in my house, and carried me away with a licence: but I was gone before as God would have it. Notwithstanding they sought every corner of my house, but could not prevail. I mistrusted they would search it again that night, and kept me abroad, and indeed there came seven of his men and the constable, and searched my house.

And when they saw that they could not meet with me, they were ready to rent their coats, that I had escaped them so, knowing they should have such a check of their master. When I heard that they had sought so for me again, I perceiving that they were greedy of their prey, came home, and my wife told me all things.

Then I supposed that they would lay all the country for me, and the sea coast, because I should not go over, and then I thought that they would not mistrust that I would dare be nigh home. So I told my wife that I would make my lodging in a wood not past a flight shot* from my house, as I did indeed, even under a tree, and there had my Bible, my pen and mine ink, and other necessaries, and there continued a six or seven weeks, my wife bringing me meat daily as I had need. Yea I thought myself blessed of God, that I was counted worthy to lie in the woods for the name of Christ. Then there came word into the country, that I was seen and spoken to in Flanders: whereupon they left laying await for me for they had laid all the country for me, and the sea coast from Portsmouth to Dover, even as God put in my mind they would.

*Woodman lodged six weeks in a wood.*

*All the country and sea coasts laid for Woodman.*

So when all was hushed, I went abroad among our friends and brethren, and at length I went beyond the sea both into Flanders and in France: but I thought every day seven year or ever I were at home again. So I came home again as soon as it was possible. I was there but three weeks, but as soon as I was come home, and it once known among Baal's priests,* they could not abide it, but procured out warrants against me, causing my house to be searched sometimes twice in a week. This continued from Saint James tide to the first Sunday in Lent. Otherwhile I went privily, otherwhile openly, otherwhile I went from home a fortnight or three weeks, otherwhile I was at home a month or five weeks together, living there most commonly and openly, doing such works as I had to do: and yet all mine enemies could lay no hands on me, till the hour was full come:* and then by the voice of the country, and by manifest proofs, mine own brother as concerning the flesh, delivered me into their hands, by that he knew that I was at home.

*Woodman delivered by his own brother into his enemies' hands.*

For my father and he had as much of my goods in their hands, as I might have fifty-six pound for by the year clear, and

'Auri sacra fames quid non mortalia cogis pectora?' Virgil.*

thereunto preyed.* It was a lordship and an honour, to pay my debts, and the rest to remain to my wife and children. But they had reported that it would not pay my debts: which grieved me sore. For it was two hundred pounds better than the debts came to. Which caused me to speak to some of my friends, that they would speak to them to come to some reckoning with me, and to take all such money again of me, as they were charged with, and to deliver me such writings and writs, as they had of mine, again, or to whom I would appoint them.

So it was agreed betwixt my father and me, that I should have it again, and the day was appointed, that the reckoning should be made and sent to me that same day that I was taken, my brother supposing that I should have put him out of most of all his occupying, that he was in: for it was all mine in a manner that he occupied, as all the country can and do well know. Whereon (as it is reported) he told one Gradillar my next neighbour, and he told some of Master Gage's men, or to Master Gage himself: and so he sent to his brother, and his brother sent twelve of his men (he being sheriff) in the night before I was taken, and lay in the bushes not far from my

Brother betrayeth the brother.

house, till about nine of the clock, even the hour that was appointed amongest themselves: for about the same time they thought to have had me within my house. . . .

Woodman put to his shifts.

So there was a place in my house that was never found which was at the least, I dare say twenty times, and sometimes almost of twenty men searched at once, both by night and by day. Into which place I went: and as soon as I was in, my

The part of a trusty wife to her husband.

wife opened the door: whereby incontinent they came, and asked for me: and she said I was not at home. Then they asked her wherefore she shut the door, if I were not at home. She said, because she had been made afraid diverse times, with such as came to search us, and therefore she shut the door. 'For it is reported' (saith she) 'that whosoever can take my husband, shall hang him or burn him straightway: and therefore I doubt they will serve me or my children so: for I think they may do so unto us as well as to him,' she said. 'Well,' said they, 'we know he is in the house, and we must search it, for we be the sheriff's men: let us have a candle. It is told us, there be many secret places in your house.' So she lighted a candle, and they sought up and down in every corner that they could find, and had given over, and many of them were gone out of my house into the churchyard, and were talking with my father, and with some that he had brought with him.

Now when they could not find me, one of them went to him that gave them word that I was at home, and said, 'We cannot find him.' Then he asked them whether they had sought over a window that was in the hall (as it was known afterward) for that same place I had told him of myself. For many times when I came home, I would send for him to bear me company: yet as it chanced I had not told him the way into it. Then they began to search anew. One looked up over the window, and spied a little loft, with three or four chests, and the way went in betwixt two of the chests, but there could no man perceive it. Then he asked my wife which was the way into it. 'Here is a place that we have not sought yet.' Then she thought they would see it by one means or other. She said, the way was into it out of a chamber they were in even now. So she sent them up, and cried, 'Away, away.' Then I knew there was no remedy, but make the best shift* for myself that I could. The place was boarded over and fast nailed, and if I had come out that way that I went in, I must needs come amongst them all in the hall. Then I had no shift but set my shoulders to the boards that were nailed to the rafters to keep out the rain, and break them in pieces, which made a great noise, and they that were in the other chamber, seeking for the way into it, heard the noise, and looked out of a window, and spied me, and made an outcry. But yet I got out, and leaped down, having no shoes on.

So I took down a lane that was full of sharp cinders, and they came running after, with a great cry, with their swords drawn, crying, 'Strike him, strike him.' Which words made me look back, and there was never a one nigh me by a hundred foot: and that was but one, for all the rest were a great way behind. And I turned about hastily to go my way, and stepped upon a sharp cinder with one foot, and saving of* it, I stepped in a great miry hole, and fell down withal, and ere ever I could arise and get away, he was come in with me. His name is Parker the Wild,

*This belike was his brother.*

*Woodman at length after long seeking found out.*

*Parker in Sussex a bloody persecutor of Woodman.*

as he is counted in all Sussex. But if I had had on my shoes, they had been like to have gone away errandless,* if there had been five hundred more, if I had caught the plain ground once, to the which I had not a stone's cast: but it was not God's will: for if it had, I should have scaped from them all, if there had been ten thousand of them.

*Woodman taken of his enemies. John Fauconer a blasphemous persecutor.*

Then they took me and led me home again to put on my shoes and such gear as I had need of. Then said John Fauconer: 'Now your master hath deceived you. You said, you were an angel, and if you had been an angel, why did you not flee away from us?' Then said I, 'What be they that ever heard me say that I was an angel? It is not the first lie by a thousand that they have made of me. Angels were never begotten of men, nor born of women: but if they had said, that they had heard me say, that I do trust I am a saint, they had not said amiss.' 'What, do you think to be a saint?' 'Yea that I do, and am already in God's

*Every true Christian man is a saint in God's sight.*

sight, I trust in God: for he that is not a saint in God's sight already, is a devil. Therefore he that thinketh scorn to be a saint, let him be a devil.' And with that word they had brought me to mine own door: where met with me my father, and willed me to remember myself.

To whom I answered: 'I praise God, I am well remembered whereabout I go. This way was appointed of God for me to be delivered into the hands of mine enemies, but woe unto him by whom I am betrayed. It had been good for that man, that he had never been born,* if he repent not with speed. The scriptures are now fulfilled on me: "For the father shall be against the son, and the brother shall deliver the brother to death,"* as

*Woodman betrayed either by his own father or by his own brother.*

it is this day come to pass.' Then said one: 'He doth accuse his father: a good child indeed.' 'I accuse him not, but say my mind: for there was no man knew me at home, but my father, my brother, and one more, the which I dare say, would not hurt me for all the good in this town.'

*George Beching brother-in-law to Woodman.*

There was one George Beching that married one of my sisters, and he thought that I had meant him, that he had betrayed me: and he said: 'Brother, I would you should not think that I was the cause of your taking.' To whom I answered, that I meant him not: I meant one that was nearer of my blood than he was. Then said one of Lewes, that had been a gospeller, and stood from them, when I was brought to a sessions to Lewes, and he said, 'I thought you would have been an honest man when you were at Lewes, and I offered Hussey the sheriff to be bound for you, that you should go home to your wife, and come to him again.' Then I remembered what he was, and said: 'Be you the pewterer?' And he said, 'Yea.' Then said I: 'It is happened to you according to the true proverb, as sayeth Saint Peter: "The dog is turned to his vomit again, and the sow that is washed, to wallow in the mire,"* and the end of all such will be worse than the beginning.' Then his mouth was stopped so, that he had nothing to say.

*A pewterer of Lewes, a turncoat.*

All this while I stood at my door without: for they would not let me go in. So I put on my shoes and my clothes, and then they put on a harness about mine arms made of a dog's slip,* which rejoiced my heart, that I was counted worthy to be bound for the name of God. So I took my leave of my wife and children, my father and other of my friends, never thinking to see them more in this world. For it was so thought of all the country, that I should not live six days after my taking: for they had so reported. But yet I knew it was not as they would, unless God would grant it. I know what God can do: but what he will do, I know not: but I am sure he will work all things for the best, for them that love and fear him.* So we drank and went our way, and came to Firle about three of the clock. And thus much touching the causes and effect of the troubles of Richard Woodman. . . .

*Woodman rejoiceth to be bound for the name of Christ.*

*Woodman taketh his leave of his wife and children.*

After these examinations thus had and commenced between Richard Woodman and the bishops, he was (as is afore told) judged by sentence of condemnation, and so deprived of his life: with whom also was burned nine other, to wit, five men and four women, which were taken not past two or three days before their judgement. The names of all which being also before expressed, here again follow in this order. Richard Woodman, George Stevens, William Maynard, Alexander Hosman his servant, Thomasin a Wood his maid, Margery Morris, James Morris her son, Dennis Burgis, Ashdown's wife, Grove's wife.

*The name of this place so far as we could gather by the copy was Firle.*

These persons here above named, and blessed martyrs, were put to death at Lewes, the twenty-second of June.

# 23. ROSE ALLIN AND OTHER COLCHESTER MARTYRS

*August 2. The martyrdom of ten godly martyrs, five men and five women, at Colchester.*

As it is no new thing in those whom we call prelates and priests of the church,* to be raisers up of persecution against Christ and his poor flock: so is it much to be marvelled or rather lamented, that noble persons, and men of honour, and worship, would be made such ministers to serve the affections of these tyrants, as commonly, as well in all the sorrowful days of the late Queen Mary, as namely in this present story is to be marked.

And first thou remembrest (gentle reader) how mention was made a little before . . . of twenty-two which were sent up prisoners together from Colchester to London by the Earl of Oxford, the Lord Darcy, Master Tyrrell of Saint Osyth's, and other commissioners and justices, et cetera. The which twenty-two (as is aforesaid) through a gentle submission put unto them, were afterward released and delivered.

In the number of these foresaid twenty-two was one William Munt of Muchbently in Essex, husbandman, with Alice his wife, and Rose Allin maid, the daughter of the said Alice Munt: which coming home again to their house at Muchbently

*William Munt, Alice his wife, Rose Allin her daughter.*

aforesaid, refrained themselves from the unsavoury service of the popish church, and frequented the company of good men and women which gave themselves diligently to reading, invocating, and calling upon the name of God through Christ: whereby they so fretted the wicked priest of the town called Sir

*Thomas Tye priest, a wicked promoter.*

Thomas Tye . . . [petitioned Lord Darcy for redress and] wrote secretly a letter to Edmund Bonner Bishop of London, wherein he maketh his account how he had bestowed his time, and complained of diverse honest men, among the which was the said William Munt and his company. The tenor of which letter hereafter followeth.

## A letter sent to Bonner Bishop of London, from Sir Thomas Tye Priest.

Right honourable Lord, after my bounden duty done in most humble wise, these shall be to signify unto your Lordship the state of our parties concerning religion. And first since the coming down, of the twenty-four rank heretics dismissed from you, the detestable sort of schismatics were never so bold since the king and queen's majesty's reigns, as they are now at this present. In Muchbently where your Lordship is Patron of the church, since William Munt, and Alice his wife, with Rose Allin her daughter came home, they do not only absent themselves from the church, and service of God but do daily allure many other away from the same, which before did outwardly show signs and tokens of obedience.

They assemble together upon the Sabbath day in the time of divine service, sometimes in one house, sometime in another, and there keep their privy conventicles and schools of heresy. The jurates saith, the Lord's Commission is out, and they are discharged of their oath. The quest men in your Archdeacon's visitation alleged that for as much as they were once presented and now sent home they have no more to do with them nor none other. Your officers saith, namely Master Boswell, that the council sent them not home without a great consideration. I pray God some of your officers prove not favourers of heretics. The rebels are stout in the town of Colchester.

The ministers of the church are hemmed at in the open streets, and called knaves. The blessed sacrament of the altar is blasphemed and railed upon in every alehouse and tavern. Prayer and fasting is not regarded. Seditious talks and news are rife, both in town and country, in as ample and large manner, as though there had no honourable Lords and Commissioners been sent for reformation thereof. The occasion riseth partly by reason of John Lone of Colchester Heath (a perverse place) which John Lone was twice indicted of heresy, and thereupon fled with his wife and household, and his goods seized within the town of Colchester, to the king and queen's majesty's use. Nevertheless the said John is come home again, and nothing said or done to him. Whereupon the heretics are wonderfully encouraged, to the no little discomfort of good and catholic people, which daily prayeth to God for the profit, unity, and restoration of his church again, which thing shall come the sooner to pass, through the travail and pains of such honourable

Lords and reverend fathers, as your good Lordship is, unto whom I wish long life and continuance, with increase of much honour.

From Colchester the eighteenth of December.

Your humble beadsman Thomas Tye Priest

When Judasly* this wicked priest had thus wrought his malice against the people of God, within a while after, the storms began to arise against those poor persecuted William Munt and his company, whereby they were enforced to hide themselves from the heat thereof. And continuing so a little space at last, the seventh day of March anno 1557 being the first Sunday in Lent, and by two of the clock in the morning, one Master Edmund Tyrrell (who came of the house of that Tyrells which murdered King Edward the fifth and his brother*) took with him the bailiff of the hundred* called William Simuell, dwelling in Colchester, and the two constables of Muchbently aforesaid named John Baker and William Harries with diverse *Tye's letter to* other, a great number: and besetting the house of the said *Bishop* William Munt round about, called to them at length to open *Bonner.* the door, which being done Master Tyrrell with certain of his *William* company, went into the chamber where the said father Munt *Simuell, John* and his wife lay, willing them to rise: 'For,' (said he), 'ye must *Baker,* go with us to Colchester Castle.' Mother Munt hearing that, *William* being very sick, desired that her daughter might first fetch her *Harries* *persecutors.* some drink: for she was (she said) very ill at ease.

*The taking of* Then he gave her leave and bade her go. So her daughter the *William* forenamed Rose Allin, maid, took a stone pot in one hand, and *wife, and Rose* a candle in the other, and went to draw drink for her mother: *Allin their* and as she came back again through the house, Tyrrell met her, *daughter.* and willed to give her father and mother good counsel, and to advertise them to be better Catholic people.

*Talk between* *Rose.* 'Sir, they have a better instructor than I. For the Holy *Edmund* Ghost doth teach them I hope, which I trust will not suffer *Tyrrell and* them to err.' *Rose Allin.*

*Tyrrell.* 'Why,' said Master Tyrrell, 'art thou still in that mind, thou naughty housewife? Marry, it is time to look upon such heretics indeed.'

*Rose.* 'Sir, with that which you call heresy, do I worship my Lord God. I tell you troth.'

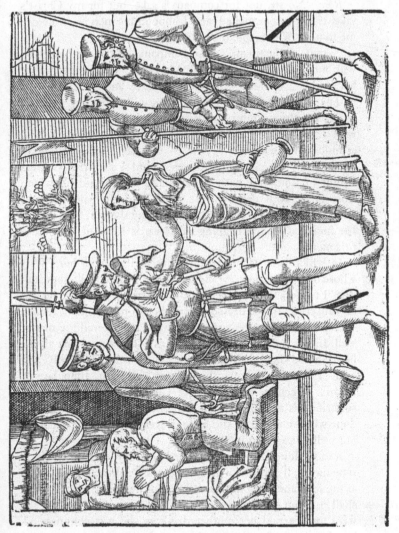

20. The burning of Rose Allin's hand

*Tyrrell.* 'Then I perceive you will burn, gossip, with the rest, for company's sake.'

*Rose.* 'No sir, not for company's sake, but for my Christ's sake, if so I be compelled, and I hope in his mercies, if he call me to it, he will enable me to bear it.'

*Tyrrell.* So he turning to his company, said: 'Sirs this gossip will burn: do ye not think it?' 'Marry sir,' quoth one, 'prove her, and you shall see what she will do, by and by.'

Then that cruel Tyrrell taking the candle from her, held her wrist, and the burning candle under her hand, burning cross wise over the back thereof, so long till the very sinews cracked asunder. Witness hereof William Candler then dwelling in Muchbently, which was there present and saw it. Also Mistress Bright of Romford, with Anne Starkey her maid, to whom Rose Allin both declared the same, and the said Mistress Bright also ministered salve for the curing thereof, as she lay in her house at Romford going up towards London with other prisoners.

*Tyrrell burneth Rose Allin's hand.*

In which time of his tyranny, he said often to her: 'Why whore wilt thou not cry? Thou young whore, wilt thou not cry?' Et cetera. Unto which always she answered, that she had no cause, she thanked God, but rather to rejoice. He had, she said more cause to weep than she, if he considered the matter well. In the end, when the sinews (as I said) brake that all the house heard them, he then thrust her from him violently, and said: 'Ha strong whore, thou shameless beast, thou beastly whore,' et cetera, with such like vile words. But she quietly suffering his rage for the time, at the last, said: 'Sir, have ye done what ye will do?' And he said, 'yea, and if thou think it be not well, then mend it.'

*The patience of the faithful.*

*Rose.* 'Mend it? Nay, the Lord mend you, and give you repentance, if it be his will. And now if ye think it good begin at the feet, and burn the head also. For he that set you a work, shall pay you your wages one day I warrant you': and so she went and carried her mother drink as she was commanded. Furthermore, after the searching of the house for more company, at the last they found one John Thurston and Margaret his wife there also, whom they carried with the rest to Colchester Castle immediately.

*The devil payeth the persecutors their wages.*

And this said Rose Allin being prisoner, told a friend of hers this cruel act of the said Tyrrell, and showing him the manner thereof, she said: 'While my one hand,' (quoth she), 'was a burning, I having a pot in my other hand, might have laid him on the face with it, if I had would? For no man held my hand to let me therein. But I thank God,' (quoth she), 'with all my heart, I did it not.'

*She revengeth not evil for evil.*

Also being asked of another how she could abide the painful burning of her hand, she said, at first it was some grief to her, but afterward, the longer she burned the less she felt, or well near none at all.

[*Following an account of the suffering of six individuals who were imprisoned at Mote Hall in Colchester, the narrator recounts the interrogation and condemnation of William and Alice Munt, Rose Allin, and another prisoner at Colchester Castle.*]

. . .William Munt of Muchbently in Essex, of the age of sixty-one years, said: that the sacrament of the altar was an abominable idol, and that if he should observe any part of their popish proceedings, he should displease God, and bring his curse upon him, and therefore for fear of his vengeance he durst not do it. This good father was examined of many things, but God be thanked, he stood to the truth and in the end therefore had sentence of condemnation read against him.

*William Munt condemned.*

John Johnson of Thorpe in Essex, widower of the age of thirty-four years, was examined as the rest, and made answer in such sort, as the papists counted them none of theirs, and therefore condemned him with their bloody sentence, as they had done the rest before. This John Johnson affirmed, that in the receiving of the sacrament, according to Christ's institution, he receiveth the body of Christ spiritually, et cetera.

*John Johnson condemned.*

Alice Munt, the wife of the said William Munt, of the age of sixty-one years, being also examined as the rest, said and confirmed the same in effect as her husband did, and was therefore also condemned by their bloody sentence in like manner.

*Alice Munt condemned.*

Rose Allin maid, the daughter of the said Alice Munt of the age of twenty years, being examined of the auricular confession, going to the church to hear mass, of the popish seven sacraments, et cetera, answered stoutly that they stank in the

*Rose Allin.*

face of God, and she durst not have to do with them for her life, neither was she (she said) any member of theirs: for they were the members of Antichrist, and so should have (if they *Rose Allin's* repented not) the reward of Antichrist. Being asked further, *answers.* what she could say of the see of the Bishop of Rome, whether she would obey his authority or no: she answered boldly, that she was none of his. 'As for his see,' (quoth she), 'it is for crows, kites, owls and ravens to swim in, such as you be, for by the grace of God I shall not swim in that sea,* while I live, neither will I have anything to do therewith.' Then read they the sentence of condemnation against her, and so sent her unto *Rose Allin* prison again unto the rest, where she sung with great joy, to the *condemned.* wonder of many.

Thus these poor condemned lambs, being delivered into the hands of the secular power, were committed again every one unto the prison from whence they came, where they remained with much joy and great comfort (in continual reading, and invocating the name of God) ever looking and expecting the happy day of their dissolution. In which time the cruel papists left not their mischievous attempts against them (although they would seem now to have no more to do with them) for bloody Bonner, whose throat never cried 'Ho,' shortly after got a writ for the burning of the foresaid ten good creatures, and to show the more diligence in the cause, he sent his own trusty man down with it, named Edward Cosin, and with him also his letter for the furtherance of the matter, the thirtieth day of July, the next month after the condemnation.

The writ being thus received of the said bailiffs, and they having then no leisure thereabouts, appointed the day of the execution thereof, to be the second day of August next following. And because the faithful souls were in two several prisons, as the Castle was for the country and the Mote Hall for the town, therefore it was agreed among them, that they in Mote Hall should be burnt in the forenoon and those at the Castle, by the sheriff of the shire, in the afternoon, as here thou mayest see it more plain how it came to pass accordingly.

The second day of August, 1557, betwixt six and seven of the clock in the morning, was brought from Mote Hall unto a plat of ground hard by the town wall of Colchester on the outward side, William Bongeor, William Purcas, Thomas Benold, Agnes Silverside alias Smith, Helen Ewring and Elizabeth Folkes aforenamed, which being there, and all things prepared for their martyrdom at the last these said constant martyrs kneeled down and made their humble prayers to God, but not in such sort as they would: for the cruel tyrants would not suffer them: especially one Master Clere among the rest (who sometime had been a gospeller) showed himself very extreme unto them: the Lord give him repentance (if it be his good will) and grace to be a better man. When they had made their prayers, they rose, and made them ready to the fire. And Elizabeth Folkes when she had plucked off her petticoat, would have given it to her mother, (which came and kissed her at the stake, and exhorted her to be strong in the Lord) but the wicked there attending, would not suffer her to give it. Therefore taking the said petticoat in her hand, she threw it away from her saying: 'Farewell all the world, farewell faith, farewell hope': and so taking the stake in her hand, said: 'Welcome love,' et cetera. Now she being at the stake, and one of the officers nailing the chain about her, in the striking of the staple, he missed the place and strake her with a great stroke of the hammer on the shoulder bone: whereat she suddenly turned her head lifting up her eyes to the Lord, and prayed smilingly, and gave herself to exhorting the people again.

When all six were also nailed likewise at their stakes and the fire about them, they clapped their hands for joy in the fire, that the standers by (which were by estimation thousands) cried generally all almost: 'The Lord strengthen them, the Lord comfort them, the Lord pour his mercies upon them,' with such like words, as was wonderful to hear.

Thus yielded they up their souls and bodies into the Lord's hands, for the true testimony of his truth. The Lord grant we may imitate the same in the like quarrel (if he so vouch us worthy) for his mercy's sake. Amen.

In like manner, the said day in the afternoon, was brought forth into the Castle yard, to a place appointed for the same, William Munt, John Johnson, Alice Munt, and Rose Allin aforesaid, which godly constant persons, after they had made their prayers, and were joyfully tied to the stakes, calling upon the name of God, and exhorting the people earnestly to flee from idolatry, suffered their martyrdom with such triumph and joy, that the people did no less shout thereat to see it, than at the other that were burnt the same day in the morning.

Thus ended all these glorious ten souls that day, their happy lives unto the Lord, whose ages all did grow to the sum of four hundred and six years or thereabouts. The Lord grant we may well spend our years and days likewise to his glory. Amen.

# 24. GEORGE EAGLES

The story and death of George Eagles, otherwise
termed Trudgeover, a most painful travailer in
Christ's gospel, who for the same gospel most cruelly
was martyred by the cruel papists.

Among other martyrs of singular virtue and constancy, one
George Eagles deserveth not the least admiration, but is so
much the more to be commended, for that he having little
learning or none, most manfully served and fought under the
banner of Christ's church. For oftentimes the will and pleasure
of God is to beautify and adorn his kingdom with the weak and
simple instruments of this world: such as in the Old Testament
Amos* was, who with many other of obscure and unknown
names, were called from the herds and folds to the honour of
prophets: as likewise we read of the Apostles that were called
from fishermen's craft, and put into churches.* Wherefore
this George Eagles is not to be neglected for his base occupation, whom Christ called thence to set forth and declare abroad
his gospel. Rather we ought to glorify God the more thereby in
his holiness, which in so blind a time inspired him with the
gift of preaching, and constancy of suffering: who after a certain time he had used the occupation of a tailor, being eloquent
and of good utterance, gave and applied himself to the profit of
Christ's church.

*George Eagles martyred.*

Which man, as before in those most bright and clear days of
King Edward the sixth he had not unfruitfully showed and
preached the power and force of the Lord: so afterward in the
tempestuous time and fall of the church (at what time the
confessors* of Christ and his gospel were turmoiled, diverse of
them murdered, part banished, and other some constrained for
fear not to show their heads) he expressed and uttered his
manly stomach. For he wandering abroad into diverse and far
countries, where he could find any of his brethren, he did there
most earnestly encourage and comfort them, not tarrying in this
town, and sometime abiding in that certain months together,

as occasions served, lodging sometime in the country and sometime for fear living in fields and woods, who for his immoderate and unreasonable going abroad, was called Trudgeover. Oftentimes he did lie abroad in the night without covert spending the most part thereof in devout and earnest prayer.

His diet was so above measure spare and slender, that for the space of three years, he used for the most part, to drink nothing but very water, whereunto he was compelled through necessity of the time of persecution: and after when he perceived that his body by God's providence proved well enough with this diet, he thought best to inure himself therewithal against all necessities.

Now when he had profited Christ's church in this sort, by going about and preaching the gospel a year or two, and especially in Colchester and the quarters thereabout, that privy enemy which envieth always the salvation and blessed estate of the good, lurketh and layeth wait by all means possible for him, so that there were diverse espies* sent out, who had in commandment, wheresoever they found him, to bring him either quick or dead.

But when this their attempt could not prevail, but all was in vain (the said Eagles with his brethren keeping in close, and hiding themselves in out and dark places, as in barns, thickets, holes, and privy closets) his adversaries went about another way to compass this their enterprise of taking him. For in the queen's name a grievous edict was proclaimed throughout [the] four shires [of] Essex, Suffolk, Kent, and Norfolk, promising the party that took him, twenty pound for his pains: doubtless a worthy hire to entice any Jew* to treachery. For being inflamed with greedy desire of the money, devised and invented all ways and reasons they could possible to be enriched with the hurt and destruction of this silly man.

At length it came to pass, that this George being seen by chance at Colchester upon Mary Magdalen's day, at which time they kept a fair in the town, should have forthwith been delivered to his adversaries, if he perceiving the same (as God would have it) had not conveyed himself away as fast as he could, a great multitude pursuing after, and seeking diligently for him. Who first hid himself in a grove, and then from thence he stole into a corn field thereby, and so lay secretly couched from the violence of his enemies, in so much as they were all, saving one, past hope of taking him, and therefore ready to depart their way.

This one having more subtlety and wicked craft in his head than the rest, would not depart thence with his fellows, but climbed up into a high tree, there to view and espy if he might see Eagles anywhere stir or move. The poor man thinking all sure enough, by reason that he heard no noise abroad, rose up upon his knees, and lifting up his hands, prayed unto God. And whether it were for that his head was above the corn, or because his voice was heard the lurker perceiving his desired prey that he hunted after, forthwith came down, and suddenly laying hands on him, brought him as prisoner to Colchester. Notwithstanding the greedy and Judas knave which had so much promised him, was fain to be contented with a very small reward, and glad to take that too, lest he should have had nothing at all.

*'Quo non mortalia pectora cogis, auri sacra fames.'\* Virgil. Aeneid. 1.*

This George, not without great lamentation of diverse good men: and great lack unto the Church of God (of which to his power he was a worthy instrument) was committed to prison there, and from thence within four days after conveyed to Chelmsford, where he abode all that night in devout prayer, and would not sleep, neither would eat or drink, but bread and water. The next day he was carried to London to the Bishop or the council,\* and there remained a certain time, and then was brought down to Chelmsford to the sessions, and there was indicted and accused of treason, because he had assembled companies together, contrary to the laws and statutes of the realm in that case provided. For so it was ordained a little before, to avoid sedition, that if men should flock secretly together, above the number of six, they should be attached of treason: which strait law was the casting away of the good Duke of Somerset\* before mentioned.

And albeit it was well known that poor Eagles did never anything seditiously against the queen, yet to cloak an honest matter withal, and to cause him to be the more hated of the people, they turned religion into a civil offence and crime, and though he defended his cause stoutly and boldly, making a full declaration of his religion or faith before the judges: yet could he not bring to pass by any means, but that he must needs be indicted (as is said) of treason, whose indictment did run much after this fashion.

*George Eagles's indictment.*

'George Eagles, thou art indicted by the name of George Eagles, otherwise Trudgeover the world, for that thou didst such a day make thy prayer, that God should turn Queen Mary's heart, or else take her away.'

He denied that he prayed that God should take her away, but he confessed that he prayed that God would turn her heart in his prayer. Well, notwithstanding he was condemned for a traitor, although the meaning thereof was for religion.

This thing done, he was carried to the new inn, called the sign of the Crown in Chelmsford, by the beastly bailiffs, which some of them were they that before did the best to take him, and being in the inn, one Richard Potto the elder, an innholder,

*Richard Potto innholder at the Cock in Chelmsford.*

dwelling at the sign of the Cock in the same town, did much trouble him in persuading him to confess he had offended the queen in his prayer which he was condemned for, and to ask her forgiveness.

To whom he said he had not offended her grace in that behalf. So in process of time he was laid upon a sled with an hurdle* on it, and drawn to the place of execution being fast bound, having in his hand a Psalm book, of the which he read very devoutly all the way with a loud voice till he came there: and, being on the ladder, this foresaid Potto did much trouble him with the matter aforesaid, when he would have uttered other things, till such time as the sheriff commanded Potto to hold his peace and trouble him no more.

So he made his confession and stood very constant still. Then he was turned off the ladder.* With him were cast certain thieves also, and the next day when they were brought out to be executed with him, there happened a thing that did much set forth and declare the innocency and godliness of this man. For being led between two thieves* to the place where he should suffer, when as he exhorted both them and all other, to stand steadfastly to the truth, one of these turned the counsel he gave, into a jesting matter, and made but a flout* of it.

'Why should we doubt to obtain heaven,' saith he, 'for as much as this holy man shall go before us, as captain and leader unto us in the way. We shall flee thither straight as soon as he hath once made us the entry.'

In this, George Eagles and that other did greatly reprove him, who on the other side gave good heed to George's exhortation, earnestly bewailing his own wickedness, and calling to Christ for mercy. But the more that the first was bid to be still and to leave off his scoffing, the more perverse did he continue in his foolishness and his wicked behaviour. At length he came to the gallows, where they should be hanged, but George was carried to another place thereby to suffer. Between the two it was the godlier's chance to go the foremost, who being upon the ladder, after he had exhorted the people to beware and take heed to themselves, how they did transgress the commandments of God, and then had committed his soul into God's hands, he ended his life after a godly and quiet manner.

The mocker's turn cometh next, which would have said likewise somewhat, but his tongue did so fumble and falter in his head, that he was not able to speak a word. Fain would he have uttered his mind, but he could not bring it out. Then did the under-sheriff bid him say the Lord's Prayer, which he could not say neither, but stutteringly, as a man would say, one word today, and another tomorrow. Then one did begin to say it, and so bade him say after.

*An example to be noted of a thief rejecting and deriding wholesome and godly preaching.*

Such as were there and saw it, were very much astonied: especially those that did behold the just punishment of God against him that had mocked so earnest a matter. George Eagles in the mean time, after he had hanged a small time, having a great check with the halter, immediately one of the bailiffs cut the halter asunder, and he fell to the ground being still alive, although much amazed with the check he had of the ladder.

The one William Swallow of Chelmsford a bailiff did draw him to the sled, that he was drawn thither on, and laid his neck thereon, and with a cleaver, such as is occupied in many men's kitchens, and blunt, did hackle* off his head, and sometime hit his neck, and sometime his chin, and did foully mangle him, and so opened him. Notwithstanding this blessed martyr of

*William Swallow tormentor of George Eagles.*

Christ abode steadfast and constant in the very midst of his torments, till such time as this tormentor William Swallow did pluck the heart out of his body. The body being divided in four parts, and his bowels burnt, was brought to the foresaid Swallow's door, and there laid upon the fish-stalls before his door, till they had made ready a horse to carry his quarters, one to Colchester, and the rest to Harwich, Chelmsford and St Rouse's.*

His head was set up at Chelmsford on the market-cross on a long pole, and there stood till the wind did blow it down, and lying certain days in the street tumbled about, one caused it to be buried in the Churchyard in the night. Also a wonderful work of God was it that he showed on this wicked bailiff Swallow, who within short space after this was so punished, that all the hair went well near off his head, his eyes were as it were closed up and could scant see, the nails of his fingers and toes went clean off. He was in such case of his body, as though he had been a leper, and now in his last age almost a very beggar, and his wife which he a little after married God hath punished with the falling sickness, or a disease like unto that: which may be a warning or glass* for all men and women to look in, that be enemies to God's true servants.

*God's just punishment upon a cruel persecutor.*

*William Swallow's wife punished with the falling sickness.*

No less token of his marvellous judgement did God show upon the foresaid Richard Potto, which did so much trouble this George Eagles in the inn, and at the place of execution, as is above specified. He lived till the beginning of Queen Elizabeth's reign, all which time he little joyed, and on a time being in a great chafe with two or three of his neighbours in his own house, feeling himself not well, he said to one of his servants: 'Go with me into the chamber,' and when he came there, he fell down on a low bed, as heavy as it had been lead, and lay there foaming at the mouth, and could never speak after, neither yet understand what was said to him, as by all means was tried by his neighbours with signs to him made, but lay as senseless as it had been a very dumb beast, and within three or four days died. God grant that this token sent of God, with many more like, may be a warning to us ever hereafter, while we shall live unto the world's end.

*God's judgement upon Richard Potto another persecutor of George Eagles.*

Besides this, God hath wonderfully showed his work. For at a time when they laid great wait for this George Eagles: so that it was thought that it was unpossible but that he should be taken being so beset, his friends did put him in a prentice apparel, that is to say, watchet* hose, as their manner is, and an old cloak, and set him on a pack of wool, as though he had ridden to carry wool to the spinners, so he rode amongst the midst of his adversaries and escaped them all for that time. Another troubler of the said George Eagles was also justice Brown, who enjoyed not his cruelty many years after, et cetera.

# 25. THE ISLINGTON MARTYRS

The order and occasion of taking certain godly men
and women praying together in the fields about
Islington, of whom thirteen were condemned by
Bonner, and after suffered in the fire for the truth's
sake, as in the story here following may appear.

*June 27.*
*Twenty-two*
*men taken.*
*Thirteen*
*martyrs*
*burned.*
Secretly in a back close* in the field by the town of Islington
were collected and assembled together a certain company of
godly and innocent persons, to the number of forty, men and
women, who there sitting together at prayer, and virtuously
occupied in the meditation of God's holy word, first cometh a
certain man to them unknown: who looking over unto them, so
stayed and saluted them, saying that they looked like men that
meant no hurt. Then one of the said company asked the man,
if he could tell whose close that was, and whether they might
be so bold there to sit. 'Yes,' said he, 'for that ye seem unto me
such persons as intend no harm,' and so departed. Within a
quarter of an hour after, cometh the constable of Islington,
*King constable*
*of Islington.*
named King, warded with six or seven other, accompanying
him in the same business, one with a bow, another with a bill,
and other with their weapons likewise. The which six or seven
persons the said constable left a little behind him in a close
place, there to be ready if need should be while he with one
with him should go and view them before. Who so doing, came
through them, looking and viewing what they were doing, and
what books they had: and so going a little forward, and returning back again, had them deliver their books. They understanding that he was constable, refused not so to do. With that
cometh forth the residue of his fellows above touched, who had
them stand and not to depart. They answered again [that] they
would be obedient and ready to go whither so ever they would
have them: and so were they first carried to a brewhouse but a
little way off, while that some of the said soldiers ran to the
Justice next at hand. But the Justice was not at home: whereupon they were had to Sir Roger Cholmley. In the mean time

some of the women being of the same number of the foresaid forty persons, escaped away from them, some in the close, some before they came to the brewhouse. For so they were carried ten with one man, eight with another, and with some more, with some less, in such sort that it was not hard for them to escape that would. In fine, they that were carried to Sir Roger Cholmley, were twenty-seven, which Sir Roger Cholmley and the recorder* taking their names in a bill, and calling them one by one so many as answered to their names, they sent to Newgate.

*Sir Roger Cholmley, and Recorder of London, persecutors.*

. . . These twenty-two were in the said prison of Newgate seven weeks before they were examined, to whom word was sent by Alexander the keeper, that if they would hear a Mass, they should all be delivered. . . .

Ye heard before of those twenty-two taken at Islington, thirteen were burned, and six escaped, albeit very hardly, and some of them not without scourging by the hands of the bishop. In the which number was Thomas Hinshaw and John Milles, according to the express picture hereafter purported. . . .

[Poem Concerning the Likeness of Bonner]

Muse not so much, that nature's work
is thus deformed now,
With belly blown, and head so swollen,
for I shall tell you how:
This cannibal in three years' space
three hundreth martyrs slew:
They were his food, he loved so blood,
he spared none he knew.
It should appear that blood feeds fat,
if men lie well and soft:
For Bonner's belly waxed with blood,
though he seemed to fast oft.
O bloody beast, bewail the death
of those that thou hast slain:
In time repent, since thou canst not
their lives restore again.

G. G.

## The scourging of Thomas Hinshaw

In the godly number above mentioned, which were apprehended at Islington, there congregated together for their exercise of prayer and reading, was this Thomas Hinshaw above named, a young man of the age of nineteen or twenty years, prentice in Paul's churchyard with one Master Pugson. Who with the rest was carried to the constable's of Islington, and there every one of them searched, and led forthwith to the chief Justice Master Cholmley, dwelling in the Old Bailey in London, and by him then the said Thomas Hinshaw was sent to Newgate, and there remaining prisoner without conference with any, about eight weeks, at the last was sent for to Bonner Bishop of London, and by him, Harpsfield and Cole* examined. After which examination he was sent to Newgate again, where he remained a three weeks following. Which time being over passed, he was sent for again before the said bishop, the day being Saturday, and with him had much talk to little purpose. The next day after also, which was Sunday, they persuaded with him very much in like manner, and perceiving they could not bend him unto their bow, in the afternoon, the Bishop going unto Fulham, took him with him, where immediately after his coming, he was set in the stocks, remaining there all the first night with bread and water.

*The story of Thomas Hinshaw.*

*W. Cholmley Justice.*

*Bonner, Harpsfield, and Cole.*

*Hinshaw carried to Fulham and there set in the stocks with bread and water.*

The next morning the bishop came and examined him himself, and perceiving no yielding to his mind, he sent Master Harpsfield to talk with him: who after long talk, in the end fell to raging words, calling the said Thomas Hinshaw 'peevish boy,' and asked him whether he thought he went about to damn his soul, or no, et cetera. Unto which the said Thomas answered, that he was persuaded that they laboured to maintain their dark and devilish kingdom, and not for any love to truth. Then Harpsfield being in a mighty rage, told the bishop thereof. Whereat the bishop fumed and fretted, that scant for anger being able to speak,* he said: 'Doest thou answer my Archdeacon so, thou naughty boy? I shall handle thee well enough, be assured': so he sent for a couple of rods, and caused him to kneel against a long bench in an arbour in his garden, where the said Thomas without any enforcement of his part, offered himself to the beating, and did abide the fury of the said Bonner, so long as the fat-paunched Bonner could endure

21. Bonner, scourging God's saints in his orchard at Fulham

*Hinshaw beaten with rods. The boy was beholding to Bishop Bonner's grand paunch.*

with breath, and till for weariness he was fain to cease, and give place to his shameful act. He had two willow rods, but he wasted but one, and so left off.

Now after this scourging, the said Thomas Hinshaw notwithstanding did sustain diverse conflicts and examinations sundry times. At last being brought before the said bishop in his chapel at Fulham, there he had procured witnesses, and gathered articles against him, which the young man denied, and would not affirm, or consent to any interrogatory there and then ministered, do what they could. . . .

Not long after this his examination, about a fortnight or such a thing, the foresaid examinate fell sick of a burning ague, whereby he was delivered upon entreaty unto his master Martin Pugson in Paul's Churchyard aforesaid: for the bishop thought verily, he was more like to die than to live. The which his sickness endured a twelvemonth or more, so that in the mean time Queen Mary died. Then he shortly after recovered health, and escaped death, being at the writing of this yet alive, both witness and reporter of the same, the Lord therefore be praised, Amen.

*Thomas Hinshaw delivered to Master Pugson his master.*

## The scourging of John Milles by Bishop Bonner.

Besides the above named, was scourged also by the hands of the said bishop one John Milles a capper,* a right faithful and true honest man in all his dealings and conditions. . . . And being brought before Bonner and there examined, was commanded to the coal house, with the foresaid Thomas Hinshaw, where they remained one night in the stocks. From thence he was sent to Fulham, where he with the said Hinshaw, remained eight or ten days in the stocks: during which time he sustained diverse conflicts with the said Bonner, who had him oft times in examination, urging him, and with a stick which he had in his hand, oft times rapping him on the head, and flirting him* under the chin and on the ears, saying he looked down like a thief. Moreover, after he had assayed all manner of ways to cause him to recant and could not, at length having him to his orchard, there within a little arbour, with his own hands beat him first with a willow rod, and that being worn well nigh to

*The story of John Milles capper.*

*John Milles with Thomas Hinshaw laid in the stocks at Fulham.*

the stumps, he called for a birchen rod, which a lad brought out of his chamber. The cause why he so beat him, was this: Bonner asked him when he had crept to the cross.* He answered, not since he came to the years of discretion, neither would to be torn with wild horses. Then Bonner bade him make a cross in his forehead, which he refused to do. Whereupon he had him incontinently to his orchard, and there calling for rods, showeth his cruelty upon him, as he did upon Thomas Hinshaw, as is above declared.

*Hinshaw and Milles beaten of Bonner.*

This done, he had him immediately to the parish church of Fulham with the said Thomas Hinshaw, and with Robert Willis, to whom there being severally called before him, he ministered certain Articles, asking if they would subscribe to the same. To the which the said John Milles made his answer according to his conscience, denying them all, except one article which was concerning King Edward's service in English.* Shortly after this beating, Bonner sent to him in prison a certain old priest lately come from Rome to conjure out the evil spirit from him, who laying his hand upon his head, began with certain words pronounced over him, to conjure as he had been wont before to do. Milles marvelling what the priest was about to do, said he trusted no evil spirit to be within him, and laughed him to scorn, et cetera.

*John Milles denyeth to subscribe to Bishop Bonner's articles.*

*An old conjuring priest.*

As this John Milles was diverse times and oft called before Bonner, so much communication and talk passed between them, which to recite all, it were too long. And yet it were not unpleasant for the reader that lusteth to laugh, to see the blind and unsavoury reasons of that bishop which he used to persuade the ignorant withal. As in the process of his other talk with this Milles, Bonner going about to persuade him not to meddle with matters of the scripture, but rather to believe other men's teaching, which had more skill in the same: first asked if he did believe the scripture: 'Yea,' said he, 'that I do.' Then the bishop: 'Why,' (quoth he). 'St Paul saith: "if the man sleep, the woman is at liberty to go to another man." If thou were asleep having a wife, wouldst thou be content thy wife to take another man? And yet this is the scripture.

'Item,* if thou wilt believe Luther, Zwingli, and such, then thou canst not go right. But if thou wilt believe me, et cetera,

*The unsavoury reasons or talk of Bishop Bonner going about to persuade John Milles.*

thou canst not err. And if thou shouldest err, yet thou art in no peril, thy blood should be required at our hands. As if thou shouldest go to a far country, and meet with a fatherly man as I am,' (for these were his terms), 'and ask the way to the head city, and he should say, "go this way," and thou wilt not believe him, but follow Luther and other heretics of late days, and go a contrary way, how wilt thou come to the place thou askest for? so if thou wilt not believe me, but follow the leading of other heretics, so shalt thou be brought to destruction, and burn both body and soul.

'As truly as thou seest the bodies of them in Smithfield burnt, so truly their souls do burn in hell, because they err from the church.'

Oft times speaking to the said John Milles, he would say: 'they call me, "bloody Bonner." A vengeance on you all. I would fain be rid of you, but you have a delight in burning. But if I might have my will, I would sow your mouths, and put you in sacks, and drown you.'

Now somewhat to say concerning the deliverance of the said John Milles, the same day that he was delivered, Bonner came unto the stocks where he lay, and asked him how he liked his lodging, and his fare.

'Well,' said Milles, 'if it would please God I might have a little straw to lie or sit upon.'

Then said Bonner: 'thou wilt show no token of a Christian man'. And upon this his wife came in unknowing unto him, being very great with child, and looking every hour for her lying down, entreating the bishop for her husband, and saying, that she would not go out of the house, but there would lay her belly in the bishop's house, unless she had her husband with her. 'How sayst you,' (quoth Bonner), 'thou heretic? If thy wife miscarry, or thy child, or children, if she be with one, or two, should perish, the blood of them would be required at thy hands.' Then to this agreement he came, that he should hire a bed in the town of Fulham and her husband should go home with her the morrow after, upon this condition, that his kinsman there present (one Robert Rouse) should bring the said Milles unto his house at Paul's the next day.

*Bonner's judgement, that we should trust more to men, than to the scriptures of God.*

*This similitude holdeth κατὰ τὴν ἐναντίωσιν.**

*Rash and presumptuous judgement of Bonner.*

*Bishop Bonner's wish in punishing God's saints.*

*The occasion and manner of delivering John Milles.*

*Milles's wife entreateth for her husband.*

*Robert Rouse kinsman to John Milles.*

Whereunto the said Milles said he would not agree, except he might go home by and by. At length his wife being importunate for her husband, and seeing that she would go no further, but there remain unless she had her husband with her, the bishop fearing belike the rumour which might come upon his house thereby, bade the said Milles make a cross and say: 'In nomine patris et filii, et spiritus sancti.* Amen.'

*The condition put to John Milles to say, 'In nomine patris', et cetera.*

Then the said Milles began to say: 'In the name of the Father, and of the Son, and of the holy ghost, Amen.' 'No, no,' saith Bonner, 'say it me in Latin,* "In nomine patris, et filii, et spiritus sancti," Amen.' Milles understanding the matter of that Latin to be but good, said the same, and so went home with his wife, his foresaid kinsman being charged to bring him the next day unto Paul's, 'either else,' said Bonner, 'if thou doest not bring him, thou art an heretic as well as he.' Notwithstanding, the charge being no greater, this kinsman did not bring him, but he of his own voluntary accord came to the said bishop within a few days after, where the bishop put unto him a certain writing in Latin to subscribe unto, containing as it seemed to him no great matter, that he needed greatly to stick at: albeit, what the bill was, he could not certainly tell. So subscribed he to the bill, and returned home. And thus much concerning the twenty-two taken at Islington.

*John Milles sent home with his wife.*

# 26. PREST'S WIFE

## The trouble and martyrdom of a godly poor woman which suffered at Exeter.

Although in such an innumerable company of godly martyrs, which in sundry quarters of this realm were put to torments of fire in Queen Mary's time, it be hard so exactly to recite every particular person that suffered, but that some escape us either unknown, or omitted: yet I cannot pass over a certain poor woman,* and a silly creature, burned under the said queen's reign, in the city of Exeter (whose name I have not yet learned:) who dwelling sometime about Cornwall, having a husband and children there, much addicted to the superstitious sect of popery: was many times rebuked of them, and driven to go to the church, to their idols and ceremonies, to shrift, to follow the cross in procession, to give thanks to God for restoring Antichrist again into this realm, et cetera. Which when her spirit could not abide to do, she made her prayer unto God, calling for help and mercy, and so at length lying in her bed, about midnight, she thought there came to her a certain motion and feeling of singular comfort. Whereupon in short space, she began to grow in contempt of her husband and children, and so taking nothing from them, but even as she went, departed from them, seeking her living by labour and spinning as well as she could, here and there for a time. In which time notwithstanding she never ceased to utter her mind, as well as she durst: howbeit she at that time was brought home to her husband again. Where last she was accused by her neighbours, and so brought up to Exeter, to be presented to the bishop and his clergy. The name of the bishop which had her in examination, was Doctor Troubleville.* His chancellor (as I gather) was Blackstone. The chiefest matter whereupon she was charged and condemned, was for the sacrament (which they call of the altar) and for speaking against idols, as by the declaration of those which were present, I understand, which report the talk between her and the bishop on this wise.*

*Bishop.* 'Thou foolish woman,' (quoth the bishop), 'I hear say that thou hast spoken certain words of the most blessed sacrament of the altar, the body of Christ. Fie for shame. Thou art an unlearned person and a woman: wilt thou meddle with such high matters, which all the doctors of the world cannot define? Wilt thou talk of so high mysteries? Keep thy work, and meddle with that thou hast to do. It is no woman's matters, at cards and tow* to be spoken of. And if it be as I am informed, thou art worthy to be burned.' *Talk between the woman and the bishop.*

*Woman.* 'My Lord,' (said she), 'I trust your Lordship will hear me speak.'

*Bishop.* 'Yea marry,' (quoth he), 'therefore I send for thee.'

*Woman.* 'I am a poor woman and do live by my hands, getting a penny truly and of that I get I give part to the poor.'

*Bishop.* 'That is well done. Art thou not a man's wife?'

And here the bishop entered into talk of her husband.

To whom she answered again, declaring that she had a husband and children: and had them not. So long as she was at liberty, she refused not, neither husband, nor children. 'But now standing here as I do,' (said she), 'in the cause of Christ and his truth, where I must either forsake Christ, or my husband, I am contented to stick only to Christ my heavenly spouse, and renounce the other.'

And here she making mention of the words of Christ: 'He that leaveth not father or mother, sister or brother, husband, et cetera,'* the bishop inferred that Christ spake that of the holy martyrs, which died because they would not do sacrifice to the false gods. *The wife renouncing her husband for Christ's sake.*

*Woman.* 'Sickerly sir, and I will rather die than I will do any worship to that foul idol, which with your Mass you make a god.'

*Bishop.* 'Yea, you callet, will you say that the sacrament of the altar is a foul idol?' *The sacrament of the altar made an idol.*

*Woman.* 'Yea truly,' quoth she: 'there was never such an idol as your sacrament is, made of your priests, and commanded to be worshipped of all men, with many fond fantasies, where Christ did command it to be eaten and drunken in remembrance of his most blessed passion our redemption.'

*Bishop.* 'See this prattling woman. Doest thou not hear, that Christ did say over the bread: "This is my body," and over the cup: "This is my blood?"'*

*Woman.* 'Yes forsooth, he said so, but he meant that it is his body and blood not carnally, but sacramentally.'

*Bishop.* 'Lo, she hath heard prattling among these new preachers, or heard some peevish book. Alas poor woman, thou art deceived.'

*Woman.* 'No, my Lord, that I have learned, was of godly preachers, and of godly books which I have heard read. And if you will give me leave, I will declare a reason why I will not worship the sacrament.'

*Reasons showing why the sacrament of the Lord's body is not to be worshipped.*

*Bishop.* 'Marry say on, I am sure it will be goodly gear.'

*Woman.* 'Truly such gear as I will lose this poor life of mine for.'

*Bishop.* 'Then you will be a martyr good wife.'

*Woman.* 'Indeed if the denying to worship that bready god* be my martyrdom, I will suffer it with all my heart.'

*Bishop.* 'Say thy mind.'

*Woman.* 'You must bear with me a poor woman,' quoth she.

*Bishop.* 'So I will,' quoth he.

*Woman.* 'I will demand of you, whether you can deny your creed, which doth say, that Christ perpetually doth sit at the right hand of his father* both body and soul, until he come again, or whether he be there in heaven our advocate and do make prayer for us unto God his father. If it be so, he is not here in the earth in a piece of bread. If he be not here, and if he do not dwell in temples made with hands,* but in heaven, what shall we seek him here? If he did offer his body once for all, why make you a new offering? If with once offering he made all perfect, why do you with a false offering make all unperfect? If he be to be worshipped in spirit and truth,* why do you worship a piece of bread? If he be eaten and drunken in faith and truth, if his flesh be not profitable to be among us, why do you say, you make his body and flesh, and say it is profitable for body and soul? Alas, I am a poor woman: but rather than I would do as you do, I would live no longer. I have said sir.'

*Bishop.* 'I promise you, you are a jolly* Protestant, I pray you in what schools have you been brought up?'

*Woman.* 'I have upon the Sundays visited the sermons, and there have I learned such things, as are so fixed in my breast that death shall not separate them.'

*Bishop.* 'O foolish woman, who will waste his breath upon thee or such as thou art? But how chanceth it that thou wentest away from thy husband? If thou were an honest woman, thou wouldest not have left thine husband and children, and run about the country like a fugitive.'

*Woman.* 'Sir, I laboured for my living: and as my master Christ counselleth me, when I was persecuted in one city, I fled unto another.'*

*Bishop.* 'Who persecuted thee?'

*Woman.* 'My husband and my children. For when I would have him to leave idolatry, and to worship God in heaven, he would not hear me, but he with his children rebuked me, and troubled me. I fled not for whoredom, nor for theft, but because I would be no partaker with him and his, of that foul idol the Mass. And wheresoever I was, as oft as I could upon Sundays and holy days I made excuses not to go to the popish church.'

*Bishop.* 'Belike then you are a good housewife, to flee from your husband, and also from the church.'

*Woman.* 'My housewifery is but small but God give me grace to go to the true church.'*

*Bishop.* 'The true church: what doest thou mean?'

*Woman.* 'Not your popish church, full of idols and abominations, but where three or four are gathered together in the name of God, to that church will I go as long as I live.'

*Bishop.* 'Belike then you have a church of your own. Well, let this mad woman be put down to prison, until we send for her husband.'

*Woman.* 'No, I have but one husband, which is here already in this city and in prison with me, from whom I will never depart:' and so their communication for that day brake off. Blackstone and others persuaded the bishop that she was a mazed creature, and not in her perfect wit (which is no new thing, for the wisdom of God to appear foolishness to carnal men of this world) and therefore they consulted together, that she should have liberty and go at large. So the keeper of the bishop's prison had her home to his house, where she fell to

*The wife persecuted by husband and children.*

spinning and carding, and did all other work as a servant in the said keeper's house and went about the city, when and whither she would, and diverse had delight to talk with her. And ever she continued talking of the sacrament of the altar. Which, of all thing[s] they could least abide. Then was her husband sent for, but she refused to go home with him, with the blemish of the cause and religion, in defence whereof she there stood before the bishop and the priests.

*Talk between the woman and the priests about the sacrament.* Then diverse of the priests had her in handling, persuading her to leave her wicked opinion about the sacrament of the altar, the natural body and blood of our saviour Christ. But she made them answer, that it was nothing but very bread and wine, and that they might be ashamed to say, that a piece of bread should be turned by a man into the natural body of Christ, which bread doth vinew and mice oftentimes do eat it, and it doth mould and is burned: 'And,' (said she), 'God's own body will not be so handled, nor kept in prison, or boxes, or ambries. Let it be your god: it shall not be mine: for my saviour sitteth on the right hand of God, and doth pray for me. And to make that sacramental or significative* bread instituted for a remembrance, the very body of Christ, and to worship it, it is very foolishness and devilish deceit.'

'Now truly,' (said they), 'the devil hath deceived thee.'

'No,' (said she), 'I trust the living God hath opened mine eyes, and caused me to understand the right use of the blessed sacrament, which the true church doth use, but the false church doth abuse.'

*Talk between the woman and a friar.* Then stepped forth an old friar, and asked what she said of the holy pope.

'I,' (said she), 'say that he is Antichrist and the devil.'

Then they all laughed.

'Nay,' (said she), 'you had more need to weep than to laugh, and to be sorry that ever you were born, to be the chaplains of that Whore of Babylon. I defy him and all his falsehood: and get you away from me: you do but trouble my conscience. You would have me follow your doings: I will first lose my life. I pray you depart.'

'Why, thou foolish woman,' (said they), 'we come to thee for thy profit and soul's health.'

'O Lord God,' (said she), 'what profit riseth by you that teach nothing but lies for truth? How save you souls, when you preach nothing but damnable lies, and destroy souls?'

'How provest thou that?' (said they).

'Do you not damn souls,' (said she), 'when you teach the *False doctrine* people to worship idols, stocks, and stones, the work of men's *of the papists* hands? and to worship a false god of your own making, of a *reproved.* piece of bread, and teach that the pope is God's vicar, and hath power to forgive sins? and that there is a Purgatory, when God's son hath by his passion purged all? and say, you make God and sacrifice him, when Christ's body was a sacrifice once for all? Do you not teach the people to number their sins in your ears, and say they be damned, if they confess not all: when God's word saith: "Who can number his sins?"* Do you not promise them trentals and dirges, and Masses for souls, and sell your prayers for money, and make them buy pardons, and trust to such foolish inventions of your own imaginations? Do you not altogether against God? Do you not teach us to pray upon beads, and to pray unto saints, and say they can pray for us? Do you not make holy water and holy bread to fray* devils? Do you not a thousand more abominations? And yet you say, you come for my profit and to save my soul. No, no, one hath saved me. Farewell you with your salvation.' Much other talk there was between her and them, which here were too tedious to be expressed.

In the mean time during this her month's liberty granted to her by the bishop, which we spake of before, it happened that she entering in Saint Peter's Church, beheld there a cunning Dutchman how he made new noses to certain fine images which were disfigured* in King Edward's time: 'What a mad man art thou,' (said she), 'to make them new noses, which within a few days shall all lose their heads.' The Dutchman accused her, and laid it hard to her charge. And she said unto him: 'Thou art accursed, and so are thy images.' He called her 'whore.' 'Nay,' (said she), 'thy images are whores, and thou art a whore-hunter: for doth not God say: "You go a-whoring after strange gods,* figures of your own making"? and thou art one of them.' Then was she sent for, and clapped* fast: and from that time she had no more liberty. . . .

In the bill of my information, it is so reported to me, that albeit she was of such simplicity and without learning, yet you could declare no place of scripture, but she would tell you the chapter: yea, she would recite to you the names of all the books of the Bible. . . .

At the last, when they perceived her to be past remedy, and had consumed all their threatenings, that by neither imprisonment nor liberty, by menaces nor flattery, they could bring her to sing any other song, nor win her to their vanities and superstitious doings, then they cried out, 'An Anabaptist,* an Anabaptist.' Then at a day they brought her from the bishop's prison to the guildhall, and after that delivered her to the temporal power, according to their custom, where she was by the gentlemen of the country exhorted yet to call for grace, and to leave her fond opinions: 'And go home to thy husband,' (said they:) 'thou art an unlearned woman, thou art not able to answer to such high matters.'

*The woman brought from the bishop's prison to the guildhall.*

*Exhortations to have her recant.*

'I am not,' said she: 'yet with my death I am content to be a witness of Christ's death: and I pray you make no longer delay with me: my heart is fixed, I will never otherwise say, nor turn to their superstitious doings.'

*The constant standing of this woman.*

Then the bishop said, the devil did lead her.

*Blasphemy of the bishop.*

'No my Lord,' (said she), 'it is the spirit of God which leadeth me, and which called me in my bed, and at midnight opened his truth to me.' Then was there a great shout and laughing among the priests and other. . . .

*How God revealed his truth unto her.*

Then the indictment being given and read, which was, that she should go to the place whence she came, and from thence to be led to the place of execution, then and there to be burned with flames till she should be consumed: she lifted up her voice and thanked God, saying: 'I thank thee my Lord my God, this day have I found that which I have long sought.' But such outcries as there were again, and such mockings were never seen upon a poor silly woman: all which she most patiently took. And yet this favour they pretended after her judgement, that her life should be spared, if she would turn and recant. 'Nay, that will I not,' (said she:) 'God forbid that I should lose the life eternal for this carnal and short life. I will never turn from my heavenly husband, to my earthly husband: from the fellowship of angels, to mortal

*Judgement given against this good woman.*

*She thanketh God for her judgement given.*

children: and if my husband and children be faithful, then am I theirs. God is my father,* God is my mother, God is my sister, my brother, my kinsman, God is my friend most faithful.'

Then was she delivered to the sheriff, and innumerable people beholding her, she was led by the officers to the place of execution, without the walls of Exeter, called Southernhay, where again these superstitious priests assaulted her: and she prayed them to have no more talk with her, but cried still, 'God be merciful to me a sinner, God be merciful to me a sinner.' And so whiles they were tying her to the stake, thus still she cried, and would give no answer to them, but with much patience took her cruel death, and was with the flames and fire consumed: and so ended this mortal life as constant a woman in the faith of Christ, as ever was upon the earth. She was as simple a woman to see to as any man might behold: of a very little and short stature, somewhat thick, about fifty-four years of age. She had a cheerful countenance, so lively, as though she had been prepared for that day of her marriage to meet the Lamb:* most patient of her words and answers, sober in apparel, meat and drink, and would never be idle: a great comfort to as many as would talk with her: good to the poor: and in her trouble, money, she said, she would take none: for she said, 'I am going to a city where money beareth no mastery: whiles I am here, God hath promised to feed me.' Thus was her mortal life ended. For whose constancy God be everlastingly praised. Amen.

Touching the name of this woman (as I have now learned) she was the wife of one called Prest, dwelling in the diocese of Exeter, not far from Launceston.

*The woman delivered to the sheriff and led to the place of execution.*

# 27. EDWIN SANDYS

A brief discourse concerning the troubles and
happy deliverance of the Reverend Father in God,
Doctor Sandys, first Bishop of Worcester, next of
London, and now Archbishop of York.

King Edward died, the world being unworthy of him, the Duke
of Northumberland* came down to Cambridge with an army
of men, having commission to proclaim Lady Jane* queen, and
by power to suppress Lady Mary, who took upon her that dignity, and was proclaimed queen in Norfolk. The duke sent for
Doctor Sandys* being Vice Chancellor, for Doctor Parker,* for
Doctor Bill, and Master Lever, to sup with him. Amongst other
speeches he said: 'Masters, pray for us that we speed well, if not,
you shall be made bishops, and we deacons.' And even so it came
to pass, Doctor Parker, and Doctor Sandys were made bishops,
and he and Sir John Gates, who was then at the table, were made
deacons ere it was long after, on the Tower Hill. Doctor Sandys
being Vice Chancellor, was required to preach on the morrow.
The warning was short for such an auditory, and to speak of
such a matter: yet he refused not the thing, but went into his
chamber, and so to bed. He rose at three of the clock in the
morning, took his Bible in his hand, and after that he had prayed
a good space, he shut his eyes, and holding his Bible before him,
earnestly prayed to God that it might fall open where a most fit
text should be for him to entreat of. The Bible as God would
have it, fell open upon the first chapter of Joshua, where he
found so convenient a piece of scripture* for that time, that the
like he could not have chosen in all the Bible. . . . And as God
gave the text, so gave he him such order and utterance, as pulled
many tears out of the eye of the biggest of them.

 In the time of his sermon one of the guard lift up to him into
the pulpit a Mass book and a grail, which Sir George Haward
with certain of the guard had taken that night in Master
Hurleston's house where Lady Mary had been a little before, and
there had Mass. The duke with the rest of the nobility, required

Doctor Sandys to put his sermon in writing, and appointed Master Lever to go to London with it, and to put it in print. Doctor Sandys required one day and a half for writing of it. At the time appointed he had made it ready, and Master Lever was ready booted* to receive it at his hands, and carry it to London. As he was delivering of it, one of the beadles named Master Adams, came weeping to him, and prayed him to shift for himself, for the duke was retired, and Queen Mary proclaimed.

Doctor Sandys was not troubled here withal, but gave the sermon written to Master Layfield. Master Lever departed home, and he went to dinner to one Master More's a beadle, his great friend. At the dinner, Mistress More's seeing him merry and pleasant (for he had ever a man's courage, and could not be terrified) drank unto him, saying: 'Master Vice Chancellor, I drink unto you, for this is the last time that ever I shall see you.' And so it was, for she was dead before Doctor Sandys returned out of Germany. The duke that night retired to Cambridge, and sent for Doctor Sandys to go with him to the market place to proclaim Queen Mary. The duke cast up his cap with others, and so laughed that the tears ran down his cheeks for grief. He told Doctor Sandys that Queen Mary was a merciful woman, and that he doubted not thereof: declaring, that he had sent unto her to know her pleasure, and looked for a general pardon. Doctor Sandys answered, 'My life is not dear unto me, neither have I done or said anything that urgeth my conscience. For that which I spake of the state, I have instructions warranted by the subscription of sixteen councillors. Neither can speech be treason, neither yet have I spoken further than the word of God, and laws of this realm doth warrant me, come of me what God will. But be you assured, you shall never escape death: for if she would save you, those that now shall rule, will kill you.'

That night the guard apprehended the duke, and certain grooms of the stable were as busy with Doctor Sandys as if they would take a prisoner. But Sir John Gates* who lay then in Doctor Sandys his house, sharply rebuked them, and drove them away. Doctor Sandys by the advice of Sir John Gates, walked into the fields. In the mean time, the University contrary to all order, had met together in consultation, and ordered, that Doctor Mouse and Doctor Hatcher, should repair to

Doctor Sandys's lodging, and fet* away the statute book of the University, the keys, and such other things that were in his keeping, and so they did, for Doctor Mouse being an earnest Protestant the day before, and one whom Doctor Sandys had done much for, now was he become a papist, and his great enemy. Certain of the University had appointed a congregation at after noon. As the bell rang to it, Doctor Sandys commeth out of the fields, and sending for the beadles, asketh what the matter meaneth, and requireth them to wait upon him to the Schools, according to their duty. So they did, and so soon as Doctor Sandys, the beadles going before him, came into the Regent House* and took his chair, one Master Mitch with a rabble of unlearned papists, went into a by-school, and conspired together to pull him out of his chair, and to use violence unto him. Doctor Sandys began his oration, expostulating with the University, charging them with great ingratitude, declaring that he had said nothing in his sermon, but that he was ready to justify, and that their case was all one with his: for they had not only concealed, but consented to that which he had spoken.

And thus while he remembered unto them how beneficial he had been to the University, and their unthankfulness to him again, in cometh Master Mitch with his conspirators about twenty in number. One layeth hand upon the chair to pull it from him, another told him that that was not his place, and another called him 'traitor.' Whereat he perceiving how they used violence, and being of great courage, groped to his dagger, and had dispatched some of them as God's enemies, if Doctor Bill and Doctor Blith had not fallen upon him, and prayed him for God's sake to hold his hands and be quiet, and patiently to bear that great offered wrong. He was persuaded by them, and after that tumult was ceased, he ended his oration, and having some money of the University's in his hands, he there delivered the same every farthing. He gave up the books, reckonings and keys, pertaining to the University, and withal, yielded up his office, praying God to give to the University a better officer, and to give them better and more thankful hearts, and so repaired home to his own College.

On the morrow after, there came unto him one Master Jerningham, and one Master Thomas Mildmay. Jerningham told him, that it was the queen's pleasure that two of the guard should attend upon him, and that he must be carried prisoner to the Tower of London with the duke. . . .

Upon this, his stable was robbed of four notable good geldings, the best of them Master Huddlestone took for his own saddle, and rode on him to London in his sight. An inventory was taken of all his goods by Master More beadle for the University. He was set upon a lame horse that halted to the ground, which thing a friend of his perceiving, prayed that he might lend him a nag. The yeomen of the guard were content. As he departed forth at the town's end, some papists resorted thither to jeer at him, some of his friends to mourn for him. He came into the rank to London, the people being full of outcries. And as he came in at Bishopsgate, one like a milk wife hurled a stone at him, and hit him on the breast with such a blow, that he was like to fall off his horse. To whom he mildly said: 'Woman, God forgive it thee.' Truth is, that journey and evil entreating so mortified him, that he was more ready to die, than to live.

As he came through Tower Hill street, one woman standing in her door, cried: 'Fie on thee thou knave, thou knave, thou traitor, thou heretic.' Whereat he smiled. 'Look, the desperate heretic,' (sayeth she), 'laugheth at this gear.' A woman on the other side of the street, answered, saying: 'Fie on thee neighbour, thou art not worthy to be called a woman, railing upon this gentleman whom thou knowest not, neither yet the cause why he is thus entreated.' Then she said, 'good gentleman, God be thy comfort, and give thee strength to stand in God's cause even to the end.' And thus he passed through fire and water into the Tower, the first prisoner that entered in that day, which was Saint James's day. The yeomen of the guard took from him his borrowed nag, and what else so ever he had. His man one Quinting Swainton brought after him a Bible, and some shirts and such like things. The Bible was sent in to him, but the shirts and such like, served the yeomen of the Guard.

After he had been in the Tower three weeks in a bad prison, he was lift up into Nun's Bower,* a better prison, where was put to him Master John Bradford.

At the day of Queen Mary's coronation, their prison door was set open, ever shut before. One Master Mitchell his old acquaintance, and had been prisoner before in the same place, came in to him and said: 'Master Sandys, there is such a stir in the Tower, that neither gates, doors, nor prisoners, are looked to this day. Take my cloak, my hat, and my rapier, and get you gone, you may go out of the gates without questioning, save yourself, and let me do as I may.' A rare friendship: but he refused the offer, saying: 'I know no just cause why I should be in prison. And thus to do were to make myself guilty. I will expect God's good will, yet must I think myself most bound unto you,' and so Master Mitchell departed.

While Doctor Sandys and Master Bradford were thus in close prison together twenty-nine weeks, one John Bowler was their keeper, a very perverse papist, yet by often persuading of him, for he would give ear, and by gentle using of him at the length he began to mislike popery and to favour the gospel, and so persuaded in true religion, that on a Sunday when they had Mass in the chapel, he bringeth up a service book, a manchet and a glass of wine, and there Doctor Sandys ministered the communion to Bradford and to Bowler. Thus Bowler was their son begotten in bonds when Wyatt was in arms, and the old Duke of Norfolk* sent forth with a power of men to apprehend him, that room might be made in the Tower for him and other his accomplices, Doctor Cranmer, Doctor Ridley, and Master Bradford were cast into one prison, and Doctor Sandys with nine other preachers were sent into the Marshalsea.

The keeper of the Marshalsea appointed to every preacher, a man to lead him in the street, he caused them go far before, and he and Doctor Sandys came behind, whom he would not lead, but walked familiarly with him. Yet Doctor Sandys was known, and the people everywhere prayed to God to comfort him and to strength[en] him in the truth. By that time the people's minds were altered, popery began to be unsavoury. After they passed the Bridge, the keeper Thomas Way said to Doctor Sandys: 'I perceive the vain people would set you forward to the fire, ye are as vain as they, if you being a young man will stand in your own conceit, and prefer your own knowledge before the judgement of so many worthy prelates, ancient, learned, and grave men as be in this realm. If you so do, you shall find me as strait a keeper as one that utterly misliketh your religion.'

Doctor Sandys answered: 'I know my years young and my learning small. It is enough to know Christ crucified, and he hath learned nothing that seeth not the great blasphemy that is in popery. I will yield unto God and not unto man. I have read in the scriptures of many godly and courteous keepers, God may make you one. If not, I trust he will give me strength and patience to bear your hard dealing with me.' Saith Thomas Way, 'do ye then mind to stand to your religion?': 'Yea,' saith Doctor Sandys, 'by God's grace.' 'Truly,' saith the keeper, 'I love you the better, I did but tempt you. What favour I can show you, you shall be sure of, and I shall think myself happy if I may die at the stake with you.' The said keeper showed Doctor Sandys ever after, all friendship: he trusted him to go into the fields alone, and there met with Master Bradford, who then was removed into the Bench, and there found like favour of his keeper. He laid him in the best chamber in the house: he would not suffer the Knight Marshal's man to lay fetters on him, as others had. And at his request he put Master Sandys into him, to be his bedfellow, and sundry times suffered his wife, who was Master Sandys's daughter of Essex, a gentlewoman, beautiful both in body and soul to resort to him. There was great resort to Doctor Sandys, and Master Saunders, they had much money offered them, but they would receive none. They had the communion there three or four times, and a great sort of communicants. Doctor Sandys gave such exhortation to the people, for at that time being young, he was thought very eloquent, that he moved many tears and made the people abhor the Mass, and defy all popery.

When Wyatt with his army came into Southwark, he sent two gentlemen into the Marshalsea to Doctor Sandys: saying, that Master Wyatt would be glad of his company and advice, and that the gates should be set open for all the prisoners. He answered: 'Tell Master Wyatt, if this his rising be of God it will take place: if not, it will fall. For my part I was committed hither by order, I will be discharged by like order, or I will never depart hence.' So answered Master Saunders, and the rest of the preachers being there prisoners.

After that Doctor Sandys had been nine weeks prisoner in the Marshalsea, by the mediation of Sir Thomas Holcroft then

Knight Marshall he was set at liberty. Sir Thomas sued earnestly to the Bishop of Winchester, Doctor Gardiner for his deliverance after many repulses, except Doctor Sandys would be one of their sect, and then he could want nothing. He wrung out of him that if the queen could like of his deliverance, he would not be against it: for that was Sir Thomas's last request. In the mean time he had procured two ladies of the Privy Chamber to move the queen in it: who was contented if the Bishop of Winchester could like of it. The next time that the bishop went into the Privy Chamber to speak with the queen, Master Holcroft followed and had his warrant for Doctor Sandys's remission ready, and prayed the two ladies, when as the bishop should take his leave to put the queen in mind of Doctor Sandys. So they did. And the queen said, 'Winchester: what think you by Doctor Sandys, is he not sufficiently punished?' 'As it please your majesty,' sayeth Winchester. That he spake, remembering his former promise to Master Holcroft, that he would not be against Doctor Sandys, if the queen should like to discharge him. Sayeth the queen: 'Then truly, we would that he were set at liberty.' Immediately Master Holcroft offered the queen the warrant, who subscribed the same, and called Winchester to put to his hand, and so he did. The warrant was given to the Knight Marshal again, Sir Thomas Holcroft. As the bishop went forth of the Privy Chamber door, he called Master Holcroft to him: commanding him not to set Doctor Sandys at liberty, until he had taken sureties of two gentlemen of his country with him, every one bound in £500 that Doctor Sandys should not depart out of the realm without licence. Master Holcroft immediately after met with two gentlemen of the North, friends and cousins to Doctor Sandys, who offered to be bound in body, goods and lands for him. . . . Doctor Sandys answered: 'I give God thanks, who hath moved your heart to mind me so well, and I think myself most bound unto you, God shall requite, and I shall never be found unthankful. But as you have dealt friendly with me, I will also deal plainly with you. I came a free man into prison, I will not go forth a bondman. As I cannot benefit my friends, so will I not hurt them: and if I be set at liberty, I will not tarry six days in this realm if I may get out. If therefore I may not go free forth, send me to the Marshalsea again, and there you shall be sure of me.'

This answer much misliked Master Holcroft: he told Doctor Sandys that the time would not long continue, a change would shortly come: the star was but a cloud, and would soon shake away. And that his cousin Sir Edward Bray would gladly receive him and his wife into house, where he should never need to come at church, and how the Lady Bray was a zealous gentlewoman, who hated popery. Adding that he would not so deal with him to lose all his labour. When Doctor Sandys could not be removed from his former saying, Master Holcroft said: 'Seeing you cannot be altered, I will change my purpose, and yield unto you. Come of it what will, I will set you at liberty: and seeing you mind over sea, get you gone so quickly as you can. One thing I require of you, that while you are there, you write nothing to come hither, for so ye may undo me.' He friendly kissed Doctor Sandys, bade him farewell, and commanded the keeper to take no fees of him: saying, 'let me answer Winchester as I may.' Doctor Sandys returned with the keeper to the Marshalsea [and] tarried all night. There on the morrow [he] gave a dinner to all the prisoners, bade his bedfellow, and sworn stake-fellow,* if it had so pleased God, Master Saunders farewell, with many tears and kissings, the one falling on the other's neck, and so departed, clearly delivered without examination or bond. From thence he went to the Bench, and there talked with Master Bradford, and Master Farrar Bishop of Saint David's, then prisoners. Then he comforted them, and they praised God for his happy deliverance. He went by Winchester's house, and there took boat, and came to a friend's house in London, called William Banks, and tarried there one night. On the morrow at night he shifted to another friend's house, and there he learned that search was made for him.

Doctor Watson and Master Christopherson coming to the Bishop of Winchester, told him that he had set at liberty the greatest heretic in England, and one that had of all other most corrupted the University of Cambridge Doctor Sandys. Whereupon the Bishop of Winchester being Chancellor of England, sent for all the constables of London, commanding them to watch for Doctor Sandys, who was then within the city, and to apprehend him, and whosoever of them should take him and bring him to him, he should have £5 for his labour. Doctor Sandys suspecting the matter, conveyed himself by night to one Master Barty's house a stranger, who was in the Marshalsea with him prisoner a while. He was a good Protestant and dwelt in Mark Lane. There he was six days, and had one or two of his friends that repaired unto him. Then he repaired to an acquaintance of his, one Hurlestone a skinner, dwelling in Cornhill. He caused his man Quinting to provide two geldings for him, minding on the morrow to ride into Essex to Master Sandys his father-in-law, where his wife was. . . .

[*After being warned by a sympathetic constable named Benjamin, Sandys altered his original plan and fled London by a different route.*]

Accordingly Doctor Sandys did, clothed like a gentleman in all respects, and looked wildly as one that had been long kept in prison out of the light. Benjamin carried him through Birching lane, and from one lane to another, till he come at Moorgate. There they went forth until they came to Bethnal Green where the horses were ready, and Master Hurleston, to ride with him as his man. Doctor Sandys pulled on his boots, and taking leave of his friend Benjamin, with tears they kissed each other, he put his hand in his purse, and would have given Benjamin a great part of that little he had, but Benjamin would take none. Yet since, Doctor Sandys hath remembered him thankfully. He rode that night to his father-in-law, Master Sandys where his wife was. He had not been there two hours, but it was told Master Sandys that there was two of the guard which would that night apprehend Doctor Sandys, and so they were appointed.

That night Doctor Sandys was guided to an honest farmer near the sea, where he tarried two days and two nights in a chamber without all company. After that he shifted to one James Mower, a shipmaster, who dwelt at Milton shore, where he expected wind for the English fleet ready into Flanders. While he was there James Mower brought to him forty or fifty mariners, to whom he gave an exhortation. They liked him so well, that they promised to die for it, or that he should be apprehended.

The sixth of May [1558] being Sunday, the wind served. He took his leave of his host and hostess, and went towards the ship. In taking his leave of his hostess who was barren, and had been married eight years, he gave her a fine handkerchief and an old royal of gold in it, thanking her much, and said: 'Be of good comfort, or that an whole year be past, God shall give you a child, a boy.' And it came to pass, for that day twelvemonth lacking one day, God gave her a fair son.

At the shore Doctor Sandys met with Master Isaac of Kent who had his eldest son there, who upon the liking he had to Doctor Sandys, sent his son with him, who afterward died in his father's house in Frankfort. Doctor Sandys and Doctor Cox,* were both in one ship, being one Cockrel's ship. They were within the kenning,* when two of the guard came thither to apprehend Doctor Sandys. They arrived at Antwerp, being bid to dinner to Master Locke. And at dinner time one George Gilpin being secretary to the English House, and kinsman to Doctor Sandys, came to him and rounded him in his ear, and said: 'King Philip hath sent to make search for you, and to apprehend you.' Hereupon they rose from their dinner in a marvellous great shower, and went out at the gate toward the land of Cleve.* There they found a wagon and hasted away, and came safe to Augsburg in Cleveland where Doctor Sandys tarried fourteen days, and then journeyed towards Strasbourg, where after he had lived one year, his wife came unto him. He fell sore sick of a flix,* which kept him nine months, and brought him to death's door. He had a child which fell sick of the plague and died. His wife at length fell sick of a consumption and died in his arms. No man had a more godly woman to his wife.

After this, Master Sampson went away to Emmanuel, a man skilful in the Hebrew. Master Grindal went into the country to learn the Dutch tongue. Doctor Sandys still remained in Strasbourg, whose sustentation then was chiefly from one Master Isaac, who loved him most dearly, and was ever more ready to give, than he to take. He gave him in the space above one hundreth marks, which sum the said Doctor Sandys paid him again, and by his other gifts and friendliness, showed himself to be a thankful man. When his wife was dead he went to Zurich, and there was in Peter Martyr's house for the space of five weeks.

Being there, as they sat at dinner, word suddenly came that Queen Mary was dead, and Doctor Sandys was sent for by his friends at Strasbourg. That news made Master Martyr, and Master Jarret then there, very joyful, but Doctor Sandys could not rejoice, it smote into his heart that he should be called to misery.

Master Bullinger* and the ministers feasted him, and he took his leave and returned to Strasbourg where he preached, and so Master Grindal and he came towards England, and came to London the same day that Queen Elizabeth was crowned.*

# 28. LADY ELIZABETH

The miraculous preservation of the Lady Elizabeth, now Queen of England, from extreme calamity and danger of life, in the time of Queen Mary her sister.

But when all hath been said and told, whatsoever can be recited touching the admirable working of God's present hand in defending and delivering any one person out of thraldom, never was there since the memory of our fathers, any example to be showed, wherein the Lord's mighty power hath more admirably and blessedly showed itself, to the glory of his own name, to the comfort of all good hearts, and to the public felicity of this whole realm, than in the miraculous custody and outscape* of this our sovereign lady, now queen, then Lady Elizabeth, in the strait time of Queen Mary her sister.

*The blessed protection of almighty God in preserving the Lady Elizabeth in her manifold dangers and troubles.*

In which story, first we have to consider in what extreme misery, sickness, fear, and peril her highness was: into what care, what trouble of mind, and what danger of death she was brought: first with great routs and bands of armed men (and happy was he that might have the carrying of her) being fetched up as the greatest traitor in the world, clapped in the Tower, and again tossed from thence, from house to house, from prison to prison, from post to pillar, at length also prisoner in her own house, and guarded with a sort of cutthroats, which ever gaped for the spoil, whereby they might be fingering of somewhat.

*The troubles of Lady Elizabeth in Queen Mary's time.*

Secondly, to consider again we have, all this notwithstanding, how strangely, or rather miraculously from danger she was delivered: what favour and grace she found with the almighty, who when all help of man, and hope of recovery was past, stretched out his mighty protection, and preserved her highness, and placed her in this princely seat of rest and quietness, wherein now she sitteth, and long may she sit, the Lord of his glorious mercy grant, we beseech him.

In which story, if I should set forth at large and at full, all the particulars and circumstances thereunto belonging, and as just occasion of the history requireth, besides the importunate length of the story discoursed, peradventure it might move offence to some being yet alive, and truth might get me hatred. Yet notwithstanding I intend (by the grace of Christ) therein to use such brevity and moderation, as both may be to the glory of God, the discharge of the story, the profit of the reader, and hurt to none, suppressing the names of some, whom here although I could recite, yet I thought not to be more cruel in hurting their name, than the queen hath been merciful in pardoning their lives.

*The history of the Lady Elizabeth.*

Therefore now to enter into the discourse of this tragical matter, first here is to be noted, that Queen Mary when she was first queen, before she was crowned, would go no whither, but would have her by the hand, and send for her to dinner and supper: but after she was crowned, she never dined nor supped with her, but kept her aloof from her, et cetera. After this it happened, immediately upon the rising of Sir Thomas Wyatt . . . that the Lady Elizabeth and the Lord Courtenay* were charged with false suspicion of Sir Thomas Wyatt's rising. Whereupon Queen Mary, whether for that surmise, or for what other cause I know not, being offended with the said Elizabeth her sister, at that time lying in her house at Ashridge, the next day after the rising of Wyatt, sent to her three of her councillors, to wit, Sir Richard Southwell,* Sir Edward Hastings,* then Master of the Horse, and Sir Thomas Cornwallis,* with their retinue and troop of horsemen, to the number of two hundred and fifty. Who at their sudden and unprovided* coming, found her at the same time sore sick in her bed, and very feeble and weak of body. Whither when they came, ascending up to her grace's Privy Chamber, they willed one of her ladies, whom they met, to declare unto her grace, that there were certain come from the court, which had a message from the queen. . . .

*Sir Richard Southwell, Sir Edward Hastings, and Sir Thomas Cornwallis sent to fetch up Lady Elizabeth, with whom also afterward was sent the Lord William Haward, et cetera. The unmannerliness of the knights.*

At whose so sudden coming into her bed chamber, her grace being not a little amazed, said unto them: 'Is the haste such, that it might not have pleased you to come tomorrow in the morning?'

They made answer, that they were right sorry to see her in that case. 'And I,' (quoth she), 'am not glad to see you here at this time of the night.' Whereunto they answered, that they came from the queen to do their message and duty: which was to this effect, that the queen's pleasure was, that she should be at London the seventh day of that present month. Whereunto she said: 'Certes, no creature more glad than I to come to her majesty, being right sorry that I am not in case at this time to wait on her, as you yourselves do see and can well testify.'

'Indeed we see it true,' (quoth they), 'that you do say: for which we are very sorry. Albeit we let you to understand, that our commission is such, and so straineth us, that we must needs bring you with us, either quick or dead.' Whereat she being amazed, sorrowfully said, that their commission was very sore: but yet notwithstanding she hoped it to be otherwise, and not so strait. 'Yes verily,' said they. Whereupon they called for two physicians, Doctor Owen and Doctor Wendy,* [and] demanded of them, whether she might be removed from thence with life, or no. Whose answer and judgement was, that there was no impediment to their judgement, to the contrary, but that she might travel without danger of life. *A strait commission from the Queen to bring the Lady Elizabeth either quick, or dead.*

In conclusion, they willed her to prepare against the morning at nine of the clock to go with them, declaring that they had brought with them the queen's litter for her. After much talk, the messengers declaring how there was no prolonging of times and days, so departed to their chamber, being entertained and cheered as appertained to their worships. *The gentleness of Queen Mary to send her horse litter to bring her sister to trouble.*

On the next morrow at the time prescribed, they had her forth as she was, very faint and feeble, and in such case, that she was ready to swoon three or four times between them. What should I speak here that cannot well be expressed, what an heavy house there was to behold the unreverent and doleful dealing of these men, but especially the careful fear and captivity of their innocent lady and mistress. . . .

Now, when she came to the court, her grace was there straight ways shut up, and kept as close prisoner a fortnight, which was till Palm Sunday, seeing neither king nor queen, nor lord, nor friend, all that time, but only then the Lord Chamberlain, Sir John Gage,* and the Vice-chamberlain, which were attendant unto the doors. About which time Sir William Sentlow was called before the Council. To whose charge was laid, that he knew of Wyatt's rebellion. Which he stoutly denied, *Lady Elizabeth taketh her journey towards the Queen.*

protesting that he was a true man, both to God and his prince, defying all traitors and rebels: but being straitly examined, he was in conclusion committed to the Tower.

Lady
Elizabeth
charged with
Sir Thomas
Wyatt's
conspiracy.

The Friday before Palm Sunday, the Bishop of Winchester, with nineteen other of the Council (who shall be here nameless) came unto her grace from the queen's majesty, and burdened* her with Wyatt's conspiracy: which she utterly denied, affirming that she was altogether guiltless therein. They being not contented with this, charged her grace with business made by

Sir Peter Carew,* and the rest of the gentlemen of the West Country: which also she utterly denying, cleared her innocency therein.

In conclusion, after long debating of matters, they declared unto her, that it was the queen's will and pleasure that she should go unto the Tower, while the matter were further tried and examined.

Whereat she being aghast, said, that she trusted the queen's majesty would be [a] more gracious Lady unto her, and that her highness would not otherwise conceive of her, but that she was a true woman: declaring furthermore to the lords, that she was innocent in all those matters wherein they had burdened her, and desired them therefore to be a further mean to the queen her sister, that she being a true woman in thought, word, and deed towards her majesty, might not be committed to so notorious and doleful a place, protesting that she would request no mercy at her hand, if she should be proved to have consented unto any such kind of matter as they laid unto her charge: and therefore in fine desired their lordships to think of her what she was, and that she might not so extremely be dealt withal for her truth.

Whereunto the lords answered again, that there was no remedy, for that the queen's majesty was fully determined that she should go unto the Tower. Wherewith the lords departed, with their caps hanging over their eyes.* But not long after, within the space of an hour or little more, came four of the foresaid lords of the Council, which were the Lord Treasurer,* the Bishop of Winchester,* the Lord Steward, [and] the Earl of Sussex,* with the guard, who warding the next chamber to her, secluded all her gentlemen and yeomen, ladies and gentlewomen, saving that for one gentleman usher, three gentlewomen, and two grooms of her chamber, were appointed in their rooms three other men of the queen's, and three waiting women to give attendance upon her, that none should have access to her grace.

*Lady Elizabeth's servants removed from her.*

At which time there were an hundreth of Northern soldiers in white coats, watching and warding about the gardens all that night, a great fire being made in the midst of the hall, and two certain lords watching there also with their band and company.

*The Queen's men, and waiting women attendant upon Lady Elizabeth.*

Upon Saturday following, two lords of the Council (the one was the Earl of Sussex, the other shall be nameless*) came and certified her grace, that forthwith she must go unto the Tower, the barge being prepared for her, and the tide now ready, which tarryeth for nobody. In heavy mood her grace requested the lords that she might tarry another tide, trusting that the next would be better and more comfortable. But one of the lords replied, that neither tide nor time was to be delayed.

And when her grace requested him that she might be suffered to write to the queen's majesty, he answered, that he durst not permit that, adding that in his judgement it would rather hurt, than profit her grace in so doing.

*The hard dealing of a certain Lord with the Lady Elizabeth.*

But the other lord, more courteous and favourable (who was the Earl of Sussex), kneeling down, told her grace that she should have liberty to write, and as he was a true man, he would deliver it to the queen's highness, and bring an answer of the same, whatsoever came thereof. Whereupon she wrote, albeit she could in no case be suffered to speak with the queen to her great discomfort, being no offender against the queen's majesty.

*The Earl of Sussex gentle to the Lady Elizabeth.*

*Lady Elizabeth writeth to the Queen but it would not serve.*

And thus the tide and time passed away for that season, they privily appointing all things ready that she should go the next tide which fell about midnight: but for fear she should be taken by the way, they durst not. So they stayed till the next day, being Palm Sunday, when about nine of the clock these two returned again, declaring that it was time for her grace to depart. She answering, 'if there be no remedy, I must be contented, willing the lords to go on before.' Being come forth into the garden, she did cast up her eyes toward the window, thinking to have seen the queen, which she could not. Whereat she said she marvelled much what the nobility of the realm meant, which in that sort would suffer her to be led into captivity, the Lord knew whither, for she did not. In the mean time commandment was given in all London, that everyone should keep the church and carry their palms,* while in the mean season she might be conveyed without all recourse of people into the Tower.

*Lady Elizabeth sent to the Tower.*

After all this, she took her barge with the two foresaid lords, three of the queen's gentlewomen, and three of her own, her gentleman usher, and two of her grooms, lying and hovering upon the water a certain space, for that they could not shoot* the bridge, the bargemen being very unwilling to shoot the same so soon as they did, because of the danger thereof: for the stern of the boat, struck upon the ground, the fall* was so big, and the water was so shallow, that the boat being under the bridge, there stayed again a while. At landing, she first stayed, and denied to land at those stairs where all traitors and offenders customably used to land, neither well could she, unless she should go over her shoe. The lords were gone out of the boat before and asked why she came not. One of the lords went back again to her, and brought word [that] she would not come.

Then said one of the lords which shall be nameless,* that she should not choose: and because it did then rain, he offered to her his cloak, which she (putting it back with her hands with a good dash) refused. So she coming out, having one foot upon the stair, said: 'Here landeth as true a subject being prisoner, as ever landed at these stairs: and before thee O God I speak it, having none other friends but thee alone.'

*The words of Lady Elizabeth entering the Tower.*

. . . After this passing a little further, she sat down upon a cold stone and there rested her self. To whom the Lieutenant then being, said: 'Madam, you were best to come out of the rain, for you sit unwholesomely.' She then replying, answered again: 'Better sitting here than in a worse place: for God knoweth, I know not whither you will bring me.' With that her gentleman usher wept: she demanding of him what he meant so uncomfortably to use her, seeing she took him to be her comforter, and not to dismay her, especially for that she knew her truth to be such, that no man should have cause to weep for her. But forth she went into the prison.

The doors were locked and bolted upon her: which did not a little discomfort and dismay her grace. At what time she called to her gentlewoman for her book,* desiring God not to suffer her to build her foundation upon the sands but upon the rock,* whereby all blasts of blistering weather should have no power against her. The doors being thus locked, and she close shut up, the lords had great conference how to keep ward and watch, every man declaring his opinion in that behalf, agreeing straightly and circumspectly, to keep her.

*The Christian prayer of Lady Elizabeth.*

Then one of them, which was the lord of Sussex swearing, said: 'My lords, let us take heed, and do no more than our commission will bear us, whatsoever shall happen hereafter. And further, let us consider that she was the king, our master's daughter, and therefore let us use such dealing, that we may answer unto it hereafter, if it shall so happen, for just dealing,' (quoth he), 'is always answerable': whereunto the other lords agreed that it was well said of him, and thereupon departed. . . .

*The lord of Sussex speaketh for Lady Elizabeth.*

The next day her grace took her journey from thence to Woodstock, where she was enclosed, as before in the Tower of London, the soldiers guarding and warding both within and without the walls, every day to the number of threescore, and in the night without the walls forty during the time of her imprisonment there.

At length she had gardens appointed for her walk, which was very comfortable to her grace. But always when she did recreate herself therein, the doors were fast locked up, in as strait manner as they were in the Tower, being at the least five or six locks between her lodging and her walks: Sir Henry [Bedingfield] himself keeping the keys, and trusting no man therewith. Whereupon she called him her jailer: and he kneeling down, desired her grace not to call him so, for he was appointed there to be one of her officers. 'From such officers,' (quoth she), 'good Lord deliver me.'. . .

But before her removing away from Woodstock, we will a little stay to declare in what dangers her life was in during this time she there remained: first through fire, which began to kindle between the boards and ceiling under the chamber where she lay, whether by a spark of fire, gotten into a cranny, or whether of purpose by one that meant her no good, the

*Lady Elizabeth in danger of fire.*

Lord doth know. Nevertheless a worshipful knight of Oxfordshire, which was there joined the same time with Sir Henry Bedingfield in keeping that Lady (who then took up the boards and quenched the fire) verily supposed it to be done of purpose.

*Lady Elizabeth in danger of killing.*

Furthermore it is thought, and also affirmed (if it be true) of one Paul Peny, a keeper of Woodstock, a notorious ruffian and a butcherly wretch, that he was appointed to kill the said Lady Elizabeth: who both saw the man being often in her sight, and also knew thereof.

*Another conspiracy of murder against Lady Elizabeth.*

Another time, one of the privy chamber, a great man about the queen, and chief darling of Stephen Gardiner, named Master James Basset, came to Blandenbridge a mile from Woodstock, with twenty or thirty privy coats, and sent for Sir Henry Bedingfield to come and speak with him. But, as God would, which disposed all things after the purpose of his own will, so it happened, that a little before the said Sir Henry Bedingfield was sent for by post to the council, leaving straight word behind him with his brother, that no man, whatsoever he were, though coming with a bill of the queen's hand, or any other warrant, should have access to her before his return again. By reason whereof it so fell out, that Master Bedingfield's brother coming to him at the bridge, would suffer him in no case to approach in, who otherwise (as is supposed) was appointed violently to murder the innocent lady.

*Lady Elizabeth preserved by the Lord's providence from execution in the Tower. Winchester's platform overthrown.*

In the life of Stephen Gardiner we declared before . . . how that the Lady Elizabeth being in the Tower, a writ came down, subscribed with certain hands of the council for her execution. Which if it were certain, as it is reported, Winchester (no doubt) was deviser of that mischievous drift: and doubtless the same Ahithophel* had brought his impious purpose that day to pass, had not the fatherly providence of almighty God (who is always stronger than the devil) stirred up Master Bridges, Lieutenant the same time of the Tower, to come in haste to the queen, to give certificate thereof, and to know further her consent touching her sister's death. Whereupon it followed, that all that devise was disappointed, and Winchester's devilish platform, which he said he had cast through the Lord's great goodness, came to no effect.

Where moreover is to be noted, that during the prisonment of this lady and princess, one Master Edmund Tremain was on the rack, and Master Smithwick, and diverse other in the Tower were examined, and diverse offers made to them to accuse the guiltless lady, being in her captivity. Howbeit all that notwithstanding, no matter could be proved by all examinations, as she the same time lying at Woodstock, had certain intelligence by the means of one John Gayer: who under a colourable pretence of a letter to Mistress Cleve from her father, was let in, and so gave them secretly to understand of all this matter. Whereupon the Lady Elizabeth at her departing out from Woodstock, wrote these verses with her diamond in a glass window.*

> Much suspected by me:
> Nothing proved can be.
> Quoth Elizabeth prisoner. . . .

*Verses written by Lady Elizabeth in the glass window.*

The next day following, her grace entered Hampton Court on the back side, into the prince's lodging, the doors being shut to her, and she guarded with soldiers, as before, lay there a fortnight at the least, or ever any had recourse unto her. . . .

Thus her grace departing, went to her lodging again, and the seventh night after was released of Sir Henry Bedingfield her jailer (as she termed him) and his soldiers, and so her grace being set at liberty from imprisonment, went into the country,* and had appointed to go with her Sir Thomas Pope,* one of Queen Mary's councillors, and one of her gentlemen ushers, Master Gage, and thus straitly was she looked to* all Queen Mary's time. And this is the discourse of her highness's imprisonment. . . .

*Lady Elizabeth by God's providence set at liberty. Sir Henry Bedingfield discharged.*

# 29. JUDGEMENT TALES

The severe punishment of God upon the
persecutors of his people and enemies to his word,
with such also as have been blasphemers, contemners,
and mockers of his religion.

*A treatise of* Leaving now Queen Mary, being dead and gone, I come to
*God's severe* them which under her were the chief ministers and doers in
*punishment* this persecution, the bishops (I mean) and priests of the clergy,
*against cruel*
*persecutors,* to whom Queen Mary gave all the execution of her power,* as
*and enemies to* did Queen Alexandra* to the Pharisees after the time of the
*his word.* Maccabees. Of whom Josephus thus writeth . . . [that] 'She
only retained to herself the name and title of the kingdom, but
all her power, she gave to the Pharisees to possess,'* et cetera.
Touching which prelates and priests, here is to be noted in like
sort the wonderful and miraculous providence of almighty
God, which as he abridged the reign of their queen, so he
suffered them not to escape unvisited: first beginning with
Stephen Gardiner the Arch-persecutor of Christ's church,
whom he took away about the midst of the queen's reign.* . . .

After him dropped other away also, some before the death of
*God's* Queen Mary, and some after, as Morgan Bishop of Saint
*punishment* David's, who sitting upon the condemnation of the blessed
*upon Doctor*
*Morgan* martyr Bishop Farrar, and unjustly usurping his room, not
*Bishop of* long after was stricken by God's hand after such a strange sort,
*Saint David's.* that his meat would not go down but rise and pick up again,
sometime at his mouth, sometime blown out of his nose most
horrible to behold, and so he continued till his death. . . .

Among other plentiful and sundry examples of the Lord's
judgement and severity practised upon the cruel persecutors of
his people, that is not the least that followeth, concerning the
story of one William Fenning, the effect and circumstance of
which matter is this.

John Cooper, of the age of forty-four years, dwelling at
Watsam in the county of Suffolk, being by science a carpenter, a
man of a very honest report and a good housekeeper, a harbourer

of strangers, that travailed for conscience, and one that favoured religion,* and those that were religious, he was of honest conversation and good life hating all popish and papistical trash.

This man being at home in his house, there came unto him one William Fenning, a serving man dwelling in the said town of Watsam, and understanding that the said Cooper had a couple of fair bullocks, did desire to buy them of him, which Cooper told him that he was loath to sell them, for that he had brought them up for his own use, and if he should sell them, he then must be compelled to buy other and that he would not do.

When Fenning saw he could not get them (for he had often assayed the matter) he said he would sit as much in his light,* and so departed, and went and accused him of high treason. The words he was charged with were these: how he should pray that if God would not take away Queen Mary, that then he should wish the devil to take her away. Of these words did this Fenning charge him before Sir Henry Doyle Knight (unto him he was carried by Master Timperley of Hinchlesam in Suffolk, and one Grimwood of Lowshaw* Constable) which words Cooper flatly denied: and said he never spake them, but that could not help.

Notwithstanding he was arraigned therefore at Berry before Sir Clement Higham, at a Lent assize, and there this Fenning brought two naughty men that witnessed the speaking of the foresaid words, whose names were Richard White of Watsam, and Grimwood of Hitcham,* in the said county of Suffolk. Whose testimonies were received as truth, although this good man John Cooper had said what he could to declare himself innocent therein, but to no purpose God knoweth. For his life was determined, as in the end appeared by Sir Clement Higham's words, who said he should not escape, for an example to all heretics, as indeed he thoroughly performed. For immediately he was judged to be hanged, drawn, and quartered, which was executed upon him shortly after, to the great grief of many a good heart. Here good Cooper is bereft of his life, and leaves behind him alive his wife and nine children with goods and cattle, to the value of three hundred marks, the which substance was all taken away by the said Sir Henry Doyle sheriff, but his wife and poor children left to the wide world in their clothes, and suffered not to enjoy one penny of that they had sore laboured for, unless they made friends to buy it with money, of the said sheriff so cruel and greedy was he and his officers upon such things as were there left.

Well, now this innocent man is dead, his goods spoiled, his wife and children left desolate and comfortless, and all things is hushed, and nothing feared of any part, yet the Lord who surely doth revenge the guiltless' blood, would not still so suffer it, but began at the length to punish it himself. For in the harvest after, the said Grimwood of Hitcham one of the witnesses before specified, as he was in his labour staking up a goaf* of corn, having his health and fearing no peril: suddenly his bowels fell out of his body, and immediately most miserably *The judgement* he died: such was the terrible judgement of God, to show his *of God upon* displeasure against this bloody act, and to warn the rest by *Grimwood.* these his judgements to repentance. The Lord grant us to honour the same for his mercy's sake. Amen. . . .

Before in the story of Master Bradford*. . . mention was *Master* made of Master Woodruff, who being the sheriff, used much to *Woodruff a* rejoice at the death of the poor saints of Christ, and so hard he *cruel sheriff,* was in his office, that when Master Rogers was in the cart going *plagued.* toward Smithfield, and in the way his children were brought unto him, the people making a lane for them to come: Master Woodruff had the carman's head should be broken* for staying his cart. But what happened? He was not come out of his office the space of a week, but he was stricken by the sudden hand of God, the one half of his body in such sort that he lay benumbed and bedridden, not able to move himself but as he was lifted of other, and so continued in that infirmity the space of seven or eight years till his dying day. . . .

Because some there be, and not a few, which have such a *A story of* great devotion in setting up the popish Mass, I shall desire *Burton bailiff* them to mark well this story following. There was a certain *of Crowland,* bailiff of Crowland in Lincolnshire named Burton, who pre- *how he was* tending an earnest friendship to the gospel in King Edward's *plagued for* days, in outward show at least (although inwardly he was a *setting up* papist or atheist,* and well known to be a man of a wicked and *Mass.*

adulterous life) set forth the king's proceedings lustily, till the time that King Edward was dead and Queen Mary placed quietly in her estate.

Then perceiving by the first proclamation concerning religion, how the world was like to turn, the bailiff turned his religion likewise: and so he moved the parish to show themselves the queen's friends, and to set up the Mass speedily. Nevertheless the most substantial of the parish, marvelling much at the bailiff's inconstant lightness, considering also his abominable life, and having not great devotion unto his request: knowing moreover that their duty and friendship to the queen stood not in setting up the Mass, spared to provide for it, as long as they might: but the bailiff called on them still in the queen's name.

At last, when he saw his words were not regarded, and purposing to win his spurs by playing the man in the Mass's behalf and the queen's, he got him to the church upon a Sunday morning, and when the curate was beginning the English service, according to the statute set forth by King Edward VI,* the bailiff cometh in a great rage to the curate and saith: 'Sirrah will you not say Mass? Buckle yourself to Mass you knave, or by God's blood I shall sheath my dagger in your shoulder.' The poor curate for fear settled himself to Mass.

Not long after this, the bailiff rode from home upon certain business, accompanied with one of his neighbours and as they came riding together upon the Fenbank homeward again, a crow sitting in a willow tree took her flight over his head, singing after he wonted note, 'knave, knave,' and withal let fall upon his face, so that her excrements ran from the top of his nose down to his beard.

*Burton earnest in setting up the Mass.*

The poisoned scent and savour whereof so noyed* his stomach, that he never ceased vomiting until he came home, wherewith his heart was so sore and his body so distempered: that for extreme sickness he got him to bed, and so lying, he was not able for the stink in his stomach and painful vomiting, to receive any relief of meat or drink, but cried out still, sorrowfully complaining of that stink, and with no small oaths, cursing the crow that had poisoned him. To make short, he continued but a few days, but with extreme pain of vomiting

*The stinking death of a popish Massmonger.*

and crying, he desperately died without any token of repentance of his former life.

Reported and testified for a certainty, by diverse of his neighbours, both honest and credible persons. . . .

*Alexander the cruel keeper of Newgate, died a rotten death.*

Alexander the keeper of Newgate, a cruel enemy to those that lay there for religion, died very miserably, being so swollen that he was more like a monster than a man, and so rotten within, that no man could abide the smell of him. This cruel wretch, to hasten the poor lambs to the slaughter, would go to Bonner, Story, Chomley, and other, crying out: 'Rid my prison, rid my prison: I am too much pestered with these heretics.'

*The sudden death of James, Alexander's son.*

The son of the said Alexander called James, having left unto him by his father great substance, within three years wasted all to naught: And when some marvelled how he spent those goods so fast: 'O,' said he, 'evil gotten, evil spent': and shortly after as he went in Newgate market, fell down suddenly, and there wretchedly died.

*John Peter, Alexander's son-in-law, rotted away.*

John Peter, son-in-law to this Alexander, an horrible blasphemer of God, and no less cruel to the said prisoners, rotted away, and so most miserably died. Who commonly when he would affirm anything, were it true or false, used to say: 'If it be not true, I pray God I rot ere I die.' Witness the printer hereof, with diverse other. . . .

*The just punishment of God upon Sir Rafe Ellerker persecutor.*

And what a notable spectacle of God's revenging judgement, have we to consider in Sir Rafe Ellerker, who as he was desirous to see the heart taken out of Adam Damlip,\* whom they most wrongfully put to death: so shortly after the said Sir Rafe Ellerker being slain of the Frenchmen, they all too mangling him, after they had cut off his privy members, would not so leave him, before they might see his heart cut out of his body. . . .

*Leaver of Abingdon, a blasphemer of God's martyrs, plagued.*

About the year of our Lord 1565 at Brightwell in the county of Berkshire, upon certain communication as touching the right reverend martyrs in Christ, Bishop Cranmer, Bishop Ridley, and Master Hugh Latimer, there came into an house in Abingdon, one whose name is Leaver, being a ploughman, dwelling in Brightwell aforesaid, and said, that he saw that evil favoured knave Latimer when he was burned: and also in despite said, that he had teeth like a horse. At which time and hour, as near as could be gathered, the son of the said Leaver most wickedly hanged himself, at Shepton in the county aforesaid within a mile of Abingdon.

These words were spoken in the hearing of me Thomas Jenens of Abingdon.

Did not Thomas Arundel, Archbishop of Canterbury give sentence against the Lord Cobham,* and died himself before him, being so stricken in his tongue, that neither he could swallow nor speak for a certain space before his death?. . .

*Thomas Arundel Archbishop of Canterbury.*

William Swallow the cruel tormentor of George Eagles,* was shortly after so plagued of God, that all the hair of his head, and nails of his fingers and toes went off, his eyes well near closed up, that he could scant see. His wife also was stricken with the falling sickness, with the which malady she was never infected before. . . .

*God's just plague upon William Swallow.*

Likewise Richard Potto, another troubler of the said George Eagles, upon a certain anger or chafe with his servants, was so suddenly taken with sickness, that falling upon his bed like a beast, there he died and never spake word. . . .

*God's just plague upon Richard Potto.*

# EXPLANATORY NOTES

## 1. THOMAS BILNEY

3 *from a child*: from childhood.

*both laws*: civil law and canon law.

*cross-keeper*: one who retains a large crucifix and carries it in procession.

*Luciferous*: Satanic.

5 *bore the swing*: possessed complete control.

*called me to knowledge*: converted me to evangelical faith.

6 *school*: Scholastic.

*I knew a man . . . and such fooleries*: on Hugh Latimer's reminiscences concerning Thomas Bilney, see *Selected Sermons of Hugh Latimer*, ed. Allan G. Chester (Charlottesville: University of Virginia Press for the Folger Shakespeare Library, 1968), 120–1, 167.

*words and examples . . . suffer his passion*: Matthew 26–7.

*New Testament of Tyndale's translation, and the Obedience of a Christian Man*: see entry for William Tyndale, in the Glossary of Persons.

*doctors, civil and canon*: learned individuals with a mastery of civil or canon law.

7 *of*: from.

*story of Haukes*: see Narrative 12.

*put away his wife*: divorced.

*four orders of friars*: the most important orders of mendicant brothers were the Franciscans (Grey Friars), Carmelites (White Friars), Dominicans (Black Friars), and Augustine (or Augustinian, or Austin) Friars.

*was at a point*: was determined.

*Doctor Pelles . . . Chancellor*: Doctor Thomas Pelles, chancellor of the diocese of Norwich.

9 *guildhall*: the governmental seat of a town or city.

*philosophy*: natural philosophy (i.e., the study of natural bodies).

*'Fear not . . . holy one of Israel'*: Isaiah 43: 1–3.

*tables*: tablets of paper or wax.

10 *Lollards' Pit*: a site where Lollards and others condemned for heresy were burnt alive.

*tarrying*: awaiting.

11 *collation*: a homily based upon comparison of biblical texts.

*'Hear my prayer . . . living be justified'*: Psalm 143: 1–2.

*for*: because of.

*Feed your flock, feed your flock*: engage in pastoral care.

12 *visor*: outward appearance, countenance.

*Credo*: 'I believe'.

*per licentiam Poeticam*: 'By poetic licence.'

*residue*: the remainder. 'Master More' is Sir Thomas More.

## 2. WILLIAM TYNDALE

14 *Enchiridion militis Christiani*: Tyndale offers this translation of Erasmus' influential guide to religious devotion to the Walshes in order to demonstrate his fluency in learned languages and therefore succeed in a bid to secure their patronage. See Erasmus, Glossary of Persons.

*doctorly*: learned (ironic).

*Tyndale*: concerning writings cited in this narrative, see the entry for Tyndale in the Glossary of Persons.

16 *Isocrates*: an ancient Greek rhetorician, a translation of whose unusually difficult prose Tyndale offers as a proof of his humanistic scholarship in an unsuccessful effort to secure patronage from Bishop Tunstall.

*Humphrey Monmouth*: a London merchant from whom Tyndale received patronage.

17 *with might and main*: with all of one's power and strength.

*wresting the scripture . . . riddles*: a reference to the fourfold method of biblical interpretation that Tyndale rejects in *The Obedience of a Christian Man*.

18 *the printer . . . Barnes*: on behalf of John Day, Foxe edited this edition of the collected doctrinal writings of Tyndale, John Frith (see Glossary of Persons), and Robert Barnes. The last-named figure was a former Augustinian friar and prior who went into exile after recanting from Lutheran beliefs. Following his return to England under the protection of Thomas Cromwell, Barnes served as a royal ambassador and was eventually burnt alive for heresy.

*as was the goddess Diana amongst the Ephesians*: Acts 19: 28–35.

19 *front*: the forward position.

20 *converted . . . household*: an allusion to the conversion of a Phillippian jailer by Sts Paul and Silas (Acts 16: 25–34).

## 3. ANNE ASKEW

22 *Secondly, he said . . . what Stephen and Paul had said therein*: on the basis of hearsay testimony concerning Askew's public exposition of the Bible, a member of a judicial inquest interrogates her concerning her understanding

of the following utterance by Sts Stephen and Paul: 'God was not in temples made with hands' (Acts 7: 48 and 17: 24).

22　*throw pearls among swine*: Matthew 7: 6.

　　*'If the trumpet . . . to the battle?'*: 1 Corinthians 14: 8.

23　*that every man . . . for the other*: James 5: 16.

　　*King's Book*: published under the formal title of *A Necessary Doctrine and Erudition for Any Christian Man* (1543), this codification of Henry VIII's theological views reaffirms traditional Roman Catholic doctrine.

　　*private Masses*: Protestants opposed Masses celebrated by unaccompanied priests.

　　*Saint Paul . . . word of God*: 1 Corinthians 14: 33–4.

24　*'By communing . . . take scathe'*: Proverbs 1: 5–7.

　　*sacrament at Easter*: laypersons were expected to receive the Eucharist only at Easter.

　　*London*: Bishop of London.

25　*was affectioned to*: was inclined to.

26　*Gray's Inn*: an institution for the study of the law, located in Holborn.

　　*willers*: wishers.

28　*And Solomon saith . . . a gift of God*: Proverbs 19: 14.

29　*houseled*: received the Eucharist.

30　*Ex. Registrum*: Latin for 'From the Register',i.e., an extract from the diocesan records of the Bishop of London.

31　*flang*: flung himself.

　　*Doctor Weston*: Doctor Hugh Weston.

34　*Doctor Shaxton*: Doctor Nicholas Shaxton recanted after his condemnation for heresy because of his denial of official doctrine concerning the Real Presence of Christ in the Eucharist. After failing in an attempt to obtain a similar recantation from Anne Askew, Shaxton preached from a portable pulpit when she and her companions were burnt at Smithfield.

　　*'He misseth, and speaketh without the book'*: Askew claims that his sermon lacks a basis in the Bible.

　　*old Duke of Norfolk*: Thomas Howard, 3rd Duke of Norfolk.

　　*'Fiat justitia'*: Latin for 'Let there be justice'.

## 4. JOHN ROGERS

35　*Merchant Adventurers*: an English trading company engaged largely in the cloth trade with Germany and the Low Countries.

　　*The Translation of Thomas Matthew*: an unauthorized English Bible translation supervised by John Rogers and printed in Antwerp in 1537.

It consists of William Tyndale's translation of the complete New Testament and of half of the Old Testament along with supplements from Miles Coverdale's translations, commentaries, and patristic writings. The pseudonym 'Thomas Matthew' is a composite of the names of two disciples, Sts Thomas and Matthew.

*unlawful vows*: Protestants rejected the taking of vows, in this case the vow of celibacy sworn by priests.

*Dutch tongue*: the German language.

36 *After the queen was come to the Tower of London*: after the collapse of the effort to install Lady Jane Grey on the throne, Mary I took up residence at the Tower. It served as a fortress, a royal palace, and a prison.

37 *I need not to tie my points*: Rogers recognizes that the haste with which he is to be executed renders it unimportant to fasten his clothing carefully.

38 *crown-shorn*: refers to the tonsure or shaven area of the heads of Roman Catholic priests and monks.

*Nebuchadnezzar*: the King of Babylonia whom the Book of Daniel represents as a powerful but overbearing ruler who ultimately went mad.

*Zerubbabel . . . Nehemiah*: after leading a group of Jews back from captivity in Babylon, Zerubbabel laid the foundation of the Second Temple in Jerusalem (Ezra 2–4); *Esdras*, commonly known as Ezra, was a priest and scribe credited with the writing down of scriptures that had been lost during the Babylonian Captivity (2 Esdras); *Nehemiah* was a governor of Jerusalem, who rebuilt its walls after the Babylonian Captivity (Nehemiah 1–7).

39 *Persians and Medes*: successor states of the Babylonian Empire.

*disparkled*: dispersed, driven apart.

*thrasonical*: boastful or vainglorious (from Thraso, a bombastic character in Terence's *Eunuchus*).

*'if judgement beginneth . . . ungodly and sinful appear'*: 1 Peter 4: 17–18.

*the printer of this present book*: John Day (see Glossary of Persons).

*Alexander, a coppersmith*: St Paul criticized a coppersmith named Alexander for doing him harm (2 Timothy 4: 14–15).

40 *Day of Judgement*: according to Christian eschatology, the period of time at the world's end during which God or his agent will determine the eternal state of all souls.

*Master Rochester*: Maurice Griffin, Bishop of Rochester.

*Sir Richard Southwell*: a Privy Councillor and Member of Parliament.

*protomartyr*: the first martyr during the reign of Mary I, with an allusion to St Stephen as the first Christian martyr (Acts 6: 8–8: 1).

## 5. LAWRENCE SAUNDERS

42 *as the private pastors of particular flocks*: as unauthorized ministers who led conventicles (i.e., clandestine religious gatherings at private locations).

43 *fantasize*: anticipate with pleasure.

*well-exercised*: well-employed.

*then was his company marvellous comfortable*: then was it profitable to be in his company.

*College at Fotheringhay*: a religious house in Northamptonshire that was dissolved during the reign of Edward VI.

44 *nothing meddling with the estate*: having nothing to do with affairs of state (i.e., his behaviour is not treasonable).

*a just plague . . . offered unto them*: Saunders preaches that the change in religion and suffering of Protestants and under Mary I constitutes a punishment for English backsliding of the kind encountered in Deuteronomic history, a term that refers to a cyclical pattern of religious infidelity, divine wrath, catastrophic punishment, renewal of faith, and providential restoration. It informs Joshua, Judges, 1 and 2 Samuel, and 1 and 2 Kings.

46 *as the apostles were brought . . . unto the rulers of the priests*: Acts 5: 19–32.

47 *Lord Chancellor*: Bishop Stephen Gardiner.

*as Annas sent Christ to Caiaphas*: John 18: 24. Protestants attacked Roman Catholic clergy by identifying them with Caiaphas, the high priest at the time of Jesus' trial.

*utter*: outer.

*tables*: the game of backgammon.

*admonished . . . by Ezekiel the prophet*: Saunders claims that he is a mouthpiece for Ezekiel's prophetic warnings concerning divine judgement (Ezekiel 7: 1–27).

48 *commanded rather to obey God than man*: Acts 5: 29.

*a book of true obedience*: Protestants mocked Stephen Gardiner for writing *De vera obedientia* (1535), a Latin defence of Henry VIII's exercise of royal supremacy over church and state. The bishop retracted this position after the accession of Mary I.

*prettily nipped and touched*: wittily mocked.

49 *Weston*: Hugh Weston, Dean of Westminster, Archdeacon of Colchester, and a leading figure in the prosecution of alleged heretics.

50 *Master Grimald*: Nicholas Grimald, poet and chaplain to Bishop Nicholas Ridley, was a co-religionist of Saunders who recanted his beliefs.

*had more store of good gifts, than of great constancy*: he had greater personal aptitude than he did religious fidelity. Narrative 3 recounts a comparable story about how Nicholas Shaxton preached, following his recantation, at the burning of Anne Askew and her fellow martyrs.

*a more bitter cup*: Matthew 27: 33–4.

51 *It is not I . . . queen's realm*: Saunders likens the confrontation between Mary I and dissident preachers to Ahab's reproof to Elijah for opposing the worship of Baal (1 Kings 18: 17–19).

*slept in the Lord*: died in a state of grace.

*Saint Lawrence*: according to tradition, St Lawrence of Rome was roasted to death on a gridiron (258 CE).

*green wood . . . burning fuel*: Saunders died slowly because the executioners tormented him by employing poor tinder to light unseasoned wood, which smouldered rather than bursting into flames.

## 6. JOHN HOOPER

53 *Six Articles*: John Foxe and other Protestants vilified the Act of Six Articles (1539) which reacted against evangelical reform by imposing stringent penalties including the death penalty for disbelief in clerical celibacy, auricular confession, celebration of private Masses, and the doctrine of transubstantiation.

*rabbis*: a term used contemptuously to identify Roman Catholic scholars with interpreters of Jewish laws during the time of Jesus Christ.

*Sir Thomas Arundel*: Sheriff of Dorset and an early patron of John Hooper, who notified Stephen Gardiner concerning the religious heterodoxy of his protégé.

54 *molested and laid for*: treated vexatiously.

*higher parts of Germany*: mountainous regions of central and southern Germany and the Alps.

*English exiles*: Protestants who left England following passage of the Act of Six Articles.

55 *Orpheus's harp*: in Greek mythology, Orpheus was capable of enchanting human beings, animals, and inanimate objects by playing on the lyre.

*liberal*: hospitable.

*sometime more free . . . epistle to Timothy*: among other qualities, St Paul expects the good bishop to exemplify moderation, hospitality, peacefulness, absence of avarice, and good management of his household (1 Timothy 3: 1–7).

56 *But I cannot tell . . . of this godly bishop*: after causing considerable scandal within the Edwardian church establishment because of his proto-Puritanical opposition to the wearing of ecclesiastical vestments, Hooper agreed to wear traditional episcopal attire as a concession to theologians such as Heinrich Bullinger, who wished to avoid dissension in the newly reformed Church of England.

57 *mathematical cap . . . into four parts*: a biretta; when worn by a bishop, the colour is commonly purple.

57 *Archbishop*: Thomas Cranmer, Archbishop of Canterbury.

*the fault . . . things themselves*: the principle of the *adiaphora* (the Greek word for 'indifferent things'), whereby the misuse of a religious practice does not rule out its appropriate use.

58 *in fine*: in conclusion.

59 *mess*: a serving of food.

60 *of*: concerning.

*close prison*: strict confinement.

61 *I paid always . . . man's table*: Hooper refers to the practice of requiring prisoners to pay for their meals.

*slave*: a contemptible person.

63 *Chandos*: Sir John Brydges, 1st Baron Chandos, Lieutenant of the Tower of London.

*the Angel*: an inn or public house.

## 7. ROWLAND TAYLOR

72 *Hadleigh*: a town in Suffolk where Rowland Taylor served as parson, as an appointee of Thomas Cranmer, whom he had served as chaplain.

*Master Thomas Bilney*: see Narrrative 1.

*sentence*: determination or opinion.

*doctor in both the civil and canon laws*: Taylor studied secular and ecclesiastical law at the University of Cambridge, where he underwent conversion to Protestantism under the influence of Hugh Latimer and others.

*did not . . . let out his benefice to a farmer*: he would not be an absentee cleric who accepts payment from a substitute who performs his duties.

*'Peter, lovest thou me? . . . feed my sheep'*: John 21: 15–17.

73 *all those virtuous qualities . . . in a true bishop*: 1 Timothy 3: 1–7. See the description of the character of John Hooper in Narrative 6.

*light . . . upon a candlestick*: Matthew 5: 15.

*Henry the eighth . . . godly kings*: the narrator idealizes Henry VIII as one who advocated religious reforms consonant to those actually implemented during the reign of his heir.

74 *Mammonist*: one who violates Jesus' admonition that one may not worship both God and Mammon (i.e., the personification of wealth). See Luke 16: 13.

*they built up . . . Palm Monday*: they replaced the communion table with a high altar in anticipation of celebration of the old-style Mass on the day after Palm Sunday.

*On the day following . . . missal sacrifice*: the narrator mocks Foster and Clerk for bringing in priests and protecting a priest who celebrated Mass as a continuing sacrifice in a theatrical style ordained by the Mass-book.

75 *'Thou traitor . . . queen's proceedings?'*: the annotator claims that the narrator alludes to an apocalyptic utterance in Daniel 8: 23–5.

*I make no commotion . . . tumults*: the marginal gloss asserts that Taylor styles himself as a latter-day Elijah who engages in conflict with priests of Baal (i.e., Roman Catholic priests as idolaters). See 1 Kings 18.

*super-altar*: a portable stone used in place of an altar in the celebration of Mass.

76 *Masser*: Roman Catholic priest (Protestant jargon).

*'The law of unrighteousness . . . without any fear'*: Wisdom of Solomon 2: 12–20.

*to their beards*: openly, in their face.

77 *forasmuch as our Saviour . . . fly into another*: Taylor styles himself and fellow martyrs as latter-day Apostles who undergo persecution in fulfilment of Jesus' prophecy (Matthew 10: 16–23).

*Saint Nicholas*: the patron saint of highwaymen (i.e., an ironic attack on Roman Catholic clerics).

78 *John Hull*: a servant of Rowland Taylor and a possible eyewitness source for elements in this narrative.

79 *Herod's oath . . . broken*: an illicit oath that is non-binding (Matthew 14: 7–9).

*'The mouth that lieth slayeth the soul'*: Wisdom of Solomon 1: 11.

*'Lord God, thou shalt destroy all that speak lies'*: Psalm 5: 6.

80 *blessed be . . . or whoredom*: in opposition to the Roman Catholic vow of clerical celibacy, Taylor cites St Paul's advocacy of marriage to those who are incapable of remaining celibate (1 Corinthians 7: 8–9).

81 *Chrysostom, and all the doctors . . . hath the church of God none*: Taylor cites St John Chrysostom and other Fathers of the Church as authorities in support of his Zwinglian view of the Lord's Supper as a commemoration of Christ's Passion as an all-sufficient offering rather than a sacrifice repeated during celebration of the Roman-rite Mass.

*As for the godly preachers . . . in corners*: many Protestant ministers who remained in England lived in secrecy in the manner of 'true' prophets hidden by Obadiah (1 Kings 18: 4).

83 *Clink*: a prison in Southwark that was located on the grounds of the palace of the Bishop of Winchester.

84 *in cheap*: of little value.

*crosier staff*: a crook carried by a bishop.

*by Saint Peter will I*: Taylor styles himself as a latter-day St Peter, who cut off the ear of a slave of the high priest (John 18: 10).

85 *against*: in front of.

89 *For he had not built . . . rock Christ*: Matthew 7: 24–7.

89  *my father's house*: heaven (see John 14: 2).

91  *fame*: reputation.

92  *waster*: a club.

93  *Sir John Shelton . . . speak Latin*: this official orders Taylor to recite the Vulgate Latin version of Psalm 51, rather than utter the prohibited English translation. Those condemned to death conventionally uttered this sorrowful prayer for deliverance as their final words.

94  *[Illustration 9]*: compositors typically set speeches in type within banderoles. We do not know why one sinuous streamer remains empty.

## 8. THOMAS TOMKINS

95  *web*: weaving, woven cloth.

96  *'Saint Paul saith . . . not worthy to eat'*: 2 Thessalonians 3: 10.

98  *the old image of King Porsenna . . . at London in Smithfield*: Bishop Bonner is likened to Lars Porsenna, an Etruscan king who besieged ancient Rome. This invader released Gaius Mucius Scaevola, a legendary figure who demonstrated heroism when he thrust his hand into a fire after attempting to assassinate Porsenna (see Livy, *History of Rome From its Foundation*, 2.12.1 – 13.5). The narrative draws a sharp contrast between the king's leniency and Bonner's insistence on following through with burning Tomkins alive.

100 *Having also likewise confessed . . . not to be allowed*: Tomkins rejects the reimposition of the Latin rite for the sacrament of baptism in place of the English service implemented by the second Edwardian Book of Common Prayer (see Introduction).

## 9. WILLIAM HUNTER

102 *in the sequel of this history*: in the following story.

 *was commanded . . . at a Mass*: laypersons were expected to receive the Eucharist at Easter.

103 *since the Bible came abroad in English*: since a change in law permitted public reading and interpretation of the Bible during the reign of Edward VI.

104 *'Except that ye eat . . . in you'*: John 6: 53.

105 *Capernaites*: residents in a Galilean town whom Jesus curses (Matthew 11: 23 – 4) and who disbelieve that they will feed spiritually or figuratively on his body and blood (John 6: 35 – 65). William Hunter uses this term to attack believers in transubstantiation.

 *'The words . . . spirit and life'*: John 6: 63.

 *Weald*: presumably the same parish as South Weald.

107 *the bread is his body*: Luke 22: 19.

*pelting chafe*: violent rage.

*consecration*: according to Roman Catholic doctrine, the elements of bread and wine undergo transubstantiation into the body and blood of Christ when the priest consecrates the sacramental elements during the sacrifice of the Mass.

*'This do in the remembrance of me'*: Zwingli and other Protestants base their view of Holy Communion as a commemorative celebration on these words (Luke 22: 19).

*he is a vine, a door*: John 15: 1 and 10: 9. Protestants base their rejection of transubstantiation on Jesus' description of himself by means of figurative language of this kind.

109 *'you can do no more than God will permit you'*: see John 19: 11.

110 *substance . . . accidences*: substance refer to the immaterial presence of Jesus Christ within the *accidents* of bread and wine. *Accidences* (accidents) is a Scholastic term for the material nature of sacramental bread and wine that undergo immaterial transubstantiation into the body and blood of Jesus Christ.

111 *'I thank you . . . the love of Christ'*: see Philippians 3: 8.

*crown of joy*: 1 Corinthians 9: 25. The crown is a traditional emblem of martyrdom.

112 *Master Higbed*: a fellow prisoner condemned to die as a heretic.

113 *groundsel*: a threshold.

*'the sacrifice of God . . . thou wilt not despise'*: Psalm 51: 17.

*'an humble spirit'*: William Tyrrell claims that William reads a Protestant mistranslation of Psalm 51: 17.

114 *element*: the sky.

## 10.  RAWLINS WHITE

115 *light*: enlightenment.

116 *vouching*: quoting.

*the leaf . . . sentence*: the exact page and sentence of White's quotations from the Bible.

117 *'I will by his favourable grace confess . . . everlasting life'*: Matthew 10: 32, John 6: 40.

*reporter*: John Dane, a confidant who brought gifts to Rowland White during his imprisonment and wrote this narrative.

118 *in quiet*: inactive.

*beware of false prophets . . . sheep's clothing*: Matthew 7: 15.

*by-dwellers*: neighbours.

119 *'Whereas two or . . . midst of them'*: Matthew 18: 20.

*'pray to your God . . . perform my desire'*: an allusion to 1 Kings 18: 24.

121 *swing*: control.

*the good old man . . . than the best*: White actively assists in building his own pyre.

122 *invection*: invective.

*clerkly*: in the manner of a cleric.

*'Do this in the remembrance of me'*: Luke 22: 19.

## 11. GEORGE MARSH

126 *unquieted*: disturbed.

128 *Bishops of London and Lincoln*: the Edwardian bishops, Nicholas Ridley (see Narrative 14) and John Taylor, whom the Marian regime had deprived of episcopal office on the ground of heresy.

*as the four symbols, or creeds*: derived from the Greek word for 'mark', *symbol* is an alternative term for a *creed* that constitutes a formulation of orthodox Christian doctrine. The Apostles', Nicene, and Athanasian creeds constitute the chief Christian doctrinal formulations. The other creeds were formulated by Sts Ambrose and Augustine, the fourth-century bishops of Milan and Hippo. Roman Catholics and Protestants shared them in common.

*Apostolorum*: Latin for 'Of the Apostles' (i.e., the Apostles' Creed).

*Austen*: St Augustine of Hippo.

129 *'Foolish and unlearned questions . . . engender strife'*: 2 Timothy 2: 23.

130 *enterprise*: attempt.

*with a lock upon his feet*: his feet were in chains.

*book*: presumably Marsh's Bible, although it might have been a devotional volume.

## 12. THOMAS HAUKES

133 *because his execution . . . tractation thereof*: because Foxe organizes martyrologies in obituary fashion (i.e., by the date of death), he inserts the 'tractation' (i.e., written account) concerning Thomas Haukes at a point different from that where he included accounts of the men with whom he was arrested.

*nobilitate*: to bestow nobility upon.

*as Saint Ambrose doth . . . write*: a citation from the writings of the fourth-century Bishop of Milan, who was a major patristic authority.

134 *Lord of Oxford*: John de Vere, 16th Earl of Oxford, a wealthy nobleman with a dissolute reputation. After originally supporting the succession of Lady Jane Grey, he went over to the side of Mary I and appears to have assisted in the burning of alleged heretics in Essex.

*that old wicked Serpent*: the Devil (see Revelation 20: 2).

136 *Lord Rich*: Richard Rich, first Baron Rich. A member of the Privy Council, he was actively involved in the prosecution of heretics and suppression of heterodoxy.

## 13. JOHN BRADFORD AND JOHN LEAF

139 *Sir John Harington*: Sir John Harington of Exton, vice-treasurer of English military forces in France, whom Bradford served as an auditor late during the reign of Henry VIII.

140 *Martin Bucer*: an influential Strasbourg theologian whom Edward VI appointed Regius Professor of Divinity at the University of Cambridge (1549–51).

142 *to try what should become of his just doing*: to decide how to respond to the restoration of Roman Catholicism.

143 *preventing his hour*: returning prior to the appointed time.

*backside*: an area at the rear of Queen's Bench and Marshalsea Prisons, which abutted each other in Southwark.

144 *to receive the sacrament at Easter in one kind*: Protestants disapproved of the Roman Catholic practice of withholding the sacramental element of wine from members of the laity, who were required to receive it once each year at Easter.

145 *your chain is now a-buying*: an executioner is now purchasing the chain to secure you to the stake.

*shifted himself*: he apparelled himself with.

146 *nurse:* one who offers support.

*wedding garment*: Bradford likens the garment in which he will die to wedding attire for his marriage to Jesus Christ as the Bridegroom (Revelation 18: 23) after death.

147 *Master Rogers's scholar*: an ironic reference to Leaf's study of the 'Matthew' Bible, in which Rogers combined English translations by William Tyndale and Miles Coverdale.

148 *Cardmaker*: John Cardmaker, a Protestant cleric and well-known preacher in London who had been executed barely one month earlier on 30 May.

149 *'Strait is the way . . . few there be that find it'*: Matthew 7: 14.

## 14. HUGH LATIMER AND NICHOLAS RIDLEY

151 *Lord Williams*: John Williams, Baron Williams of Thame. As Sheriff of Oxfordshire, he oversaw the executions of Latimer, Ridley, and Cranmer.

*all ready to*: prepared for.

*Bocardo*: the prison over North Gate, Oxford, where Latimer, Ridley, and Thomas Cranmer were jailed prior to execution.

*Friar Soto*: Pedro de Soto, a Spaniard who received appointment as Professor of Hebrew at the University of Oxford during the reign of Mary I.

151 *pretty way*: considerable distance.

152 *of*: from.

> *Doctor Smith*: Richard Smith recanted and then went into exile during the reign of Edward VI. He received appointment as chaplain to Mary I and Philip of Spain and resumed duties as Lecturer in Theology at the University of Oxford.
>
> *if I yield my body to the . . . nothing thereby*: 1 Corinthians 13: 3.
>
> *the goodness of the cause . . . maketh the holiness of the person*: Protestants and Catholics alike subscribed to this patristic definition of martyrdom.
>
> *Oecolampadians*: followers of Johannes Oecolampadius.
>
> *old Church of Christ, and the Catholic faith*: Protestants contested this claim to authority on the basis of apostolic succession (i.e., direct succession from the apostles of the early Christian church).

153 *Vice . . . Oxford*: Richard Smith.

> *form*: platform.
>
> *Doctor Marshall*: Doctor Richard Marshall, Dean of Christ Church. The marginal gloss incorrectly designates Marshall, rather than Smith, as Vice Chancellor of Oxford University.
>
> *poesy*: motto or epigram.
>
> *there is . . . opened*: Latimer would have recalled that Jesus uttered this aphorism (Matthew 10: 26) in the context of a prophetic warning against fear of persecutors 'who kill the body but cannot kill the soul' (Matthew 10: 28). Latimer's cryptic consolatory message suggests that he models his death on the crucifixion of Jesus.
>
> *suffered*: permitted.
>
> *them*: themselves.
>
> *Sir Henry Lee*: despite his Protestantism, he remained in favour under Mary I and filled the office of Master of the Leash.
>
> *races*: roots.

154 *lightly*: readily.

> *truss*: a snug garment.
>
> *brother . . . gunpowder in a bag*: Ridley's brother-in-law, George Shipside, mercifully supplies gunpowder in the expectation that its ignition would kill the victims before their bodies were consumed by fire.
>
> *play the man*: an allusion to Eusebius' account of a voice from heaven that exhorted St Polycarp, the second-century martyr whose elderliness corresponded to that of Latimer, to 'play the man' when he entered the Roman arena where he would die (*Ecclesiastical History*, 4.15.17). These words have the appearance of an artful embellishment, because they were added in the second edition fifteen years after Latimer's death.
>
> *light such a candle . . . never put out*: Protestants interpreted the text from the Sermon on the Mount (Matthew 5: 14–16) to which Latimer alludes as a prefiguration of the Reformation.

*The church . . . saints*: this gloss stresses the figurative nature of Latimer's epigrammatic utterance.

156 *'Lord, Lord, receive my spirit'*: a free translation of the Latin text of Luke 23: 46.

*evil*: unskilful.

*goss*: gorse employed as kindling.

*fire burned . . . the wood*: the fire smouldered beneath the piled faggots without igniting sufficiently to kill Ridley.

*poise*: weight.

## 15. STEPHEN GARDINER

158 *the nineteenth day of October*: the chronology is problematic because Thomas Howard, 3rd Duke of Norfolk, died on 25 August 1554, long in advance of the execution of Latimer and Ridley and putative onset of Gardiner's illness on 19 October 1555. In actual fact, Bishop Gardiner addressed Parliament on 21 October 1555.

159 *like*: apparent.

## 16. JOHN PHILPOT

160 *advowson*: preferment to a benefice.

*Doctor Ponet*: having succeeded Stephen Gardiner as Bishop of Winchester during the reign of Edward VI, Doctor John Ponet appointed John Philpot to serve as Archdeacon of Winchester Cathedral. Ponet lost episcopal office and fled into exile during the reign of Mary I.

161 *room and degree*: office and rank.

*the Archdeacon of London's servant*: the servant of John Harpsfield.

*blind*: closed in.

163 *God's commandment in visiting the prisoners*: an ironic comment on a cleric's obligation to visit prisoners.

164 *The true report of the disputation*: published anonymously, Philpot's *The True Report of the Disputation Had and Begun in the Convocation House at London*, which concerns a debate that began 17 October 1553, was printed during the following year at Emden. This East Frisian seaport provided a safe haven for the printing of propaganda written by English Protestants. A false imprint misleadingly assigns publication to a printer in Basle named A. Edmunds.

*true ancient Catholic fathers*: the Fathers of the Church.

*Bishop of Bath*: Gilbert Bourne, Bishop of Bath and Wells.

166 *lay my gown to gage*: offer my gown as a forfeit.

*limbo*: strict confinement.

168 *with all his examinations that came to our hands*: despite the harshness of his imprisonment, Philpot, like other prisoners, succeeded at obtaining writing materials in order to record transcripts of their examinations for heresy.

*of his keeper*: by his keeper.

*John Careless*: a weaver from Coventry, who corresponded with and copied manuscripts for Protestant prisoners during his incarceration in London.

*the way to . . . narrow gate*: Matthew 7: 14.

170 *neither life neither death is able to separate us from the love of Christ's gospel*: see Romans 8: 38–9.

*careless . . . careful*: just as Philpot includes many puns on 'careless' and 'careful' in writing to Careless, Careless includes puns on full and empty pots in writing a letter to Philpot that is not included in this collection of narratives.

171 *The Devil must rage for ten days*: an allusion to Revelation 2: 10.

*Master F.*: Master Fokes (*FBMO*, n. on p. 1834).


## 17. BARTLETT GREEN

172 *Thomas Whittle*: a prisoner with whom John Philpot was incarcerated at Bishop Bonner's coal house (see Narrative 16).

*the fountain . . . woman of Samaria*: John 4: 10–15.

*compartner*: a copartner.

173 *his one testimony*: his own testimony.

*adversary*: Satan, the literal meaning of whose name in Hebrew is 'adversary'.

*the devil . . . may devour*: 1 Peter 5–8.

*A patient . . . conquereth towns and cities*: Proverbs 16: 32.

174 *synagogue of Rome*: Roman Catholic Church (Protestant jargon).

*Christopher Goodman*: this Protestant cleric, who was a close associate of Pietro Martire Vermigli, went into exile because of his religious convictions. His treatise, *How Superior Powers Ought to Be Obeyed of Their Subjects* (Geneva, 1 January 1558), advocates resistance to tyrants, notably Mary I.

175 *this letter . . . not yet dead*: in sending this confirmation to Christopher Goodman, Green inadvertently invited a charge of treason for condoning the death of Mary I.

*the anointed sort*: the clerics.

*Sir John Bourne*: secretary to Mary I and a commissioner who examined many alleged heretics.

*importable*: capable of being brought in (meaning obscure).

176 *that they received . . . only grace added thereto*: with this response, Green denies the Roman Catholic doctrine of transubstantiation.

177 *in a strange tongue . . . in both kinds*: Green rejects celebration of the Mass in the Latin language and reservation of wine for priests, who only administered Eucharistic bread to members of the laity.

*with the rest above named*: Green underwent interrogation with prisoners named Thomas Whittle, John Tudson, John Went, Thomas Brown, Isabel Foster, and Joan Lashford.

178 *Chrysostom*: St. John Chrysostom, a fourth-century Father of the Church.

*'Ask . . . opened unto you'*: Matthew 7: 7.

180 *shamefast*: self-effacing.

181 *pitiful*: sympathetic.

## 18. THOMAS CRANMER

182 *state*: personal condition.

*ancient parentage . . . to be deducted*: descended from ancestry that may be traced back to the Norman Conquest.

*it chanced him . . . fellowship there*: he was forced to resign his fellowship because he failed to meet the requirement of celibacy.

*Buckingham College*: a forerunner of Magdalene College of Cambridge University.

183 *lecture*: a lecturer?

*whereof certain friars . . . rejected by him*: Cranmer rejected the qualifications for degrees in theology of members of religious orders who were knowledgeable in Scholastic authorities, but not the Bible.

*a white friar*: a Carmelite Friar.

184 *Cardinal Wolsey's college in Oxford*: Cardinal College, later refounded as Henry VIII's College, and then as Christ Church.

*Lady Catherine Dowager of Spain*: Catherine of Aragon, first wife of Henry VIII and mother of Mary Tudor.

*canonists, civilians*: *canonists* were experts in canon law; *civilians* experts in civil law.

*Waltham Abbey*: a town between Cambridge and London, which takes its name from a monastery at this location.

*Cardinal Campeius*: Lorenzo Campeggi (Campeggio), cardinal, papal legate, Protector of England, and Bishop of Salisbury.

*commission from the pope . . . pretended wife*: Pope Clement VII appointed Cardinals Campeggi and Wolsey to adjudicate Henry VIII's petition for a divorce from Catherine of Aragon.

184 *Dukes of Norfolk and Suffolk*: the pre-eminent nobles, Thomas Howard and Charles Brandon.

185 *Greenwich*: site of a favoured royal palace downriver from London.

*harbingers*: individuals who precede a royal party in order to arrange lodging for its members.

*Doctor Stephens secretary*: Stephen Gardiner, Secretary to Henry VIII (*FBMO*, n. on p. 1860).

*It were better . . . word of God*: Cranmer's advocacy of deciding the divorce question on the basis of scriptural authority, rather than papal prerogative, reflects Henry VIII's interpretation of Leviticus 18: 16 as a prohibition against his marriage to the widow of his late brother, Arthur.

*frustratory*: producing defeat.

*unbolted out by*: unsubstantiated with.

186 *colourable*: having the semblance of truth.

*hath the sow by the right ear*: is on the right track.

188 *Earl of Wiltshire*: Thomas Boleyn, father of Anne Boleyn.

*the Bishop of . . . the scripture*: scriptural authority nullifies that of the pope.

*ambassage*: ambassadorship.

189 *his foot to be . . . that idolatry*: Foxe and his fellow Protestants regarded kissing the pope's foot as an idolatrous act of fealty.

*a prognosticate of . . . See of Rome*: a foreshadowing of England's schism from the Church of Rome in 1534.

*smiling in their sleeves*: experiencing inward amusement.

*to be defended*: to advocate.

*Jure divino*: Latin for 'by divine law'.

190 *penitentiaryship*: appointment as an official charged with considering ecclesiastical cases related to penance.

*Emperor*: Charles V, Holy Roman Emperor, nephew of Catherine of Aragon, cousin to Mary Tudor and father of Philip of Spain.

*Cornelius Agrippa*: Heinrich Cornelius Agrippa, a German scholar who served as the historiographer of Charles V.

*Agrippa fell into such displeasure . . . as it was reported*: in actual fact, Agrippa died at Grenoble after being released from imprisonment for his criticism of Louise of Savoy, the mother of Francis I, King of France.

*Bishop Warham*: William Warham, appointed Archbishop of Canterbury by Henry VII in 1503, whose death in 1532 opened the way to Cranmer's appointment as primate of the Church of England.

191 *love of this world is hatred against God*: 1 John 2: 15.

192 *'It is hard for a rich man . . . the kingdom of heaven'*: Matthew 19: 23.

*'He that hath the substance . . . loveth God'*: 1 John 3: 17.

'*Weep you and howl . . . against the last day*': James 5: 1–3.

*colour*: external appearance.

*I believe in God . . . heaven and earth*: the opening words of the Apostles' Creed.

*catholic faith*: universal Christian faith, as opposed to the contested claim to universality of the Church of Rome.

193 *my book against the Bishop of Winchester*: He refers to *An Answer of . . . Thomas Archbishop of Canterbury, unto a Crafty Cavillation by Stephen Gardiner* (London: Reyner Wolfe, 1551). This treatise reprints Bishop Gardiner's *An Explication and Assertion of the True Catholic Faith, Touching the Most Blessed Sacrament of the Altar* (Rouen: Robert Caly, 1551) in the course of responding to it in the conventional pro and con fashion of an academic disputation. According to the imprint of the second edition of Cranmer's treatise, which was printed in 1580 by Foxe's publisher, John Day, this exposition of Protestant sacramental theology was 'revised, and corrected by the archbishop before his martyrdom'. Prefaced to Day's edition is a biography of Cranmer extracted out of the *Book of Martyrs* and illustrated with its woodcut portrayals of his being pulled down from a platform at the University Church of St Mary the Virgin and ensuing execution (see Illustrations 17–18).

194 *barker*: one who harshly cries out against.

196 *Ely*: William Ely, Vice Principal of Brasenose College.

'*Lord Jesus, receive my spirit*': in emulation of the last words of St Stephen (Acts 7: 59), the first Christian martyr, many Marian martyrs uttered these words at the point of death.

## 19. THE GUERNSEY MARTYRS

198 *fact*: an act performed by.

*member*: an outlying district.

199 *attached*: indicted.

*taken by inventory*: inventoried and seized.

*durance*: imprisonment.

200 *dean*: the Dean of Guernsey is a cleric who serves as the local representative of the Bishop of Winchester and functions as judge of the island's ecclesiastical court.

201 *complices*: accomplices.

*bailiff and jurats*: on the island of Guernsey, this court of justice is made up of the chief magistrate and a body of twelve magistrates with life tenure. They function both as judges and as members of a jury. Because the Bailiwick of Guernsey is a residual part of the Duchy of Normandy, rather than a formal part of the English kingdom, it falls under the jurisdiction of Norman common law.

202 *sat upon*: went into session concerning.

　　*deposed*: testified.

203 *Herodian cruelty*: cruelty in the manner of Herod the Great, who ordered the massacre of infant boys in an attempt to kill Jesus, whom the Magi heralded as 'the new-born king of the Jews' (Matthew 2: 2, 16–18).

## 20. JOAN WASTE

205 *repeat one chapter upon a price*: read a chapter in return for payment.

　　*notorious*: commonly known.

206 *why was not Christ able . . . as to turn water into wine*: in interrogating Joan Waste concerning her dissent from Roman Catholic Eucharistic doctrine, Ralph Bayne, Bishop of Coventry and Litchfield, and Doctor Anthony Draycot, chancellor of Coventry, liken transubstantiation of the elements of bread and wine into the body and blood of Jesus Christ (see Matthew 26: 26) to his transformation of water into wine at the wedding at Cana (John 2: 1–11).

　　*raise Lazarus from death*: Luke 16: 19–31.

207 *De haeretico comburendo*: Latin for 'concerning the heretic who is to be burnt'. Legislated in 1401, this statute imposed the penalty of being burnt alive on those condemned for heresy on the basis of reading the Bible in English translation, notably the Lollard version inspired by John Wyclif. Parliament abrogated this law during the reign of Edward VI and then reinstated it under Mary I.

## 21. WILLIAM DANGERFIELD

209 *the story of . . . at Derby*: Narratives 19–20.

　　*repaired*: returned

　　*Doctor Brooks*: Doctor James Brooks, Bishop of Gloucester.

　　*fretted off*: worn away.

210 *as the serpent did with Eve*: the narrator likens the bishop's deception of Dangerfield to the temptation of Eve (Genesis 3: 1–6).

　　*your first vow made to Christ in baptism*: on behalf of infants undergoing baptism, parents make a vow of fidelity to Jesus Christ.

## 22. RICHARD WOODMAN

212 *ironmaker*: one who smelts iron.

　　*turning head to tail*: making an about face.

　　*Richard Woodman . . . he was apprehended*: he was arrested for accusing a priest named Fairbank of renouncing his marriage, which was permissible during the reign of Edward VI, following the reimposition of clerical celibacy under Mary I.

*Doctor Story*: Doctor John Story, whom Henry VIII had appointed Regius Professor of Civil Law, was imprisoned and went into exile during the reign of Edward VI, and then returned to England under Mary I. As Chancellor of London and Oxford and Dean of Arches, he played an active role in the prosecution of Protestants.

214 *carnal gospellers*: Protestant jargon for hypocritical Christians who fail to act upon knowledge of the New Testament.

*God . . . oven*: Exodus, Daniel 6, Daniel 3. These texts contain prefigurations of divine deliverance.

215 *king*: Philip of Spain.

216 *battle*: a psychomachia (i.e., a conflict within the mind).

217 *flight shot*: an arrow shot.

*Baal's priests*: Canaanite priests (Protestant jargon for Roman Catholic priests).

*till the hour was full come*: an allusion to John 12: 23.

218 *preyed*: preyed upon.

*'Auri . . . pectora?' Virgil*: 'Accursed desire for gold, to what do you not drive mortal hearts?' Virgil, *Aeneid*, 3. 56.

219 *shift*: a means for accomplishing a goal.

*saving of*: while avoiding.

220 *errandless*: without success.

*but woe . . . been born*: Matthew 26: 24.

*'For the father . . . brother to death'*: Matthew 10: 21.

221 *'The dog . . . mire'*: 2 Peter 2: 22.

*slip*: a leash.

*I am sure . . . love and fear him*: an allusion to Romans 8: 28.

## 23. ROSE ALLIN AND OTHER COLCHESTER MARTYRS

222 *prelates . . . of the church*: Roman Catholic clergy.

224 *Judasly*: treacherously.

*who came of the house . . . his brother*: who was a relative of Sir James Tyrrell, the putative murderer of Edward V and his brother, Prince Richard, at the Tower of London (*c.*1483).

*hundred*: district of a county or shire with a law court.

228 *sea*: with a sarcastic pun on the papal see.

## 24. GEORGE EAGLES

231 *Amos*: a shepherd whose prophesying is recorded in the Book of Amos.

*Apostles . . . churches*: Matthew 4: 18–22.

231 *confessors*: individuals who openly avow religious conviction.

232 *espies*: spies.

*Jew*: a Roman Catholic (Protestant innuendo).

233 *'Quo . . . fames'*: 'To what do you not drive human hearts, accursed thirst for gold!' Virgil, *Aeneid*, 3. 56.

*council*: the Privy Council.

*Duke of Somerset*: Edward Seymour.

234 *hurdle*: a frame on a sledge on which condemned individuals were dragged to execution.

*he was turned off the ladder*: Potto pushed him off the ladder in order to hang him by the neck until he died.

*between two thieves*: Luke 23: 39–43.

*flout*: a mockery.

235 *hackle*: hack.

236 *George Eagles . . . St Rouse's*: it was the fate of condemned traitors to be hung by the neck, cut down while still alive, have their intestines drawn out and burned, and then to be cut in quarters that were displayed at city gates as a warning to potential malefactors.

*glass*: a mirror (in the figurative sense of prophetic reflection).

237 *watchet*: light blue.

## 25. THE ISLINGTON MARTYRS

238 *back close*: an enclosed portion of a field, adjacent to houses. It is the site of an out-of-door gathering of Protestants who engaged in the study of the Bible and other books. Many of them were among the last individuals to die for heresy prior to the death of Mary I.

239 *recorder*: an official charged with keeping track of legal proceedings, precedents, and customs of a city such as London.

240 *Harpsfield and Cole*: John Harpsfield (see Glossary of Persons) and Henry Cole, Dean of St Paul's Cathedral.

*scant for anger being able to speak*: almost unable to speak because he was so angry.

242 *capper*: a maker of caps.

*flirting him*: striking him sharply or suddenly.

243 *crept to the cross*: they observed a Good Friday ritual whereby parishioners crawled to a cross prior to its placement in a wooden chest symbolic of the tomb in which Jesus' body was placed following the crucifixion. Forbidden at the end of Henry VIII's reign, this practice was restored after the accession of Mary I.

*King Edward's service in English*: see Introduction.

*Item*: likewise, also.

244 κατὰ τὴν ἐναντίωσιν. 'in accordance with his opposition'. See *FBMO*.

245 *In nomine . . . sancti*: Matthew 28: 19 (a text used in baptismal liturgy).

*say it me in Latin*: Bishop Bonner demands that Milles recite the liturgy in Latin, rather than use the vernacular version authorized under Edward VI.

## 26. PREST'S WIFE

246 *a certain poor woman*: a woman who was known only by the surname of her husband, a man named Prest.

*Doctor Troubleville*: Doctor James Turberville, Bishop of Exeter.

*on this wise*: in this manner.

247 *cards and tow*: cards are instruments for combing fibre into a form suitable for spinning; tow is flax prepared for spinning.

'*He that leaveth . . . et cetera*': Mark 10: 29–31.

248 '*This is my body*' . . . '*This is my blood*': Mark 14: 22–4.

*bready god*: Eucharistic bread.

*your creed, which . . . of his father*: Apostles' Creed.

*dwell in temples made with hands*: Isaiah 66: 1–2, Acts 7: 48.

*worshipped in spirit and truth*: John 4: 24–5.

*jolly*: arrogantly presumptuous.

249 *when I was persecuted . . . unto another*: Matthew 10: 23.

*true church*: the invisible church of 'true' Christians, rather than the officially established church.

250 *significative*: pertaining to the external sign of Christ's sacrifice, rather than its commemorative signification in holy communion.

251 '*Who can number his sins?*': Psalm 19: 12.

*fray*: ward off.

*disfigured*: damaged by iconoclastic attack.

*a-whoring after strange gods*: Deuteronomy 31: 16.

*clapped*: shut up (i.e. imprisoned).

252 *Anabaptist*: a member of a radical sect in disfavour with Roman Catholics and magisterial Protestants.

253 *God is my father*: Matthew 6: 9.

*marriage . . . Lamb*: Revelation 19: 9.

## 27. EDWIN SANDYS

254 *Duke of Northumberland*: John Dudley.

*Lady Jane*: Lady Jane Grey.

254 *Doctor Sandys*: Doctor Edwin Sandys.

*Doctor Parker*: Doctor Matthew Parker, Master of Corpus Christi College, Cambridge, who was deprived of his offices and lived in obscurity during the reign of Mary I; later appointed Archbishop of Canterbury.

*convenient . . . scripture*: Joshua 1: 16–18 concerns the Israelites' declaration of allegiance to Joshua following the death of Moses.

255 *ready booted*: he was dressed and ready to go.

*John Gates*: a supporter who was executed with John Dudley.

256 *fet*: fetch.

*Regent House*: a meeting place for governing body of the University of Cambridge.

257 *Nun's Bower*: a prison chamber.

258 *Duke of Norfolk*: Thomas Howard, 3rd Duke of Norfolk.

261 *stake-fellow*: one who has been condemned to die by being burnt alive as a companion to another victim.

263 *Doctor Cox*: Doctor Richard Cox, former tutor of Edward VI and Vice Chancellor of the University of Oxford. He went into exile after imprisonment at Marshalsea Prison.

*kenning*: derived from *ken* ('area within sight'), this word refers to the furthest distance visible at sea (i.e., approximately 20 miles).

*Cleve*: also known as Kleve or Cleveland, the Duchy of Cleves was a Dutch-speaking principality in the Rhineland that offered a haven to English Protestant exiles.

*flix*: a flux (i.e., dysentery).

264 *Master Bullinger*: Heinrich Bullinger.

*the same day that Queen Elizabeth was crowned*: 15 January 1559.

## 28. LADY ELIZABETH

265 *outscape*: an escape.

266 *Lord Courtenay*: Edward Courtenay, Earl of Devonshire. Having been rejected as a suitor to Mary I, he hoped to marry Lady Elizabeth and to make her queen.

*Sir Richard Southwell*: a Privy Councillor, Member of Parliament, and diplomat.

*Sir Edward Hastings*: a soldier and key supporter of Mary I before and during her reign.

*Sir Thomas Cornwallis*: a Privy Councillor and Member of Parliament.

*unprovided*: unprepared.

267 *Doctor Owen and Doctor Wendy*: Doctor George Owen and Doctor Thomas Wendy were royal physicians and Members of Parliament.

*Sir John Gage*: a Member of the Privy Council and Comptroller of the Queen's Household.

268 *burdened*: accused.

*Sir Peter Carew*: the leader of a rebellion in Devon.

*caps hanging over their eyes*: in shame.

*Lord Treasurer*: Sir William Paulet (1474/5?–1572), 1st Marquess of Winchester.

*Bishop of Winchester*: Stephen Gardiner.

*Earl of Sussex*: Henry Radcliffe.

269 *the other shall be nameless*: Foxe conceals the identity of Sir William Paulet, who was still alive when the first two editions of the *Book of Martyrs* were published (*FBMO*, n. on p. 2092).

270 *carry their palms*: in the Palm Sunday ritual restored under Mary I.

*shoot*: cruise under.

*fall*: a descent.

*one of the lords . . . nameless*: Sir William Paulet.

271 *her book*: the Bible.

*to build her foundation . . . upon the rock*: Matthew 7: 24–7.

272 *Ahithophel*: the narrator likens Gardiner to a counsellor who betrayed King David (2 Samuel 15–17).

273 *wrote these verses . . . a glass window*: during the early modern era, well-to-do individuals were known to inscribe epigrams of this kind and other sentiments in windows with diamonds.

*went into the country*: she went to Hatfield House, which was then a royal palace located to the north of London. It was a favourite residence of Elizabeth I both before and after she was crowned queen. Only later did this estate come into the hands of Robert Cecil, who built the edifice that presently occupies this site.

*Sir Thomas Pope*: officer of the Court of Augmentations and a member of the Privy Council.

*looked to*: observed.

## 29. JUDGEMENT TALES

274 *I come to them . . . execution of her power*: Foxe diminishes the accountability of Mary I by assigning responsibility for persecution to those whom she charged to serve as her agents.

*Queen Alexandra*: a Hasmonean ruler of Judaea (76–69 BCE).

*'She only retained . . . to possess'*: Josephus, *Antiquities of the Jews*, 13.16.2.

*Stephen Gardiner . . . queen's reign*: see Narrative 15.

275 *favoured religion*: i.e., favoured Protestantism.

275 *he would sit as much in his light*: he would take revenge by accusing him falsely.

   *Grimwood of Lowshaw*: William Grimwood, of Hitcham, Suffolk.

   *Grimwood of Hitcham*: the same person as 'Grimwood of Lowshaw' (*FBMO*, nn. on p. 2099).

276 *goaf*: a stack.

   *story of Master Bradford*: see Narrative 13.

   *carman's head should be broken*: i.e., he was punished by being hit in the head.

   *atheist*: an impious person.

277 *statute . . . Edward VI*: the Act of Uniformity of 1549.

   *noyed*: annoyed.

278 *Adam Damlip*: the alias of George Bucker, a Protestant executed for treason at Calais in 1543.

279 *Lord Cobham*: Sir John Oldcastle, a Lollard martyr whom authorities burnt alive for heresy in 1417. His martyrology and the woodcut of his execution are memorable features of the *Book of Martyrs*.

   *George Eagles*: see Narrative 24.

# GLOSSARY OF WORDS AND TERMS

**accompt** account (noun and verb).

**advouch** avouch (i.e., certify).

**advouterer** an adulterer.

**affected to** moved to embrace.

**ague** a severe fever.

**allure** attract.

**almoner** one who gives alms on behalf of a notable individual.

**ambries** cupboards.

**anchoress** a nun.

**anon** immediately.

**Antichrist, the** the ultimate enemy of Jesus Christ and God (1 John 2: 18–22; 4: 3), whom Protestants identified with the pope.

**apert** open, unconcealed.

**ap(p)ertly** openly, evidently.

**arms** heraldic arms.

**assize** circuit court.

**assoil** forgive.

**astonied** astonished.

**attained** convicted.

**auditory** an audience.

**auricular confession** private confession (i.e., only within the hearing of a priest), rather than congregational confession of sins.

**avoid** void, evacuate.

**Babylonical** a quasi-biblical reference to idolatry that Protestants employed to attack Roman Catholic clerics as unfaithful Christians.

**bailiff** a royal officer who might be a sheriff, magistrate, or mayor.

**begon** partaken of, embarked upon, accomplished.

**benefice** an endowed clerical appointment.

**benet and collet** lower clerical orders beneath the rank of sub-deacon.

**betimes** early.

**bill** a pickaxe, halberd.

**braid** an assault, suffering.

**bread** the Mass bread or wafer.

**broil** to agitate, engage in conflict.

**broom** a flowering shrub.

**bruiting** spreading rumours.

**buckler** a small shield.

**buskins** boots.

**butcher** a persecutor or executioner of Protestants (Protestant jargon). See Isaiah 53: 7 and Romans 8: 36. See also *lamb* and *sheep*.

**butt** a mound.

**callet** a strumpet.

**carnal(ly)** Protestant jargon for belief in transubstantiation and the Roman-rite Mass. Used as an antonym for *spiritual(ly)*.

**catchpole** a contemptuous term for a sheriff's officer.

**certes** certainly.

**chancellor** an official who oversees cases brought before diocesan courts conducted on behalf of a bishop.

**check** an obstruction.

**chid** rebuked.

**chimere** an episcopal robe.

**common** commune, discuss.

**consistory** a diocesan court that considers ecclesiastical offences.

**contentation** satisfaction, acceptance.

**convented** summoned.

**conventicle** clandestine religious gathering.

**corn** grain.

**Council** the Privy Council.

**creed** a formal affirmation of religious belief, most commonly with reference to the Apostles' Creed.

**curate** a cleric in charge of a parish, usually as a salaried assistant to the incumbent who holds the benefice (see above).

**cure** the office of a curate.

**customably** customarily.

**darkness** ignorance (metaphoric sense).

**deacon** a cleric below the rank of priest.

**degradation** formal removal from ecclesiastical office.

**degrade** to remove from ecclesiastical office.

**dial** a pocket sundial.

**disgrade** to remove from ecclesiastical office.

**divine** a theologian.

**divinity** theology.

**doctor** a learned person.

**doublet** informal masculine attire that may possess or lack sleeves.

**effectuously** earnestly.

**eftsoons** soon afterwards.

**endued** endowed.

**erst** before.

**examinate** a person undergoing interrogation concerning heresy.

**examination** a formal legal inquiry into whether the beliefs of alleged heretics were in accord with Roman Catholic doctrine.

**exercise** customary practice, declamation, meditation.

**except** unless.

**faggot** a bundle of wood employed in the burning heretics.

**faggot, to bear a** an action symbolic of death penalty escaped by an alleged heretic who has recanted.

**fain** adj. and adv. that signifies happiness, agreement, necessity, or obligation.

**firkin** a small cask.

**flock** a Christian congregation. See *lamb* and *sheep*.

**foins** marten furs.

**freeman** one who is licensed to engage in a trade.

**fretted off** worn away.

**gear** equipment, apparatus; practice (pp. 103 and 248); clothing (p. 220).

**ghost** the spirit or soul.

**ghostly** spiritual, spiritually.

**glaive** a spear.

**gleaves** spears.

**glozing** deceiving.

**godly** pious.

**gospeller** an evangelical reformer with an extreme reliance on scripture rather than ecclesiastical tradition and authority in religious matters.

**Gramercies** an expression of gratitude.

**great with child** pregnant.

**groat** a fourpenny piece.

**halberd** a spearhead, or a sharp blade with a pointed end that combines the functions of a battle-axe and spear.

**hardly** barely, scarcely.

**hose(n)** garment(s) for the legs, trousers.

**hostler** a groom who attends horses at an inn (used as an insult that implies that an individual is of a very low social rank).

**hugger mugger** in secrecy.

**hundreth** hundred.

**idols** religious images.

**imagination** an imagined human belief, rather than an enduring spiritual truth.

**incontinent(ly)** immediately.

**in fine** finally.

**insured** assured.

**intermeddling** intermingling.

**interrogatories** examinations, questions.

**Judas** traitor(ous).

**juggling** jargon employed by Protestants to mock fourfold Scholastic interpretation of the Bible and other allegedly mystifying practices of the Church of Rome. See Narrative 2.

**justicer** one who renders judgements.

**lamb** a faithful Christian who undergoes martyrdom in the manner of a lamb led to slaughter (see Acts 8: 32), which constitutes a type of the crucifixion of Jesus. See *butcher*, *flock*, and *sheep*.

**let** prevent.

**letted** prevented.

**libel** written allegation.

**light** the truth (metaphoric sense).

**list** to wish.

**litany** this consists of a sequence of penitential petitions by a cleric, to which the congregation responds in unison. Modelled on earlier Christian liturgies, it was introduced late in the reign of Henry VIII and then incorporated into the first and second Books of Common Prayer promulgated during the reign of Edward VI.

**loath** reluctant, averse, hostile.

**maidenly** gentle, timid.

**mammetry** idolatry.

**manchet** wheat (p. 140), wheat bread (p. 258).

**marry** a word that signifies assertion, interjection, or exclamation.

**maugre** in spite of.

**mazed** mad.

**Miserere** Psalm 51, one of the Penitential Psalms, which begins 'Miserere mei, Deus' ('Have mercy upon me, O God').

**mistrusted** doubted.

**naughty** wicked.

**neither** neither, nor.

**notted** shaven.

**or** ere.

**orderly** duly or fittingly.

**ordinary** a meal open to uninvited visitors (p. 13); a bishop with full jurisdiction over ecclesiastical cases within his diocese (pp. 99, 161).

**pains** attentive effort.

**participate** to share, give.

**party** one side in a dispute.

**Pharisees** Jews who adhered strictly to religious law and tradition; Protestant jargon for Roman Catholic clerics.

**play** to exercise the capacity of.

**points** ribbons or laces used to fasten clothing, especially hose and shoes.

**prebend** revenue granted to a canon or member of a chapter house at a collegiate church or cathedral.

**prebendary** a recipient of a prebend.

**prefer** to offer patronage.

**pregnant** compelling, forceful.

**press** a crowd.

**pretenced** pretended.

**privily** privately, inwardly, secretly.

**privy** private, inward, secret.

**professor** an individual who makes an open declaration of beliefs or religious conviction.

**prophets** preachers, clerics.

**provincial** the head of an ecclesiastical body.

**provost** an official in charge of an execution.

**pursuivant** an officer who is charged with the execution of warrants.

**pyx** a container for the consecrated host.

**quest** an inquest, official inquiry.

**quick** living.

**quickeneth** revives.

**quod, quoth** these verbs precede the subject and signify that a speaker's words are repeated.

**refel** refute.

**register** a diocesan record book.

**retractation** recantation.

**rochet** a vestment typically worn by bishops or abbots.

**roisting** swaggering, blustering.

**rood** a cross (or possibly an archaic spelling for 'road').

**ruddish** ruddy, reddish.

**scaffold** a platform.

**scant** scarcely.

**school** one of the faculties that make up the University of Oxford or Cambridge.

**sembled** dissembled, pretended.

**session(s)** period(s) during which law courts are in session.

**sheep** a Christian believer; a martyr (Isaiah 53: 7, Romans 8: 36). See *flock*, *lamb*, and *shepherd*.

**shepherd** a pastor (from the Latin word *pastor*, i.e., 'shepherd'). Jesus states: 'I am the good shepherd; the good shepherd lays down his life for the sheep' (John 10: 11).

**shirt** a loose garment resembling a shirt, or a shirt-like undergarment for the upper body.

**shoggling** shaking.

**shrift** the sacrament of confession.

**shrive** to hear confession and administer absolution for sins.

**shriven** confessed, absolved.

**sickerly** surely, without doubt.

**silly** innocent, blameless, naïve, pitiable.

**sirrah** an expression of contempt or reprimand.

**sistern** sisters.

**sithens** since.

**smell** to perceive by intuition.

**sore** arduously.

**spiritual(ly)** Protestant usage referring to Holy Communion as a commemorative ceremony and religious observance grounded on faith rather than external ritual. Used as an antonym for *carnal(ly)*.

**staid** resolute.

**staple** a metal attachment to affix a chain to a stake.

**stays** supports.

**stile** a set of stairs to allow a person to pass over a fence in a pasture without permitting livestock to escape.

**stomach** anger, peevishness.

**strait** narrow, restricted, strict, stringent.

**stringling** struggling.

**suffragan** a bishop who lacks independent authority and serves as a deputy of a diocesan bishop.

**summoner** one who is empowered to summon individuals to legal proceedings.

**sureties** bail bonds.

**thrall** enslaved.

**tippet** in clerical attire, a fabric band around the neck with two ends descending from the shoulders.

**tipstaff** a metal-tipped staff carried by a constable or other court official.

**tongues** languages.

**towardness** aptness.

**tragical** pertaining to *de casibus* tragedy, which concerns the fall of illustrious individuals from an exalted position in society.

**travail** a hardship, suffering.

**trental** a cycle of thirty Requiem Masses, or a payment made in return for their celebration.

**trow** to believe.

**trumpery** deceit, worthless trash (Protestant jargon for Roman Catholic beliefs and practices).

**tush** an expression of impatience.

**twain** two.

**unmeetest** most unfit.

**unneath** underneath.

**videlicet** namely.

**vinew** become mouldy.

**vocation** a calling, usually with reference to perceiving a divine summons to become a cleric.

**void** depart from.

**vouchsafe** to confer or grant in a gracious or condescending manner.

**vulgar tongue** vernacular language (e.g., English).

**ward** (n. and vb.) a prison or guarded chamber; to guard.

**wit** knowledge, understanding, wisdom, prudence, mental acuity, or quick wittedness.

**withal** in addition.

**without** outside.

**Whore of Babylon** Protestant jargon for the Church of Rome (see Revelation 17: 1–6).

**wolf** a hypocritical or dissembling Roman Cleric (Protestant jargon).

**wont** a customary practice.

**worshipful** distinguished, entitled to honourable respect

# GLOSSARY OF PERSONS

**Arundel, Thomas** (1353–1414) as Archbishop of Canterbury (1396–1414), he was notorious among Protestants such as Foxe for his advocacy of burning Lollard heretics alive and for his promulgation of a set of *Constitutions* (1407) that promoted strict enforcement of religious orthodoxy.

**Bilney, Thomas** (*c*.1495–1531) after ordination as a priest, he fell under the influence of Erasmus's Latin–Greek New Testament and subscribed to the doctrine of justification by faith based upon Luther's interpretation of the Pauline epistles. Not only did he convert Hugh Latimer, who became the spiritual leader of the first generation of English Protestants, but his iconoclastic attacks against the use of relics and religious images, intercession of the saints, pilgrimages to shrines, and other elements of traditional religion incurred the disapproval of Cardinal Thomas Wolsey. Bilney approved of translation of parts of the Bible into the vernacular. After a period of imprisonment in the Tower of London, he preached in the open air because withdrawal of his preaching licence denied him access to churches. For these violations he was burnt alive at Norwich on 19 August 1531. Bilney does not conform to conventional expectations of Protestant martyrs because he always maintained orthodox positions concerning the papal authority, the doctrine of transubstantiation, the Roman-rite Mass, and clerical celibacy.

**Bonner, Edmund** (1500?–69) this religious conservative served as Bishop of London during the latter part of the reign of Henry VIII, the early part of the reign of Edward VI, and the reign of Mary I. As a consequence of the Protestant settlement of religion during the reign of Edward VI, Bonner was deprived of his bishopric and imprisoned. Restored to the bishopric of London under Mary, he earned the nickname of 'Bloody Bonner' for his persecution of Protestants and strenuous enforcement of Roman Catholic orthodoxy. He was incarcerated at Marshalsea Prison during the reign of Elizabeth I.

**Bradford, John** (1510?–55) after serving as an agent of the Crown in France, he studied law at the Inner Temple and underwent conversion under the influence of Hugh Latimer. Shifting to classical and biblical studies, he became a Fellow of Pembroke Hall, Cambridge, before entering the ministry under the influence of Martin Bucer and Nicholas Ridley, Bishop of London. Appointments as chaplain to Edward VI and Ridley followed. After the accession of Mary I, he was imprisoned for unauthorized preaching even though he had calmed a mob that became enraged by a conformist sermon delivered by Bishop Gilbert Bourne at Paul's Cross. Following imprisonment and condemnation, he was burnt alive at Smithfield in the company of an apprentice named John Leaf on 1 July 1555.

**Bullinger, Heinrich** (1504–75) this Protestant theologian succeeded Ulrich Zwingli as the spiritual leader of the church in Zurich. John Hooper studied with him prior to his return to England during the reign of Edward VI. Bullinger exerted a powerful influence on leaders of the Protestant movement in England, with whom he engaged in energetic correspondence. When Edwin Sandys went into exile, Bullinger offered hospitality to him.

**Chedsey, William** (1510–74) as a prebendary at St Paul's Cathedral and St George's Chapel, Windsor, he was an active participant in the prosecution of Protestant leaders during the reign of Mary I. At Oxford he engaged in disputation concerning the Eucharist with Thomas Cranmer, Hugh Latimer, and Nicholas Ridley.

**Chester, Sir William** (*c.*1509–95?) an Alderman and Sheriff of London, he was later elected Lord Mayor during the reign of Elizabeth I. Unlike David Woodruff, his fellow sheriff, he treated Protestant prisoners sympathetically.

**Cholmley, Sir Roger** (*c.*1485–1565) after serving as Lord Chief Justice of the King's Bench during 1552, he served as a commissioner of the peace who persecuted alleged heretics during the reign of Mary I.

**Clement VII** (1478–1534) a member of the Medici family like his cousin, Leo X, he was elected pope in 1523. After failing to approve of a divorce between Henry VIII and Catherine of Aragon, this pope excommunicated the king following his divorce and marriage to Anne Boleyn in 1533. England then entered into schism from the Church of Rome.

**Coverdale, Miles** (1488–1569) this Bible editor, translator, and religious propagandist assimilated translations by William Tyndale into the Coverdale Bible (1535) and oversaw publication of the Great Bible (1539). It remained the authorized version of the English Bible until its reading was prohibited during the reign of Mary I. Appointed Bishop of Exeter during the reign of Edward VI, he exerted a powerful influence on England's movement toward Protestantism. After going into exile following the king's death, he returned under Elizabeth I. In his old age, he remained active as a preacher within a group of evangelically minded divines in London.

**Cranmer, Thomas** (1489–1556) appointed Archbishop of Canterbury in 1533, he was the architect of the English church service introduced during the reign of Edward VI and reintroduced, with some modifications, under Elizabeth I. Deprived from office and imprisoned during the reign of Mary I, he recanted his religious beliefs only to retract his recantation shortly before he was burnt at the stake at Oxford on 21 March 1556.

**Day, John** (1521/2–84) a London printer, publisher, and bookseller, he was notable for his commitment to the dissemination of Protestant propaganda. He engaged in surreptitious publication during the reign of Mary I. John Rogers mentions that he encountered Day as a fellow prisoner at Newgate (see Narrative 4). Forming a close association with John Foxe during the reign of Elizabeth I, Day published the *Book of Martyrs*, other items connected to Foxe, the sermons of Hugh Latimer, and other writings by Marian martyrs.

**Edward VI** (1537–53) King of England, he was the son of Henry VIII and Jane Seymour. Upon his accession to the throne in 1547 at age 9, the Council of Regency appointed by Henry VIII appointed the young king's uncle, Edward Seymour, to serve as Protector of the Realm. He was later overthrown by John Dudley, Duke of Northumberland. Edward VI commonly received praise as a New Josiah on the ground that the boy king who purged Israel of idolatrous images and shrines (2 Kings 22–3) provided a precedent for pursuing a legally dubious policy of religious reform during King Edward's minority. His reign is notable for the implementation of a Protestant settlement of religion under the direction of Seymour, John Dudley, and Thomas Cranmer. Protestants regarded his early death as a great catastrophe that led to the reversal of religious policy by his half-sister, Mary I.

**Elizabeth I** (1533–1603) born Princess of England, she underwent illegitimation after her father, Henry VIII, countenanced the execution of her mother, Anne Boleyn, on grounds of adultery. In danger of death when she was suspected of treason following the rebellion of Sir Thomas Wyatt, she escaped the fate of Lady Jane Grey by remaining steadfastly silent concerning her religious and political beliefs. She became queen when Mary I died on 17 November 1558. Although she was the recipient of the dedicatory epistle to the *Book of Martyrs*, which is illustrated with a grandiose historiated initial capital *C*, her desire to synthesize Protestant theology with religious practices suggestive of Catholicism (e.g., the wearing of clerical vestments and kneeling during the communion service) ran counter to the views of evangelically minded individuals including John Foxe and members of the nascent presbyterian movement.

**Erasmus, Desiderius** (*c*.1466–1536) the leading opponent of Scholasticism, this humanistic scholar exerted a profound influence on Western European thought. A friend of Sir Thomas More, he received patronage from high-ranking ecclesiastics during his residences in England. Published by Johannes Froben in Basle in 1516, with a dedication to

Pope Leo X, his Latin–Greek New Testament served the needs of readers who were not fluent in Greek. His advocacy of the translation of the Bible into vernacular tongues, so that even ploughmen and weavers could understand it, supplies a model for many of the less learned martyrs whose narratives are included in the *Book of Martyrs*. Although he opposed Lutheranism, his biblical scholarship, including *Annotations on the New Testament*, had an important impact on Protestant humanists including William Tyndale. Published in 1503, his most important devotional treatise, *Enchiridion militis Christiani* (*Handbook of the Christian Soldier*), advocates emulation of the 'philosophy of Christ' embodied in the Gospels.

**Feckenham, John** (*c.*1510–84) after imprisonment during the reign of Edward VI, he received appointment as a chaplain to Mary I, Abbot of Westminster, and Dean of St Paul's Cathedral. He was present at the execution of Lady Jane Grey, interrogated Princess Elizabeth, and was present when Thomas Cranmer, Hugh Latimer, and Nicholas Ridley engaged in theological disputation at Oxford.

**Ferrar, Robert** (d. 1555) bishop of St David's (1548–54), he was deprived of office under Mary I and burnt alive as a heretic on 30 March 1555.

**Frith, John** (1503–33) an associate of William Tyndale, he may have collaborated on his translation of the New Testament. Frith independently wrote a sequence of polemical tracts influenced by the thinking of Martin Luther and Philip Melanchthon. After returning to England, Frith was imprisoned and then burnt at the stake at Smithfield on 4 July 1533.

**Gardiner, Stephen** (*c.*1495–1555) an expert in civil law, canon law, and theology, this royal administrator gained favour with Henry VIII for advancing the king's unsuccessful effort to secure papal approval for a divorce from Catherine of Aragon. He received appointment as Bishop of Winchester in 1531 and was a powerful member of the Privy Council until King Henry's death. Gardiner wrote *De vera obedientia* (1535), a defence of royal supremacy in ecclesiastical affairs, and was a prime mover behind the Act of Six Articles (1539), which affirmed adherence to Catholic doctrines in the face of Protestant challenges. Following the accession of Edward VI, he was deprived of his bishopric and imprisoned at the Tower of London. After his restoration as Bishop of Winchester and appointment as Lord Chancellor by Mary I, he led the persecution of Protestants. Attacking him for dissembling and concealment of his true religious convictions during Henry VIII's reign, Protestants vilified him as the 'Winchester Wolf' who bore responsibility for the slaughter of innocent 'lambs' (i.e., martyrs).

**Grey, Lady Jane** (1537–54) the nine-day Queen of England, she was enthroned during the interregnum that followed the death of Edward VI (10–19 July 1553). Although Lady Jane was convicted of treason, Mary I planned to pardon her when the new queen gave birth to a male heir. A new course of action followed the rebellion led by Sir Thomas Wyatt the Younger, however, and she was decapitated following the execution of her husband, Lord Guildford Dudley. He was the son of John Dudley, Duke of Northumberland, who had encouraged their marriage in order to perpetuate his power.

**Grindal, Edmund** (1519?–83) after serving as chaplain to Edward VI and Bishop Nicholas Ridley, this scholar went into exile during the reign of Mary I. He played a seminal role in the gathering of documents that John Foxe absorbed into the *Book of Martyrs*. After Elizabeth I appointed him to serve first as Bishop of London and then as Archbishop of York, he received appointment as Archbishop of Canterbury in 1576. He fell out of favour and the queen suspended him from performing his duties after he failed to take vigorous steps to stem the nascent Puritan movement.

**Harpsfield, John** (1516–78) chaplain to Bishop Edmund Bonner and Archdeacon of St Paul's Cathedral, this strenuous opponent of Protestant reform engaged in theological disputation with Thomas Cranmer, Hugh Latimer, and Nicholas Ridley before their execution at Oxford. Following deprivation from office under Elizabeth I, he was incarcerated with his brother, Nicholas, at Fleet Prison from 1559 until 1574.

**Harpsfield, Nicholas** (1519–75) an expert in canon law, he emigrated to Louvain during the reign of Edward VI. Returning to England after the accession of Mary I, he received appointment as a proctor of the Court of the Arches and Archdeacon of Canterbury. He engaged vigorously in the prosecution of heresy. Deposed from his offices under Elizabeth I, he was imprisoned at the Fleet during the same time as his brother, John (1559–74). While in prison, he wrote *Dialogi Sex*, published in Antwerp in 1566, which contains the first extended critique of the *Book of Martyrs*. Foxe took great pains to counter his criticism in the second edition (1570).

**Henry VIII** (1491–1547) crowned King of England in 1509, he defended religious orthodoxy against attack by Martin Luther and then initiated England's schism from the Church of Rome as a result of the failure of Pope Clement VII to grant him a divorce from Catherine of Aragon. Parliament took the radical step of declaring the monarch Supreme Head of the Church of England. Despite this administrative rupture, he condoned retention of Catholic ritual and theology. The religious convictions of his wives (notably Catherine of Aragon, Anne Boleyn,

Jane Seymour, and Catherine Parr) and his offspring (Edward VI, Mary I, and Elizabeth I) had a profound impact on English politics and religion during the remainder of the sixteenth century and beyond.

**Hooper, John** (*c.*1497–1555) going into exile after the Act of Six Articles (1539) imposed harshly punitive measures against religious reformers, he was greatly influenced by the views of Heinrich Bullinger, Zwingli's successor at Zurich. After returning to England during the reign of Edward VI, he called for abolition of clerical vestments and institution of the Lord's Supper as a commemorative service. Appointed to the bishopric of Gloucester (1551) and the combined bishopric of Worcester and Gloucester (1552), he promoted revision of the Book of Common Prayer along thoroughgoing Protestant lines (1552). He was burnt alive as a heretic on 9 February 1555. The *Book of Martyrs* memorializes him as an exemplary Protestant saint.

**Howard, Thomas** (1473–1554) 3rd Duke of Norfolk of the Howard line. An opponent of Thomas Wolsey and Thomas Cromwell, he was a proponent of the Act of Six Articles (1539). Condemned to death near the end of the reign of Henry VIII, this foremost Roman Catholic peer was imprisoned in the Tower of London under Edward VI and then released by Mary I, who restored him to the Privy Council.

**Latimer, Hugh** (*c.*1485–1555) he was the spiritual father of many members of the first generation of English Protestant clergy and of aristocratic women. Henry VIII appointed him Bishop of Worcester in 1535, but he resigned when his style of evangelical episcopacy lost favour with the monarch. A vigorous opponent of clerical abuses and the selfishness of wealthy individuals, he was arguably the greatest English preacher of his time. A recipient of patronage from Catherine Parr and the Duchess of Suffolk, he seems to have had an obscure connection to Anne Askew. After imprisonment at Oxford with Thomas Cranmer and Nicholas Ridley, he was burnt alive with Ridley on 16 October 1555.

**Leo X** (1513–21) the second son of Lorenzo ('il Magnifico'), Giovanni de' Medici (1475–1521) was elected pope in 1513 prior to his ordination as a priest and consecration as a bishop. His promotion of the sale of indulgences in order to finance extravagant expenditure on St Peter's Basilica and other projects triggered Martin Luther's *Ninety-Five Theses*. After condemning Lutheranism in his bull, *Exsurge Domine* (1520), he excommunicated Martin Luther in 1521.

**Luther, Martin** (1483–1546) this Augustinian monk and Professor of Biblical Theology at the University of Wittenberg initiated the Protestant Reformation with his *Ninety-Five Theses* (1517), which question the validity of the sale of indulgences. Based on his understanding of Paul's Epistle to the Romans, he propounded the doctrine of justification by

faith alone (*sola fide*—'by faith alone') in place of the doctrine of justification by good works, which underlay the sale of indulgences,
pilgrimages, and the entire penitential system of the Church of Rome.
In his *Babylonian Captivity of the Church* (1520), he rejected papal
authority and reduced the number of sacraments from seven (including
confirmation, marriage, extreme unction, and ordination) to the two
that possessed scriptural warrant (the Eucharist and baptism) in addition to penance, to which he soon denied sacramental status. His
other fundamental principles are the primacy of divine grace (*sola
gratia*—'by grace alone') and the self-sufficiency of the Bible in religious affairs (*sola scriptura*—'by scripture alone'). Although his ideas
were anathema to Henry VIII, he greatly influenced William Tyndale,
Miles Coverdale, and other members of the first generation of English
Protestants.

**Mary I** (1516–58) the daughter of Henry VIII and Catherine of Aragon,
she underwent illegitimation after her mother's failure to deliver a
male heir triggered revolutionary changes in church and state conse-
quent upon her father's insistence upon a divorce. When she succeeded
Edward VI in 1553, she sought to restore Roman Catholic worship and
to reconcile England with the Church of Rome. The rebellion of Sir
Thomas Wyatt the Younger in opposition to her marriage to Prince
Philip (later Philip II) of Spain led to the imprisonment of her half-
sister, Elizabeth, and the decapitation of Lady Jane Grey. During her
reign, hundreds of Protestants were burnt alive as heretics and many
of their co-religionists went into exile. Her death on 17 November 1558
halted persecution of Protestants.

**Martyr, Peter** see *Vermigli, Pietro Martire*.

**Melanchthon, Philip** (1497–1560) this close associate of Martin Luther
was a Professor of Greek at the University of Wittenberg and a prime
mover of the Protestant Reformation. His more irenic views contributed
to the more conciliatory position that he adopted toward the Church of
Rome. His compilation of a Lutheran confession of faith, the Augsburg
Confession (1530), was unequivocally rejected by Roman Catholic theologians, notably Luther's antagonist, Johann Eck.

**More, Sir Thomas** (1478–1535) the successor to Cardinal Wolsey
as Lord Chancellor, he was England's leading supporter of Roman
Catholic orthodoxy. He engaged in bitter propagandistic warfare with
Luther, Tyndale, Frith, and other advocates of ecclesiastical reform.
Following his failure to subscribe to replacement of papal authority with
royal headship of the Church of England, he was convicted of treason
and beheaded at the Tower of London on 6 July 1535. He was canonized
as a saint in 1935.

**Oecolampadius, Johannes** (1482–1531) this humanistic scholar assisted Erasmus in his compilation of his Latin–Greek edition of the New Testament (1516). Under the influence of Martin Luther, he left monastic orders and rejected the doctrine of transubstantiation. A close associate of Ulrich Zwingli, he defended the sacramental theology of the Zurich reformer.

**Philip of Spain** (1527–98) as the consort of his cousin, Mary I, he was titular King of England from 1554 until her death. He governed Spain as Philip II from 1556 until 1598.

**Philpot, John** (1515/16–55) deprived of office as archdeacon of Winchester and excommunicated during the reign of Mary I, he was imprisoned first at Queen's Bench Prison and then at both the coal house used as a prison by Bishop Bonner and a tower at St Paul's Cathedral. Despite great duress, he engaged in active correspondence with fellow Protestants and wrote detailed accounts of his heresy examinations that later fed into the *Book of Martyrs*. He was burned as a heretic at Smithfield on 18 December 1555.

**Ridley, Nicholas** (c.1502–55) during the reign of Edward VI, he was involved in the creation of the Book of Common Prayer. When Edmund Bonner was deprived of episcopal office in 1550, Ridley succeeded him as Bishop of London. On his deprivation from office under Mary I, Bonner succeeded Ridley. He was imprisoned at Oxford before being burnt alive in the company of Hugh Latimer on 16 October 1555.

**Rogers, John** (c.1500–55) as chaplain to English merchants in Antwerp, he became acquainted with William Tyndale. Supplementing Tyndale's translation with his own work and that of Miles Coverdale, Rogers then edited an edition of the English Bible under the pseudonym of Thomas Mathew. After returning to England, he became active in reformist circles under Edward VI. He is called the proto-martyr because, following imprisonment at Newgate, he was the first Protestant to be burnt alive as a heretic during the reign of Mary I. He died at Smithfield on 4 February 1555.

**Sandys, Edwin** (1509?–88) after receiving high clerical appointments and serving as Vice Chancellor of the University of Cambridge during Edward VI's reign, he was imprisoned under Mary I and then escaped to continental Europe. Returning to England after her death, he was appointed by Elizabeth I to serve as Bishop of Worcester (1559), Bishop of London (1570), and finally Archbishop of York (1576).

**Saunders, Lawrence** (d. 1555) after the death of Edward VI, under whom he received appointment as reader at Litchfield Cathedral and rector at All Hallows, Bread Street, in London, he was deprived of office, imprisoned and burnt alive at Coventry on 8 February 1555.

**Seymour, Edward** (*c.*1500–52) the elder brother of Jane Seymour, he was a military leader who sympathized with evangelical reform. At the outset of the reign of Edward VI, his 9-year-old nephew, he was appointed Lord Protector of the Realm and Duke of Somerset by the Council of Regency designated by Henry VIII's will to govern during the royal minority. Following risings in different parts of England, which were triggered by economic difficulties and the imposition of a Protestant settlement of religion, he was overthrown by nobles led by John Dudley, who was created Duke of Northumberland in 1551. Beheaded on 22 January 1552, Seymour receives praise in the *Book of Martyrs* as the 'good duke'.

**Smith, Richard** (1499/1500–1563) after receiving appointment as Regius Professor of Divinity at Oxford University, he was deprived of office under Edward VI and went into exile at the University of Louvain. Restored to office during the reign of Mary I, he preached prior to the burning of Hugh Latimer and Nicholas Ridley and presided over the trial of Thomas Cranmer. Under Elizabeth, he returned to Louvain.

**Stephen, St** he was the first Christian martyr or proto-martyr (Acts 6: 8–8: 1), on whom many Protestants modelled their comportment as they approached execution under Mary I.

**Taylor, Rowland** (d. 1555) he served as chaplain to Hugh Latimer and Thomas Cranmer, who appointed him rector at Hadleigh, Suffolk, in 1544. He was burnt alive in the vicinity of this town on 9 February 1555. The *Book of Martyrs* memorializes him as an ideal provincial parson.

**Tunstall, Cuthbert** (1474–1559) as Bishop of London, he declined to offer patronage for William Tyndale's translation project. He was translated to the see of Durham in 1530, only to be deprived under Edward VI and then restored to this bishopric by Mary I. He lost this position, yet again, under Elizabeth I.

**Tyndale, William** (*c.*1494–1536) under the influence of Erasmus and Luther, this humanistic scholar earned the antipathy of members of the ecclesiastical hierarchy by advocating translation of the Bible into the vernacular. He went into exile in Germany and the Low Countries in order to accomplish this project. His English New Testament, the first complete edition of which was published in 1526, for ever altered the religious landscape of his homeland. Also printed abroad and smuggled into England were his influential Bible commentaries and polemical treatises, the most notable of which are *The Parable of the Wicked Mammon* (8 May 1528) and *The Obedience of a Christian Man* (2 October 1528). He was burnt at the stake at Vilvorde, Brabant, on or about 6 October 1536.

**Vermigli, Pietro Martire** (1499–1562) the prior of an Augustinian monastery at Lucca in Italy, he underwent conversion under the influence of Juan de Valdès and went into exile in 1542. This influential Protestant theologian then immigrated to England during the reign of Edward VI and received appointment Regius Professor of Divinity at the University of Oxford, where his lectures on 1 Corinthians aroused a Eucharistic controversy. Returning to the Continent under Mary I, he lectured on the Bible and philosophy before receiving appointment as Professor of Old Testament at Zurich in 1556.

**Weston, Hugh** (c.1510–58) appointed Lady Margaret Professor of Divinity at Cambridge University under Henry VIII, he was imprisoned during the reign of Edward VI for resisting ecclesiastical reform. Mary I then appointed him to serve as one of her chaplains and as Dean of Westminster. A vigorous interrogator of alleged heretics, he engaged in disputation with Hugh Latimer, Nicholas Ridley, and Thomas Cranmer at Oxford.

**Winchester, Stephen** see *Gardiner, Stephen*.

**Wolsey, Thomas** (c.1470/1–1530) Archbishop and Cardinal of York, he became Lord Chancellor of England in 1515. When Leo X named him legate *a latere*, he even outranked the Archbishop of Canterbury. Living in a grandiose style that rivalled that of Henry VIII, he dominated both church and state until 1529, when he lost power during tortuous negotiations concerning the king's request for a divorce from Catherine of Aragon. Wolsey died while under arrest during the following year.

**Woodruff, David** (fl. 1554–5) unlike his fellow Sheriff of London, Sir William Chester, Woodruff expressed great hostility toward condemned prisoners, whom he harassed and mocked prior to their execution.

**Wriothesley, Thomas** (1505–50) Earl of Southampton and Lord Chancellor, he collaborated with Stephen Gardiner in the persecution of Protestant heretics and played a prominent role in the interrogation, torture, and subsequent burning of Anne Askew.

**Wyatt, Sir Thomas, the Younger** (c.1521–54) the son of Sir Thomas Wyatt, the poet, he was beheaded after raising troops and leading them to attack London on 7 February 1554 in a failed attempt to overthrow Mary I and place her half-sister, Elizabeth, on the throne.

**Zwingli, Ulrich** (1484–1531) an early convert to Protestantism, he dominated religious life at Zurich as pastor of Grossmünster. Although he joined Luther's attack on indulgences and clerical celibacy, he diverged in his support of iconoclasm and rejection of the Real Presence of Christ in the Eucharist. He instead viewed Holy Communion as a wholly memorial celebration of the Passion.

# GLOSSARY OF PLACES

**Bench, The** see *Queen's Bench Prison* and *King's Bench Prison*.

**Blackfriars** the site of a dissolved Dominican monastery south-west of St Paul's Cathedral, whose buildings came into the possession of Sir Thomas Cawarden, Master of the Revels.

**Cheapside** London's chief marketing district, which is located immediately to the east of St Paul's Cathedral.

**coal house** a structure at the London palace of the Bishop of London, used as an ad hoc prison.

**Counters** debtors' prisons in the City of London, one located at Bread Street, before it was moved to Wood Street in 1555, and the other at the Poultry.

**English House** a walled residential community inhabited by English merchants in Antwerp. William Tyndale preached to members of this community, and John Rogers served as chaplain. In all likelihood, residents engaged in the smuggling of their books and other clandestine publications into England.

**Fleet Prison** also known as the Fleet, it was located alongside the Fleet River immediately to the west of the City of London and served as a site for incarceration of prisoners convicted by the Court of Chancery and Court of the Star Chamber.

**Fulham** during the sixteenth century, it was a village up the River Thames from Westminster where Fulham Palace, the suburban manor of the Bishop of London, was located.

**Guildhall** the governmental seat of the City of London.

**Hampton Court** a magnificent royal palace located up the River Thames from the City of London and Westminster.

**Inner Temple** an institution for the study of law located on the River Thames west of the City of London.

**Islington** during the sixteenth century, it was a village about ½ mile north of the City of London.

**London, City of** the 1-mile square city demarcated roughly by London Wall and located at the centre of present-day Metropolitan London.

**King's Bench Prison** during the reign of Mary I, it should have been called Queen's Bench Prison (see below).

**Marshalsea Prison** an important prison located alongside the Queen's Bench in Southwark.

**Newgate** a gate at the western end of London Wall, where a law court and prison were located.

**Old Bailey** a law court located at Newgate.

**Queen's Bench Prison** a prison in Southwark attached to Queen's Bench law court and located alongside Marshalsea Prison.

**Paul's** St Paul's Cathedral.

**Paul's Cross** a pulpit within the precincts of St Paul's Cathedral, where large congregations gathered to hear sermons delivered in the open air.

**St Paul's Cathedral** the cathedral of the City of London.

**Shoreditch** during the sixteenth century, it was a hamlet north of the City of London.

**Smithfield** a site north-west of London Wall, where alleged heretics were burnt alive.

**Southwark** a borough on the south bank of the River Thames that was connected to the City of London by London Bridge.

**Steelyard** a walled trading enclave alongside the River Thames that was occupied by Hanseatic merchants resident in London.

**Temple** see *Inner Temple*.

**Tower** Tower of London.

**Tower of London** a Thames-side location at the south-east corner of London Wall, this imposing edifice functions to the present day as a fortress, royal palace, and prison. During the Middle Ages and early modern era, it was notorious as a site for the imprisonment, torture, and/or the beheading of condemned prisoners of high rank.

# CONCORDANCE OF PAGE REFERENCES

# INDEX

Bold numbers denote references to illustrations

# BIBLICAL TEXTS CITED

American Literature

British and Irish Literature

Children's Literature

Classics and Ancient Literature

Colonial Literature

Eastern Literature

European Literature

Gothic Literature

History

Medieval Literature

Oxford English Drama

Philosophy

Poetry

Politics

Religion

The Oxford Shakespeare

A complete list of Oxford World's Classics, including Authors in Context, Oxford English Drama, and the Oxford Shakespeare, is available in the UK from the Marketing Services Department, Oxford University Press, Great Clarendon Street, Oxford OX2 6DP, or visit the website at www.oup.com/uk/worldsclassics.

In the USA, visit www.oup.com/us/owc for a complete title list.

Oxford World's Classics are available from all good bookshops. In case of difficulty, customers in the UK should contact Oxford University Press Bookshop, 116 High Street, Oxford OX1 4BR.

| | |
|---|---|
| | **The Anglo-Saxon World** |
| | **Beowulf** |
| | **Lancelot of the Lake** |
| | **The Paston Letters** |
| | **Sir Gawain and the Green Knight** |
| | **The Poetic Edda** |
| | **The Mabinogion** |
| | **Tales of the Elders of Ireland** |
| | **York Mystery Plays** |
| GEOFFREY CHAUCER | **The Canterbury Tales**<br>**Troilus and Criseyde** |
| GUILLAUME DE LORRIS<br>and JEAN DE MEUN | **The Romance of the Rose** |
| HENRY OF HUNTINGDON | **The History of the English People**<br>**1000–1154** |
| JOCELIN OF BRAKELOND | **Chronicle of the Abbey of Bury**<br>**St Edmunds** |
| WILLIAM LANGLAND | **Piers Plowman** |
| SIR JOHN MANDEVILLE | **The Book of Marvels and Travels** |
| SIR THOMAS MALORY | **Le Morte Darthur** |

Classical Literary Criticism
The First Philosophers: The Presocratics
   and the Sophists
Greek Lyric Poetry
Myths from Mesopotamia

APOLLODORUS | The Library of Greek Mythology

APOLLONIUS OF RHODES | Jason and the Golden Fleece

APULEIUS | The Golden Ass

ARISTOPHANES | Birds and Other Plays

ARISTOTLE | The Nicomachean Ethics
Politics

ARRIAN | Alexander the Great

BOETHIUS | The Consolation of Philosophy

CAESAR | The Civil War
The Gallic War

CATULLUS | The Poems of Catullus

CICERO | Defence Speeches
The Nature of the Gods
On Obligations
Political Speeches
The Republic and The Laws

EURIPIDES | Bacchae and Other Plays
Heracles and Other Plays
Medea and Other Plays
Orestes and Other Plays
The Trojan Women and Other Plays

HERODOTUS | The Histories

HOMER | The Iliad
The Odyssey

Travel Writing 1700–1830

Women's Writing 1778–1838

WILLIAM BECKFORD    **Vathek**

JAMES BOSWELL    **Life of Johnson**

FRANCES BURNEY    **Camilla**
**Cecilia**
**Evelina**

ROBERT BURNS    **Selected Poems and Songs**

LORD CHESTERFIELD    **Lord Chesterfield's Letters**

JOHN CLELAND    **Memoirs of a Woman of Pleasure**

DANIEL DEFOE    **A Journal of the Plague Year**
**Moll Flanders**
**Robinson Crusoe**
**Roxana**

HENRY FIELDING    **Jonathan Wild**
**Joseph Andrews and Shamela**
**Tom Jones**

JOHN GAY    **The Beggar's Opera and Polly**

WILLIAM GODWIN    **Caleb Williams**

OLIVER GOLDSMITH    **The Vicar of Wakefield**

MARY HAYS    **Memoirs of Emma Courtney**

ELIZABETH INCHBALD    **A Simple Story**

SAMUEL JOHNSON    **The History of Rasselas**
**Lives of the Poets**
**The Major Works**

CHARLOTTE LENNOX    **The Female Quixote**

MATTHEW LEWIS    **The Monk**

| | |
|---|---|
| JANE AUSTEN | **Emma** |
| | **Persuasion** |
| | **Pride and Prejudice** |
| | **Sense and Sensibility** |
| ANNE BRONTË | **The Tenant of Wildfell Hall** |
| CHARLOTTE BRONTË | **Jane Eyre** |
| EMILY BRONTË | **Wuthering Heights** |
| WILKIE COLLINS | **The Moonstone** |
| | **The Woman in White** |
| JOSEPH CONRAD | **Heart of Darkness and Other Tales** |
| | **The Secret Agent** |
| CHARLES DARWIN | **The Origin of Species** |
| CHARLES DICKENS | **Bleak House** |
| | **David Copperfield** |
| | **Great Expectations** |
| | **Hard Times** |
| GEORGE ELIOT | **Middlemarch** |
| | **The Mill on the Floss** |
| ELIZABETH GASKELL | **Mary Barton** |
| THOMAS HARDY | **Jude the Obscure** |
| | **Tess of the d'Urbervilles** |
| WALTER SCOTT | **Ivanhoe** |
| | **Waverley** |
| MARY SHELLEY | **Frankenstein** |
| ROBERT LOUIS STEVENSON | **Strange Case of Dr Jekyll and Mr Hyde and Other Tales** |
| BRAM STOKER | **Dracula** |
| W. M. THACKERAY | **Vanity Fair** |
| OSCAR WILDE | **The Picture of Dorian Gray** |
| WORDSWORTH and COLERIDGE | **Lyrical Ballads** |